MEDIATED PERSPECTIVES

MEDIA OWNERSHIP, LITERACY, AND EFFECTS

Revised First Edition

By Bick Treut

Raritan Valley Community College

Bassim Hamadeh, CEO and Publisher
Michael Simpson, Vice President of Acquisitions
Jamie Giganti, Managing Editor
Jess Busch, Graphic Design Supervisor
John Remington, Acquisitions Editor
Brian Fahey, Licensing Associate
Mandy Licata, Interior Designer

First published in the United States of America in 2014 by Cognella, Inc.

Cover image copyright: © 2011 by Depositphotos / Maxim Kazmin.
© 2013 by Depositphotos / Hongqi Zhang.

Printed in the United States of America

ISBN: 978-1-62661-846-6 (pbk) / 978-1-62661-847-3 (br)

www.cognella.com   800-200-3908

CONTENTS

READINGS

PERSPECTIVES

PREFACE

A year ago, I would have never have even dreamed of writing a textbook on the mass media. Not that it isn't favorite topic of mine—along with others like communication theory, psychology, radio and television production, modern American history, cooking, and stand-up comedy. I follow our (U.S.) media system closely by reading industry publications like *Broadcasting & Cable* magazine and remain entranced by the latest findings on media effects published in journals like *Media Psychology*. I was right in the middle of my pursuit of a PhD in General Psychology, with an emphasis on media, when I received a call from Cognella Publishing asking if I would be interested in writing this textbook. As an Assistant Professor of Communication Studies at Raritan Valley Community College, I felt humbled and honored by the invitation. I decided to give it a go.

My students are fascinated by the fact that I have remained unplugged from broadcast, cable, and/or satellite television for five years. This lifestyle change was made after a close reading of findings from George Gerbner's Cultural Indicators Project, which suggests the fallout from watching all of the violence on American television isn't that viewers commit more violence. Rather, heavy television viewers fear violence being committed against them. I was also concerned about the "conspicuous consumerism" associated with frequent exposure to television ads, the objectification of women and men, and, after 9/11, all of the fear-mongering about terrorists and terrorism. I called Comcast and told them to disconnect the cable.

After studying media systems globally, I have learned: Media systems provide elites the power to systematize and naturalize certain values and perspectives that perpetuate their place in a culture. It is easier to see these relationships outside of our own society but, after a great deal of reflection, see it happening here. The big question is: Why would the power elite want us to live in a culture of fear?

I have lots of heroes. These include people like Professor Walt Littlefield at Emerson College who told me, back in 1979, to keep learning because I was a natural student, Marshall McLuhan who got me wildly excited about media ecology, Douglas Rushkoff who wrote masterpieces like *Media Virus* and *Coercion* and who provided valuable guidance and encouragement while writing this book, Neil Postman who is one of my favorite authors on media ecology, Tom Valasek at Raritan Valley Community College who has always been my mentor and supporter and took the risk of hiring on a non-PhD candidate as full-time professor, and all of my colleagues in Communication Studies including Mark Bezanson, Sara Banfield, and Traci Shanewolfe.

But this book would not have been written without the steadfast love, encouragement, patience, and insight of my brilliant wife, Dana Nelson. Dana and I met at the college during our new faculty orientation session in August 2006. We fell in love shortly there-after and married in 2011. While writing this text, Dana, Allie, Nathan, Danny (the kids), Bailey (the cat), and Whitey and Brownie (the guinea pigs) surrounded this computer that sits in the living room of our modest Somerville, NJ apartment. All have contributed either substantially or through errant keystrokes. I would have never agreed to commit to writing this book had I not been with Dana who is the consummate encourager, healer, thinker, hugger, neck rubber, and snuggler. Thank you, Dana, for making my life so damn nice.

GETTING STARTED

How do we know what we know? How much of what we know is based on *direct*, first-hand knowledge or contact with people, places, things, and events? Let's call this direct knowledge. And, how much of what we know is acquired indirectly through *mediated channels* of communication such as television, movies, videos, magazines, books, and newspapers? Let's call this mediated knowledge.

I like to begin a course in Introduction to Mass Communication by asking these questions. Here is what students say (an average after teaching this course for more than ten years):

> Mediated: 85%
> Direct: 15%

Figure I.1 Mediated forms of communication are those that do not require face-to-face contact or the act of physically being there.

What are the *real* percentages? They don't exist. After searching for years, I've learned that researchers have failed to answer the question quantitatively—most likely because it would be nearly impossible to do. Maybe this could be the study you consider when you attend graduate school.

But we do know that children and young adults spend more time attending to nearly all screen-based mediums (e.g., television, Internet, video games) than they spend in conversation with their parents. The rule of thumb, reinforced by the students' hunches, is that most of our experiences with life in the early 21st century are mediated. And, based on good statistics covering the use of mediated sources, this trend is expected to grow into the foreseeable future.

Figure I.2 Grand Master Jay calls for an end to violence in Detroit (2010).

With so much of our knowledge coming to us indirectly, it is important to understand more about how the forms of mediated communication, such as television, Internet, video games, music, and reading books affect us. It is also critical to understand whether or not the providers of mediated communication, the senders, have an agenda or bias. And, based on our frames of reference, or the knowledge we use to decode or interpret people, actions, ideas, events, images, and/or words, how media effects the ways we see the world.

Many communication scholars believe that media have a significant impact on how we view and interact with the world around us. Early research into media effects focused on whether or not viewing violence in movies or on television led to aggressive or violent behaviors among viewers. These studies indicated that there is a relationship between viewing violence and acting aggressively or violently, but that the effect was minimal after considering issues such as a predisposition (based, for instance, on relations with close family members) to act aggressively. Later studies suggested that viewing violence had a more significant impact—that of audiences fearing violence directed toward themselves. Heavy viewers of television, the research revealed, led viewers to believe that the world was as dangerous a place as depicted on television and in films where violence is a staple, industrial ingredient, used to increase the numbers of viewers and hold them through commercial breaks. Violence on television, including that shown on television news, grossly exaggerates the incidence of violence in real life. Heavy viewers, those who watch television for more than 4 hours per day, begin to perceive the real world around them as

Figure I.3 Recent research suggests that the effect of repeated exposure to media violence is an increase of fear among heavy television viewers in the population.

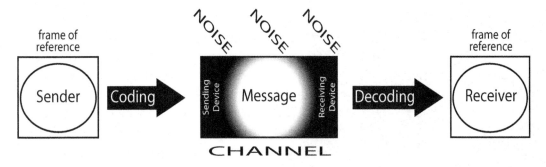

Figure I.4 Symbolic Interactionism

similar to that viewed on their television sets. Less-frequent viewers say that their likelihood of being a crime victim is as likely as it is in real life.

For instance, 2010 was the least affected by serious crime in the United States in almost forty years. The decrease includes all types of such crime, with violent and property crimes having reached an all-time low. The homicide rate in particular decreased 51% between its record high point in 1991.

More recent research on media effects focus on the notion of *acculturation*—how we observe and absorb values, attitudes, and beliefs by way of mediated communication, especially as depicted in fictional stories (i.e., from cartoons, situation comedies, dramas, and reality shows). It is in this sphere that most students of mass communication should be concerned. Television, film, music, videogames, and books harbor a fairly narrow perspective of reality. This view may or may not reinforce cultural perspectives that we learn from our families, schools, religions, and communication with others who attend to media systems. Media's perspective drives our sense of reality in that we select, organize, and interpret the things, people, and events we perceive using the frameworks that construct our frames of reference.

Symbolic interactionism, which forms the baseline of modern thinking on human communication, suggests that objects (people, things, words, ideas, and actions) have no inherent meaning in and of themselves. Rather, meanings are created by recipients as their minds decode the symbols they receive. Meanings attributed to objects are based on the things we learned from specific others, including parents, siblings, relatives, and teachers, along with generalized others; the things we learn through our culture as manifest through its media system. These are noted in figure I.4 as "frame of reference." To the extent that these don't *match*, the meaning conveyed by the sender and that decoded by the receiver will not match.

The way media affects acculturation—our adoption of cultural norms—results in similar frames of reference for senders and the receivers within the same culture. In the United States, our media system is perhaps the most significant influencer of the meanings we

Figure I. 5 In the television studio, producers use color, lighting, camera tilts, framing, and sound to effect our perceptions and interpretation of programs.

attribute to symbols. It also helps us to make similar judgments about what's right and wrong, good and bad. We share a significant common experience by way of the television, films, music, websites, and books we attend to.

Since the media is so influential, it is important for students to know more about how the U.S. media system evolved as a commercialized system, how this system compares with others, how media works from a business perspective, who the companies are that own the media, what their agendas are, the effects that researchers have deduced from prolonged exposure to the media, and perspectives on the future of our media system. These are the goals of this textbook along with one more very important goal: to increase readers' media literacy—the ability to think critically about what you watch on television, at the movies, and on the web. Considering the vast amount of media we consume, it startles this author to think that American schoolchildren expend so much time mastering literacy of the written word while spending a small fraction of time, if any, on mastering the vocabulary of visual and aural media production. Knowledge about framing, color, camera tilts, shot distance, sound and laugh tracks, along with identification of subtext by way of actors' nonverbal behaviors, will go a long way in helping students understand why visual media have such a strong impact on our lives.

MEDIA HISTORY

A Media Ecology Perspective

n this section, we will explore the history of mass media including books, newspapers, magazines, radio, film, television, and new media (made possible through the digitization of content and Internet distribution). Each of these mediums heralded changes in the sensibilities of the people who used them as their predominant source of information. In turn, these changes led to more widespread social, cultural, economic, and political transformations.

The study of how a mass medium affects users and societies is called *media ecology*. Media ecology examines how media and communication processes affect human perception and understanding (West and Turner, 2010). According to Neil Postman, a NYU Communication Professor and founder of the media ecology program there, "Media ecology looks into the matter of how media of communication affect human perception, understanding, feeling, and value; and how our interaction with media facilitates or impedes our chances of survival."

Figure 1.1 The Pike Place News Stand in Seattle, WA sells print publications from all over the world.

Media ecologists view predominant mediums historically, and mediums available today, as a part of our environment—similar to the air we breathe, the water we drink, and the food we eat. We surround ourselves with our media. Later on, we will learn just how immersed we are in this environment.

Each major medium developed since our tribal ancestors shared information verbally, be it one-on-one (interpersonally) or one-to-many (oratory), has been considered and explored by media ecologists. Their findings provide an interesting perspective from which to view the technological and historical progression of the mass media along with our social, economic, political, and cultural evolution.

A NOTE ON PROCESS VERSUS FORM

Mass media are technologies that make the process of mass communication possible. The process of mass communication contrasts with other processes of communication, which include intrapersonal communication (communication with oneself), interpersonal communication (in-person communication between two people), group communication (in-person communication between members of a group), and oratory or rhetoric (in-person communication between a speaker and a group). Mass communication may be defined as communication between a sender and a large, heterogeneous, and geographically dispersed audience, typically unknown to the sender. In this regard, mass communication is a mediated, or non-in-person, form of communication that requires a medium.

A medium of communication is a technology used to send a message. Mediums include: print (real books, magazines, and newspapers); radio, recorded music (vinyl, tapes, CDs, MP3s); motion pictures; and television.

Mediums should not be confused with distribution channels, which define how we receive the medium's content. Distribution channels include over-the-air broadcast, Internet, satellite, cable, cellular network, shipped direct via U.S. Mail, UPS, or FedEx, and brick-and-mortar retailers (e.g., Barnes & Noble, WalMart). Distribution channels for print (books, magazines, newspapers) differ between hard copies (Amazon, bookstores, supermarkets, discount stores) and digital (websites, blogs, eBooks, posts, and tweets). Radio is distributed through broadcast (AM and FM channels), satellite (Sirius XM), and Internet (streaming of broadcast, satellite stations, and Internet-native radio). Recorded music is distributed through peer-to-peer networks, iTunes, and brick-and-mortar retailers. Movies are distributed through movie theaters, DVDs (Amazon, other online retailers, Red Box), brick-and-mortar stores (FYE, Barnes & Noble), and Internet (peer-to-peer, NetFlix, Amazon). Television is distributed through broadcasting (over the air), cable television, and Internet (websites like Hulu, YouTube, and NetFlix).

THE MASS MEDIA

Mass media enable mass communication. Each medium not only provides senders (e.g., authors, publishers, producers) with the power to persuade, but each medium has an effect on the way people interpret the world around them. Neil Postman states, "The forms of our media ... are rather like metaphors, working by unobtrusive but powerful implication to enforce their special definition of reality" (p. 10). The medium(s) we attend to "direct us to organize our minds and integrate our experience of the world, it imposes itself on our consciousness and social institutions in myriad forms" (p. 18).

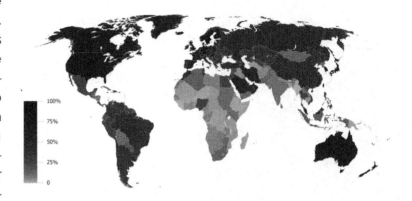

Figure 1.2 Internet penetration rates around the world (percentage of people with access).

The world of print is logical and linear. Writing forces us to capture experience in the form of an algebraic expression: subject, verb, and predicate. In a text-based world, reading is believing. The world of television is visual and emotional. We process movies and television in the right hemisphere of the brain adjacent to our emotional centers.Recent fMRI studies show that the prefrontal cortex, which ties logic to emotion in our brain, is shut down shortly after beginning to watch. Television and film compel us to believe that "seeing is believing." Postman states, "A major new medium changes the structure of discourse; it does so by encouraging certain uses of the intellect, by demanding a certain kind of content—in a phrase, by creating a new kind of truth-telling" (p. 27). When people watch television, they ask, "Did you see the story about ...?" When they've heard it on the radio, they answer, "Yes, I heard about that." If they read about it in a newspaper, they'll say, "I saw (or read) that too."

Media ecologists seek to draw associations between our symbolic environment (i.e., oral vs. print, print vs. electronic) and natural environment (i.e., quality of air, water, plants, light). "They are both gradual and additive at first, and then, all at once, a critical mass is achieved, as the physicists say" (Postman, p. 27). McLuhan saw each medium as an extension of man. Print is an extension of the visual faculty, "which intensified perspective and a fixed point of view" (p. 172).

Figure 1.3 Philosopher of communication theory Marshall McLuhan (1911–1980) was visionary in his perspective that mediums themselves, regardless of content, have significant effects on their users. He coined the terms "global village" and "the medium is the message."

Ernst Cassirer wrote in *An Essay on Man* (1956):

Physical reality seems to recede in proportion as man's symbolic activity advances. Instead of dealing with the things themselves man is in a sense constantly conversing—with himself. He has so enveloped himself in linguistic forms, in artistic images, in mythological symbols or religious rites that he cannot see or know anything except by the interposition of an artificial medium.

BOOKS

Between the time Joan of Arc was burned at the stake in France (1431) and the Protestant Reformation began in Germany (1521), Johannes Gutenberg developed movable metal type (1446) in Mainz, Germany. Gutenberg experimented with metal alloys and cast each letter of the alphabet into unique pieces that could be assembled, inked, and pressed onto paper. Fifty years later, printing presses were operational throughout Western Europe and some 40,000 books produced.

Movable metal type made print media, including books, newspapers, and magazines possible. But in the first two centuries after the development of the printing press, books predominated as the leading printed medium. The social, political, cultural, and economic effects of books in Europe and America were huge. Marshal McLuhan, in *Understanding Media: The Extensions of Man* (1964), documents significant shifts occurring as a result of books, including a rise in nationalism, industrialism, literacy, and education. The replication of storytelling, knowledge, and persuasion over a broad landscape replaced the power of oration, which tended to reinforce more localized control of information and power. Postman (1985) states that print freed people from the local and immediate, while making a stronger impact than actual, first-person-observed events. In other words, print liberated people from the people, ideas, and events that took place in their villages, towns, or cities and what they read seemed more "real."

The print era, according to West and Turner (2010), signaled the beginning of mass production, and the industrial revolution, because the same text could be reproduced identically and sold to a vast, geographically diverse set of readers. When Margaret

Figure 1.4 Gutenberg.

Mead, who studied non-industrial cultures, brought along a few copies of a book to a Pacific Island, the natives were stumped. According to Marshall McLuhan, "The natives had seen books, but only one copy of each, which they assumed to be unique. Their astonishment at the identical character of several books was a natural response to what is after all the most magical and potent aspect of print and mass production. It involves a principle of extension by homogenization that is the key to understanding Western power" (p. 174).

Mass production not only produces quantities of the same product but, according to McLuhan, citizens who are similar to each other. West and Turner state, "The same content is delivered over and over again by the same means. This visual dependent era, however, produced a fragmented population because people could remain in isolation reading their mass-produced media" (p. 434).

But books, by their very nature, are quite personal. Baran (2008) considers books a medium that "encourages personal reflection to a greater degree than other media" (p. 73). We read and use our experiences and perspectives to visualize the stories that we read. We consider the ideas, visualize the action, and contemplate the plot lines on our own.

The first printing press came to the United States in 1638 and books, along with shorter pamphlets, were central to the Colonists' revolt against the British in the 1770s. Most of the early publications were religious but the Stamp Act, which levied taxes on printing to fund the French and Indian War while limiting expression, resulted in open revolt by printers while doubling the price of publications. Subsequent books by John Adams, Thomas Jefferson, and James Wilson openly challenged British rule. Thomas Paine's *Common Sense*, which ran all of 47 pages, sold 120,000 copies in 3 months—which is amazing considering the colonies harbored approximately 400,000 adults.

American book publishers thrived after the American Revolution and the newspaper industry

Figure 1.5 Reproduction of Gutenberg-era Press on display at Printing History Museum in Lyon, France. Photograph taken by George H. Williams in July, 2004

Figure 1.6 Margaret Mead, American cultural anthropologist.

grew quickly from publishers who operated a mix of coffeehouse or tavern and back-room print shop. During the 1880s, printing experienced improvements including the use of continuous-roll paper, steam-powered printing, and low-cost paper production. But the most significant improvement resulted from Ottmar Mergenthaler's linotype machine (1884) that enabled printers to set type mechanically instead of manually. American publishers John Wiley & Sons and Harper Brothers began publishing novels like Nathaniel Hawthorne's *The Scarlet Letter*, Herman Melville's *Moby Dick*, and Mark Twain's *Adventures of Huckleberry Finn*.

As mass production increased, so did the need for mass media. Factories lured rural people to the cities. According to Sterling and Kittross (1978), "The growing cities furnished an industrial base, great amounts of information and people who wanted it, and a market for mass-produced entertainment and information. The density of the population made it easy. The local tavern continued to serve as a center of communications as it had for hundreds of years, but information now came as posted broadside advertisements or printed newspapers in addition to the traditional word of mouth from travelers" (p. 7).

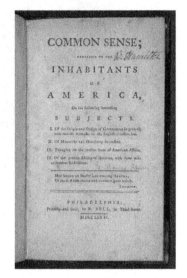

Figure 1.7 Inside cover of Common Sense; Addressed to the Inhabitants of America.

In the late 1930s, inexpensive paperback books were introduced and sold in newsstands, train stations, and department stores. Called "dime novels," but sold at 25 cents, publishers like Pocket Books sold titles such as *Catcher in the Rye* and *The Titans*.

But while books failed to attract mass audiences, they did, nevertheless, appeal to those attracted to the titles or topics of the printed works. While not advertising-supported, this medium could appeal to narrow or unspecified audiences. Likewise, books, to this day, do not have to pass the test of appealing to corporate sponsorship. Baran (2008) states, "Because books are less dependent than other mass media on attracting the largest possible audience, books

Figure 1.8 Author Thomas Paine. Painting by Auguste Milliere.

Figure 1.10 A View of Murton Colliery near Seaham, County Durham, England. Painting by John Wilson Carmichael (1843).

Figure 1.9 Mass production of cars: Ford Motor Company assembly line in 1928.

are more able to and more likely to incubate new, challenging, or unpopular ideas. As the medium least dependent on advertiser support, books can be aimed at extremely small groups of readers, challenging them and their imaginations in ways that many sponsors would find unacceptable in advertising-based mass media" (p. 69).

Figure 1.11 Books are the first mass produced media. Books challenged earlier sources of information including local leaders and the Church. Today, books remain as one of the most intimate, persuasive, personal, and enlightening mediums in existence.

Postman (1985) states "typography fostered the modern idea of individuality, but it destroyed the medieval sense of community and integration. Typography made modern science possible but transformed religious sensibility into mere superstition. Typography assisted in the growth of the nation state but thereby made patriotism into a sordid if not lethal emotion," (p. 29).

In 2012, the American Association of Book Publishers reported that book sales reached $7.1 billion, up 6% from 2011. This growth was bolstered by the sale of ebooks, which now account for 23% of total book sales. By contrast, U.S. box office receipts for movie tickets were $10.2 billion. Electronic book readers, such as the Kindle, contribute to a four-fold increase in books read by users, according to maker Amazon.

NEWSPAPERS

McLuhan (1964) writes that both books and newspapers "are confessional in character, creating the effect of the inside story by their mere form, regardless of their content" (p. 205).

Newspapers similar to those we recognize today began in 1620. Corantos, a one-page "sheet," was printed in Holland, exported to England, and sold in bookstores. In England, the monarchy authorized the publication of the Oxford Gazette in 1665.

In America, Benjamin Harris, a printer/bookseller/coffeehouse owner, printed the broadsheet *Publick Occurrences Both Foreign and Domestick*, the nation's first daily newspaper, which was printed for just one day because Harris failed to obtain a license. In 1704, Boston Postmaster John Campbell began printing the *Boston News-Letter*. The newspaper, which published shipping news, English newspaper article reprints, and government-issued announcements, survived until the beginning of the Revolutionary War (1775). Benjamin Franklin's brother, James, began publishing a government-supported paper called the *New-England Courant* in 1721. Jailed for criticizing the governor of Massachusetts, James handed the paper off to his brother, Benjamin, who later moved to Philadelphia to print the *Pennsylvania Gazette*. The newspaper gained advertiser support, which provided cover for criticizing its governor and other elected leaders. By relying less on government funding, Franklin learned that he gained some freedom from government intervention.

After the Revolutionary War, America's first Congress enacted the first ten amendments, called the Bill of Rights, to the Constitution. The First Amendment reads:

Congress shall make no law respecting an establishment of religion, or prohibiting the free exercise thereof; or abridging the freedom of speech, or of the press; or of the right of the people to peacefully assemble, and to petition the Government for redress of grievances.

Democracy, government by the people, needs press freedom. The members of the first Congress knew this based on their experiences with European monarchies, which is where most of the inhabitants of America at the time had emigrated from. More recently, they recognized that local governments had shut down newspapers because they

Figure 1.12 First issue of the *Boston News-Letter*, regarded as the first continuously published newspaper in British North America. Published April 24, 1704.

criticized elected officials. Media scholar McChesney (2004) states, "The more democratic a society, the more likely the decisions about how best to regulate social life will be the result of widespread debate. The less democratic a society, the more likely those decisions will be made by powerful self-interested parties with a minimum of popular participation" (p. 19).

There is a range of interpretation of the First Amendment. Supreme Court Hugo Black, writing an opinion in 2005, wrote:

> No law means no law. My view is, without deviation, without exception, without any ifs, buts, or whereases, that freedom of speech means that government shall not do anything to people, either for the views they have or the views they express, or the words they speak or write.

Figure 1.13 Issue of the New-England Courant that resulted in a jail sentence for Benjamin Franklin's brother James.

But this is a fundamentalist perspective. Subsequent threats to First Amendment freedoms have challenged this definition, including:

- Attacks on the amendment from government sources other than Congress. What if laws are passed by states, city councils, or the courts? This is still an open question, from a legal perspective.
- Attacks on the definition of "the press" and "speech." What falls under these definitions today?
    - Movies (according to *Burstyn v. Wilson*) in 1952
    - Television networks (according to *CBS v. Democratic National Committee*) in 1973 where Justice William O. Douglas wrote "…that TV and radio are all included in the concept of 'press' as used in the First Amendment and therefore are entitled to live under the laissez faire regime which the First Amendment sanctions."
    - Advertising. In 1942, *Valentine v. Christen,* the Supreme Court ruled that all media are, in effect, commercial (advertising supported), although they ruled against the advertiser. The case went a long way toward protecting advertiser rights.
    - For entertainment fare, *Time, Inc. v. Hill,* confirmed that entertainment television carries the same rights for Freedom of Speech as non-entertainment programming.
    - During times of war. In *Schenck v. United States*, a case about the distribution of a pamphlet decrying the military draft during World War I, Justice Oliver

Wendell Holmes wrote, "the words used are used in such circumstances and are of such a nature as to create a clear and present danger that they will bring about the substantive evils that Congress has a right to prevent. Free speech should not protect a man in falsely shouting fire in a theatre and causing panic."

Newspapers with limited circulations continued in the United States through the early 1800s. Postman (1985) states that by 1730, seven newspapers were published on a regular basis. By 1800, there were more than 180. But the first truly "mass circulated" daily newspaper did not arrive until September 3, 1833 when Benjamin Day began publishing *The Sun* in New York City. Day's breakthrough was a new business model: sell the newspaper for a penny, attract a large readership, and sell the readers to advertisers. In this regard, Day innovated the commercial media model that later supported the burgeoning newspaper, radio, magazine, and television industries. Cutting the cost of a newspaper to a penny was significant considering established dailies were priced at 6 cents a copy. Starr's (2004) analysis of the origins of U.S. media states, "Depending entirely on revenue from readers and advertisers, the publishers of penny papers proclaimed their independence of any political party and represented themselves as the unfettered champions of the public in reporting the news" (p. 132).

This isn't to say that advertising failed to appear in earlier newspapers. From the start, newspapers typically included paid advertisements, although their form and approach differed significantly from today's. Postman states that early ads exemplified the typographic mind—the way in which books, pamphlets, and newspapers conditioned their users to think. "They assumed that potential buyers were literate, rational, analytical," he wrote. Three appeared in *The Boston Newsletter* (1704) including a reward for the capture of a thief, the sale of a property on Long Island, and a reward for the return of a lost anvil. In total, they took up four inches in a single column of the paper.

Between 1704 and the late 1800s, advertising messages maintained their appeals to logic, rationality, and understanding by boasting product or service attributes and price. At times, these product claims may have proven false. But the craft of advertising remained static in its approach for almost 200 years. Things changed in the 1890s when newspapers began publishing photographs. During the same decade, advertisers also began to develop and use slogans. By the turn of the century, Postman states, "advertisers no longer assumed rationality on the part of their potential customers. Advertising became one part depth psychology, one part aesthetic theory. Reason had to move itself to other arenas" (p. 60).

On the heels of *The Sun,* several other penny papers were launched in New York City including James Gordon Bennett's *New York Morning Herald* and Horace Greeley's *New York Tribune.* The *Herald* was the first to use correspondents, reporters in other cities, who filed stories using the telegraph, which became available for sending news stories in the 1840s. The *Tribune* was a Whig-leaning (later Republican) newspaper and considered "non-sensationalistic, issues-oriented, and humanitarian" and "established the mass newspaper as a powerful medium of social action" (Baran, 2008, p. 103).

THE TELEGRAPH AND WIRE SERVICES

In 1837, Samuel Morse successfully transmitted signals representing text with his invention—the telegraph. By the 1860s, telegraph networks enabled the sending and receiving of text from most major cities. Telegraph was the first technology to decouple people, space, and communication from one another. Before telegraph, information could move only as fast as a human could carry it. If someone carried the information on a train, that would be roughly 35 miles per hour.

Figure 1.14 Benjamin Day publisher of The New York Sun, penny press innovator.

Telegraph lines were most commonly called "lightning lines" by people just learning about their function. Parades and festivals heralded the introduction of lightning lines to their home towns. In New Jersey, the closing stock market index was telegraphed from Manhattan to the telegraph operator in the town's train station. Later, a train arrived with a gentleman physically carrying the same closing index. The residents erupted in cheers of amazement and disbelief when the numbers matched.

The telegraph matured to later carry personal messages, news stories, and even photographs. In 1856, six New York City papers including *The Sun, New York Morning Herald,* and *New York Tribune* established the first pooled newsgathering organization, the New York Associated Press. Other wire services followed including Associated Press (1900), United Press International (1907), and International News Service (1909).

Henry David Thoreau, philosopher and author of *Walden*, mourned the arrival of the telegraph. It brought "important" stories from Maine to Texas to local newspaper readers. Before the advent of the telegraph, all stories were written locally and covered local events. The telegraph, he argued, introduced impotence and irrelevance to the news. "We are in great haste to construct a magnetic telegraph from Maine to Texas; but Maine and Texas, it may be, have nothing important to communicate" (Thoreau, 1882, p. 84).

The concept of news impotence is an important one that is not discussed frequently enough in Mass Communication texts. The question behind the concept is: What can we really do about the news that we watch or read? With local coverage of news, people would fill their city or town halls to make personal appeals about their perspectives. After the telegraph, news from other places began to take up space in newspapers. As Postman states, "The local and the timeless had lost their central position in newspapers, eclipsed by the dazzle of distance and speed" (p. 66).

Over time, people have focused more of their attention to national issues and events considered "spectacular" by news editors. The telegraph made the unusual, the violent, the disgraceful, and the bizarre from all over the country, and later the globe, available

to print. As Thoreau suggested, "telegraphy made relevance irrelevant" (Postman, p. 67). Contextualization of the news, that is the lack of placing news stories into some kind of context with other stories or trends, apparently waned with the introduction of new and strange news stories from other places.

Postman asks, "How often does it occur that information provided to you on morning radio or television, or in the morning newspaper, causes you to alter your plans for the day, or to take some action you would have not otherwise taken, or provides insight into some problem you are required to solve?" (Postman, 68)

I always challenge students to attend a local town hall, council, or committee meeting. How many people attend these? As a local reporter for a few years, I can tell you that only a handful of people do.

Figure 1.15 Telegraph wires in New York City (1890).

Generally, I would watch the sessions, take notes, see one or two spectators, and write an article. It's sad how few people actually attend these meetings considering how important they are. People pay the majority of their taxes to their local municipalities and most of these fees go to local schools.

But, the modern media compel us to look at the world all upside down. We focus on national issues while the most important ones take place close to home. Economically, our attention should be on local news. But, we have learned to devalue localness due to the introduction of "global" news.

Postman writes about an information-action ratio. The idea behind it is that readers calculate the importance of

Figure 1.16 The Associated Press Building in New York City.

what they read based on the range of actions they can do about it. Since there was less and less people could do about what they had read, the notion of information overload or glut crept into our culture. What can we really do about the Pentagon, the CIA, the Middle East, or terrorism? The question perpetuates the information-impotence ratio.

Before telegraphy, with news stories locally produced, readers believed that they could do something about the things they read about. As Postman writes, "The telegraph introduced a kind of public conversation whose form had startling characteristics: Its language was the language of headlines—sensational, fragmented, impersonal. News took the form of slogans, to be noted with excitement, to be forgotten, with dispatch" (p. 70).

Figure 1.17 Henry David Thoreau. Portrait by Benjamin D. Maxham (daguerreotype).

The telegraph also introduced a stranglehold of sorts on the news people read from distant places. Blondheim (2004) described the relationship between Associated Press and Western Union, the monopoly telegraph company, as "symbiotic" and that it raised "troubling issues about who was controlling news and information and presenting it as unbiased when, in fact, it had lots of political bias as demonstrated during the 1876 election of Rutherford B. Hayes." After the Civil War, Blondheim argues that the close ties between Western Union and Associated Press established a monopoly on news, and "opened up troubling questions about the control of information. This led to a rise of anti-monopolist sentiment that called for government takeover of the Associated Press in order to safeguard the flow of information as a public good and limit harmful discrimination. … In the 1880s, for instance, the Associated Press entered into a secretive agreement to distribute exclusive news to regional news-brokers while excluding others in return for a kickback. The Associated Press worked to cultivate a veneer of objectivity in news reporting while simultaneously engaging in extremely biased coverage."

Schudson (1978) reports that the Associated Press claimed to have adopted an "objective" approach so its style wouldn't run contrary to its client newspapers. However, the author believes this to be a shallow argument. If anything, the Associated Press contributed to the sensationalism that ran rampant with the later "yellow journalism" phase of journalism. Yellow journalism, according to Baran (2008), "was a study in excess—sensational sex, crime, and disaster news; giant headlines; heavy use of illustrations; and reliance on cartoons and color" (p. 105). In addition, while attracting broad audiences, newspapers skewed their coverage in favor of conservative political positions and pro-business or pro-corporate perspectives. The peak of "yellow journalism" coincided with the newspaper circulation wars between Joseph Pulitzer's *New York World* and William Randolph Hearst's *New York Journal* (1895–1898) but continued into the early

20th century. Some observers believe local television news is currently engaged in "yellow journalism." What do you think?

It is important to recognize that the "customers" of major newspapers are its advertisers. Readers are the commodity sold to these customers. Playing by these rules, the most important thing a publisher can do is to produce a paper that attracts the largest possible audience that may, in turn, be sold (at the highest possible cost)

Figure 1.18 Western Union Telegraph Building, New York City. Built in 1875 at 195 Broadway and destroyed in 1914. The building housed 100 telegraph operators who worked 24 hours a day.

Figure 1.19 Peak of yellow journalism? The cause of the Maine's sinking remains the subject of speculation. Suggestions have included an undetected fire in one of her coal bunkers, a naval mine and her deliberate sinking to drive the U.S. into a war with Spain. The cause and responsibility for her sinking remained unclear after a board of inquiry. Nevertheless, popular opinion in the U.S., fanned by inflammatory articles printed in the "Yellow Press" by William Randolph Hearst and Joseph Pulitzer, blamed Spain.

to its advertisers. In the newspaper business, editors and journalists call the portion of the paper where they place their stories the "news hole." While laying out each page of the paper, the revenue-producing content (the ads) is always placed first. The remaining space is used for the stories (the filler).

In today's political and social environment, many people believe the media, in general, are liberally biased. When newspapers and television news are attacked for not being objective, they are typically accused of being the "liberal news media." According to McChesney (2004), this perspective is "kept alive by hardcore political organizing. Launched in earnest in the 1970s by financial backers with deep pockets, conservatives blamed the liberal media for losing the Vietnam War and for fomenting dissent in the United States" (p. 111). He reports that these organizers spent about $1 billion to get Americans to question its media establishment. Beyond this, "the campaign to alter the media has entailed funding the training of conservative and business journalists at universities and bankrolling right-wing student newspapers to breed a generation of pro-business Republican journalists" (p. 112).

According to the Newspaper Association of America, about 44 million newspapers are sold daily in the United States (2011 data). About half of our population reads a newspaper daily. But this average hides an important demographic trend. While almost 80% of people over age 35 read a newspaper, only 19% of adults under age 35 report doing so.

As newspaper readership deteriorates, so too does an important medium that follows news in your town or local area. At Raritan Valley Community College (North Branch, NJ), several local newspapers covered stories about the campus and events or news in the local area. Many of these have either gone out of business or have significantly scaled back their operations in the last few years, including the *Courier-News*, *Hunterdon County Democrat*, *Somerset Messenger-Gazette*, and *Home News*. Most of these once-independent and well-staffed newsrooms now share resources (i.e., have reporters cover much larger "beats" and/or geographic areas). Searching the web for these papers points readers to <mycentraljersey.com> (Gannett Newspapers, which owns 80 daily newspapers including *USAToday*, with $5.4 billion in annual revenues) or to <nj.com> (Advance Publications, a division of Newhouse, that owns 19 papers, with $7.6 billion in annual revenues).

IBIS World states, "As the internet becomes the go-to news source for many readers, newspapers will experience a mass exodus of advertisers and readers. The growing popularity of real-time reporting and customizable ad campaigns means that

The US Newspaper Industry at Crossroads?

In the second quarter of 2007, the print ad revenue of the US newspapers decreased by 10.2% to $10.5 billion, compared to the same period in 2006. At the same time, the advertising in the online versions of newspapers moved up 19% than that of 2006, to hit $796 million.[1] According to Newspaper Association of America (NAA)[2], the print ad revenue of the US newspapers has been declining since 2005. NAA pointed out that the industry players have been in financial crisis because of the high

[1] Douglas McIntyre A., "Gannett And The New York Times: Newspaper Revenue Drop Quickens", http://www.247wallst.com/2007/09/gannett-and-the.html, September 3rd 2007
[2] The Newspaper Association of America (NAA) is a trade association in the US which represents the country's largest daily newspapers. It provides services including market research, technology education and support.

overhead costs associated with the print newspapers. Decreasing circulations of newspapers due to the increasing popularity of digital media is also said to have contributed to the losses of the industry. While many analysts predict that the US newspaper industry will go completely online in the near future, many others believe that the print newspapers are here to stay. It is generally believed the newspaper companies will retain their local divisions in the print format as local advertising and circulations are significant revenue sources for the companies, while their national and international editions will eventually be diluted. Analysts view the aggressive cost cutting strategies, being initiated by many companies in the industry, as an effort to protect their print newspapers. However, speculation is rife that the newspapers will undergo a paradigm shift from print medium to online medium.

US Newspaper Industry: An Insight

The United States is considered to be the largest and most technologically powerful economy in the world. In 2006, the US economy had the world's highest GDP of $13.21 trillion, with a per capita GDP of $43,500.[3] The United States is considered to be the 4th largest newspaper market in the world, in terms of circulation.[4] Newspaper publishing is one of the oldest and largest segments of the media industry in the country. According to NAA, as of 2006, newspaper publishing is a $59 billion industry in the US which employs approximately 356,000 people.[5] The US newspaper industry consists of daily (morning and evening dailies), weekly, monthly, and Sunday newspapers, and the online newspapers. In the US, large circulation newspapers are usually produced daily, and the community newspapers are usually weeklies. The industry also constitutes controlled- circulation papers and free newspapers.

The history of US newspapers dates back to the 14th century, when the handwritten newsletters were widely circulated, in order to provide information on government and politics. The first news report in the Americas was printed in Mexico in 1541.[6] According to Mitchell Stephens, an industry analyst, Britain's American colonies entered the world of the newspaper relatively late because of their sparse populations and strict governments.[7] In the 16th and 17th centuries, printed newsbooks, short pamphlets reporting on a news event, and news ballads, were popular in the European colonies in America. The first printed American newspaper was published in 1690.[8]

The US newspaper industry witnessed growth through the 17th and 18th centuries. There were about 200 newspapers in the US in 1801.[9] The number of players in the industry increased exponentially over

3   "The World Fact Book", https://www.cia.goV/library/publications/the-world-factbook/geos/us.html#Intro, November 1st 2007
4   Balding Timothy, "World Trends in the Newspaper Industry: An Update", http://extranet.anj.org.br/palestras/cbj2006/timothy_balding.ppt, 2006
5   Jones Jonathan, "What You Should Know about the Newspaper Industry", http://www.pbs.org/wgbh/pages/frontline/newswar/part3/newspaperprimer.html, February 27th 2007
6   Stephens Mitchell, "History of Newspapers", http://www.nyu.edu/classes/stephens/Collier's%20page.htm, May 2005
7   Ibid.
8   "A Newspaper Timeline", http://www.wan-press.org/article2822.html, 2004
9   "History of Newspapers", op.cit.

the years. In 1830, the number of newspapers published in the US was 715, which increased to 5,091 by 1870.[10]

The early newspapers faced high overhead costs, as they had to incur the same initial outlays for equipment, typesetting and editorial matter, regardless of the number of copies printed. In the initial years of publishing, the high operating costs were covered with the help of government or political parties, on which the newspapers were heavily dependent. Rapid urbanisation of the US, following industrialisation, resulted in overall economic development of the country. By late 18th century, people required more information about markets and price listings, following increased commerce. By this time, the population in the US also began to grow and literacy rate increased. This increased the popularity of newspapers, which helped the publishers to spread their overhead costs over more readers. And the newspaper companies gradually became stand-alone entities, independent of government or other bodies. The urbanisation and increased information requirements of people, also transformed the newspapers to a daily from a weekly publication.

When the circulation increased, the newspapers gained popularity as an advertising medium. The US wholesalers, who were trying to catch the attention of the other merchants, were the first advertisers in the newspapers. By the late 1880s, with productive capacity increasing in all industries in the US, retail advertising aimed at a mass market became prominent. By 1900, the newspapers were flooded with commodity advertisements like for instance, the ads of soap and patent medicines. And the dailies in the big cities earned significant revenue through selling their advertising space. In early 1900s, such dailies were earning between 70% and 80% of their revenues through advertising. [11]

In the early 1900s, the American newspaper industry was dominated by small, family-owned newspapers. But they faced stiff competition from other daily and weekly newspapers. The industry became more competitive with the entrance of a number of new players. David Demers, of Washington State University, in his study titled, Media Concentration in the United States, said, "In 1910, there were about 2202 dailies in the US. There were 559 cities with a daily, or 61% of the total, had two or more competing newspapers".12 The new companies competed on content quality and price, and sold their newspapers, with more emphasis on local news, for a half or a third of the price of the older newspapers.

However, many of the new players could not sustain their growth, due to the high operating cost of newspapers, and many small companies went out of business. The increased newsprint and other operating cost affected the old family-owned newspapers also, and many of those companies fell in deep financial crisis. Mitchell Stephens said, "The capital requirement for the newspaper industry was high, and many budding players were not able to cope up with the high operating costs. Numerous new

10   "A Newspaper Timeline", op.cit.
11   "Newspapers, Politics and the State", http://www.thecanadianencyclopedia.com/index.cfm?PgNm=TCE&Params=A1S EC825182, 2007
12   Jolly Rhonda, "Media ownership deregulation in the United States and Australia: in the public interest?", http://www.aph. gov.au/Library/pubs/RP/2007-08/08rp01.pdf, July 24th 2007

papers were founded, bought, merged, sold or abandoned."[13] In the early 1910s, the US newspaper industry witnessed many mergers and acquisitions whereby smaller newspapers were acquired by other financially sound companies.

By 1914, the US newspaper industry witnessed the formation of large newspaper chains which owned multiple newspapers. In 1914, the Scripps-McRae League, the first large newspaper chain in the US, was publishing 23 newspapers. In 1922, William Randolph Hearst, owned the second largest chain in the US, whose media conglomerate consisted of 20 daily and 11 Sunday newspapers.[14] By the end of 1920s, the number of newspapers under chain ownership increased to 20%, from 1.4% in 1900.[15]

According to analysts, the US newspaper industry was stable in the 1930s and 1940s. Elizabeth M. Neiva (Neiva) at Columbia University said, "There were no significant technological innovations and the industry had enjoyed years of relative stability".[16] She added, "The origin of the newspaper industry's transformation can be traced to the post World War II (WW II) years. After the WW II, government had lifted wartime wage freezes, production workers began demanding substantial salary increases. Production costs, made worse by postwar inflation, soared. But most publishers were illequipped to cope with these sudden cost increases." [17]

According to a 1953 Harvard Business School study, "Publishers of the period had little knowledge of, and considerable contempt for, the skills normally associated with running a business. Publishers viewed their papers as local institutions, not as commercial enterprises".[18] According to the study, the situation changed when radio and later television, entered the communication landscape of the US. It threatened the dominance of newspapers in the US communication arena. According to Neiva, by 1960, the newspaper industry landed in a crisis, mainly due to the competition from radio and TV. This resulted in the industry witnessing some consolidations. By 1970s, two-thirds of the nation's 1,700 dailies were owned by 170 newspaper groups. Neiva also mentioned, "By 1970s, the pool of available independent newspapers had all but dried up. The big companies needed to continue expanding, but there was nothing to buy. Many therefore began exploring other news-related ventures".[19] Between 1969 and 1973, many newspaper companies, like for instance The New York Times, Washington Post, and Times Mirror, went public.

The growth crisis created by radio and TV continued through 1980s, and the nation's publicly traded papers were in immense trouble. The newspaper giants like Gannett Company[20], ventured into new

---

13   "History of Newspapers", op.cit.
14   Ibid.
15   Demers David, "Media Concentration in the United States", http://www.cem.ulaval.ca/CONCetatsUnis.pdf, 2001
16   Neiva Elizabeth M., "Chain Building: The Consolidation of the American Newspaper Industry, 1955-1980", http://www.h-net.msu.edu/~business/bhcweb/publications/BEHprint/v024n1/p0022-p0026.pdf, 1995
17   Ibid.
18   Ibid.
19   Ibid.
20   Gannett Company Inc., a leading international news and information company, founded by Frank E. Gannett in 1906. The Washington headquartered company publishes 85 daily newspapers and nearly 1,000 non-daily publications, and operates 23

growth areas. Gannett unveiled the first national newspaper, USA Today, in 1982, and many other firms diversified into cable television. Many other chains also began to channel their profit into new businesses. By late 1980s, the state of the US newspaper industry improved, and in 1987 the circulation of US newspapers peaked at 63 million.21 (Exhibit I). By the late 19th century, large, publicly traded media conglomerates dominated the industry.

Exhibit I: The Circulation of Newspapers in the US 1960-2004

YEAR	MORNING	EVENING	TOTAL M&E	SUNDAY
1960	24,028,788	34,852,958	58,881,746	47,698,651
1965	24,106,776	36,250,787	60,357,563	48,600,090
1970	25,933,793	36,173,744	62,107,527	49,216,602
1975	25,490,186	35,165,245	60,655,431	51,096,393
1980	29,414,036	32,787,804	62,201,840	54,671,755
1985	36,361,561	26,404,671	62,766,232	58,825,978
1990	41,311,167	21,016,795	62,327,962	62,634,512
1991	41,469,756	19,217,369	60,687,125	62,067,820
1992	42,387,813	17,776,686	60,164,499	62,159,971
1993	43,093,866	16,717,737	59,811,594	62,565,574
1994	43,381,578	15,923,865	59,305,436	62,294,799
1995	44,310,252	13,883,145	56,193,397	61,229,296
1996	44,784,812	12,198,486	56,983,290	60,797,814
1997	45,433,888	11,294,021	56,727,902	60,486,463
1998	45,643,495	10,538,603	56,182,092	60,065,892
1999	45,997,367	9,981,971	55,979,332	59,894,381
2000	46,772,497	9,000,350	55,772,847	59,420,999
2001	46,821,480	8,756,566	55,578,046	59,090,364
2002	46,617,163	8,568,994	55,186,157	58,780,299
2003	46,930,215	8,255,136	55,185,351	58,494,695
2004	46,887,440	7,738,648	54,626,138	57,753,013

Source: "The Source—Newspapers by the Numbers" http://web.naa.org/thesource/2005/the_source_newspapers_by_the_numbers.pdf, 2005

---

television stations in the US, as of 2007.
21   "Media Concentration in the United States", op.cit.

Exhibit II: Circulation Revenue of the US Newspapers 1975-2005

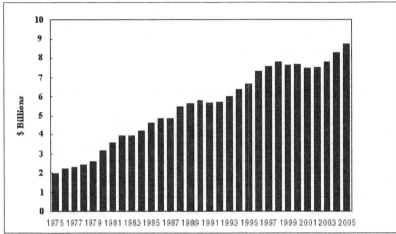

Source: Bone Allison, "Revenue Fluctuations for Newspaper Publishers",
http://www.statcan.ca/english/research/63F0002XIE/63F0002XIE2007051.htm, January 22nd 2007

In 2000, there were 1483 dailies in the US with a total circulation of 55 million, and the number of ownership entities was 436. The number of weekly newspapers was about 8,000 with a total circulation of 75 million. As of 2000, 80% of all the newspapers in the US, were under chain or group ownership. In 2001, there were 124 newspaper chains in the US and each of these chains owned nine newspapers, on an average. The leading chains like Gannett, Knight-Ridder, Newhouse and Times Mirror, accounted for more than one-fourth of the total US newspaper circulations.[22]

In 2005, there were about 2000 companies in the US newspaper industry with combined annual revenue of $50 billion. The large companies included Gannett, Knight Ridder, Advance Publications, Tribune Company, Washington Post, and New York Times. The industry was highly concentrated, where over 60% of the market was controlled by the top 20 companies, as of 2005.[23] When a few newspapers like the Wall Street Journal, USA Today, Los Angeles Times, Washington Post, and New York Times managed a circulation of more than 1 million, almost 85% of the newspapers had circulation under 50,000.[24] And the total daily circulation of all the US newspapers was slightly less than 60 million.[25] Exhibits II shows the annual revenues of the US newspaper industry from circulations.

According to analysts, the US newspaper industry was a loose oligopoly dominated by around ten chains, as of 2006. These top ten companies owned 14 of the top 20 newspapers, and 60 of the top 100 newspapers in the US. These chains also accounted for more than half of the 50 million circulations in the US.[26]

---

22   Ibid.

23   "The US Newspaper Industry is Highly Concentrated with the Top 20 Companies Controlling Over 60% of the Market", http://findarticles.com/p/articles/mi_m0EIN/is_2005_Sept_22/ai_n15626002, September 22nd 2005

24   "The State of the News Media",http://www.stateofthenewsmedia.org/2005/narrative_newspapers_audience. asp?cat=3&media=2, 2005

25   "The US Newspaper Industry is Highly Concentrated with the Top 20 Companies Controlling Over 60% of the Market", op.cit.

26   "US Newspapers", http://www.oligopolywatch.com/2004/02/08.html, February 8th 2004

However, through the ages, managing cost continued to be a critical factor for the success of a newspaper. The major operating cost components of US newspapers include printing costs, labor costs and distribution costs. The newsprint costs and other printing costs account for a major share of operating cost; labor and distribution costs come next. The major revenue sources of US newspapers are advertising and circulations. All the US newspapers earn money through advertising and paid circulations, except the free newspapers whose sole revenue source is advertising. By 2000, about 80% of the industry revenue was from sales of advertising space, and about 20% came from single-copy sales and subscription.27 Exhibits III shows the increase in the ad spending in the US newspapers from 1965 to 2004 and Exhibits IV represents the increase in ad revenue of the print medium between 1975-2005.

Exhibit III: Growth in US Newspaper Ad Spending

YEAR	NATIONAL ADVERTISING (MILLIONS)	RETAIL ADVERTISING (MILLIONS)	CLASSIFIED ADVERTISING (MILLIONS)	TOTAL PRINT NEWSPAPER ADVERTISING (MILLIONS)
1965	$783	$2,429	$1,214	$4,426
1970	891	3,292	1,521	5,704
1975	1,109	4,966	2,159	8,234
1980	1,963	8,609	4,222	14,794
1985	3,352	13,443	8,375	25,170
1990	4,122	16,652	11,506	32,280
1991	3,924	15,839	10,587	30,349
1992	3,834	16,041	10,764	30,639
1993	3,853	16,859	11,157	31,869
1994	4,149	17,496	12,464	34,109
1995	4,251	18,099	13,742	36,092
1996	4,667	18,344	15,065	38,075
1997	5,315	19,242	16,773	41,330
1998	5,721	20,331	17,873	43,925
1999	6,732	20,907	18,650	46,289
2000	7,653	21,409	19,608	48,670
2001	7,004	20,679	16,622	44,305
2002	7,210	20,994	15,898	44,102
2003	7,797	21,341	15,801	44,939
2004	8,083	22,012	16,608	46,703

Source: "The Source—Newspapers by the Numbers"http://web.naa.org/thesource/2005/the_source_newspapers_by_the_numbers.pdf, 2005

Exhibit IV: Advertising Revenue of the US Newspapers 1975-2005

Source: Bone Allison, "Revenue Fluctuations for Newspaper Publishers", http://www.statcan.ca/english/research/63F0002XIE/63F0002XIE2007051.htm, January 22nd 2007

---

27 "The US Newspaper Industry is Highly Concentrated with the Top 20 Companies Controlling Over 60% of the Market". op.cit.

According to analysts the overhead costs of the US newspapers have increased substantially over the

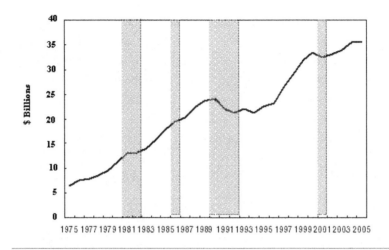

years. However, companies have adopted various strategies to reduce their operating costs. According to EDGAR Online[28], "Over the last several years, newspapers have used a clustering strategy consisting of owning and managing papers with geographic proximity in order to achieve both revenue and cost benefits. Newspaper clusters are able to offer advertisers broader, bundled purchasing compared to the narrower reach of a single newspaper. Clusters can also facilitate cost efficiencies by consolidating printing facilities, distribution channels, sharing editorial resources and other types of centralized cost savings".[29]

However it is felt that the print medium is losing its dominance in US communication arena, in spite of all its cost cutting initiatives. The decreasing circulation of US newspapers is a strong indication of the downward trend in the popularity of the medium. Statistics indicate that the newspaper circulation in the US is decreasing every year. According to a study conducted by World Association of Newspapers (WAN)[30], in 2005 the circulation of the US newspapers declined by 2.4%, compared to the year before. While the circulation of morning dailies decreased by 1.6%, the evening dailies' circulation was down by 6.6%. The decline in overall newspaper circulation for a five year period ended in 2005 was 4.2%. During the same period, the daily newspaper circulation was down by 1.4% and the evening daily circulation decreased by 17.5%. In 2005, the Sunday newspaper circulation was also decreased by

28   EDGAR Online, Inc. is a leading provider of interactive business and financial data on global companies to financial, corporate and advisory professionals.
29   "Hollinger Inc. - Information on the Company", http://sec.edgar-online.com/2003/09/17/0000909567-03- 001081/Section4. asp, September 17th 2003
30   World Association of Newspaper (WAN), founded in 1948, represents about 18,000 newspapers worldwide. The Paris- based organisation was established to promote press freedom worldwide.

6.5%, from that of 2004, and the total loss in the five year period was 4.3%. At the same time, the non daily newspaper of the US witnessed an increase in their circulations. In 2005, the non daily newspaper circulation increased by 6% over 2004, and recorded a total growth of 2.5% in the five year period till 2005.[31] According to NAA, the average daily circulation of US newspapers fell 2.8% to about 43.8 million copies for the first half of 2006.[32]

According to industry experts, many factors have contributed to the decline in the US newspaper circulations. Some industry analysts believed that, the National Do Not Call Registry[33], which has forced newspapers to rely less on telemarketing to secure subscribers, has added to the worries of newspaper industry. John Kimball, chief marketing officer for the NAA said, "Of all the things that have happened, [the change in telemarketing rules] had the single largest impact." Kimball added, "Newspapers relied on telemarketing to acquire an average of 60 to 65% of their home delivery subscribers. As a result of the registry, newspapers have cut that figure down to 50 or 55%."[34]

Many analysts like Kimball believed that a shift in strategy among major newspapers, to focus less on short-term promotions, which generally help acquire new readers, have also contributed to industry losses. Kimball said, "Newspapers are focusing less on short-term promotions and more on going after people who are likely to subscribe for a longer period. Such subscribers 'take a lot longer to acquire in the first place, and acquisition costs are higher.'"[35]

Another factor that seemed to have affected the newspaper industry is the increased popularity of TV and radio, as news sources. According to a 2006 survey conducted by Pew Internet & American Life Project, a US Internet research project, TV and radio were the most popular news sources for Americans. As per the survey, 59% of Americans depended on TV channels and 44% of Americans were listening to radio for news updates. The survey also mentioned that the popularity of newspapers is decreasing as a news medium, and only 38% of Americans read various Us newspapers on a typical day in 2006.[36]

According to analysts, the increasing popularity of digital media was another major factor which contributed to the decline in newspaper circulations. Fredric A. Emmett, an industry expert said, the principal trend represented by the interactive media, fueled by the advance of digital technology and the growing convergence of the computer, telephone and cable television, affected the newspaper industry.[37]

---

31 "World Trends in the Newspaper Industry: An Update", op.cit.

32 "US newspaper circulation down 2.8%", http://www.itfacts.biz/index.php?id=P7641, October 30th 2006

33 The National Do Not Call Registry (NDNC Registry) is intended to give the US consumers an opportunity to limit the telemarketing calls they receive. It was initiated in June 2003, by the US Federal Trade Commission. The primary objective of the Registry is to curb Unsolicited Commercial Communication (UCC). The subscribers can register their numbers to the registry to avoid telemarketing calls. The registry only applies to residential lines, not to business lines.

34 Shin Annys, "Newspaper Circulation Continues to Decline", http://www.washingtonpost.com/wp- dyn/content/article/2005/05/02/AR2005050201457.html, May 3rd 2005

35 Ibid.

36 "Online News: For many home broadband users, the Internet is a primary news source", http://www.pewinternet.org/pdfs/PIP_News.and.Broadband.pdf, March 22nd 2006

37 Emmert Fredric, "US Media in the 1990s", http://usinfo.state.gov/usa/infousa/media/files/media1cd.htm, 2000

Digital Media: The Changing Trend

According to analysts, the US media landscape has come a long way from the time when the newspapers were considered the only source of news. Digital media and the Internet had a dramatic impact on the communication landscape of the US. By the mid 1990s, digital computers and Internet became widely popular in the US. This was followed by the invention of various media like interactive television[38], mobile devices, podcasting[39] and graphic user interface technology[40]. By 2000, the industry of the US was dominated by these media, collectively known as new media[41]. The dot-com boom of 2000, made Internet more popular among the American mass, and it started grabbing some market share from the traditional media in the US. As of 2006, digital media was a $20 billion industry in the US. It is estimated that by 2011 the US digital media industry will grow to $80 billion.[42]

Analysts at Rossiter & Co, a UK based consulting firm, pointed out interactivity, freedom of choice, instant availability and cost effectiveness of new media as certain factors which gave them an advantage over the traditional media.[43] According to analysts, the costs associated with the new media like Internet, were comparatively lesser than that of traditional media.[44]

According to Nielsen/NetRatings[45] reports, Internet usage increased in the US, especially after the dot-com boom of 2000. Nielsen/NetRatings reported, "As of December 2000, more than 158 million people in the US had access to the Internet".[46] By the end of 2000, approximately 69.6 million or 71% of the total home users in the US had internet access. This was an increase of about 95%, compared to the 35.6 million home users in the US who had access to Internet in 1999. Nielsen/NetRatings also reported that, in 2000, the number of US homes which had access to broadband Internet increased to approximately 11.7 million. This was 148% increase, when compared to the 4.7 million home users who

---

38   Interactive TV is the programming that blends traditional TV viewing with the interactivity of a personal computer, and provides interactive content.

39   Podcasting is the process of transmitting an audio file to be downloaded and viewed/heard by other Internet users either on a computer or MP3 player. Podcasting is a method of releasing files to the Internet, allowing users to subscribe and receive new files automatically.

40   Graphic use interface technology is the term given to that set of items and facilities which provide the user with a graphic means for manipulating screen data rather than being limited to character based commands.

41   According to analysts at Rossiter & Co (UK), the emergence of new media happened in three phases - video, multimedia, and websites.

42   "Digital Marketing, Privacy & the Public Interest", http://www.democraticmedia.org/current_projects/privacy, April 3rd 2007

43   "Public Communication and the New Media", http://www.rundfunk-institut.uni-koeln.de/institut/pdfs/13100.pdf, December 2000

44   Ibid.

45   Nielsen//NetRatings is a part of Nielsen Online unit of The Nielsen Company, a global information and media company. The services of Nielsen//NetRatings include, Internet audience measurement, online advertising intelligence, user lifestyle and demographic data, e-commerce and transaction metrics, and custom data and research and analysis.

46   "Digital Media Industry", http://www.lib.washington.edu/business/guides/dig.html, March 2002

had Internet access in 1999.[47] It was also reported that the number of households which have access to high speed Internet was also on the rise.

With the increasing popularity of Internet, the ad spend on the medium increased. It is reported that the internet advertising revenue outpaced the cable and broadcast television significantly, in comparable early growth periods. In 2005, the internet advertising accounted for nearly 5% of total

US advertising revenue, up from less than 4% reported in 2004.[48] Pete Petrusky, Director, PricewaterhouseCoopers LLP said, "Continued strong growth in online advertising documents that an increasing number of advertisers and marketers see the Internet as an essential brand-building component in their media planning. The Internet delivers the right audience at the right time - a winning combination for all types of marketers. We expect to see continued growth in Internet advertising spend."[49]

Many analysts believed that the traditional medium is becoming the last choice for many advertisers. TNS Media Intelligence reported that, in 2005, newspaper advertising witnessed the slowest rate of growth within the media industry. The combined national and local newspaper advertising rose by a mere 1.8% to about $28.6 billion, when the internet advertising rose 13% to $8.3 billion.[50] In 2006, print newspapers accounted for 18.7% of the total advertising expenditure in the US, which was 1.2% less than that of 2005.[51] According to figures compiled by the NAA, in Q2 of 2007, print-only advertising in the US newspapers slumped 10.2% to $10.5 billion. It was the fifth consecutive quarter of decline in the print advertising in the US newspapers, as per NAA estimates. [52]

The biggest decline in print ad was in the classified ads category, which was considered to be a large source of revenue for the newspapers. Peter Zollman (Zollman), Editor, Classified Intelligence[53] said, "Classified ads contribute a good share of most the newspapers' revenue. The decline in print classified ads has affected the US newspapers badly".[54] Zollman continued, "Newspapers are losing recruitment, automotive, real estate, and other ad revenue to online competitors".[55] According to Zollman, the newspapers are doing little to hold on to, or grow their classified franchises. He added that the newspapers are

---

47 Ibid.
48 "IAB Internet Revenue Report-An Industry Survey", http://www.ameinfo.com/pdf/iab/IAB_PwC_2005full.pdf, April 2006
49 Ibid.
50 MacMillan Robert, "US newspapers weigh choices in struggling market", http://www.newswatch.in/news- analyses/markets-companies/5089.html, June 8th 2006
51 "U.S. Advertising Expenditures Increased 4.1 Percent in 2006; Online Advertising Shows Biggest Gain", http://www.rtoonline.com/Content/Article/Mar07/2006AdvertisingExpenditures031407.asp, March 14th 2007
52 Sutel Seth, "Advertising at U.S. papers falls 8.6%", http://cnews.canoe.ca/CNEWS/MediaNews/2007/08/31/pf- 4461543.html, August 31^ 2007
53 Classified Intelligence, publishers of Classified Intelligence Report, is a leading consulting group in traditional and interactive advertising. It was founded by Peter M. Zollman.
54 Evans Blanche, "Newspapers Continue to Price Themselves Out of Ads", http://realtytimes.com/rtapages/20050309_newspapers.htm, March 9th 2005
55 Ibid.

losing the private party buyers and sellers, landlords and tenants, auto dealers, home buyers, romance seekers, and the rest of the consumer spectrum.[56]

According to analysts, the advertisers prefer online media to print, mainly because of the interactive nature of online media, especially for the classified advertising. The Center for Digital Democracy (CDD)[57] reported, "The interactive marketing through new media has the power to deeply engage you in what is being sold".[58] Zollman, supports this while saying that, the newspapers failed to create the kinds of interactive marketplaces like eBay[59] and Craigslist[60].[61] He continued, "Craigslist has stamped out marketplaces in nearly 100 cities worldwide with an easy memorable URL: cityname.craigslist.org. eBay doesn't do this - but imagine the effect if it began parsing its massive database by locality, i.e., yourcity.ebay.com. If you're a newspaper classifieds director, it should send chills up your spine".[62]

Zollman cites the high cost for advertising in the newspaper, as another reason for decreasing ad spend on the medium. He said, "With few exceptions, most papers are an improbable place for the private party who just wants 25 bucks for her old kitchen table, or the family hoping to raise a couple hundred dollars in a garage sale when it costs that much to advertise in the paper".[63] A survey conducted by Classified Intelligence with Belden Associates pointed out that, pricing and options for print and online merchandise classifieds is making it difficult for newspapers to compete. After surveying 71 US newspapers of all sizes, Zollman said, "The pricing and packaging for private-party merchandise ads seems to be driven by what it costs to put a few lines of ink on a page or a half-tone in print".[64]

The survey explained that the merchandise ads are subordinate to employment, real estate, and automotive advertising, where these online media find the biggest accounts, most repeat business, and their best revenue.[65] In the opinion of Blanche Evans, the editor of Realty Times (an online real estate news service provider), "Print costs are too much for small advertisers, which is where low-cost, high-traffic online sites get their feet in the door, but what's at stake is that sites like eBay are also leaching away eyeballs from core employment, real estate, and automotive ads".[66]

Another reason cited for the increasing popularity of Internet among advertisers is the measurability of online advertising. According to analysts, measuring advertising effectiveness in print media is far more difficult than measuring online advertising. They believed that there were no standard tools existing which gave accurate details about print advertising reach. Rich Gordon, a Northwest University

---

56 Ibid.
57 The Center for Digital Democracy (CDD) is a nonprofit organisation, founded in 2001. The Washington, D.C. based organisation contributes towards the development of sustainable online communities and services.
58 "Digital Marketing, Privacy & the Public Interest", op.cit.
59 eBay.com is a worldwide online auction and shopping website which enables people and businesses buy and sell goods and services. eBay has also established localised websites in several countries.
60 Craigslist is a centralised network of online communities, featuring free classified advertisements and forums on various topics. It was established in 1995.
61 "Newspapers Continue to Price Themselves Out of Ads", op.cit.
62 Ibid.
63 Ibid.
64 Ibid.
65 Ibid.
66 Ibid.

professor, quoted some publishers, "Internet is the most measurable medium ever - one that allows accurate measurement of site usage and advertising effectiveness".[67]

However, as of 2005, newspapers made up the largest category of overall advertising expenditures in the United States (Exhibit V). According to TNS Media Intelligence report, the traditional media accounted for the largest share in the overall advertising expenditure in the US in 2006. But, the report indicated that the traditional media is losing its advertisements to the emerging digital media. A study released by the media investment firm Veronis Suhler Stevenson (VSS), predicted that the overall Internet ad spending in the US, including the advertising on websites of traditional media outlets, will surpass print newspaper advertising in 2010, to become the largest advertising category.[68] (Exhibit VI).

Exhibit V: Advertising Expenditure in Various Media in the US (in $ Millions)

	2003	2004	2005
Newspapers	$46,155	$48,244	$49,436
National	$7,797	$8,083	$7,910
Retail	$21,341	$22,012	$22,178
Classified	$15,801	$16,608	$17,312
Online[1]	$1,216	$1,541	2,027
Magazines	$11,435	$12,247	$12,847
Broadcast TV	$41,932	$46,267	44,293
Cable TV	$18,814	$21,527	23,654
Radio	$19,100	$19,581	19,640
Direct Mail	$48,370	$52,191	55,218
Yellow Pages	$13,896	$14,002	14,229
Miscellaneous[2]	$31,990	$34,654	35,692
Business papers	$4,004	$4,072	4,170
Outdoor	$5,443	$5,770	6,232
Internet[3]	$4,434	55,312	5,737
TOTAL ALL MEDIA	$245,573	$263,867	271,148

1. Advertising in newspaper websites
2. Includes weeklies and pennypffss
3. Non-newspaper internet advertising

Source: "The Source—Newspapers by the Numbers," http://web.naa.org/thesource/2005/the_source_newspapers_by_the_numbers.pdf, 2005

67   Gordon Rich, "Sizing Up Online Audience Measurement Services", http://www.naa.org/Resources/Articles/Digital-Edge-Sizing-Up-Online-Audience-Measurement-Services/Digital-Edge-Sizing-Up-Online-Audience-Measurement-Services.aspx, June 8th 2007

68   "Online ads to overtake US newspapers", http://www.ft.com/cms/s/0/6098d396-4448-11dc-90ca- 0000779fd2ac,dwp_uuid=e8477cc4-c820-11db-b0dc-000b5df10621.html?nclick_check=1, August 7th 2007

Exhibit VI: Growth Forecast of the US Internet Advertising (in $ Millions)

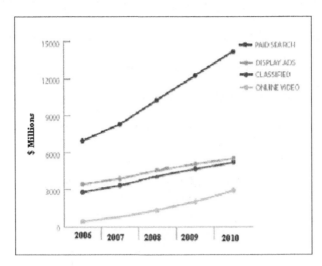

Source: "Future of Media Report", http://www.rossdawsonblog.com/Future_of_Media_Report2007.pdf, July 2007

Industry at Crossroads?

As per the industry sources, the increasing number of web users and growing ad revenue of the Internet persuaded the US newspaper companies to venture into online newspapers. Chicago Tribune launched the first online newspaper service Chicago Online, in the US, in 1992.[69]According to NAA reports, 11 newspapers had an online presence in the US, by the end of 1992. However, by the end of 2006, almost 90% of the US newspapers had their online editions.[70] The increasing number of web users turning to Internet to obtain news is said to have increased the popularity of online newspaper websites. As per MSNBC survey in 1998, daily about 20 million people in the US used Internet to obtain news.[71] As per the statistics compiled by NAA, on a typical day in 2006, 50 million Americans turned to the Internet for news.[72] According to NAA US newspaper websites witnessed a rise in the number of unique visitors per month of 15% to reach 57.3 million - a third of all Internet users - in the second half of 2006, compared to the same period in 2005.[73]

---

69   Carlson David, "The Online Timeline", http://iml.jou.ufl.edu/carlson/1990s.shtml, 2007
70   Ibid.
71   Breecher Maury, "The newspaper of the future", http://www.columbia.edu/cu/21stC/issue-3.2/breecher.html, 1998
72   Horrigan John, "For many home broadband users, the internet is a primary news source", http://www.pewinternet.org/pdfs/PIP_News.and.Broadband.pdf, March 22nd 2006
73   MacMillan Robert, "U.S. newspapers press for more positive image", http://www.reuters.com/article/industryNews/idUSN3043527620070402, April 2nd 2007

It was widely felt that the increasing popularity of online newspapers affected the print versions of the US newspapers. The industry's initiatives to cut costs by shrinking the newsprint size and reducing the employee population were considered as significant efforts to sustain in the market. In August 2007, New York Times (NYT) reduced its page size by an-inch-and-a-half, as a measure to offset the escalating printing and distribution costs.[74] In the same month, Chicago Tribune, owned by the Tribune Co., reduced its page width by one-and-a-half inch to 12 inch.[75] These were not the only instances of US newspapers trying to cut their overhead costs through reducing their page size. Earlier, Wall Street Journal had cut its page size.

Some industry experts were concerned about the impact on the content that the smaller newspaper size will have. Analyst Joe Strupp (Strupp), however, believed that the smaller newspaper size would not affect the quality of content, as smaller print paper would not have the stark impact on coverage. According to Strupp, smaller page size means fewer-words-per-page, not-as-many-letters-on-the-editorial-page.[76]

To obtain cost benefit, many of the US newspapers have also reduced their employee population and continue doing it. According to NAA, the US newspaper industry cut the employee population by 18%, between 1990 and 2004.[77] In its October 2007 report, Forbes magazine said, "As anyone who works in the news business can attest, sagging ad revenue, rising newsprint costs and Internet competition are quickly changing this industry. Large metropolitan dailies have cut jobs and the size of their papers. Of course there will always be a demand for news, but the government projects news jobs will grow at a meager 5% by 2014".[78]

Industry experts opine that it is difficult for the newspapers to reduce their operating costs substantially due to various reasons. According to Chris C., Vice President of Product Development at PlatformQ, a leading virtual event management company, "Printing, distribution, content creation, ad sales and unions—all make it difficult to lower operating costs to compete effectively or invest in new areas, for the newspapers".[79]

In 2006, a research conducted by PrintCity (an alliance of over 40 independent companies, in the graphic arts industry) on the US newspaper industry found out that focusing only on cost reduction will not help the print newspapers. According to the research report, more innovative approach to industry

74 Strupp Joe, "Today, A Smaller 'NYT': Tomorrow, None at All?",
http://www.mediainfo.com/eandp/columns/rewrite_display.jsp?vnu_content_id=1003621983, August 6th 2007
75 "Chicago Tribune to reduce page size", http://cnews.canoe.ca/CNEWS/MediaNews/2007/08/17/pf-4426037.html, August 17th 2007
76 Ibid.
77 "Newspaper industry shed 18% of its jobs between 1990 and 2004", http://www.itfacts.biz/index.php?id=P7696, November 12th 2006
78 Ibid.
79 "Future of the Newspaper Industry?", http://www.linkedin.com/answers/financial-markets/equity-markets/MKT_EQU/7441-1213, 2006

opportunities is required to generate new readers and revenue.[80] The WAN's 2005 report on the newspaper industry titled, *Innovations in Newspapers*, suggested that the newspapers have to bring their own print quality closer to the standards of commercial printers. The report said that increasing the print quality will help the newspapers produce more in-house ads, which in turn contribute to the newspapers' revenue.[81] The PrintCity research supported this approach: "Newspapers can attract more advertisers by providing advertising space for premium double-page and cover advertising and giant pull-out posters. This will attract higher revenues to the newspaper, by adding to its differentiation".[82]

According to the PrintCity research report, focusing more on the quality of content will help the newspapers. According to the report, "Newspapers that want to survive in print form will need to provide in depth journalism and commentary that is less time sensitive. That's what made people buy newspapers in the past".[83]

In 2007, the General Social Survey (GSS)[84] reported that the core problem faced by the US newspapers was not specific to the emergence of World Wide Web or some other factors; but with the relevance of content that the newspapers provided, in an increasingly rich media mix. As Steve Yelvington, a media analyst rightly said, "The core problem faced by newspapers is not a migration of consumption from their print products to their Internet products. The core problem faced by newspapers is a loss of readers across the board".[85] Zollman makes it clear, "What we've yet to see is any U.S. newspaper that is willing to lead with its online pricing, allowing print to be the upsell. Yet, it's clear that this is what they must do-to regain market share, audience, and relevance".[86]

Analysts like Joe Strupp thought that the significance of print newspaper is lost. Mentioning the *New York Times*, Strupp said, "As each major daily cuts back in size, space, or expands on the Web, which the Times has been doing steadily for years with more blogs, online video and audio, and expanded posting of background information and poll data, the relevance of the print product has somewhat diminished."[87] According to Steve Osgoode, the director of online marketing at HarperCollins, Canada, the new generations are going to be people who have grown up using screens and it is going to be the tipping point.[88]

---

80   "Innovative newspaper products generate revenue, readership", http://www.newsandtech.com/issues/2006/12-06/nt/12-06_printcity_special.htm, December 2006
81   Ibid.
82   "Innovative newspaper products generate revenue, readership", op.cit.
83   Ibid.
84   The General Social Survey (GSS), started in 1972, is one of NORC's flagship surveys. National Opinion Research Center or NORC conducts regional, national and international studies on various topics. NORC was founded in 1941, and headquartered in Chicago.
85   Wilson Steve, "Preserving the American Community Newspaper in an Age of New Media Convergence and Competition", http://etd.gsu.edu/theses/available/etd-04282005-184258/unrestricted/wilson_stephen_m_200505_ma.pdf, 2005
86   "Newspapers Continue to Price Themselves Out of Ads", op.cit.
87   "Today, A Smaller 'NYT': Tomorrow, None at All?", op.cit.
88   Ibid.

Many analysts question the significance of print newspapers in the Internet age, and consider it essential for the newspapers to undergo a paradigm shift from print to online medium. Warren Buffett, chairman, Berkshire Hathaway Inc., opined on the state of newspaper industry, "Almost all newspaper owners realize that they are constantly losing ground in the battle for eyeballs. If cable and satellite broadcasting, as well as the Internet, had come along first, newspapers as we know them probably would never have existed."[89]

Many analysts believed that the future of the US newspaper industry, and the global newspaper industry in general, is in the Internet. In November 2006, Piers Morgan, former editor of the Daily Mirror, said, "Every newspaper has a great future online. End of story. Within five years every newspaper will be free and they'll all be online."[90] Morgan cited the increasing online ad revenue of the US newspapers. In the second quarter of 2007, online advertising in the US newspaper websites rose 19.3% to $795.7 million, compared to the same period in 2006.[91]The statistics compiled by NAA shows that, the contribution of online ads to total newspaper revenues continued to rise through the first quarter of 2007. As per NAA reports, online ad revenues accounted for 5.4% of the total revenues of the US newspapers in Q1 of 2006, and increased to 7% by Q1 of 2007.[92] However, the combined revenue of the US newspaper companies from the print and online advertising has been decreasing. The combined advertising revenue of the US newspapers fell by 2.2% in the fourth quarter of 2006 compared to the same period in 2005, and fell 8.6% to $11.3 billion in the first quarter of 2007, compared to that of Q1 of 2006.[93]

Citing the increasing ad revenues at newspapers' websites, many analysts believed that many newspapers, including some of the national dailies would soon go completely online. According to Sir Martin Sorrell, CEO WPP Group, the newspapers do have a future, but they have to adapt to the digital revolution.[94] In the opinion of the industry onlookers, many of the industry players have already started their effort to transform completely into an online medium.

It is believed that the transition from print to completely online will not be an easy task for many newspapers. Analysts are of the opinion that the small-town and suburban newspapers are here to stay, mainly because of their localised content.[95] Media analyst John Morton wrote, "Most newspapers

---

89   Serafino Phil, "India, China newspaper shares surge as US media nosedives", http://www.newswatch.in/news- analyses/markets-companies/7375.html, April 23rd 2007
90   "The Facts about Newspapers in 2007...Not the Myths", http://www.wanpress.org/IMG/pdf/WAN_Capital_Market_2007.pdf, 2007
91   Levitt Leon, "Aggregating and Segmenting Audience", http://www.naa.org/Resources/Articles/Events-NAA-2006-Annual-ConventionPresentations/~/media/Events/Events%20NAA%202006%20Annual%20Convention%20Presentations/0403%20215%20Aggregating_Levitt%20pdf.ashx, 2006
92   "Advertising at U.S. papers falls 8.6%", op.cit.
93   "Economic Data Update", http://www.clevelandfed.org/research/edata/2007/03/index.cfm, 2007
94   "The Facts about Newspapers in 2007...Not the Myths", op.cit.
95   "'Forbes' Puts Journalists on Endangered Species List", http://www.editorandpublisher.com/eandp/search/article_display.jsp?vnu_content_id=1003657563, October 11th 2007

are moving rapidly onto the Internet … to protect their local information franchises".[96]According to Morton, local franchises of many major newspapers contribute significantly to their revenues and so those organisations would retain their local franchises in the print format and continue to rely on their local content and local reader base. Supporting their claims, the statistics show an increase in the overall advertising spending in the US. TNS Media Intelligence[97] has forecasted that, in 2007, the total advertising spending in the US media would increase by 1.7% to $152.3 billion, from that of the year before.[98]

Many analysts believed that going completely online will not solve the problems of the US newspaper industry, and future of newspaper industry may not be secure. According to Robert MacMillan, "Newspapers are threatened on nearly every front".[99]

Analysts predict a bleak future for the US newspaper industry, citing the overall decrease in the total advertising revenue of the US newspapers, when both the print and online advertising are considered. Analysts believe that the traditional medium needs to find new ways to make money. Deborah Rosser, VP and Publisher of Rogers Consumer Publishing, said that as long as the newspaper companies remain focused on what people want and the consumer behaviour, there is a future for them as content providers. However, the US newspapers have to be smart, understand their customer base and respond to it, she added.[100]

A number of analysts believed that the business models of most the US newspapers are broken, and a new business model, which is not solely dependent on the advertising revenue, is to be framed, in order to sustain in the market. The American Press Institute report in 2006 says, "The newspapers have not done enough to look beyond the traditional revenue model. Most signs indicate that the newspaper itself is likely to shrink into a boutique product, serving an ever-smaller audience and advertiser base. The pace of shrinkage appears to be accelerating."[101]

Helen Boaden, Head of News, BBC, said, "I think the challenge for traditional media is how they make money in this new world".[102] However, Helen was not optimistic about the future of online newspapers. Many analysts like Helen, believed that it was difficult for the newspapers to sustain in a hyper competitive environment, while citing the decreasing number of visitors to the US newspaper websites. LeeAnn Prescott, an industry expert, compiled the statistics, "In March 2007, the top 10 news websites accounted for 28.13% of visits to the industry. This represents a decline of 3.8% from March 2006, when the top 10 websites accounted for

96   "The newspaper of the future", op.cit.
97   TNS Media Intelligence is a part of London-based TNS Group, which provides marketing information to various companies worldwide.
98   "TNS Media Intelligence Forecasts 1.7 Percent Increase in U.S. Advertising Spending for 2007", http://www.tns- mi.com/news/06122007.htm, June 12th 2007
99   "US newspapers weigh choices in struggling market", op.cit.
100   "Traditional media fights back", http://www.cbc.ca/theend/print.html, 2007
101   "US Newspapers to Review Business Model", http://www.bapla.org.uk/news/index.php?a=show&id=672&from=, October 6th 2006
102   "The Facts about Newspapers in 2007...Not the Myths", op.cit.

29.24% of industry visits".[103]According to Prescott, the decreasing number of visitors to the US news and media websites point to the fragmentation of online news consumption.[104] Prescott also said that the growth rate of online ad revenue of newspapers is also not promising. He cited the statistics compiled by NAA which says, "The online ad revenue growth rate of 19.3% in the second quarter of 2007, was lower than the 22.3% gain recorded in the first quarter of 2007 and the 35% gain in the fourth quarter of 2006".[105]

According to Blanche Evans, an industry analyst, the increasing popularity of websites like Google, Yahoo and AOL, as information providers also pose threat to the online newspapers. Evans, quoting a survey conducted by Classified Intelligence says, "In addition to new competitors online, newspapers have to contend with existing behemoths such as Google, MSN, Yahoo, and AOL which are all expanding their ability to capture local advertising revenue with local, targeted contextual searches".[106]

However, some analysts are of the opinion that the newspaper websites can compete effectively with the giants like Google. According to Stephen Gray, MD, Newspaper Next, newspapers could compete with Google and Yahoo. He said, "We thought that was fascinating. Newspaper websites (collectively) have a substantial user base that can be competitive".[107] However it remains to be seen how successful the online formats of the newspapers would turn out to be in the near future. As Nathan Stoll of Google News rightly says, "My sense is that newspapers will continue to exist [but] the forms are still being experimented with, the ones that are going to work out".[108]

According to the 2006 report of NAA, "The key to the future of newspapers is the effort to build a broad portfolio of products around the core product, the traditional newspaper, and to connect with both general and targeted audiences. Newspapers across the country have established their presence on the Web and are aggressively developing additional online products. They are launching niche publications and reaching out to new audiences, particularly minorities. It's all part of a critical transformation: from newspaper companies to information companies."[109]

---

103   Prescott LeeAnn, "Hitwise US News and Media Report (Excerpts)", http://www.masternewmedia.org/news/2007/05/09/us_new_media_trends_and.htm, March 2007
104   Ibid.
105   "Advertising at U.S. papers falls 8.6%", op.cit.
106   "Newspapers Continue to Price Themselves Out of Ads", op.cit.
107   "US Newspapers to Review Business Model", op.cit.
108   "The Facts about Newspapers in 2007...Not the Myths", op.cit.
109   "The Source-Newspapers by the Numbers",http://web.naa.org/thesource/the_source_newspapers_by_the_numbers.pdf, 2006

newspapers must find ways to expand their traditional print offerings onto the internet. To counter these trends, industry firms will develop mobile platforms to make themselves more accessible to readers."

MAGAZINES

A magazine is a regularly produced publication, ink on paper, containing articles and illustrations, covering a specific topic for a specific audience. Top magazines today include *Reader's Digest*, *National Geographic Magazine*, *Time*, and *People*. Magazines are another advertising-supported medium (like most newspapers, radio, and television channels) but revenue is also derived through newsstand sales and subscriptions.

While magazines have been published since the mid-1700s in American and England, less expensive printing and growing literacy rates propelled *The Saturday Evening Post* (1821–1968), *Harper's* (1850–today), and the *Atlantic Monthly* (1857–today). Magazines provide readers with more in-depth coverage of stories written by specialists in a topic along with detailed illustrations. Social movements like labor reform and abolitionism contributed to interest in such magazines and writers.

Magazine circulations increased dramatically after the Civil War as America's middle class emerged along with the concept of national advertising. The Postal Act of 1879, which allowed magazines to be sent inexpensively and from coast to coast with the expansion of the railroad, and advances in printing that kept costs down, made magazines affordable for most working people. The period also saw increased industrialization, urbanization, the creation of consumer-goods brands, and the development of advertising agencies.

Photographs were an important feature in early magazines; magazines emerged as the first source of photojournalism, the use of pictures to tell or supplement a story in print. Halftone, developed in the 1880s, made it possible to print photographs by breaking them down into a sequence of pixels, or dots, that appear as shades of gray. Magazine (and newspaper) photographs resulted in, from a media ecology perspective, a significant shift in readers' sensibilities. Postman (1985) states, "the photograph presents the world as object; language, the world as idea. For even the simplest act of naming a thing is an act of thinking—of comparing one thing from others, selecting certain features

Figure 1.20 News stands like this one in New York City feature dozens of mass circulated magazines, a still vibrant mass medium.

in common, ignoring what is different, and making an imaginary category." He continued, "For countless Americans, seeing, not reading, became the basis for believing."

"It is one of the peculiar characteristics of the photo that it isolates single moments in time," Marshall McLuhan writes in *Understanding Media: The Extensions of Man.* "Both the monocle and camera tend to turn people into things, and the photograph extends and multiplies the human image and proportions of mass-produced merchandise. The movie stars and matinee idols are put in the public domain by photography."

Magazines are described by Baran (2008) and others as "America's first national mass medium. … What these magazines (e.g., *Good Housekeeping, Life,* and *Look*) all had in common was the size and breadth of readership. They were mass market, mass circulation publications, both national and affordable" (p. 137). With the advent of television in America (1940s), the readership for magazines began to change. Quickly, especially in contrast to the adoption of earlier mediums, television became the dominant mass medium that forced magazine publishers to focus on more specialized and lifestyle topics to compete. *Look* and *Life,* which went out of business in 1971 and 1972, respectively, gave way to titles like *Surfing, Ski,* and *Flyfishing.*

America after World War II saw even further intensification in urbanization and industrialization resulting in more leisure time and disposable income. Magazines, perhaps more than any other medium, picked up on the trend and responded accordingly:

> Magazines often are harbingers of change. When large social, economic, or technological shifts begin to reshape the culture, magazines frequently are the first media to move, and the structure of the industry is one reason. Unlike newspapers, most magazines are not so tied to a specific geographic area, but are instead centered on interest or niches. Writers are looking for trends (Project for Excellence in Journalism, 2004).

Since the late 1980s, the number of magazine titles published in the U.S. has grown steadily. Today, over 20,000 magazine titles are in print (up from 13,000 in 1989). Paxson (2010) states that the number of consumer magazines decreased during this period while trade magazines (aimed at people who work in specific businesses) have increased. Magazine circulation peaked in 2007 with the sale of 369,793,587 magazines (322,359,612 by subscription and 47,434,075 copies sold at newsstands) according to the Magazine Publishers Association. In 2012, magazine circulation dropped to 312,478,313 in total, including subscription and newsstand sales.

The increase in the number of magazine titles coupled with declines in total readership, or circulation, is symptomatic of a phenomenon called *fragmentation.* Fragmentation occurs when audiences are provided with a greater number of media choices. Paxson (2010) refers to fragmentation as disaggregation—an environment

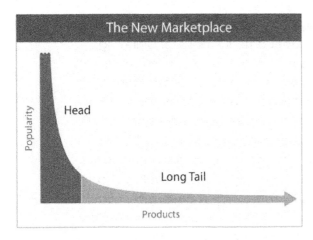

Figure 1.21 The New Marketplace. The narrow right side of the figure, or long tail, shows a standard demand curve that could apply to any industry from entertainment to hard goods.

where there are more magazines, but each has a smaller circulation. Chris Anderson, editor of *Wired* magazine, and author of a book entitled *The Long Tail*, describes fragmentation or disaggregation as follows:

The theory of the Long Tail is that our culture and economy is increasingly shifting away from a focus on a relatively small number of "hits" (mainstream products and markets) at the head of the demand curve and toward a huge number of niches in the tail. As the costs of production and distribution fall, especially online, there is now less need to lump products and consumers into one-size-fits-all containers. In an era without the constraints of physical shelf space and other bottlenecks of distribution, narrowly-targeted goods and services can be as economically attractive as mainstream fare.

One example of this is the theory's prediction that demand for products not available in traditional brick and mortar stores is potentially as big as for those that are. But the same is true for video not available on broadcast TV on any given day, and songs not played on radio. In other words, the potential aggregate size of the many small markets in goods that don't individually sell well enough for traditional retail and broadcast distribution may someday rival that of the existing large market in goods that do cross that economic bar.

The term refers specifically to the long tail of the sales chart above, which shows a standard demand curve that could apply to any industry, from entertainment to hard goods. The vertical axis is sales; the horizontal is products. The head of the curve is the hits, which have dominated our markets and culture for most of the last century. The long tail is the non-hits, or niches, which is where the new growth is coming for entertainment now and in the future.[1]

---

1   Copyright © 2004 by Chris Anderson, (CC BY 2.0) at: http://www.thelongtail.com/about.html.

Thanks to reductions in publication and distribution costs, accelerated by the Internet, mass communication is more specialized and less "mass." Media companies, including magazine publishers, can now focus on the more narrow interests of its readers and users while charging higher prices to its advertisers who would rather pay for specific rather than broad audiences. Hanson (2008) states that:

> When a movie comes to a local theater, it needs to attract about 1,500 people over a two-week period for the run to be a success.... A CD has to sell at least four copies a year for it to justify the shelf it takes up on the shelf.... Even if it will sell 5,000 copies nationwide, if it can't sell four copies in your local store, your local store can't pay the rent on the half an inch of shelf space the CD takes up.

The "long tail," according to Hanson (2008), is characteristic of:

1. High number of goods available
2. Low cost of reaching markets
3. Ease of finding niche products
4. Flattening the demand curve for mainstream hits
5. Size of collective market
6. Tailoring to personal tastes.

FILM

Movies, or motion pictures, are a descendant of photography, already popularized in the 1830s, and the efforts of inventors to create or replicate movement or motion. In France, Etienne-Jules Marey captured the circulation of blood in the human body and the movement of animals. In 1882, he developed a photographic gun that took 12 exposures per second but recorded them on a single frame of film. In England, Eadweard Muybridge captured motion by setting up multiple single-frame cameras spaced evenly in a location. The frames were then viewed using a zoetrope—a spinning cylinder. Thomas Edison, often credited with developing the motion picture industry in the United States, presented his first film, a 30-second film called "Blacksmith Scene," on May 9, 1893. His film was not projected onto a screen but viewed in an arcade-like device called the kinetoscope, similar to a "peep show."

But in France, brothers Auguste-Marie and Louis-Jean Lumière worked on Edison's idea and improved it substantially by creating a portable movie camera that doubled as a projector. They called it the cinématographe. The Lumières also established

Figure 1.22 A photo of flying pelican taken by Étienne-Jules Marey around 1882.

standards for the format and speed of the film later adopted by Edison. On December 28, 1895, they showed several of their short films that captured a slice of life in Paris—street scenes, factory shift changes, and families at the Grand Café in Paris. In attendance was an actor and illusionist by the name of Georges Méliès who offered the Lumière brothers 10,000 francs for one of the machines. Unfortunately, the Lumière brothers refused. Méliès sought filmmaking equipment worldwide and settled on equipment manufactured in England and went on to produce and direct 531 films between 1896 and 1913, ranging in length from one to forty minutes. He was also the first director to use film to tell a story: A Trip to the Moon (1902) included special effects, including a space craft slamming into the eye of the man on the moon.

In the United States, Edwin S. Porter, while working on film production for Edison, saw A Trip to the Moon and resolved to work on his own narrative film called The Great Train Robbery (1903). The 12-minute action movie, about outlaws robbing a high-speed train, broke new ground in using film to tell a story including the use of "cross-cutting," or the cutting away from one action sequence to another while suggesting that both are occurring at the same time. The twelve-scene multi-location footage was craftily edited, considering its vintage. The film toured the United States for several years and became the premiere attraction in the first nickelodeon (1905).

Harry Davis and John P. Harris opened a small theater, called the Nickelodeon (by combining "nickel" with the Greek word for an enclosed theater, adopted by the famous 18th century Odéon in Paris), in Pittsburgh, Pennsylvania on June 19, 1905. This wasn't the first theater to show films, but perhaps the most influential.

According to media historian Daniel Czitrom, "Of all the facets of motion picture history, none is so stunning as the extraordinarily rapid growth in the audience during the brief period between 1905 and 1918" (p. 41). Two things transpired together to make it happen. First, films with story lines, lasting up to 15 minutes, replaced short one- to two-minute films. These works included those produced by Méliès, Porter, and Griffith. Second, movie theaters emerged, beginning in New Orleans and Chicago as early as 1896, that presented continuous films for as little as a dime. But Davis and Harris's Nickelodeon concept, and even its name, swept the nation. "All over America adventurous exhibitors converted penny arcades, empty store rooms, empty lofts, and almost

Figure 1.23 a Auguste-Marie and Louis-Jean Lumiere invented a movie camera that doubled as a movie projector in the 1890s.

any available space into movie theaters. ... By 1907, between three and five thousand nickelodeons had been established" (p. 41). In 1908, around eight thousand nickelodeons were showing films and by 1910 as many as 26 million Americans (28% of America's total population) visited these theaters every week (Bowser, Eileen, 1990).

Nickelodeons swept into converted storefronts, tenements, arcades, and empty storerooms, and may have seated fewer than 200. Larger nickelodeons could accommodate well over 1,000 patrons. They were filled with working-class and immigrant audiences. And the "sudden and staggering boom in movie attendance evoked strenuous reactions from the nation's cultural traditionalists," according to Czitrom (p. 43). In just a few years, theaters were packed while parks, playgrounds, libraries, museums, recreation centers, YMCAs, and church-sponsored fellowship saw sharp declines in attendance or use. The growth of movie audiences signaled "a fundamental shift in the values of American civilization" (p. 43). Indeed, commercial amusements posed a significant threat to recreation. In 1914, New York Commissioner of Immigration and author Frederic C. Howe warned that "commercialized leisure is molding our civilization—not as it should be molded but as commerce dictates. ... And leisure must be controlled by community, if it is to become an agency of civilization rather than the reverse" (p. 44).

The nickelodeons provided an effective respite and escape from the monotony and drudgery of factory jobs rampant in urban centers at the time. Keep in mind, the rise in popularity of nickelodeons occurred just as a large influx of immigrants came to America and as rural farmers migrated to the cities to work in

Figure 1.23 b First camera/projector of the Lumière brothers at the French Museum of Photography in Bièvres, Essonne, France.

Figure 1.24 George Melies' film studio in Montreuil, France.

Figure 1.25 Screenshot from *Le Voyage dans la lune* (*A Trip to the Moon*), 1902.

higher-paying industrial jobs. A 1911 Russell Sage study of New York theatergoers estimated that about three fourths of movie audiences were working class. Those working the longest hours spent the most time at the shows and those who earned less than $10 per week went the most often.

Films viewed at nickelodeons were effective at acculturating immigrants and members of the working class. But perhaps more influenced by films were children, particularly in the area of peer socialization, according to Chicago progressive and humanitarian Jane Addams. "The act of moviegoing created an important new subculture centered outside of the home," Addams said (Czitrom, p. 51). A 1907 investigation by numerous agencies and Chicago police department identified 18 nickelodeons in a mile-and-a-half stretch on Milwaukee Avenue alone. The investigators were "greatly agitated by both the large numbers of children at the shows and the large proportion of objectionable films: movies with scenes of robbery, murder, shoplifting, skirt-lifting, and bedrooms" (p. 51). Addams' perspective was that children should attend the movies, but that their content had to be regulated. "What is needed," Addams stated, "is a regulation of the theatres. They are useful in providing a place of amusement for those who cannot go to a regular theater and can be made instructive. ... Young people attended movie theaters in groups with something of the gang instinct. ... What is seen and heard there becomes the sole topic of conversation, forming the ground pattern of their social life." While this was seen as a pro-social benefit of film attendance, Addams also "lamented the tendency of movies to erase the ethnic heritage from the minds of so many children" (p. 52).

In New York City, the motion picture industry organized its National Board of Censorship of Motion Pictures to pre-empt government interference in film content (1909). The board,

Figure 1.26 Boys in front of the movie theatre on Dundas Street, Toronto, Canada. The silent film showing in the theatre, *Let 'Er Run*, starred Dorothy Devore and George Stewart and had been released almost a year earlier, in October 1922. Similar theaters, called Nickelodeons, popped-up throughout the United in the 1890s and early 1900s.

Figure 1.27 a and b Working-class adults and children flocking Nickelodeons watched films like Edwin Porter's *Great Train Robbery* and D.W. Griffith's *Those Awful Hats* a short film designed to compel women at the theatre to take off their hats.

composed of cultured and socially active doctors, lawyers, clergy, and businessmen, presumed a "very simple psychology at the core of the moviegoers experience," according to Czitrom. "Those who are educated by the movies are educated through their hearts and their sense impressions and that sort of education sticks. Every person in an audience has paid admission and for that reason gives his attention willingly. ... Therefore he gives it his confidence and opens the window of his mind. And what the movie says sinks in" (p. 53).

Some saw the creation of the board as a step toward retargeting film content toward the middle and upper classes. By 1914, some extended narrative silent films such as *Queen Elizabeth*, a 53-minute French film starting Sarah Bernhardt, demanded higher ticket prices and attracted more well-to-do audiences. In 1915, The *Prisoner of Zenda*, a silent directed by Edwin S. Porter (*The Great Train Robbery*) and produced by Adolf Zukor, who purchased an armory on 26th Street in Manhattan and converted it into Chelsea Studios to shoot the film, a movie studio that is still in use today. But most movie historians point to D. W. Griffith as the creator of the modern feature-length film. His silent *Birth of a Nation* (1915)

Figure 1.28 Nickelodeons provided a much needed respite from the drudgery of work. For example, in this photo Mrs. Battaglia, her daughter Tessie (age - 12 years), and Tony (age - 7 years) at 170 Mulberry St. in New York City. Mrs. Battaglia works in the shop every day except Saturdays, when the children sew with her at home. The Battaglia's earned 2 or 3 cents a pair finishing men's pants. They could earn $1 to $1.50 on Saturday. Father disabled and earns very little.

chronicled the rise of the Ku Klux Klan after the Civil War. The three-hour film had a $110,000 production budget and grossed $50,000,000.

By the 1920s, movie making was an important industry in America. Major studios like Paramount, Warner Brothers, MGM, and Columbia had been established. Until the mid-1920s, all movies were silent. But in 1927, The Jazz Singer was released by Warner Brothers, which included two talking and singing segments. The film is regarded as a "talkie," a movie with synchronized sound, but it was Harry Warner's vision that "if it can talk, it can sing" that helped build Warner Brothers into one of the

Figure 1.29 Chelsea Studios in New York City. Formerly the location of the Famous Players movie studio where early film producer Adolf Zukor shot films like the Prisoner of Zenda in 1915.

world's premiere movie studios. The film is a story about a Jewish man who wants to be a jazz singer but learns that the genre emerges from African Americans. He uses blackface and attempts to build a career as an entertainer, but his professional ambitions ultimately come into conflict with the demands of his heritage.

The film was highly successful. With a production budget of $442,000, it grossed close to $7 million. The film used Warner Brother's Vitaphone sound system. Vitaphone was the analog sound-on-disc system and the only one that was widely used and commercially successful.

The soundtrack was not printed on the film itself, but issued separately on phonograph records. The discs, recorded at 33-1/3 rpm (a speed first used for this system) and typically 16 inches in diameter, would be played on a turntable physically coupled to the projector motor while the film was being projected. This sound system differed dramatically from sound-on-film, which refers to sound-film processes where the sound accompanying picture is physically recorded onto photographic film,

Figure 1.30 The Birth of a Nation (originally The Clansman) is a 1915 silent drama film directed by D. W. Griffith and based on the novel and play The Clansman by Thomas Dixon, Jr. According to Dixon, he wrote the book as a message to Northerners to maintain racial segregation. Griffith responded to the film's negative critical reception with his next film, Intolerance. Birth of a Nation was a commercial success.

Film Distribution

Film distribution includes the marketing and shipping of films to movie theaters or theater chains. The distributor enters into a contract with the theaters setting the percentage of ticket sales to be paid by the theater after first deducting a "house allowance" or "nut." Squire (2004) (The Movie Business Book, Google Books) reports that 90% of theater revenues go to the distributor the first week of the movie's run with an increasing percentage going to the movie theater each successive week. The distributor collects the amount due, audits ticket sales, and sends the balance to the production company.

The distributor makes sure that sufficient film prints are produced for shipment to all contracted exhibitors and verifies that the film is shown. Distributors also make sure the films are returned to the distributor at the end of their run.

The distributor is also responsible for advertising the film to attract the largest possible audience. Today, this is equal, on average, to 50% of production costs while, during the hey-day of films, it might have only involved sending promotional materials to the theater owners. Baran (2011) reports that while Sony spent $350 million to produce Spider-Man 3, it spent an additional $250 million was spent on marketing and promotion. The film returned $891 million. Today, on average, Hollywood films spend $35 million in the United States and another $50 million overseas on advertising.

TOP 25 FILM DISTRIBUTION COMPANIES 1995 TO 2012 (WORLDWIDE)

	MOVIES	TOTAL GROSS	AVERAGE GROSS	MARKET SHARE	
1	Warner Bros.	532	$29,135,050,869	$54,765,133	15.25%
2	Walt Disney Pictures	453	$27,024,974,288	$59,657,780	14.15%
3	Sony Pictures	534	$24,744,320,642	$46,337,679	12.96%
4	Paramount Pictures	352	$22,915,131,099	$65,099,804	12.00%
5	20th Century Fox	364	$21,288,127,358	$58,483,866	11.15%
6	Universal	338	$19,832,959,028	$58,677,394	10.38%
7	New Line	196	$7,407,184,271	$37,791,756	3.88%
8	DreamWorks SKG	77	$5,988,394,230	$77,771,354	3.14%
9	Miramax	377	$5,621,593,306	$14,911,388	2.94%

10	MGM	229	$5,059,893,917	$22,095,607	2.65%
11	Lionsgate	227	$3,872,078,001	$17,057,612	2.03%
12	Fox Searchlight	156	$2,183,689,011	$13,998,006	1.14%
13	Summit Entertainment	42	$1,741,124,456	$41,455,344	0.91%
14	Miramax/Dimension	28	$1,403,648,516	$50,130,304	0.73%
15	Focus Features	95	$1,357,800,901	$14,292,641	0.71%
16	Sony Pictures Classics	358	$1,087,280,101	$3,037,095	0.57%
17	Weinstein Co.	90	$878,207,038	$9,757,856	0.46%
18	Newmarket Films	25	$574,995,333	$22,999,813	0.30%
19	Artisan	61	$570,201,518	$9,347,566	0.30%
20	Gramercy	58	$476,848,774	$8,221,531	0.25%
21	IFC Films	233	$437,326,825	$1,876,939	0.23%
22	Paramount Vantage	86	$433,971,729	$5,046,183	0.23%
23	USA Films	27	$417,558,635	$15,465,135	0.22%
24	IMAX Films	71	$380,175,334	$5,354,582	0.20%
25	Overture Films	23	$361,123,706	$15,701,031	0.19%

Source: http://www.the-numbers.com/market/Distributors.

usually, but not always, the same strip of film carrying the picture. Sound-on-film processes can either record an analog soundtrack or digital soundtrack, and may record the signal either optically or magnetically. Later generations of sound-film production used more advanced versions of sound-on-film technology.

By the early 1930s, the talkies were a global phenomenon. In the United States, they helped secure Hollywood's position as one of the world's most powerful cultural/commercial systems. While the United States suffered the Great Depression, the industry grew substantially with upward of 25% of American's recreational spending going to movies. The 1930s also saw the creation of the studio system where films were mass produced much like factories produced cars or breakfast cereal. Paramount Pictures,

Figure 1.31 *The Jazz Singer* starred Al Jolson as a Jewish entertainer who resorts to black face make-up to draw larger audiences. As the first major "talkie," the film changed the artform from a photographically focussed medium to a photo and sound medium. Sound changed the industry in many significant ways. Actors required voices that matched their personaes and music added a new emotional dimension.

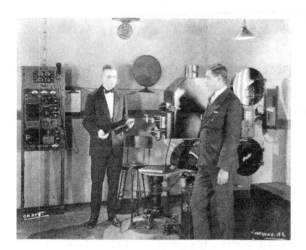

Figure 1.32 Vitaphone was the first major sound film system in the United States. Developed by Western Electric (a division of AT&T), sound was recorded on 33 1/3 rpm records and played synchronously with the film projector. The system was later replaced by "sound on film" technology developed by Lee deForest.

Warner Brothers, and MGM were major studios that hired writers, directors, actors (called "contract players"), and technicians who worked for weekly salaries. The studios also controlled the distribution of films.

In 1938, the United States Justice Department began an investigation of the movie studio system for engaging in non-competitive business practices. Paramount Pictures was identified as a

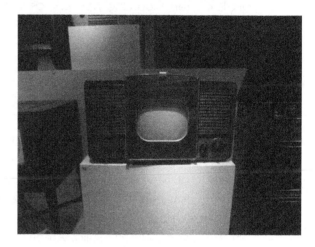

Figure 1.33 Ten-inch RCA 630-TS television, 1946, on display at the Museum of the Moving Image, New York City.

test case for charges that the studios (which also controlled distribution) conspired to set terms for the exhibition of Hollywood films. The studios had also conspired to keep films that were not produced by major studios out of the theaters they either owned or coerced, according to the Justice Department. Vertical integration, the control of an industry from production to sales, factored into the investigation. According to

Baran (2011), the five major studios also owned 75% of first-run movie screens in America. After the Paramount case, they were ordered to sell all of them.

In 1940, Paramount signed off on a government-instituted consent decree, or agreement that would end its investigation. Terms of the decree prevented Paramount from block booking (insisting that theaters show groups of movies, some inferior, to secure a better one) and "pre-selling" (the practice of collecting up-front money for films not yet in production). In turn Paramount produced fewer films, from sixty-plus pictures to a more modest twenty annually during World War II. But, with war-time theatrical attendance reaching all-time highs, Paramount and the studios made more money than ever.

Television affected the size and influence of the movie industry. At the end of World War II, Hollywood found itself competing with a new medium growing at a heady rate. In 1946, ten thousand households in the United States owned a television. This figure jumped to more than ten million in 1950 and 54 million in 1960. Movie attendance plummeted 25% by 1955.

HOLLYWOOD "BLACK LIST"

If Americans were not clear on whether or not Hollywood movies affected American culture, their thoughts were solidified in 1947 when conservative congressman J. Parnell Thomas of New Jersey, chairman of the House Un-American Activities Commission (HUAC), traveled to Hollywood to meet with film industry executives with a view of exposing what he believed was Communist infiltration of motion picture content by members of the Screen Writers Guild. America's response to victory in World War II was fear of Communism's ideology being spread in the United States. Returning to Washington, D.C., he shifted the focus of the committee to what he called "subversives" working in the film business.

The Hollywood Ten

The following people were cited for contempt of Congress and blacklisted after refusing to answer HUAC questions about their alleged involvement with the Communist Party by stating the questions asked by the committee, including "Are you or have you ever been a member of the Communist Party?" were a violation of their civil rights:

- Alvah Bessie, screenwriter
- Herbert Biberman, screenwriter and director
- Lester Cole, screenwriter
- Edward Dmytryk, director

- Ring Lardner Jr., screenwriter
- John Howard Lawson, screenwriter
- Albert Maltz, screenwriter
- Samuel Ornitz, screenwriter
- Adrian Scott, producer and screenwriter
- Dalton Trumbo, screenwriter

Others jailed included:

- Hanns Eisler, composer
- Bernard Gordon, screenwriter
- Joan Scott, screenwriter

Abe Burrows, playwright and lyricist   William Sweets, radio personality   Garson Kanin, writer and director
Fredi Washington, actress   Irene Wicker, singer and actress   J. Raymond Walsh, radio commentator   Michael Blankfort, screenwriter[c]
Lena Horne, singer and actress   Madeline Lee, actress[d]   Alexander Kendrick, journalist and author   Lee J. Cobb, actor
Vera Caspary, writer   Arthur Gaeth, radio commentator   Dorothy Parker, writer   Morton Gould, pianist and composer
Allan Sloane, radio and TV writer   Robert Lewis Shayon, former president   E. Y. "Yip" Harburg, lyricist   Alfred Drake, actor and singer
Artie Shaw, jazz musician   of radio and TV directors' guild   Luther Adler, actor and director   Rose Hobart, actress
Joseph Losey, director   José Ferrer, actor   Theodore Ward, playwright   Peter Lyon, television writer   John Brown, actor
Selena Royle, actressGypsy Rose Lee, actress and ecdysiast   John Garfield, actor   Myron McCormick, actor   Philip Loeb, actor
Howard K. Smith, journalist   Aline MacMahon, actress   Tom Glazer, folk singer   Leo Hurwitz, director   Aaron Copland, composer   Jean Muir, actress
Martin Wolfson, actor   Ruth Gordon, actress and screenwriter   Roger De Koven, actor   True Boardman, screenwriter   Pete Seeger, folk singer
Minerva Pious, actress   Leon Janney, actor   Edward Chodorov, screenwriter and producer   Sam Jaffe, actor   Ben Myers, attorney
Paul Stewart, actor   Robert St. John, journalist   Will Geer, actor   Richard Dyer-Bennett, folk singer   Millen Brand, writer   Edward G. Robinson, actor
Dashiell Hammett, writer   Pert Kelton, actress   Meg Mundy, actress
Joe Julian, actor   George Keane, actor   **Blacklisted for Suspected**   Olin Downes, music critic   Hilda Vaughn, actress
Howard Duff, actor   Walter Bernstein, screenwriter   **Communism in Hollywood**   Mady Christians, actress   Helen Tamiris, choreographer
Betty Todd, director   Lloyd Gough, actor   Langston Hughes, writer   Larry Adler, actor and musician   Jerome Chodorov, writer
Tony Kraber, actor   Norman Corwin, writer   Himan Brown, producer and director   Morris Carnovsky, actor   Margo, actress and dancer
Shirley Graham, writer   Charles Irving, actor   Ray Lev, classical pianist   William L. Shirer, journalist   Lisa Sergio, radio personality
Elliott Sullivan, actor   Roderick B. Holmgren, journalist   Nat Hiken, writer and producer   Felix Knight, singer and actor   Burgess Meredith, actor
Donna Keath, radio actress   Arthur Laurents, writer   Ben Grauer, radio and TV personality   Martin Gabel, actor   Ann Shepherd, actress
Lesley Woods, actress   Paul Draper, actor and dancer   Horace Grenell, conductor and music producer   Richard Yaffe, journalist
Paul McGrath, radio actor   Marc Blitzstein, composer   Marsha Hunt, actress   Norman Rosten, writer
Hester Sondergaard, actress   Judy Holliday, actress and comedienne   Irwin Shaw, writer   Dean Dixon, conductor   Stella Adler, actress and teacher   Louis Untermeyer, poet
Arthur Miller, playwright   Lillian Hellman, playwright and screenwriter   Avon Long, actor and singer   Gale Sondergaard, actress
Betty Winkler (Keane), actress   William N. Robson, radio and TV writer   Clifford J. Durr, attorney   Burl Ives, folk singer and actor   Alan Lomax, folklorist and musicologist
Edith Atwater, actress   John La Touche, lyricist   Bernard Reis, accountant   Paul Mann, director and teacher   Howard Koch, screenwriter
Millard Lampell, screenwriter   Adelaide Klein, actress   Johannes Steel, journalist   Robert P. Heller, television journalist   Sam Wanamaker, actor
Louise Fitch (Lewis), actress   Howard Da Silva, actor   Zero Mostel, actor and comedian   Harold Rome, composer and lyricist
Uta Hagen, actress and teacher   Margaret Webster, actress, director and producer   Joseph Edward Bromberg, actor
Ella Logan, actress and singer   Samson Raphaelson, screenwriter and playwright   Arnold Perl, producer and writer
Henry Morgan, actor   Coby Ruskin, TV director   Anne Revere, actress   Lyn Murray, composer and choral director
Ralph Bell, actor   Oscar Brand, folk singer   Lionel Stander, actor   Hazel Scott, jazz and classical musician
Earl Robinson, composer and lyricist   Kenneth Roberts, writer   Orson Welles, actor, writer and director
Mitchell Grayson, radio producer and director   Josh White, blues musician   Marc Connelly, playwright
William S. Gailmor, journalist and radio commentator
Leonard Bernstein, composer and conductor   Jack Gilford, actor and comedian   Howard Bay, scenic designer

People blacklisted between January 1948 and June 1950:

- Ben Barzman, screenwriter
- Paul Draper, actor and dancer
- Sheridan Gibney, screenwriter
- Paul Green, playwright and screenwriter
- Lillian Hellman, playwright and screenwriter
- Canada Lee, actor
- Paul Robeson, actor and singer*
- Edwin Rolfe, screenwriter and poet
- William Sweets, radio personality
- Richard Wright, writer

Red Channels: The Report of Communist Influence in Radio and Television was an anti-Communist pamphlet published during the peak of the Cold War (June 1950). It

Charles Chaplin, actor, director and producer   Ben Bengal, screenwriter
Harry Belafonte, actor and singer
Lewis Leverett, actor   Carl Lerner, editor and director   Gordon Kahn, screenwriter   Stanley Prager, director
Daniel James, screenwriter   Shimen Ruskin, actor   Dolores del Río, actress   Madeleine Sherwood, actress
Donald Ogden Stewart, screenwriter   John Wexley, screenwriter   John Hubley, animator   Ray Spencer, screenwriter
Karen DeWolf, screenwriter   John Ireland, actor   John Bright, screenwriter[97]
Arnold Manoff, screenwriter   Rosaura Revueltas, actress   Sol Barzman, screenwriter   Phil Eastman, cartoon writer
Larry Parks, actor   Anne Froelick, screenwriter   Irving Lerner, director   Jay Gorney, screenwriter   Lee Grant, actress
Frederic I. Rinaldo, screenwriter   Michael Uris, writer   Phoebe Brand, actress   Joshua Shelley, actor   Howard Fast, writer
Maurice Clark, screenwriter   Frances Farmer, actress   Jules Dassin, director   Dorothy Comingore, actress   Alfred Lewis Levitt, screenwriter
Michael Wilson, screenwriter   Alan Campbell, screenwriter   Ian McLellan Hunter, screenwriter
Charles Dagget, animator   Philip Stevenson, writer   Alexander Knox, actor   Waldo Salt, screenwriter   Faith Elliott, animator
Louise Rousseau, screenwriter   Kim Hunter, actress   Vladimir Pozner, screenwriter
Henry Myers, screenwriter   Bill Meléndez, animator   Albert Bein, screenwriter   Bert Gilden, screenwriter   Paul Trivers, screenwriter
Dorothy Tree, actress   John Henry Faulk, radio personality   Jack T. Gross, producer   Bert Gilden, screenwriter   Seymour Bennett, screenwriter
Josef Mischel, screenwriter   Arthur Strawn, screenwriter   Nedrick Young, actor and screenwriter   Seymour Bennett, screenwriter
Leo Penn, actor   Tamara Hovey, screenwriter
Luis Buñuel, director   Mitch Lindemann, screenwriter   Viola Brothers Shore, screenwriter   Frank Tarloff, screenwriter
Phil Brown, actor   Julian Zimet, screenwriter   **Blacklisted After June 1950**   John Randolph, actor   Irving Pichel, director
John Weber, producer   Roman Bohnen, actor   Karen Morley, actress
John McGrew, animator   Bernard Vorhaus, director   Richard Attenborough, director and producer   Jerry Fielding, composer
Naomi Robison, actress   Norman Lloyd, actor   Alfred Palca, writer and producer
W. L. River, screenwriter   Howard Dimsdale, writer   Lew Amster, screenwriter   Bill Scott, voice actor   Lester Koenig, producer
George Tyne, actor   Guy Endore, screenwriter   Oliver Crawford, screenwriter   Anne Green, screenwriter
Art Smith, actor   Val Burton, screenwriter   Hy Kraft, screenwriter   William Pomerance, animation executive
Reuben Ship, screenwriter   Edward Eliscu, screenwriter   Louis Pollock, screenwriter   Edward Huebsch, screenwriter
Richard Weil, screenwriter   Harold Buchman, screenwriter   Martha Scott, actress   Cy Endfield, screenwriter and director
Robert Lees, screenwriter   John Berry, actor, screenwriter and director   Victor Kilian, actor   Sidney Kingsley, playwright
Barbara Bel Geddes, actress   John "Skins" Miller, actor
George Sklar, playwright   Richard Collins, screenwriter   Eddie Albert, actor   Hannah Weinstein, producer
Louis Solomon, screenwriter and producer
Shepard Traube, director and screenwriter   David Robison, screenwriter   George Corey, screenwriter
Norma Barzman, screenwriter   Paul Jarrico, producer and screenwriter   Margaret Gruen, screenwriter   Mickey Knox, actor
Bess Taffel, screenwriter
Morton Grant, screenwriter   Arnaud d'Usseau, screenwriter   Harold Goldman, screenwriter
John Sanford, screenwriter   Janet Stevenson, writer   Carl Foreman, producer and screenwriter
Abraham Polonsky, screenwriter and director   Herschel Bernardi, actor
Jeff Corey, actor   Lee Gold, screenwriter   Marguerite Roberts, screenwriter   John Cromwell, director   Lester Fuller, director
Martin Ritt, actor and director   Peter Viertel, screenwriter   Danny Dare, choreographer   Robert L. Richards, screenwriter
Allen Boretz, screenwriter and songwriter   Julius Tannenbaum, producer   Irwin Corey, actor and comedian
Orson Bean, actor   David Hilberman, animator   Ludwig Donath, actor
Charles Collingwood, radio commentator
Madeleine Ruthven, screenwriter   Charles Korvin, actor   Jean Rouverol (Butler), actress and writer
Laurie Blankfort, artist   Leslie Edgley, screenwriter   Francis Edward Faragoh, screenwriter   Henry Blankfort, screenwriter
Hugo Butler, screenwriter   Helen Slote Levitt, screenwriter   Ben Maddow, screenwriter
Constance Lee, screenwriter   Ruth McKenney, writer   Leonardo Bercovici, screenwriter
Michael Gordon, director   Sidney Buchman, screenwriter   Paula Miller, actress
Maurice Rapf, screenwriter
Mortimer Offner, screenwriter

Figure 1.34 SURRENDER—Charged with contempt of Congress, nine Hollywood men give themselves up to U.S. Marshal yesterday. From left, Robert Adrian Scott, Edward Dmytryk, Samuel Ornitz, Lester Cole, Herbert Biberman, Albert Maltz, Alvah Bessie, John Howard Lawson and Ring Lardner Jr. (original caption from the *Los Angeles Times*, December 11, 1947).

Figure 1.35 Image of cover of Red Channels, a pamphlet-style book issued by the journal Counterattack in 1950.

was prepared by the right-wing journal *Counterattack*. The journal, published by Alfred Kohlberg, an importer of Chinese textiles and member of the anti-Communist *China Lobby*, was staffed by former FBI agents, who called themselves *American Business Consultants Inc*. Kohlberg was also a founding director of the ultra-rightwing John Birch Society, whose self-declared purpose was to identify communist influences in America.

The report named 151 actors, writers, musicians, broadcast journalists, and others as players in the "Communist manipulation of the entertainment industry." Some of those listed were already denied employment because of their political beliefs, history, or mere association with suspected "subversives." Those cited were effectively placed on the industry's black list without a hearing, legal representation, or trial.

Instead of defending their rights, and fearing negative public opinion, the studios refused to hire (or "blacklisted") those cited by the HUAC and Red Channels document. Those listed lost their jobs, or in some cases worked under pseudonyms, until the "Red Scare" ended in 1957. Baran (2011) states, "Rather than defend its First Amendment rights, the film industry abandoned those who were even mildly critical of the 'Red Scare,' jettisoning much of its best talent at a time when it could least afford to do so. In the fight against television, movies became increasingly tame for fear of being too controversial" (p. 154).

Marshall McLuhan on the Film Medium

In *Understanding Media: The Extensions of Man* (1964), media ecologist Marshall McLuhan likens movies to novels (books) and believes the linear logic of literacy is a requirement, or pre-requisite, for film literacy.

The business of the writer or the film-maker is to transfer the reader or viewer from one world, his own, to another, the world created by typography and film. That is so obvious and happens so completely, that those undergoing the experience accept it subliminally and without critical awareness.... Movies as a nonverbal form of experience are like photography, a form of statement without syntax. In fact, however, like the print and photo, movies assume a high level of literacy in their users and prove baffling to the nonliterate. Our literate acceptance of the mere movement of the camera eye as it follows or drops a figure from view is not acceptable to an African film audience. If somebody disappears off the side of the film, the African wants to know what happened to him. A literate audience, however, accustomed to following printed imagery line by line without questioning the logic of lineality, will accept film sequence without protest.... The close relation, then, between the reel world of film and the private fantasy of the printed word is indispensable to our Western acceptance of the film form.

What Is Digital Cinema?

Lev Manovich

Cinema, the Art of the Index

Thus far, most discussions of cinema in the digital age have focused on the possibilities of interactive narrative. It is not hard to understand why: since the majority of viewers and critics equate cinema with storytelling, digital media are understood as something that will let cinema tell its stories in a new way. Yet as exciting as the ideas of a viewer participating in a story, choosing different paths through the narrative space, and interacting with characters may be, they address only one aspect of cinema that is neither unique nor, as many will argue, essential to it: narrative.

The challenge that digital media pose to cinema extends far beyond the issue of narrative. Digital media redefine the very identity of cinema. In a Hollywood symposium on the digitization of the cinema, one of the participants provocatively referred to movies as "flatties" and to human actors as "organics" and "soft fuzzies."[1] As these terms accurately suggest, what used to be cinema's defining characteristics have become just the default options, with many others available. When one can "enter" a virtual three-dimensional space, viewing flat images projected on the screen is hardly the only option. When, given enough time and money, almost everything can be simulated in a computer, filming physical reality is just one possibility.

This "crisis" of cinema's identity also affects the terms and the categories used to theorize about cinema's past. French film theorist Christian Metz wrote in the 1970s that "Most films shot today, good or bad, original or not, 'commercial' or not, have as a common characteristic that they tell a story; in this measure they all belong to one and the same genre, which is, rather, a sort of 'super-genre.'"[2] In identifying fictional films as a "supergenre" of twentieth-century cinema, Metz did not bother to mention another characteristic of this genre because at that time it was too obvious: fictional films are *live action* films. These films consist largely of unmodified photographic recordings of real events that took place in real physical space. Today, in the age of computer simulation and digital compositing, invoking this live-action characteristic becomes crucial in defining the specificity of twentieth-century cinema. From the perspective of a future historian of visual culture, the differences between classical Hollywood films, European art films, and avant-garde films (apart from abstract ones) may appear to be less significant than this common feature: they relied on lens-based recordings of reality. This essay is concerned with the effect of the so-called digital revolution on cinema, as defined by its "supergenre" as fictional live-action film.[3]

During cinema's history, a whole repertoire of techniques (lighting, art direction, the use of different film stocks and lenses, etc.) was developed to modify the basic record obtained by a film apparatus. And yet behind even the most stylized cinematic images we can discern the bluntness, the sterility, the banality of early nineteenth-century photographs. No matter how complex its stylistic innovations, the cinema has found its base in these deposits of reality, these samples obtained by a methodical and prosaic process. Cinema emerged out of the same impulse that engendered naturalism, court stenography, and wax museums. Cinema is the art of the index; it is an attempt to make art out of a footprint.

Even for Andrey Tarkovsky, film-painter par excellence, cinema's identity lay in its ability to record reality. Once, during a public discussion in Moscow sometime in the 1970s, he was asked whether he was interested in making abstract films. He replied that there can be no such thing. Cinema's most basic gesture is to open the shutter and to start the film rolling, recording whatever happens to be in front of the lens. For Tarkovsky, an abstract cinema was thus impossible.

But what happens to cinema's indexical identity if it is now possible to generate photorealistic scenes entirely in a computer by using 3D computer animation; to modify individual frames or whole scenes with the help of a digital paint program; to cut, bend, stretch and stitch digitized film images into something that has perfect photographic credibility, although it was never actually filmed?

This essay will address the meaning of these changes in the filmmaking process from the point of view of the larger cultural history of the moving image. Seen in this context, the manual construction of images in digital cinema represents a return to nineteenth-century precinematic practices, when images were hand-painted and hand-animated. At the turn of the twentieth century, cinema was to delegate these manual techniques to animation and define itself as a recording medium. As cinema enters the digital age, these techniques are again becoming commonplace in the filmmaking process. Consequently, cinema can no longer be clearly distinguished from animation. It is no longer an indexical media technology but, rather, a sub-genre of painting.

This argument will be developed in three stages. I will first follow a historical trajectory from nineteenth-century techniques for creating moving images to twentieth-century cinema and animation. Next I will arrive at a definition of digital cinema by abstracting the common features and interface metaphors of a variety of computer softwares and hardwares that are currently replacing traditional film technology. Seen together, these features and metaphors suggest a distinct logic of a digital moving image. This logic subordinates the photographic and the cinematic to the painterly and the graphic, destroying cinema's identity as a media art. Finally, I will examine different production contexts that already use digital moving images— Hollywood films, music videos, CD-ROM games and artworks—in order to see if and how this logic has begun to manifest itself.

A Brief Archaeology of Moving Pictures

As testified by its original names (kinetoscope, cinematograph, moving pictures), cinema was understood, from its birth, as the art of motion, the art that finally succeeded in creating a convincing illusion of dynamic reality. If we approach cinema in this way (rather than as the art of audiovisual narrative, or the art of a projected image, or the art of collective spectatorship, etc.), we can see it superseding previous techniques for creating and displaying moving images.

These earlier techniques shared a number of common characteristics. First, they all relied on hand-painted or hand-drawn images. The magic lantern slides were painted at least until the 1850s; so were the images used in the Phenakistiscope, the Thaumatrope, the Zootrope, the Praxinoscope, the Choreutoscope, and numerous other nineteenth-century procinematic devices. Even Muybridge's celebrated Zoopraxiscope lectures of the 1880s featured not actual photographs but colored drawings painted after the photographs.[4]

Not only were the images created manually, they were manually animated. In Robertson's Phantasmagoria, which premiered in 1799, magic lantern operators moved behind the screen in order to make projected images appear to advance and withdraw.[5] More often, an exhibitor used only his hands, rather than his whole body, to put the images into motion. One animation technique involved using mechanical slides consisting of a number of layers. An exhibitor would slide the layers to animate the image.[6] Another technique was to move a long slide containing separate images slowly in front of a magic lantern lens. Nineteenth-century optical toys enjoyed in private homes also required manual action to create movement: twirling the strings of the Thaumatrope, rotating the Zootrope's cylinder, turning the Viviscope's handle.

It was not until the last decade of the nineteenth century that the automatic generation of images and their automatic projection were finally combined. A mechanical eye became coupled with a mechanical heart; photography met the motor. As a result, cinema—a very particular regime of the visible—was born. Irregularity, nonuniformity, the accident, and other traces of the human body, which previously had inevitably accompanied moving image exhibitions, were replaced by the uniformity of machine vision.[7] A machine that, like a conveyer belt, was now spitting out images, all having the same appearance, all the same size, all moving at the same speed, like a line of marching soldiers.

Cinema also eliminated the discrete character of both space and movement in moving images. Before cinema, the moving element was visually separated from the static background, as in a mechanical slide show or Rey-naud's Praxinoscope Theater (1892).[8] The movement itself was limited in range and affected only a clearly defined figure rather than the whole image. Thus, typical actions would include a bouncing ball, a raised hand or eyes, a butterfly moving back and forth over the heads of fascinated children—simple vectors charted across still fields.

Cinema's most immediate predecessors share something else. As the nineteenth-century obsession with movement intensified, devices that could animate more than just a few images became increasingly popular. All of them—the Zootrope, the Phonoscope, the Tachyscope, the Kinetoscope—were based on loops, sequences of images featuring complete actions that could be played repeatedly. The Thaumatrope (1825), in which a disk with two different images painted on each face was rapidly rotated by twirling a strings attached to it, was in its essence a loop in its simplest form: two elements replacing one another in succession. In the Zootrope (1867) and its numerous variations, approximately a dozen images were arranged around the perimeter of a circle.[9] The Mutoscope, popular in America throughout the 1890s, increased the duration of the loop by placing a larger number of images radially on an axle.[10] Even Edison's Kinetoscope (1892–1896), the first modern cinematic machine to employ film, continued to arrange images in a loop.[11] Fifty feet of film translated to an approximately twenty-second-long presentation. The genre's potential development was cut short when cinema adopted a much longer narrative form.

From Animation to Cinema

Once the cinema was stabilized as a technology, it cut all references to its origins in artifice. Everything that characterized moving pictures before the twentieth century—the manual construction of images, loop actions, the discrete nature of space and movement—was delegated to cinema's bastard relative, its supplement, its shadow: animation. Twentieth-century animation became a depository for nineteenth-century moving-image techniques left behind by cinema.

The opposition between the styles of animation and cinema defined the culture of the moving image in the twentieth century. Animation foregrounds its artificial character, openly admitting that its images are mere representations. Its visual language is more aligned to the graphic than to the photographic. It is discrete and self-consciously discontinuous: crudely rendered characters moving against a stationary and detailed background; sparsely and irregularly sampled motion (in contrast to the uniform sampling of motion by a film camera—recall Jean-Luc Godard's definition of cinema as "truth 24 frames per second"); and space constructed from separate image layers.

In contrast, cinema works hard to erase any traces of its own production process, including any indication that the images we see could have been constructed rather than recorded. It denies that the reality it shows often does not exist outside of the film image, the image that was arrived at by photographing an already impossible space, which itself was put together through the use of models, mirrors, and matte paintings, and which was then combined with other images through optical printing. It pretends to be a simple recording of an already existing reality—both to a viewer and to itself.[12] Cinema's public image stressed the aura of reality "captured" on film, thus implying that cinema was about photographing what existed before the camera, rather than about "creating the 'never-was'" of special effects.[13] Rear projection and blue screen photography, matte paintings and glass shots, mirrors and miniatures, push development, optical effects, and other techniques that allowed filmmakers to construct and alter the moving images, and thus could reveal that cinema was not really different from animation, were pushed to cinema's periphery by its practitioners, historians, and critics.[14]

Today, with the shift to digital media, these marginalized techniques move to the center.

What Is Digital Cinema?

A visible sign of this shift is the new role that computer-generated special effects have come to play in Hollywood industry in the last few years. Many recent blockbusters have been driven by special effects; feeding on their popularity, Hollywood has even created a new minigenre, "The Making of ..." videos and books that reveal how special effects are created.

To illustrate some of the possibilities of digital filmmaking, I will make reference to the use of special effects in a few recent, key Hollywood films. Until recently, Hollywood studios were the only places that had the money to pay for digital tools and for the labor involved in producing digital effects. However, the shift to digital media affects not just Hollywood but filmmaking as a whole. As traditional film technology is universally being replaced by digital technology, the logic of the filmmaking process is being redefined. What I describe below are the new principles of digital filmmaking that are equally valid for individual or collective film productions, regardless of whether they are using the most expensive professional hardware/software packages or their consumer equivalents.

Consider, then, the following principles of digital filmmaking:

1. Rather than filming physical reality, it is now possible to generate film-like scenes directly in a computer with the help of 3D computer animation. Therefore, live-action footage is displaced from its role as the only possible material from which the finished film is constructed.

2. Once live-action footage is digitized (or directly recorded in a digital format), it loses its privileged indexical relationship to pro-filmic reality. The computer does not distinguish between an image obtained through the photographic lens, an image created in a paint program, and an image synthesized in a 3D graphics package, since they are made from the same material: pixels. And pixels, regardless of their origin, can be easily altered, substituted one for another, and so on. Live-action footage is reduced to just another graphic, no different from images that were created manually.[15]

3. If live-action footage was left intact in traditional filmmaking, now it functions as raw material for further compositing, animating, and morphing. As a result, while retaining visual realism unique to the photographic process, film obtains the plasticity that previously was possible only in painting or animation. To use the suggestive title of a popular morphing

software, digital filmmakers work with "elastic reality." For example, the opening shot of *Forrest Gump* (Robert Zemeckis, Paramount Pictures, 1994; special effects by Industrial Light and Magic) tracks an unusually long and extremely intricate flight of a feather. To create the shot, the real feather was filmed against a blue background in different positions; this material was then animated and composited against shots of a landscape.[16] The result: a new kind of realism, that can be described as "something which is intended to look exactly as if it could have happened, although it really could not."

4.   Previously, editing and special effects were strictly separate activities. An editor worked on ordering sequences of images together; any intervention within an image was handled by special-effects specialists. The computer collapses this distinction. The manipulation of individual images via a paint program or algorithmic image processing becomes as easy as arranging sequences of images in time. Both simply involve "cut and paste." As this basic computer command exemplifies, modification of digital images (or other digitized data) is not sensitive to distinctions of time and space or of differences of scale. Thus, reordering sequences of images in time, compositing them together in space, modifying parts of an individual image, and changing individual pixels become the same operation, conceptually and practically.

5.   Given the preceding principles, we can define digital film in this way:

digital film = live-action material + painting + image processing + compositing + 2D computer animation + 3D computer animation.

Live-action material can be recorded either on film or video or directly in a digital format.[17] Painting, image processing, and computer animation are the processes of modifying already existent images as well as of creating new ones. In fact, the very distinction between creation and modification, so clear in film-based media (shooting versus darkroom processes in photography, production versus postproduction in cinema), no longer applies to digital cinema, since each image, regardless of its origin, goes through a number of programs before making it to the final film.[18]

Let us summarize the principles discussed thus far. Live-action footage is now only raw material to be manipulated by hand: animated, combined with 3D computer-generated scenes, and painted over. The final images are constructed manually from different elements; and all the elements are either created entirely from scratch or modified by hand.

We can finally answer the question "What is digital cinema?" Digital cinema is a particular case of animation that uses live-action footage as one of its many elements.

This can be reread in view of the history of the moving image sketched earlier. Manual construction and animation of images gave birth to cinema and slipped into the margins ... only to reappear as the foundation of digital cinema. The history of the moving image thus makes a full circle. *Born from animation, cinema pushed animation to its boundary, only to become one particular case of animation in the end.*

The relationship between "normal" filmmaking and special effects is similarly reversed. Special effects, which involved human intervention into machine-recorded footage and which were therefore delegated to cinema's periphery throughout its history, become the norm of digital filmmaking.

The same applies to the relationship between production and postproduction. Cinema traditionally involved arranging physical reality to be filmed through the use of sets, models, art direction, cinematography, and so on. Occasional manipulation of recorded film (for instance, through optical printing) was negligible compared with the extensive manipulation of reality in front of a camera. In digital filmmaking, shot footage is no longer the final point but just raw material to be manipulated in a computer, where the real construction of a scene will take place. In short, the production becomes just the first stage of postproduction.

The following examples illustrate this shift from rearranging reality to rearranging its images. From the analog era: for a scene in *Zabriskie Point* (1970), Michelangelo Antonioni, trying to achieve a particularly saturated color, ordered a field of grass to be painted. From the digital era: to create the launch sequence in *Apollo 13* (Universal, 1995; special effects by Digital Domain), the crew shot footage at the original location of the launch at Cape Canaveral. The artists at Digital Domain scanned the film and altered it on computer workstations, removing recent buildings, adding grass to the launch pad, and painting the skies to make them more dramatic. This altered film was then mapped onto 3D planes to create a virtual set that was animated to match a 180-degree dolly movement of a camera following a rising rocket.[19]

The last example brings us to yet another conceptualization of digital cinema—as painting. In his book-length study of digital photography, William J. Mitchell focuses our attention on what he calls the inherent mutability of a digital image:

> The essential characteristic of digital information is that it can be manipulated easily and very rapidly by computer. It is simply a matter of substituting new digits for old. … Computational tools for transforming, combining, altering, and analyzing images are as essential to the digital artist as brushes and pigments to a painter.[20]

As Mitchell points out, this inherent mutability erases the difference between a photograph and a painting. Since a film is a series of photographs, it is appropriate to extend Mitchell's argument to digital film. With an artist being able to easily manipulate digitized footage either as a whole or frame by frame, a film in a general sense becomes a series of paintings.[21]

Hand-painting digitized film frames, made possible by a computer, is probably the most dramatic example of the new status of cinema. No longer strictly locked in the photographic, it opens itself

Composited launch sequence from *Apollo 13*. Publicity photo from Universal Studios.

toward the painterly. It is also the most obvious example of the return of cinema to its nineteenth-century origins—in this case, to hand-crafted images of magic lantern slides, the Phenakistiscope, the Zootrope.

We usually think of computerization as automation, but here the result is the reverse: what previously was automatically recorded by a camera now has to be painted one frame at a time. But not just a dozen images, as in the nineteenth century, but thousands and thousands. We can draw another parallel with the practice, common in the early days of silent cinema, of manually tinting film frames in different colors according to a scene's mood.[22] Today, some of the most visually sophisticated digital effects are often achieved by using the same simple method: painstakingly altering thousands of frames by hand. The frames are painted over either to create mattes (hand-drawn matte extraction) or to change the images directly, as in *Forrest Gump*, where President Kennedy was made to speak new sentences by altering the shape of his lips, one frame at a time.[23] In principle, given enough time and money, one can create what will be the ultimate digital film: ninety minutes of 129,600 frames completely painted by hand from scratch, but indistinguishable in appearance from live photography.[24]

Multimedia as "Primitive" Digital Cinema

3D animation, compositing, mapping, paint retouching: in commercial cinema, these radical new techniques are mostly used to solve technical problems while traditional cinematic language is preserved unchanged. Frames are hand-painted to remove wires that supported an actor during shooting; a flock of birds is added to a landscape; a city street is filled with crowds of simulated extras. Although most Hollywood releases now involve digitally manipulated scenes, the use of computers is always carefully hidden.[25]

Commercial narrative cinema continues to hold on to the classical realist style where images function as unretouched photographic records of some events that took place in front of the camera.[26] Cinema refuses to give up its unique cinema effect, an effect that, according to Christian Metz's penetrating analysis made in the 1970s, depends upon narrative form, the reality effect, and cinema's architectural arrangement all working together.[27]

Toward the end of his essay, Metz wonders whether in the future nonnarrative films may become more numerous; if this happens, he suggests that cinema will no longer need to manufacture its reality effect. Electronic and digital media have already brought about this transformation. Since the 1980s, new cinematic forms have emerged that are not linear narratives, that are exhibited on a television or a computer screen rather than in a movie theater—and that simultaneously give up cinematic realism.

What are these forms? First of all, there is the music video. Probably not by accident, the genre of music video came into existence at exactly the time when electronic video effects devices were entering editing studios. Importantly, just as music videos often incorporate narratives within them, but are not linear narratives from start to finish, so they rely on film (or video) images, but change them beyond the norms of traditional cinematic realism. The manipulation of images through hand-painting and image processing, hidden in Hollywood cinema, is brought into the open on a television screen. Similarly, the construction of an image from heterogeneous sources is not subordinated to the goal of photorealism but functions as an aesthetic strategy. The genre of music video has been a laboratory for exploring numerous new possibilities of manipulating photographic images made possible by computers—the numerous points that exist in the space between the 2D and the 3D, cinematography and painting, photographic realism and collage. In short, it is a living and constantly expanding textbook for digital cinema.

A detailed analysis of the evolution of music video imagery (or, more generally, broadcast graphics in the electronic age) deserves a separate treatment, and I will not try to take it up here. Instead, I will discuss another new cinematic nonnarrative form, CD-ROM games, which, in contrast to music videos, relied on the computer for storage and distribution from the very beginning. And, unlike music video designers who were consciously pushing traditional film or video images into something new, the designers of CD-ROMs arrived at a new visual language unintentionally, while attempting to emulate traditional cinema.

In the late 1980s, Apple began to promote the concept of computer multimedia; and in 1991 it released QuickTime software to enable an ordinary personal computer to play movies. However, for the next few years the computer did not perform its new role very well. First, CD-ROMs could not hold anything close to the length of a standard theatrical film. Second, the computer would not smoothly play a movie larger than the size of a stamp. Finally, the movies had to be compressed, which degraded their visual appearance. Only in the case of still images was the computer able to display photographic-type detail at full screen size.

Because of these particular hardware limitations, the designers of CD-ROMs had to invent a different kind of cinematic language in which a range of strategies, such as discrete motion, loops, and superimposition, previously used in nineteenth-century moving-image presentations, in twentieth-century animation, and in the avant-garde tradition of graphic cinema, were applied to photographic or synthetic images. This language synthesized cinematic illusionism and the aesthetics of graphic collage, with its characteristic heterogeneity and discontinuity. The photographic and the graphic, divorced when cinema and animation went their separate ways, met again on a computer screen.

The graphic also met the cinematic. The designers of CD-ROMs were aware of the techniques of twentieth-century cinematography and film editing, but they had to adapt these techniques both to an interactive format and to hardware limitations. As a result, the techniques of modern cinema and of nineteenth-century moving image have merged in a new hybrid language.

We can trace the development of this language by analyzing a few well-known CD-ROM titles. The best-selling game *Myst* (Broderbund, 1993) unfolds its narrative strictly through still images, a practice that takes us back to magic lantern shows (and to Chris Marker's *La Jetee*).[28] But in other ways *Myst* relies on the techniques of twentieth-century cinema. For instance, the CD-ROM uses simulated camera turns to switch from one image to the next. It also employs the basic technique of film editing to subjectively speed up or slow down time. In the course of the game, the user moves around a fictional island by clicking on a mouse. Each click advances a virtual camera forward, revealing a new view of a 3D environment. When the user begins to descend into the underground chambers, the spatial distance between the points of view of each two consecutive views decreases sharply. If earlier the user was able to cross a whole island with just a few clicks, now it takes a dozen clicks to get to the bottom of the stairs! In other words, just as in traditional cinema, *Myst* slows down time to create suspense and tension.

In *Myst*, miniature animations are sometimes embedded within the still images. In the next best-selling CD-ROM, *7th Guest* (Virgin Games, 1993), the user is presented with video clips of live actors superimposed over static backgrounds created with 3D computer graphics. The clips are looped, and the moving human figures clearly stand out against the backgrounds. Both of these features connect the visual language of *7th Guest* to nineteenth-century procinematic devices and twentieth-century cartoons rather than to cinematic verisimilitude. But like *Myst, 7th Guest* also evokes distinctly modern cinematic codes. The environment where all action takes place (an interior of a house) is rendered by using a wide-angle lens; to move from one view to the next, a camera follows a complex curve, as though mounted on a virtual dolly.

Next, consider the CD-ROM *Johnny Mnemonic* (Sony Imagesoft, 1995). Produced to complement the fiction film of the same title, marketed not as a "game" but as an "interactive movie," and featuring full-screen video throughout, it comes closer to cinematic realism than the previous CD-ROMs—yet it is still quite distinct from it. With all action shot against a green screen and then composited with graphic backgrounds, its visual style exists within a space between cinema and collage.

It would not be entirely inappropriate to read this short history of the digital moving image as a teleological development that replays the emergence of cinema a century earlier. Indeed, as computers' speed keeps increasing, the CD-ROM designers have been able to go from a slide show format to the superimposition of small moving elements over static backgrounds, and finally to full-frame moving images. This evolution repeats the nineteenth-century progression: from sequences of still images (magic lantern slide presentations) to characters moving over static backgrounds (for instance, in Reynaud's Praxinoscope Theater) to full motion (the Lumie `res' cinematograph). Moreover, the introduction of QuickTime in 1991 can be compared with the introduction of the Kinetoscope in 1892:

both were used to present short loops, both featured images approximately two by three inches in size, both called for private viewing rather than collective exhibition. Finally, the Lumières' first film screenings of 1895, which shocked their audiences with huge moving images, found their parallel in recent titles in which the moving image—here full-screen, full-motion video—finally fills the entire computer screen. Thus, exactly a century after cinema was officially "born," it was reinvented on a computer screen.

But this is only one reading. We no longer think of the history of cinema as a linear march toward only one possible language, or as a progression toward more and more accurate verisimilitude. Rather, we have come to see its history as a succession of distinct and equally expressive languages, each with its own aesthetic variables, each new language closing off some of the possibilities of the previous one—a cultural logic not dissimilar to Thomas Kuhn's analysis of scientific paradigms.[29] Similarly, instead of dismissing visual strategies of early multimedia titles as a result of technological limitations, we may want to think of them as an alternative to traditional cinematic illusionism, as a beginning of digital cinema's new language.

For the computer/entertainment industry, these strategies represent only a temporary limitation, an annoying drawback that needs to be overcome. This is one important difference between the situation at the end of the nineteenth and the end of the twentieth centuries: if cinema was developing toward the still open horizon of many possibilities, the development of commercial multimedia, and of corresponding computer hardware (compression boards, storage formats such as Digital Video Disc), is driven by a clearly defined goal: the exact duplication of cinematic realism. So if a computer screen more and more emulates the cinema screen, this is not an accident but a result of conscious planning.

The Loop

A number of artists, however, have approached these strategies not as limitations but as a source of new cinematic possibilities. As an example, I will discuss the use of the loop in Jean-Louis Boissier's *Flora petrinsularis* (1993) and Natalie Bookchin's *The Databank of the Everyday* (1996).[30]

As already mentioned, all nineteenth-century procinematic devices, up to Edison's Kinetoscope, were based on short loops. As "the seventh art" began to mature, it banished the loop to the low-art realms of the instructional film, the pornographic peepshow, and the animated cartoon. In contrast, narrative cinema has avoided repetitions; like modern Western fictional forms in general, it put forward a notion of human existence as a linear progression through numerous unique events.

Cinema's birth from a loop form was reenacted at least once during its history. In one of the sequences of the revolutionary Soviet montage film, *A Man with a Movie Camera* (1929), Dziga Vertov shows us a cameraman standing in the back of a moving automobile. As he is being carried forward by the automobile, he cranks the handle of his camera. A loop, a repetition created by the circular movement of the handle, gives birth to a progression of events—a very basic narrative that is also quintessentially modern: a camera moving through space recording whatever is in its path. In what seems to be a reference to cinema's primal scene, these shots are intercut with the shots of a moving train. Vertov even restages the terror that the Lumie `res' film supposedly provoked in its audience; he positions his camera right along the train track so the train runs over our point of view a number of times, crushing us again and again.

Early digital movies share the same limitations of storage as nineteenth-century procinematic devices. This is probably why the loop playback function was built into the QuickTime interface, thus giving it the same weight as the VCR-style "play forward" function. So, in contrast to films and video-tapes, QuickTime movies are supposed to be played forward, backward, or looped. *Flora petrinsularis* realizes some of the possibilities contained in the loop form, suggesting a new temporal aesthetics for digital cinema.

The CD-ROM, which is based on Rousseau's *Confessions*, opens with a white screen containing a numbered list. Clicking on each item leads us to a screen containing two frames, positioned side by side. Both frames show the same video loop but are slightly offset from each other in time. Thus, the images appearing in the left frame reappear in a moment on the right and vice versa, as though an invisible wave is running through the screen. This wave soon becomes materialized: when we click on one of the frames, we are taken to a new screen showing a loop of a rhythmically vibrating water surface. As each mouse click reveals another loop, the viewer becomes an editor, but not in a traditional sense. Rather than constructing a singular narrative sequence and discarding material that is not used, here the viewer brings to the forefront, one by one, numerous layers of looped actions that seem to be taking place all at once, a multitude of separate but coexisting temporalities. The viewer is not cutting but reshuffling. In a reversal of Vertov's sequence where a loop generated a narrative, the viewer's attempt to create a story in *Flora petrinsularis* leads to a loop.

The loop that structures *Flora petrinsularis* on a number of levels becomes a metaphor for human desire that can never achieve resolution. It can be also read as a comment on cinematic realism. What are the minimum conditions necessary to create the impression of reality? As Boissier demonstrates, in the case of a field of grass, or a close-up of a plant or a stream, just a few looped frames become sufficient to produce the illusion of life and of linear time.

Steven Neale describes how early film demonstrated its authenticity by representing moving nature: "What was lacking [in photographs] was the wind, the very index of real, natural movement. Hence the obsessive contemporary fascination, not just with movement, not just with scale, but also with waves and sea spray, with smoke and spray."[31] What for early cinema was its biggest pride and achievement—a faithful documentation of nature's movement—becomes for Boissier a subject of ironic and melancholic simulation. As the few frames are looped over and over, we see blades of grass shifting slightly back and forth, rhythmically responding to the blowing of nonexistent wind that is almost approximated by the noise of a computer reading data from a CD-ROM.

Something else is being simulated here as well, perhaps unintentionally. As you watch the CD-ROM, the computer periodically staggers, unable to maintain a consistent data rate. As a result, the images on the screen move in uneven bursts, slowing and speeding up with humanlike irregularity. It is as though they are brought to life not by a digital machine but by a human operator cranking the handle of the Zootrope a century and a half ago. …

If *Flora petrinsularis* uses the loop to comment on cinema's visual realism, *The Databank of the Everyday* suggests that the loop can be a new narrative form appropriate for the computer age. In an ironic manifesto that parodies their avant-garde precursors from the earlier part of the century, Bookchin reminds us that the loop gave birth not only to cinema but also to computer programming. Programming involves altering the linear flow of data through control structures, such as "if/then" and "repeat/while"; the loop is the most elementary of these control structures. Bookchin writes:

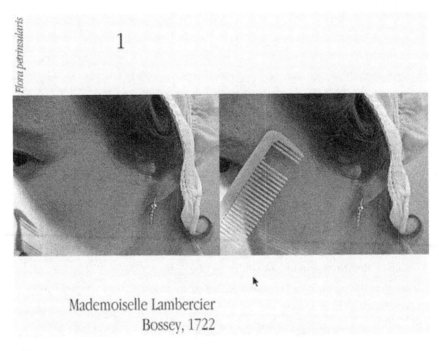

Mademoiselle Lambercier
Bossey, 1722

Flora petrinsularis: the repetitive image. Jean-Louis Boissier and the ZKM.

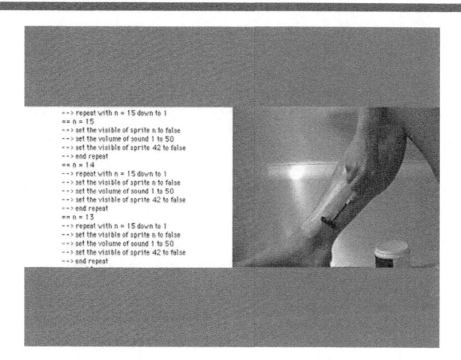

```
--> repeat with n = 15 down to 1
== n = 15
--> set the visible of sprite n to false
--> set the volume of sound 1 to 50
--> set the visible of sprite 42 to false
--> end repeat
== n = 14
--> repeat with n = 15 down to 1
--> set the visible of sprite n to false
--> set the volume of sound 1 to 50
--> set the visible of sprite 42 to false
--> end repeat
== n = 13
--> repeat with n = 15 down to 1
--> set the visible of sprite n to false
--> set the volume of sound 1 to 50
--> set the visible of sprite 42 to false
--> end repeat
```

The Databank of the Everyday: the loop as action and as code. Courtesy of Natalie Bookchin.

As digital media replaces [sic] film and photography, it is only logical that the computer program's loop should replace photography's frozen moment and cinema's linear narrative. The Databank champions the loop as a new form of digital storytelling; there is no true beginning or end, only a series of the loops with their endless repetitions, halted by a user's selection or a power shortage.[32]

The computer program's loop makes its first "screen debut" in one particularly effective image from *The Databank of the Everyday*. The screen is divided into two frames, one showing a video loop of a woman shaving her leg, the other a loop of a computer program in execution. Program statements repeating over and over mirror the woman's arm methodically moving back and forth. This image represents one of the first attempts in computer art to apply a Brechtian strategy; that is, to show the mechanisms by which the computer produces its illusions as a part of the artwork. Stripped of its usual interface, the computer turns out to be another version of Ford's factory, with a loop as its conveyer belt.

Like Boissier, Bookchin explores alternatives to cinematic montage, in her case replacing its traditional sequential mode with a spatial one. Ford's assembly line relied on the separation of the production process into a set of repetitive, sequential, and simple activities. The same principle made computer programming possible: a computer program breaks a task into a series of elemental operations to be executed one at a time. Cinema followed this principle as well: it replaced all other modes of narration with a sequential narrative, an assembly line of shots that appear on the screen one at a time. A sequential narrative turned out to be particularly incompatible with a spatialized narrative that played a prominent role in European visual culture for centuries. From Giotto's fresco cycle at the Scrovegni Chapel (1305–1306) in Padua to Gustave Courbet's *Burial at Ornans* (1850), artists presented a multitude of separate events (which sometimes were even separated by time) within a single composition. In contrast to cinema's narrative, here all the "shots" were accessible to a viewer at once.

Cinema has elaborated complex techniques of montage between different images replacing each other in time, but the possibility of what can be called "spatial montage" between simultaneously coexisting images was not explored. *The Databank of the Everyday* begins to explore this direction, thus opening up again the tradition of spatialized narrative suppressed by cinema. In one section we are presented with a sequence of pairs of short clips of everyday actions that function as antonyms—for instance, opening and closing a door, or pressing Up and Down buttons in an elevator. In another section the user can choreograph a number of miniature actions appearing in small windows positioned throughout the screen.

Conclusion: From Kino-Eye to Kino-Brush

In the twentieth century, cinema has played two roles at once. As a media technology, its role was to capture and to store visible reality. The difficulty of modifying images once they were recorded was exactly what gave cinema its value as a document, assuring its authenticity. The rigidity of the film image has defined the limits of cinema as I defined it earlier—that is to say, the super-genre of live-action narrative. Although it includes within itself a variety of styles—the result of the efforts of many directors, designers, and cinematographers—these styles share a strong family resemblance. They are all children of the recording process that uses lenses, regular sampling of time, and photographic media. They are all children of a machine vision.

The mutability of digital data impairs the value of cinema recordings as documents of reality. In retrospect, we can see that twentieth-century cinema's regime of visual realism, the result of automatically recording visual reality, was only an exception, an isolated accident in the history of visual representation, which has always involved, and now again involves, the manual construction of images. Cinema becomes a particular branch of painting—painting in time. No longer a kino-eye, but a kino-brush.[33]

The privileged role of the manual construction of images in digital cinema is one example of a larger trend: the return of pre-cinematic moving-images techniques. Marginalized by the twentieth-century institution of live-action narrative cinema that relegated them to the realms of animation and special effects, these techniques reemerge as the foundation of digital filmmaking. What was supplemental to cinema becomes its norm; what was at its boundaries comes into the center. Digital media return to us the repressed of the cinema.

As the examples discussed in this essay suggest, the directions that were closed off at the turn of the century, when cinema came to dominate the modern moving-image culture, are again beginning to be explored. Moving-image culture is being redefined once more; cinematic realism is being displaced from its dominant mode to become only one option among many.[34]

Movies, in 1946, sold over 4 billion tickets. In 2011, 1.3 billion tickets were sold. But movies are still a major industry, thanks to television and new distribution technologies that enable films to continue earning revenue after theater release. According to the Motion Picture Association of America (MPAA), box office receipts in 2011 were $10.2 billion in the U.S. and $32.6 billion worldwide. While U.S. revenues were down 4% from previous years, the International box office revenues jumped 35% thanks to increases in ticket sales in China and Russia. In the United States, about two-thirds of the population went to the movies at least once in 2011. Frequent moviegoers (10% of the population) purchase half of all movie tickets. Hispanics and 12- to 24-year-olds go to the movies most frequently compared to their counterparts in other demographic categories.

Globally, MPAA reports that there are 124,000 movie screens (2011), up 3% from 2010 figures due to the rapid increase in movie theater screens in China. About half of these are digital screens (up 79% from 2010).

RADIO

On November 20, 1920, KDKA broadcast the first bona fide radio programs from a shack on the property of Pittsburgh's Westinghouse factory. These weren't the first sounds transmitted by radio, a technology intended to send Morse code for the telegraph companies, including ship-to-shore, without wires—hence the term "wireless." On Christmas Eve 1906, Reginald Fessenden broadcast Christmas carols to understandably surprised ship operators and several reporters. Lee de Forest made several broadcasts in 1907 and 1908. But these broadcasts were intermittent. According to Kittross (1978) the broadcaster who should claim the title of "first to broadcast intentionally" and on a schedule is Charles D. "Doc" Herrold, who ran a station out of the College of Engineering and Wireless in San Jose, California. In 1909, he broadcast news reports and music on a scheduled basis. Herrold built radios that people could use in hotel lobbies and at the 1915 San Francisco Exhibition, where the station remained on the air eight hours per day.

Figure 1.36 David Sarnoff was the general manager and vice-president of RCA, the Radio Corporation of America. Photo taken and published in September 1922.

In 1916, Russian immigrant and later chairman of RCA and NBC David Sarnoff, at the time an employee of American Marconi, a company that used radio to transmit and receive telegraph messages, sent his superiors the "Radio Music Box

Memo" that outlined the concept of radio broadcasting. In the memo, Sarnoff wrote about:

> ... a plan of development which would make radio a 'household utility' in the same sense as a piano or phonograph. The idea is to bring music into the house by wireless. ... The receiver can be designed in the form of a simple 'Radio Music Box' and arranged for several different wavelengths, which should be changeable with the throwing of a single switch or the pressing of a single button.

At the end of World War I (1918), migration rates from America's rural areas to its cities increased and immigration from other countries was slowed due to restrictive legislation. The mass production of goods and services was moving the nation toward a "mass society." During this stage of change, radio broadcasting began.

In 1921, the government forced various holders of critical technologies associated with radio (Marconi, General Electric, AT&T, and Westinghouse) to merge, which created the Radio Corporation of America (RCA).

Figure 1.37 Photograph of the election night Eveready Hour broadcast from AT&T's WEAF in New York City on November 4, 1924. Will Rogers (standing far right), Art Gillham, Wendell Hall, Carson Robison, the Eveready Quartet, Graham McNamee, and the Waldorf-Astoria Dance Orchestra. Republican Calvin Coolidge won the presidency by a landslide.

Sarnoff, then 28, was made its General Manager. That same year, the U.S. Commerce Department issued licenses to five companies to broadcast, and by early 1923, more than 600 stations were operating.

In 1922, AT&T launched WEAF in New York City, the first station to sell commercials to advertisers—something AT&T called "toll broadcasting." This was a highly controversial move. According to Campbell, Martin, and Fabos (2011), "most people in radio at the time recoiled at the idea of using the medium for crass advertising, viewing it instead as a public information service" (p. 117). Other stations that had attempted advertisements had received orders to stop doing so by the Commerce Department.

Up to this point, many broadcast stations played recorded music, talked, or invited artists to perform on the air. In 1923, a lawsuit brought by the American Society of Composers, Authors, and Publishers (ASCAP) claimed that radio stations were cheating its members out of their royalties. The stations countered that by playing the songs, sales of sheet music and records would increase. But the stations struck a deal with

Figure 1.38 Photograph of a young girl listening to the radio during the Great Depression.

ASCAP called the blanket licensing agreement where stations would pay ASCAP a flat fee (originally $250 per year). In turn, it could play all ASCAP-licensed music on the air. A similar agreement was reached with the other major licensing organization Broadcast Music, Inc. (BMI).

Since radio signals travel across state lines, Congress adopted the Radio Act of 1912, which defined radio waves, from a legal perspective, as a natural resource that could not be owned but rather licensed. The Act charged the Commerce Department with issuing licenses to commercial entities, amateurs (who used the waves to transmit point-to-point, as in "ham" radio operation), churches, and educational institutions. The concept that radio is a natural resource, or a part of "the public domain," led to the idea that radio needed to benefit American citizens and operate "in the public interest." But by the early 1920s, radio spectrum became a scarce resource. As a result, channel interference—the noise associated with two or more stations coming in on radio sets on the same frequency, led equipment manufacturers and broadcasters alike to demand action. In 1924, the Commerce Department ordered stations on the same frequency to share time. But a Chicago station challenged the edict by jamming the airwaves and broadcasting on unauthorized frequencies. A court challenge in 1926 found that while Commerce was granted the authority to grant licenses, it could not restrict stations from broadcasting in any way.

As a result, Congress passed the Radio Act of 1927, which established a different premise. A radio operator could license a frequency but only as long as they broadcast in "the public interest, convenience, and necessity." The Act established the Federal Radio Commission. Seven years later, with the passage of the Communication Act of 1934, Congress dismantled the FRC and formed the Federal Communication Commission (FCC) with broader oversight of radio, telephone, and telegraph. The FCC still exists today and it also regulates television, CATV, and the Internet.

Figure 1.39 14-year old "ham" radio operator John Iringle with a well-equipped radio outfit, which he constructed, in Chicago, Ill. Photo taken in 1922.

But along with the passage of the Communication Act of 1934 came a ringing endorsement by Congress and President Franklin Roosevelt of advertising-supported broadcasting, rather than public, educational, and citizen broadcasters, as best suited to serve "the public interest, convenience, and necessity." Debate in Congress led to an amendment setting aside 25% of the airwaves to non-profit institutions and organizations. But the amendment was defeated. The Act lay the groundwork for the predominantly commercial, advertising-supported broadcast mediums (radio and television) that have influenced our perception, desire, and self-image ever since.

Radio provided the captains of mass production with an ideal medium for changing American culture. Consider the following observations from Czitrom (1982):

> The triumph of commercial broadcasting represented a substantial victory for the ideology of consumption in American life. With the accelerated mass production of consumer goods, advertising began playing a greatly expanded role in American business during the 1920s. Advertisers sold not merely products but a way of life: happiness through buying, personal fulfillment from the purchase. (p. 77).

> Advertisers 'recognized radio's extraordinary power to carry them into the intimate circle of family life at home." In 1927, radio merchandiser Edgar Felix exclaimed, "What a glorious opportunity for the advertising man to spread his sales propaganda. Here was a countless audience, sympathetic, pleasure seeking, enthusiastic, curious, interested, approachable in the privacy of their own homes' (p. 77).

> Harry P. Davis of Westinghouse said, 'broadcast advertising is modernity's medium of business expression. It made industry articulate. American business men, because of radio, are provided with a latch key to nearly every home in the United States' (p. 77).

The period between the 1920s and 1940s is known as the "golden age of radio." This is when radio dominated as a mass medium, much like television does today. Radio programming featured live music, dramas, action adventures (like *The Lone Ranger*),

Figure 1.40 The longest running program in broadcast history is Music and the Spoken Word, a weekly 30-minute radio and television program sponsored by The Church of Jesus Christ of Latter-day Saints. The program has been run weekly since 1929 (on radio) and after the advent of television on both of these mediums. The photo shows the Mormon Tabernacle Choir and Orchestra at Temple Square performing on the program's 75th anniversary.

and soap operas. For example, *The Guiding Light* was first broadcast on CBS radio in 1937. It moved to television in 1952 and survived until 2009. While not the longest-running program in broadcast history—that honor goes to *Music and the Spoken Word*, weekly broadcasts of the Mormon Tabernacle Choir (since 1929)—it has more total episodes (18,000) than any other broadcast in history.

Other personalities and programs from this era include Bing Crosby, Bob Hope, Burns and Allen, *Little Orphan Annie*, Amos 'n' Andy, and *Orson Welles' Mercury Theatre on the Air* who on October 30, 1938 performed a radio adaptation of *The War of the Worlds* by H. G. Wells that sounded so realistic that it set off a mild panic nationwide.

But where radio made clear inroads, most at the expense of newspapers, was with the transmission of news broadcasts. For the first time, news stories could be covered where they occurred and broadcast live into people's homes. According to Dave McQuown at University of Chicago (Theories of Media):

> From the 1920s until the invention of television, radio was at its peak as a culturally-relevant medium. It was during this period that radio had a truly unique niche as a form of mass entertainment and a source of breaking news. Radio was able to bring comedy and drama into the home of a listener like no medium before it. Also, early broadcasts of sporting events like boxing and baseball were extremely popular because live radio was able to capture the excitement of these events and actually bring the sounds of these events into a listener's home. (Gordon and Falk 47) Likewise, radio was able to bring the excitement of world events to home listeners, lending personality and imme-diacy to the news. In 1940, Edward R. Murrow gained fame by standing on a London rooftop and providing live news coverage of the Battle of Britain, and the sound of explosions around him. (Gordon and Falk 28)

Media Ecologist Marshall McLuhan likened radio to "a kind of nervous information system" (p. 298) that tied all of humanity into a single device (the radio). "News bulletins, time signals, traffic data, and, above all, weather reports now served to enhance the native power of radio to involve people in one another." He continued:

> Even more than the telephone or the telegraph, radio is that extension of the central nervous system that is matched only by human speech itself. Is it not worthy of our mediation that radio should be specially attuned to that primitive extension of our central nervous system, that aboriginal mass medium, that vernacular tongue? (p. 302).

McLuhan believed that radio helped to shift America from a staunchly individualistic society (from print) toward a more collectivist culture (broadcast), which may explain, from his perspective, why FDR was able to push his New Deal forward. According to McLuhan:

> For the intensely literate population, however, radio engendered a profound unlocalizable sense of guilt that sometimes expressed itself in the fellow-traveler attitude. A newly found human involvement bred anxiety and insecurity and unpredictability. Since literacy had fostered an extreme of individualism, and radio had done just the opposite in reviving the ancient experience of kinship webs of deep tribal involvement, the literate West tried to find some sort of compromise in a larger sense of collective responsibility (p. 301).

> The power of radio to retribalize mankind, its almost instant reversal of individualism into collectivism, either Fascist or Marxist, has gone unnoticed (p. 304).

With the advent of television after WWII, radio successfully morphed from a medium that people sat down and listened to—that's what they did with a radio after buying one—to a medium that complemented other tasks such as working, driving, and doing chores. In essence, television became the new radio by mimicking its national, networked, and star- and personality-oriented program formats. Radio aligned with the music industry to help sell records (the precursors to CDs and downloads) and made other changes to survive. These include:

1. Providing local advertisers with a cost-effective alternative to newspapers and television. In turn, content—especially news—is locally focused.
2. Offering content that appeals to more specialized audiences. News, Christian, Hispanic, conservative talk, sports, and genres of music (e.g., country, rock, 50s, etc.) are ways to narrow the range of content and to fragment the audience. Advertisers like this so they can develop messages that appeal to these audiences.
3. Creating an interpersonal relationship between the host (e.g., DJ, commentator, announcer), the program content, and the audience. Radio, in this regard, is considered a "personal medium."
4. Allowing for mobility by way of car, portable, and (now) streamed access. The National Association of Broadcasters (NAB) in 2012 is lobbying to incorporate radio receivers in cellphones for the purposes of receiving emergency broadcasts in situations such as super storm Sandy (2012 hurricane that devastated the northeastern U.S.).

The Telecommunications Act of 1996 eliminated national ownership limits of radio stations earlier mandated by the Communication Act of 1934 and later legislation. As

a result of the 1996 law, which aligned with the popularized concept of deregulation in the United States as initiated by President Ronald Reagan (1980–1988), no national ownership limits (with one corporation allowed to control up to 8 stations in a single market) was established—just so long as more than one owner ran a station in smaller markets. After the 1996 Act was signed, about 10,000 (of the 14,000) stations in the U.S. were sold and the number of owners has declined by one third. Today, in most major markets, just three corporations claim 80% of its listeners.

Figure 1.41 Family sits down to watch television in 1957.

TELEVISION

Television is the most ubiquitous and fast-growing medium in history. Many media scholars call it the "800-pound gorilla" when it comes to its growth and effect on American audiences. Television brought a world of video and sound into the living rooms of 9% of American households by 1950, 65% of households; by 1955, 87% of households by 1960; and 98% by 1980, according to the Television Bureau of Advertising (2010).

Today, the average household has one or more TV sets turned on for over 8 hours per day. Men watch about 5 hours, women 5½ hours, and kids 3½ hours of television per day. According to A.C. Neilson, the average U.S. household has 2.24 TV sets (66% of U.S. households have more than 3 sets). Half of Americans believe they watch too much TV and two-thirds of American households watch television while eating dinner.

Television rearranged our social landscape in a significant way. Today, children watch an average of four hours of TV per day, but converse with their parents in a meaningful way for just seven minutes. Additionally, the average American youth spends 900 hours per year in school and 1,500 watching television. Never has a medium absorbed so much time and attention, and had such a significant effect on as many people as television. Among households with television, 75%

Figure 1.42 TV dinners, a generic trademark originally used for a brand of packaged meal developed in 1953 by C.A. Swanson & Sons. The company stopped using the name "TV Dinner" in 1962 but it remains synonymous with any prepackaged dinner purchased frozen and heated at home.

have one in the living room, 64% in the master bedroom, 29% in the family room, 23% in bedrooms, and 12% in kitchens (Television Bureau of Advertising, 2012).

Justin Lewis: Observations from his book The Ideological Octopus (1991)

> In the average home in the United States, the TV is on for more than seven hours a day, and by the time children finish high school, they will have spent more hours watching TV than in school.

> It is not unusual for technological developments to occur more rapidly than our ability to understand their social consequences.

> Television began life, not so long ago, as a gimmick, an amusing diversion from the radio. Its prodigious growth in the 1950s and 1960s turned it into a monster, a creature whose tentacles squirmed into almost every avenue of our cultural life.

> The breadth of our ignorance is remarkable. We do not really know what role television plays in the formation of attitudes and beliefs about ourselves and our world.

> Conrad Lodziak (1986) contends that television's main effect is 'not on our consciousness at all, but on its tendency to monopolize our leisure time.'

According to the Frankfurt School, the work of Theodor Adorno, Max Horkheimer, and Herbert Marcuse, "Capitalism, empowered by technology that could reach whole populations" was "in a position to restrict and control cultural life as never before. Mass cultural forms (like television) would create a 'mass culture' that was uniform and banal, reducing cultural life to the lowest common denominator available in the marketplace" (p. 6).

Figure 1.43 Television, and film, introduced celebrity culture to the US. Pop artists in the 1960s and 1970s focussed on the concept of image and emotional replication in response to the excessive sameness of the capitalistic ideology.

Figure 1.44 1949 issue of Radio-Electronics featuring cover story on how to get a better picture using a television set.

Figure 1.45 Photo of the complete cast of The Honeymooners (1955). This was the premiere episode on CBS as it moved from the DuMont network. From left: Jackie Gleason (Ralph Kramden), Audrey Meadows (Alice Kramden), Art Carney (Ed Norton), Joyce Randolph (Trixie Norton).

"Where does the power—the power to create and solidify meanings—really lie? Does it rest in the hands of the TV producer or in the TV consumer? Do we create our own meanings, or are they passed on to us, prewrapped in an attractive, well-designed package?" (p. 6).

The history of research about audiences of television is as old as the medium. The key question was: What is the effect of television on the people who watch it? Between the 1950s and 1960s, the focus of research attention was on violence in television and on television's impact on peoples' political sensibilities. This became known as the "direct effects" school of media research. What resulted could be summarized, according to Lewis (1991), as "inconclusive or confusing" (p. 7). The findings were so discomforting that by the 1960s, the direct-effects approach was abandoned.

Right after WWII, just six TV stations, one per market, were on the air in New York, Washington, Schenectady, Chicago, Philadelphia, and Los Angeles, broadcasting just a few hours per day. These, and other new television station owners, had to improvise the problems of station construction, programming, and operation. Veterans returning from the war had to quickly learn new jobs as producers, directors, technicians, and writers. The only pattern they knew was radio, and they adapted those approaches to the new medium. Aside from program development and genres, this led to the rapid "networking" of television stations throughout the United States.

One of the big controversies in early television was the debate over whether television should be supported by advertising or direct payments from viewers. Zenith, a major radio and television set manufacturer, argued for pay-TV. Several companies developed technologies for the scrambling of television signals that allowed paying viewers the ability to unscramble them. Backers of pay-TV included professional

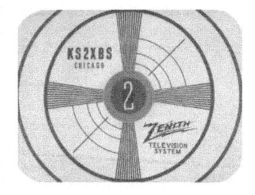

Figure 1.46 Test patterns like this one were typically broadcast during the early days of television before and after the stations went off the air. The author remembers watching test patterns, along with recorded symphonic music, early in the morning in the 1960s before broadcasting commenced—generally at 5:30am.

sports teams and cultural entertainment such as city symphonies. Opposed were theater owners, film producers, and commercial broadcasters who worried that the system would undercut their revenues. In 1952, Zenith petitioned the Federal Communication Commission to call for pay-TV. The FCC wouldn't decide on the matter until 1968.

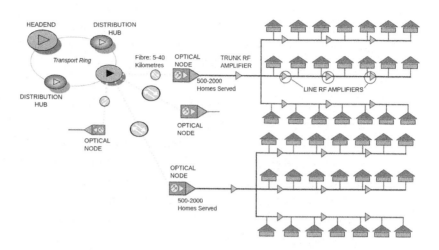

Figure 1.47 Diagram of a cable television network. The cable signal originates at a regional head-end, where stations are received by satellite transmission or over-the-air (local). The channels are transmitted on an optical fiber cable carried on utility poles or underground. The optical fiber trunk lines fan-out from distribution hubs to optical nodes that serve local neighborhoods. Here the signal from the optical fiber is translated from light beams to radio signals and carried on coaxial cable, which distribute it to individual households.

At the time, the commercial television broadcast band contained up to 12 stations per geographic market (e.g., New York). Figuring that these would run out fast, in 1952 the FCC expanded the number of stations by adding UHF stations (channels 14–80) to the existing VHF band (channels 2–13). Initially, four television networks dominated: DuMont (which went out of business in 1955), NBC, CBS, and ABC. By 1960, 87% of U.S. households had a television set and after about ten years of fits and starts, color came to television that same year. NBC began broadcasting its primetime line-up in color. CBS and ABC followed suit in 1965 and, for the first time, the sale of color sets outstripped black and white sets.

In June 2009, television broadcasting in the U.S. switched from analog to digital, which resulted in better picture quality, the ability to compress more signals into existing broadcast bandwidth, high-definition television (HDTV), and, down the road, the ability to further converge television signals with computing and telecommunications—bringing with it the possibility of increased interactivity. At the same time, flat-panel display screens began to outsell CRTs (cathode ray tubes), those big old clunky (and heavy) TVs. LCDs (liquid crystal displays) are most popular today, providing a large-screen, high-definition, near-theater-quality system to households at a reasonable price.

While over-the-air broadcasts dominated the distribution of television until the early 1970s, today just 15% of households in the U.S. receive TV to their primary set this way. Most primary television sets are connected to cable TV systems (68%) or DBS (direct broadcast satellite).

Cable television and DBS offer users up to 500 different channels—a far cry from the limited number available by way of over-the-air broadcasting. The increase in television fare increased television viewership (or, the number of hours people watch television per day) but has also greatly decreased the share of the primetime television audience that watches broadcast networks—ABC, CBS, NBC, and Fox. In 1975, 89% of primetime viewers watched broadcast network fare but by 2008 this had dropped to just 46%. The splintering of the television audience in the U.S. that occurred as a result of the numbers of stations available to watch is called "audience fragmentation." Now, rather than necessarily seeking large audiences, advertisers can find market segments that are attracted to specific interests and programs.

With the advent of DVRs (digital video recorders) that allow viewers to select and store broadcast content, as well as "zap" commercials, and broadband Internet connections that provide for streaming content from sites like Netflix.com, Hulu.com, and Youtube.com, television has moved away from an appointment- to a demand-based medium. Appointment-based mediums follow schedules where viewers must make themselves available to watch a specific show when it's broadcast. For example, if you wanted to watch the next new episode of *NCIS*, you would have to stop what you're doing and turn on the TV at 8pm on Tuesday. But more and more television is being viewed when users want to watch it.

Digitization also makes it possible to receive television content from smart phones, laptops, and iPads almost anywhere Wi-Fi or 3G cellular networks serve as a distribution capability. The TV networks have made significant investments in Internet program services to disseminate their programming outside of the traditional broadcast sphere. Ubiquitous access to television program and film content is ushering an explosion in hours spent by people watching videos wherever they may be.

With these new ways of acquiring television and other video programming, the number of households with television is actually, and for the first time, declining. In 2012, A.C. Nielsen reported that 500,000 fewer households have a television with over-the-air, cable, or satellite access. Instead, these households rely on websites distributing television via the Internet.

Online video viewing, according to Television Bureau of Advertising (2010), has increased to 47.3 million households. Online video users watch videos longer (for an average of 6 minutes) than they did in the past. This trend is poised to continue as broadband penetration increases from 75 million households (65%) in 2009 to 99 million (or 84%) by the end of 2016.

Significant increases in exposure to video content made possible through distribution channels that have emancipated television from the household, gym, and sports bar, suggests that the media ecological effects of the medium are poised to intensify. Consider the following perspectives.

From Chris Hedges (*Empire of Illusion: The End of Literacy and the Triumph of Spectacle*, 2010)

In *The Image: A Guide to Pseudo-Events in America*, Daniel Boorstin writes that in contemporary culture the fabricated, the inauthentic, and the theatrical have displaced the natural, the genuine, and the spontaneous, until reality itself has been converted into stagecraft. Americans, he writes, increasingly live in a 'world where fantasy is more real than reality.

And a culture dominated by images and slogans seduces those who are functionally literate but who make the choice not to read. There have been other historical periods with high rates of illiteracy and vast propaganda campaigns. But not since the Soviet and fascist dictatorships, and perhaps the brutal authoritarian control of the Catholic Church in the Middle Ages, has the content of information been as skillfully and ruthlessly controlled and manipulated.

And according to Marshall McLuhan in *Understanding Media: The Extensions of Man*:

Since TV, children—regardless of eye condition—average about six and a half inches from the printed page. Our children are striving to carry over to the printed page the all-involving sensory mandate of the TV image" (p. 308).

The Macworth head-camera, when worn by children watching TV, has revealed that their eyes follow, not the actions, but the reactions. The eyes scarcely deviate from the faces of the actors, even during scenes of violence (p. 309).

U.S. TV Households Fall a Second Consecutive Year But Perhaps 'TV Household' Is Due for a Redefinition

The number of U.S. TV households fell by 500,000, reflecting the popularity of online viewing and results of the 2010 census, according to Nielsen, producer of the weekly ratings that help set advertising rates.

The cut in U.S. TV households to 114.2 million took effect Aug. 27 and will apply to the television season starting this week, Nielsen Holdings said today in an e-mailed statement.

Nielsen said it's working with TV and advertising clients on what should constitute a TV home and TV device, suggesting online content may be counted. This is the second straight year Nielsen has decreased the number of homes with TVs. In May 2011, Nielsen reduced the number to 114.7 million, a 1% drop and the first decline since 1990.

In the past year, three of the four largest broadcast networks experienced drops in audiences ranging from 2% to more than 8%. Comcast's NBC, bolstered by the Olympics and football, increased its viewership by 19%, according to Nielsen data.

Andy Fixmer, from "Nielsen Cuts 500,000 U.S. TV Homes on Census, Web Viewing," Bloomberg News; September 25, 2012. Copyright © 2012 by Bloomberg LP. Read the entire article here: http://www.bloomberg.com/news/2012-09-25/nielsen-cuts-u-s-tv-homes-by-500-000-on-census-shift-to-web.html.

Figure 1.48 Facebook booth at 2010 ad:tech tradeshow in London. This was the sixth year in the UK for the online marketing and advertising community to gather at ad:tech to reveal the latest trends and market figures, share best practices and address industry challenges. Notice the "find your customers before they search" on the wall on the booth. Photo by Derzsi Elekes Andor.

NEW MEDIA

New mediums, including social networks (facebook), blogs, wikis, YouTube, and GPS-based services, are made possible through the evolution of two technologies: the Internet and the digitization of media content.

The Internet, which became a method of commercial content distribution in 1994, arose from ARPANET, the U.S. Defense Department's Advanced Research Project Agency (ARPA) network in the 1960s, that provided a means for researchers from universities and the government to share research and messages. The network's first universities on the system included UCLA, Stanford, UC Santa Barbara, and the University of Utah (1969). Five years later, more than 20 universities and government research centers along with European research centers were "on the net."

But before 1993, the Internet was a command-line service. That year, the National Center for Supercomputing Applications released a graphical user interface available to the public, called "Mosaic." This was the first "web browser," and with the release of a graphics-friendly operating system for Windows-based computers in 1995 (Windows '95), the adoption of the Internet became mainstream.

In 2012, some 2.5 trillion Internet users were identified around the world by Miniwatts Marketing Group (2013). Interestingly, just over 10% of worldwide users are from the U.S. and Canada. Just under half (45%) of people on the Internet are from Asian countries such as China and Japan. European users comprise one in five (22%) of those accessing the net. Africans, Middle Easterners, and Latin Americans are the fastest growing geographical areas gaining access.

About one-third of the people on planet earth have access to the Internet. As Asian and African countries' penetration rates increase, so too will this total percentage in a fairly rapid manner.

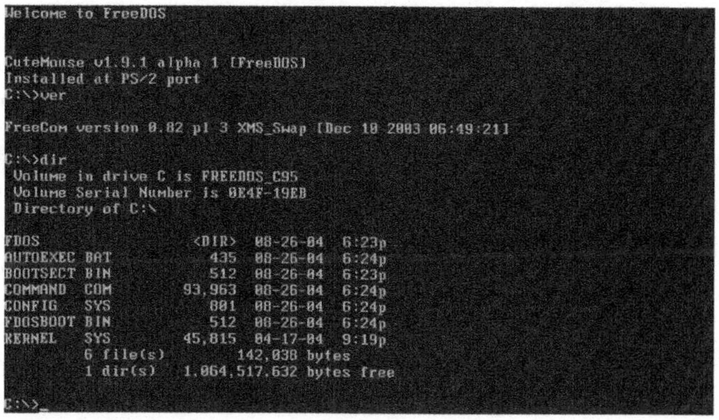

With digitization, the process where a medium (books, newspapers, magazines,

Figure 1.49 Command line interface. This is what the Internet, and computers, looked like before the advent of graphical user interfaces (GUIs).

radio, television, or film) is transformed into computer-readable form, content can be delivered to a much wider range of devices. Before digitization, media were analog— especially radio and television. Analog broadcasts relied on a carrier wave analogous to the fluctuations of the sound or image itself and necessitated the use of specialized devices such as record players, radios, and televisions to receive program content. But the term "analog" is now used to refer to all non-digitized media, including print, audio and video recordings, film, and film-based photography.

While digitization allows for easy transportability of print, music, video, and film across devices and platforms (i.e., television broadcast, Internet, 3G), it does so through content compression and the translation of wave lengths into 0s and 1s. Digital files are simply representations of their analog originals. Douglas Rushkoff reports that people who listen exclusively to MP3s lose, through brain plasticity (the use it or lose it aspect of perception), the ability to hear certain ranges of musical sound—including those that their parents can hear because their brains were developed listening to analog recordings (records, LPs, and tapes).

New media have emerged from digitization of old mediums, the evolution of new technologies that align themselves with the Internet (again, mostly through digitization), and the creativity of software developers. We can anticipate new forms to emerge, or converge, from traditional media, game developers, GPS (global positioning system) and mapping providers. Just within the past few years, social networks (e.g., Facebook, MySpace) have grown exponentially thanks to the creative forces who understood that technologies traditionally led to further alienation of users. While Facebook has reunited lots of people, and led the social networking charge, it has also led to other social problems including increased alienation from those we are physically closest to-- such as family members and the friends we "hang with."

Videogames are an $11.7 billion market (2008) in the U.S. according to the ESA (Entertainment Software Association). In this regard, videogames are a bigger market than movies (estimated at $10 billion according to the Motion Picture Association of America). There are three major platforms for computer games: PC-based, console-based, and arcade games. Most PC and console-based games are also played with others using Internet connections. The ESA study found that over two-thirds of US households play video games. The average videogame player is 35 and the number of older and female players is growing.

At the community college where I teach, video game development majors are required to take Introduction to Mass Communication—and use this textbook. They understand that games are a major communication medium replete with in-game

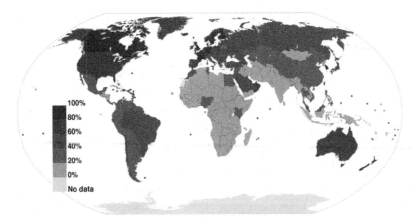

Figure 1.50 Map is colored to show the level of Internet penetration (number of Internet users as a percentage of a country's population). Map produced by Jeff Ogden based on data from Wikipedia's list of countries by number of Internet users. For 2011, this source placed the percentage of Americans using the Internet at 78%. Globally, the figure is thought to be 35%. Global population in 2011 is estimated at 7 billion people.

ads, significant revenues for content providers (such as Metallica for Guitar Hero), and a sense of realism nearing productions produced by their Digital Video/Film—Narrative and Documentary major counterparts. Massively Multiplayer Online Role Playing Games (MMORPGs), like World of Warcraft or Guild Wars, dominate this environment.

Virtual worlds such as Second Life, with 126 million hours logged-in in by users in 2009, allow for the creation of avatars—the graphic depiction of oneself online. But with the ability to represent oneself however one likes, participants can vary their race, sex, hair color, and other physical characteristics. According to Paxson (2010), "This ability to change one's identity in a variety of ways is one of the virtual

Figure 1.51 Google Digitization signs appeared all over the Michigan engineering library in 2007. The company is attempting to digitize most non-digital texts (books). Photo by Timothy Vollmer.

world's primary attractions to participants. A teenager can assume the identity of a much older person, although more likely, this process works in the opposite direction."

GPS (global positioning system) technology is also a digital technology that can converge with text, audio, video, and games (including virtual reality). GPS can trigger content based on the location of the user. Today, GPS may let users know where

Figure 1.52 Bruce Hack is the CEO of Vivendi Games, the publisher that's responsible for the output of Blizzard (including World of Warcraft) and other titles such as F.E.A.R., Scarface, and Crash Bandicoot.

a chain store is located—for instance, where a user could find a McDonald's. In the future, users may encounter coupons from a nearby retailer, specials at a restaurant, or encouragement to travel to a different location in order to find a better and cheaper hotel to spend the night. The author has also recently seen apps in development that let you find the location of friends on maps (nearby), and, an app that responds to an earpiece that registers users emotions, allowing subscribers to find where people in the area are happy, sad, frustrated, or looking for a friend.

Clearly, creativity is the most limiting factor as technologies and applications (including entertainment content) converge in such a manner. The integration of everything digital will lead, in an ever increasing rate of "breakthroughs," to new mediums and applications that one can scarcely dream about today.

STUDENT PERSPECTIVES

Who was Paul Robeson?

Paul Robeson was born on April 9, 1898. Throughout his life, Robeson has accomplished many things and has been a well rounded individual, successful at almost everything he decided to overtake. Yet, many have never even heard of him. Robeson was an actor who won many awards for best acting performance in shows such as Othello and Showboat, leaving his mark behind in everything he appeared in. He starred in over 10 films and wrote and sang music to promote African and African American history and culture.

During his time, Robeson was an icon worldwide. He was known as a citizen of the world, and traveled from country to country singing for peace and justice in 25 languages. Today, Robeson is barely mentioned. He has almost been erased from history. This has been all due to the fact that, although Robeson has done many great things in his past, he was also blacklisted.

To become blacklisted means that you are set-aside on a list of persons or organizations that are considered under suspicion, untrustworthy, or disloyal. As a result, that person is to be boycotted. They are not to be hired, served, or otherwise accepted. The reason as to why Robeson was blacklisted was unjust. As a very outspoken passionate man, Robeson constantly protested against the growing Cold War and headed an organization that challenged President Truman to support an anti-lynching law. He was a peacemaker and was quick to speak out against racism, and so during time of war Robeson openly questioned why African Americans should fight for a government that tolerated racism. This eventually led to the House of Un-American Activities Committee to accusing Robeson of being a Communist, and so he was blacklisted.

Paul Robeson's story is not known as well as it should be nationwide. Even more unfortunate, it's not known as much as it should be locally. Locally, every New Jerseyan should know Paul Robeson's story and share it with much pride. It is very important that this story is known, especially locally because Paul Robeson, like myself was a New Jersey resident.

Robeson was born in Princeton NJ, less than an hour from where I live. Even closer to home, he attended Rutgers University located only 8 minutes from where I live now. He played for the Scarlet Knights and was twice named to the All-American Football team. He won 15 varsity letters in sports and received the Phi Beta Kappa key in his junior year. After he was blacklisted, it's as if he was wiped out of the face of the earth. But, his story is still alive and history can be hidden but it can never be erased. It wasn't until 1995 that Paul Robeson was inducted into the College Football Hall of Fame, a big reminder that this man left a mark on our nation. As fellow residents, we should keep this alive and continue sharing his story.

—Harol Margarin
Professor Treut
Intro to Mass Comm.

Who is this Paul Robeson guy seen all over campus? This mysterious man has a whole room named after him – he must be something! It turns out Robeson was very successful and prominent during his time. His accomplishments in New Jersey and worldwide reflect why he is such an important figure locally. He was an athlete, actor, singer, lawyer, and an activist all in one lifetime. Paul Robeson was born on April 9, 1898 in Princeton, New Jersey to Anna Louisa and William Drew Robeson. After his mother passed when he was 6, their family moved to Somerville where Robeson excelled in school. He received a full scholarship to Rutgers University in 1915. Robeson won 15 varsity letters in sports (baseball, basketball and track) and graduated from Rutgers as valedictorian. He continued his studies at Columbia Law School and became a successful lawyer. Eventually, Robeson left the practice to promote equality through his artistic talents in singing and acting.

Robeson used singing and acting as a means of spreading the history of different cultures and to speak against racism. He knew the power of his publicity could promote change, especially in labor forces. Some believed he was a "citizen of the world" because of his extreme passion for peace between all peoples. According to www.cpsr.cs.uchicago.edu, in the 1940's he spoke and performed at strike rallies, conferences, and labor festivals worldwide. At the time, the tension between the United States and the Soviet Union had begun what is known as the Cold War. As a passionate believer of peace, he protested against the Cold War and promoted friendship and respect between the U.S and the USSR. He also questioned the president, who at the time was Truman, and asked why African-Americans should fight in an international war when they were being poorly treated at home. Due to Robeson's courage and straightforwardness, the government revoked his passport in 1950. He was accused of being a communist by the House Un-American Activities. This did not stop the determined Paul Robeson from continuing his role as an African-American activist. He pursued his quest by learning about world peace, singing and writing. After eight years, Robeson regained his passport and was finally able to prosper in acting and travel again.

—Ashley Cardoso
September 26, 2013
Paul Robeson

Media Ecology

Film is a dying art. As technology advances, so does the method in which we capture, store and enjoy visual media.

We are in a time of great renaissance when it comes to art of cinema. A child, with a phone capable of taking video, can now shoot and edit his/her own video on such device. Further more that video can be uploaded to the world wide web and viewed by virtually anyone with access to the web. A Hollywood producer spends millions of dollars on a cinematic experience they think will be big. After countless weeks of shooting and just as many weeks editing, the finished project is ready for public consumption. Thousands, if not millions of people will pay a premium price to see a showing of such film. Yet this number is rapidly decreasing due to the rapid expansion of the way we view videos. Like the kid who created a video from his phone, cheap and direct methods of capturing motion pictures has sullied the film industry. And digital video is the culprit.

Film, true film, is the art of taking physical film roll and capturing motion upon it. Digital video on the other side of the argument is the capturing of video onto a card or a file. All too often people will call a digital video they had seen a *film*. I often and most commonly call digital video a film. This however, according to Dan Streible is all too common slip of the tongue. In Streible's article *Moving Image History and the F-Word; or, "Digital Film" Is an Oxymoron* digital video is made out to be blight on the face of film. The majority of the article makes no mistake in separating the two motion capture methods. Sure, digital video and film are not the same thing. And yes, the majority of the public hasn't the slightest clue about the difference between film and digital video. But then again the separation and classification of calling video a film or not shouldn't be the issue at hand necessarily. What I found to the true crisis at hand, something that Streible only briefly touches upon, is that film is dying.

The film era is being ushered to welcome in the new more advanced digital technologies that are used by most film companies nowadays. However I will state this, digital video is not a bad thing; in fact I believe it to be a very good thing in the cinema and general movie making industry. Yet film, the originating source of motion pictures has all but vanished from the industry. Since digital video's inception 30 ought years ago filmmakers have slowly begun teaching the out the art of film and incepting the art of *digital film*. Now, even the top film schools, in the US, do not offer true film courses as required subject of study. In fact very schools have the knowledge and know how to teach such subject. Even films already subjected to motion capture are going digital. Most universities and film libraries have begun to transmute film into digital video for numerous reasons. The most pressing being that film does not last.

Film can only last for a few decades before the acidy of the grain itself degrades the film and renders it useless. Film simply was not made to stand the test of time. The irony is unbearable.

It's a sad day for film. But like all technologies after time they become obsolete. So perhaps we should simply accept that film has no place in the motion picture industry, and welcome the digital heralds of our time. We should simply say a big farewell to film. And maybe a thank you too.

—Jake Raab
Intro to Mass Comm.

MEDIA OWNERSHIP AND THE CORPORATIZATION OF THOUGHT

I believe that when we deny our own vulnerability to media we are actually increasing the degree to which we can be manipulated. If you do not know you are vulnerable—indeed, if you think you are invulnerable—you will not think and act in ways that protect you. Two basic errors in judgment that we make are (1) believing that fantasy stories in no way shape our realities and (2) believing that media's reason for being is to entertain rather than to persuade us.

—Karen Dill, How Fantasy Becomes Reality.

In 1945, roughly 80 percent of American newspapers were privately owned, often by families that were willing to sacrifice potential profits to maintain their journalistic principles and preserve their readers' trust. Today, however, more than 80 percent of American newspapers are owned and operated by publicly traded corporations, many of which are merely subsidiaries of larger conglomerates whose executives are unwilling to compromise income for the good of cities they rarely visit or towns they've never seen.

—Eric Klinenberg, The Battle to Control America's Media (2010).

Though today's media reach more Americans than ever before, they are controlled by the smallest number of owners than ever before... in 1983, there were fifty dominant media corporations, today there are five.

—Ben Bagdikian

Freedom of the press is great if you own a press.

—Will Rogers

INTRODUCTION

Think about your media system—the channels and content of the mediasphere that surrounds us, that we both actively and passively attend to. In 2009, The Kaiser Foundation reported that the average 8- to 18-year-old had nearly 11 hours of media exposure per day. Consider all of the television stations, Internet sites, radio stations, Hollywood movies, magazines, record labels, and book publishers that touch your life. These media could take on any form and present a wide variety of content—but they tend to show or play or print content that seems familiar and entertaining to us.

And, at the same time, there seems to be a disconnection between the world as we see it and the mediated world. Why does television news cover urban crime but ignore white-collar crime? Why does it cover fires but not global warming? Why, in difficult economic times, does it show stories on government-deficit reduction but not on job creation?

The corporately controlled media system in the United States tends to offer a narrow range of content to audiences. This is because broadcasters are reluctant to offend or adversely affect the businesses of their advertisers, even indirectly. Advertising-supported media systems, like ours, suffer from the "corporatization perspective"—the alignment of program content that fits the needs of advertisers.

In the United States, most television channels (except PBS, and subscription-based channels like HBO), radio stations (except public radio and college stations), newspapers, and magazines are advertising-supported. For these businesses, the business goal is to sell viewers, listeners, and readers to advertisers. The users of these mediums, people like us, are commodities who are sold

Figure 2.1 Our mediasphere, Earth from space. This photo was taken by the crew of Apollo 17 on their way to the Moon. Antarctica, Africa, the Arabian Peninsula, Madagascar, and part of Asia are visible.

to advertisers at a negotiated CPM (cost per thousand). In other words, we are not the customers—the customers are the businesses that buy commercials or ad space.

While working for a local newspaper ten years ago, I stumbled upon a story about a local environmental hazard. A local farm, an EPA Superfund site, was once a production facility for arsenic and later DDT. These carcinogens were sold to nearby farmers to keep pests off of peaches and other fruits. Children who lived near the site suffered from adult cancers and other ailments. While digging into the story, an oncologist (cancer doctor) told me that we could expect cancer cases to emerge wherever people lived where there once was an orchard. In other words, this fast growth area could expect hundreds, if not thousands, of cancer cases because arsenic and DDT linger in soil and drinking water (most of the people in this area received their water from wells).

I wrote the story and handed it to my editor. He read it and walked into the publisher's office. A few minutes later, I was called in to his office and was told that the story would not run. It would result in the devaluation of much of the area's properties and result in the "pulling of ads" from real estate and other advertisers. So the story was killed.

This was a small local newspaper. Can you imagine the pressure that is placed upon reporters, directors, and producers of television stations when it comes to selecting the stories of the day? While we cannot criticize the work of individual producers (television) or publishers (newspapers) in protecting the interests of their major advertisers, one can criticize the system that results in the death of some stories and the promotion of others. Consider the major advertisers of television news—cars, pharmaceuticals, and financial institutions. Is it little wonder that most Americans don't know that the single most dangerous thing they do each day is to get behind the wheel of their cars? That prescription drugs kill more people each year than illegal drugs? That financial institutions did more to cause our current economic woes than any other institution, including the government?

In 1970, Congress enacted the Public Health Cigarette Smoking Act that banned television and radio advertisements for smoking. Shortly afterward, people began to learn about the dangers of smoking—in many cases from studies conducted twenty or more years earlier—from the news media. Why didn't network television news cover findings from major health organizations prior to this? Because the cigarette industry spent about $1 billion per year advertising cigarette brands on television

Figure 2.2 New York City stencil *Soft Brains Watch the Screen and Buy the Jeans*, 1980. The U.S. media system is among the most commercialized, supported by corporate advertising, than any others around the world. John Fekner photo.

Figure 2.3 The primary goal of commercial television, radio, magazines, and newspapers is to sell audiences to advertisers. Viewers, readers, and listeners are the commodity media outlets sell to those who buy ads.

and radio. With advertisers as the broadcasters' primary customers, it only follows that we view the world from a corporatized perspective.

With corporate advertisers as our media's customers, it is little wonder that we receive a view of the world that placates, or at a minimum fails to offend, corporations. As stated earlier, viewers, readers, and listeners (that means us) are the commodity sold to corporate advertisers. The programs, songs, and news we enjoy watching, listening to, and reading are developed to attract and hook our attention so we will also watch, listen to, or read the advertisements that accompany the content we seek.

Americans began to prefer television news over newspapers shortly after the assassination of President John F. Kennedy in 1963. Television covered the developments of the assassination and its aftermath in close to real time. Newspapers were limited to covering the story within the confines of newspaper press cycles (i.e., weekly, daily, morning, evening). As Bob Schieffer, former CBS Evening News anchor and reporter during the assassination at the *Fort Worth Star-Telegram* stated, before the Kennedy assassination people believed things that they read, in black and white. Afterward, television dominated as the preferred medium for news. Today, according to schools.com, 60% of Americans get their news from television, 29% from newspapers, and the balance from radio, social media, and other online sources

HOW TO WATCH TV NEWS

Neil Postman and Steve Powers wrote an important book in 1992 entitled *How to Watch TV News* that warned viewers: anyone who relies exclusively on TV for his or her knowledge of the world is making a serious mistake. Television news is, at its heart, entertainment designed to hold viewers through commercial breaks. While the entertainment comes in the form of news stories, directors select from the most visually appealing (or upsetting) images to lead the news, which relates to the industry's maxim that "if it bleeds ... it leads." I have a friend who is a news director at a New York local television station who told me, "If you want the news, go buy a newspaper. That isn't what I produce. I put together a program that holds audiences. Otherwise, I'd have to go find another job."

Postman and Powers tell an industry tale where a news director, upon beginning a job at a new station, is told that if his ratings (i.e., size of his audience) drop, he is to open the three envelopes in his desk drawer. After several months, his ratings dropped so he opened the first envelope. Its contents read, "Hire a new anchor." So he fired the anchor and hired a new one. The next month, the ratings dropped again. The note in the second envelope read, "Change the set." So, he had the set remodeled and the color scheme changed. The ratings didn't drop for a while but a few months later did. He opened the third envelope, and the note read, "Put three envelopes in the drawer and look for a new job." He was fired the next day.

Platforms Used to Get News Yesterday, by Age, June 2010. (% of customers)	18–24	25–29	30–39	40–49	50–64	65+	Total
Traditional Platforms							
TV	39	44	49	60	65	75	58
Radio	22	31	38	42	38	25	34
Print newspaper	7	11	15	24	35	46	26
One or more	53	64	70	80	83	83	75
Digital Platforms							
Online*	32	36	46	40	36	18	34
Email	13	11	15	15	16	9	14
RSS/custom webpage	12	17	18	10	9	2	10
Social networking/Twitter	13	15	21	9	5	1	9
Mobile phone/smartphone	15	14	14	11	6	1	9
Podcast	5	7	5	4	4	1	4
One or more	48	48	57	49	44	23	44
Summary							
Traditional only	20	30	25	39	44	62	39
Digital only	16	15	12	9	5	1	9
Both	32	34	45	41	39	21	36
No news yesterday	31	21	18	12	11	16	17

Note: respondents were asked "Where did you get news yesterday?"; numbers may not add up to 100% due to rounding; *includes those who reported reading a newspaper online
Source: Pew Research Center for the People and the Press, "Ideological New Sources: Who Watches and Why" conducted by Princeton Survey Research Associates International, Sep 12, 2010

News programs, according to Postman and Powers, are "re-presentations" of actual events, and not the events themselves, presented using videos or pictures and words. Notice that, while watching the vast majority of news stories, the event described isn't shown. Rather, news crews rush to the scene to cover the aftermath or implications of an event. Perhaps a graphic or security footage may be used to present the event itself. The authors suggest viewers consider how language, as an "abstracted representation," is used to explain what happened. Newscasters should limit themselves to description of events but often transcend this and perform an evaluative, or worse, an inferential perspective on the event.

Levels of language abstraction used on television news are:

1. Description—describes the event (e.g., Bob Frelanger is 5 feet 8 inches tall and weighs 250 pounds)

2. Evaluation—evaluates the event (e.g., Bob Frelanger is fat)
3. Inference—infers what is unknown on basis of what's known (e.g., Bob Frelanger clearly eats too much).

The authors also suggest viewers look out for connotative meanings in newscasts. Is an attitude suggested or presented in the way the newscaster describes the story? Does the newscaster use emotion-laden or loaded words? Or, when you think about a newscaster's words, do they seem ambiguous (unclear or inexact)?

One should also keep in mind that all of the words spoken in a full one-hour news broadcast can be printed on one page of a newspaper. Can we really expect to learn all about the day's events in a single page of newsprint?

From a media ecological perspective, it's important to recognize that television (images and sound) is an ideal medium for the "showing off" of objects, rather than the discussion of ideas, which is the province of print (newspapers, magazines, and books). Television tends to be processed emotionally and moving pictures tend to favor images that change, including fires, something violently destroyed, blood-covered bodies on gurneys, earthquakes, and hurricanes. These make for compelling news images.

A substantial amount of subjectivity lies behind news selection (i.e., determining which stories are actually shown) and, as previously mentioned, a great deal of pressure lies in holding audiences and not upsetting sponsors. Since stories are sequenced in a manner designed to maximize audience interest, they are not clearly organized but instead are presented in a fragmented and chaotic style—leaving the viewer to assume that there is logic to the flow of stories. This sequencing, in and of itself, leaves many to believe that the world is a much more chaotic and unpredictable place than it really is. After viewing a murder attempt, several fires, an earthquake in India, a typhoon in

Figure 2.4 Behind the scenes at *NBC Nightly News*. This view is from the control room where the director, technical director, audio engineer, and others direct the production of the evening news broadcast. Photo by Jeff Maurone.

Indonesia, and a volcano in Peru, is it little wonder that we might say to ourselves, "the world is falling apart"?

By the 1970s, media scholars and critics began to complain that the media in America was "undermining their role in democratic life, first by concentrating media power in the hands of particular social interests—those of business especially—and second, by shifting the purpose of the press from the expression of political viewpoints to the promotion of consumerism" (Hallin and Mancini, p. 203).

Media scholar Robert McChesney states, "Democratic theory posits that society needs journalism to perform three main duties: to act as a rigorous watchdog of the powerful and those who wish to be powerful; to ferret out truth from lies; and to present a wide range of informed positions on key issues" (p. 57). He and others believe U.S. journalism fails on all three of these duties. "The problem stems directly from the system of profit-driven journalism in largely noncompetitive markets that began to emerge over a century ago," says McChesney. Under the advertising-supported model, where newspapers sell readers to advertisers, building readership (called circulation in the newspaper industry) is imperative. As a result, newspapers resorted to sensationalism and, according to McChesney, "outright lying," to increase circulation. He continued:

> Throughout this era, socialists, feminists, abolitionists, trade unions, and radicals came to regard the mainstream commercial press as the mouthpiece of their enemies and established their own media to advance their interests. In the classic 1887 utopian novel *Looking Backward* the journalist Edward Ballamy wrote longingly of a time when newspapers would write the truth and not serve as pawns of the wealthy. Robert McChesney, *The Problem of the Media*, p. 59).

But today, and with ever-increasing access to and use of media (about 12 hours per person per day) via Internet, television, radio, etc., "our era (has become) increasingly depoliticized; traditional notions of civic and political involvement have shriveled. Elementary understanding of social and political affairs has declined. Turnout for U.S. elections—admittedly not a perfect barometer—has plummeted over the past thirty years" (McChesney, 1999).

> "... the media have become a significant antidemocratic force in the United States and, to varying degrees, worldwide. The wealthier and more powerful the corporate media giants have become, the poorer the prospects for participatory democracy. I am not arguing that all media are getting wealthier, of course. Some media firms and sectors are faltering and will falter during this turbulent era. But, on balance, the dominant media firms are larger and

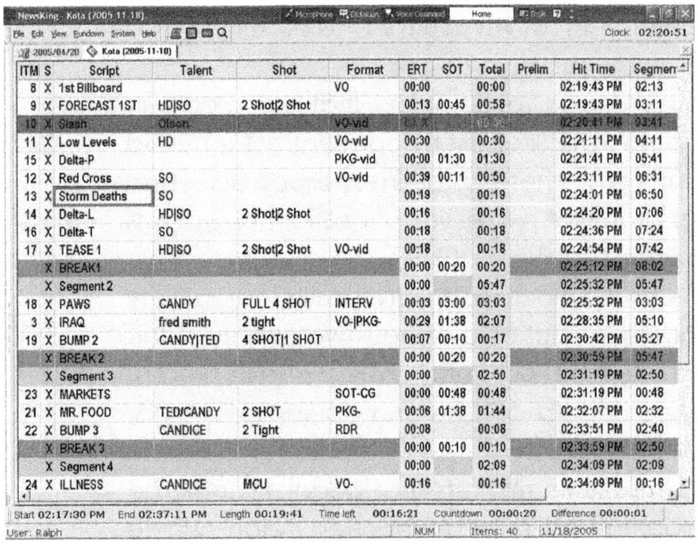

Figure 2.5 Automated broadcast news rundown is a computer program that lists the story sequences, lengths, and other important story information for news directors. Note from this example how the stories are not organized by topic but rather by the quality of the video or relative sensationalism—such as violent weather, deaths, or war.

more influential than ever before, and the media writ large are more important in our social life than ever before. Nor do I believe the media are the sole or primary cause of the decline of democracy, but they are a part of the problem and closely linked to many of the other factors. Behind the lustrous glow of new technologies and electronic jargon, the media system has become increasingly concentrated and conglomerated into a relative handful of corporate hands. This concentration accentuates the core tendencies of a profit-driven, advertising-supported media system: hypercommercialism and denigration of journalism and public service. It is a poison pill for democracy." (McChesney from *Rich Media, Poor Democracy*, 1999)

Or, consider the perspective of Mark Crispin Miller, Professor of Communication Studies at New York University ("The Death of News," *The Nation*, July 3, 2006):

Contrary to the counterclaims in 1996, there was, as The Nation noted then, copious hard evidence of corporate meddling with the news, and also, even more important, lots of subtler evidence of reportorial self-censorship throughout the media cartel. And yet what stood out as egregious back then seems pretty tame today, now that the press consistently tunes out or plays down the biggest news, while hyping trivialities, or, if it covers a disaster, does so only fleetingly and without "pointing fingers." (New Orleans is now forgotten.) The press that went hoarse over Monica Lewinsky's dress is largely silent on the Bush regime's subversion of the Constitution; its open violation of the laws here and abroad; its global use of torture; its vast surveillance program(s); its covert propaganda foreign and domestic; its flagrant cronyism; its suicidal military, economic and environmental policies; and its careful placement of the federal establishment into the hands of Christianist extremists. Whether it's such tawdry fare as Jeffrey Gannon's many overnights at Bush's house, or graver matters like the Patriot Act, or the persistent questions about 9/11, or the President's imperial "signing statements" or—most staggering of all—the ever-growing evidence of coast-to-coast election fraud by Bush & Co., the press has failed in its constitutional obligation to keep us well informed about the doings of our government.

In short, our very lives and liberty are at unprecedented risk because our press has long since disappeared into "the media"—a mammoth antidemocratic oligopoly that is far more responsive to its owners, big shareholders and good buddies in the government than it is to the rest of us, the people of this country.

WHAT CORPORATIZATION MEANS

At News World 2000, an international discussion held among journalists and academics in Barcelona, Spain, the question of corporate influence on the news was discussed. The main question raised for debate read:

> The world's media is being concentrated in the hands of fewer and fewer companies. Is it just paranoia to suggest global media giants are willing to forgo journalistic quality and ethics in exchange for shareholder return? Mass media has always been influenced and controlled by megalomaniacs; will the corporations be any different? Do corporate companies meddle in the news-room, slipping in product placement or curtailing investigations that might bite the hand that feeds?

There were mixed responses. Academics attacked journalists by raising examples of stories not covered (e.g., global warming, job loss, targeting news to upper-middle class and higher economic audiences) while most journalists generally held their ground, insisting that major news organizations work diligently to present the top stories of the day in a non-judgmental manner.

The only journalist to break ground from the others, Neil Docherty, produces at CBC (Canadian Broadcast System, a non-commercial state-sponsored network in Canada). He offered some interesting insights into what corporatization of the media means when he stated:

I produced a documentary in 1996 about events that took place in 1995 when both ABC and CBS gave in to tobacco pressure. Let me briefly outline what happened. On September 6, 1995, Lowell Bergman, Don Hewitt, and Mike Wallace are called to Black Rock, the corporate headquarters of CBS. In thirteen years at CBS it is the first time Lowell Bergman had been invited to Black Rock. They are told that they can't run a story that they have for legal reasons. It turned out that the story was one of the most important stories. These were historic pieces of journalism and at a time when the tobacco issue was very much a frontrunner issue in the States. In the case of CBS, it started when Jeffrey Wigand agreed to talk to CBS. Jeffrey Wigand was the first high-level executive from the tobacco industry who agreed to talk, to revel secrets never heard before, which were of enormous public importance. They were told they couldn't run that story because Jeffrey Wigand also had an agreement with his former employers, Brown and Williamson Tobacco, which tied him to confidentiality; if he talked to "60 Minutes" he would be breaking that and the program would be liable. But what the journalists don't know at the time is that there are a lot of corporate machinations happening behind the scenes.

At that point CBS is owned by the Tisch family, Lawrence Tisch. The Tisch family gets 60-70 percent of its profits not from broadcasting but from tobacco. They own lots of tobacco brands. Months earlier Andrew Tisch, the son of Lawrence, had gone before the U.S. Congress in the famous hearing in which seven CEOs swear on the Bible that tobacco is not addictive. Among them is Andrew Tisch, who repeatedly makes that claim. The Department of Justice launches a criminal investigation of perjury on those seven individuals. This is going on the same time when the journalists are doing their story on Wigand. It also turns out that the Tisch family is buying up brands from Brown and Williamson Tobacco, the employers of Jeffrey Wigand. And more important than all of that, and to confound the problems further, we have Westinghouse currently negotiating with Lawrence Tisch to take over CBS. Lawrence Tisch of course stands to gain about 22 million dollars by this. The people making the decision not to run this story, General Counsel Ellen Kaden and News Division President Eric Ober, stand to make about 1.2 million dollars if the merger goes ahead. Eventually the story runs; on both occasions the path was cleared by the Wall Street Journal.

Corporatization not only concerns itself with which stories run or what the slant of a story may be, but also, and probably more importantly, on the creation of a climate favorable to corporate interests. This is understandable when one considers that the advertising-supported media's mission is to sell viewers to advertisers—the customer and revenue producers for media companies.

> By the time we reach the age of sixty-six, most of us will have seen approximately two million television commercials. Time-wise, that's the equivalent of watching eight hours of ads seven days a week for six years straight (*Buyology: Truth and Lies About Why We Buy*. Martin Lindstrom and Paco Underhill)

And these ads are very effective. According to Ben Bagdikian, $80 billion per year in advertising expenditures paid toward the largest media conglomerates (see the Big 5 below) from a total, in 2011, of $171 billion in total advertising expenditures, triggers about $6 trillion in U.S. consumer spending each year. According to psychologist and author Jean Kilbourne, "We are each exposed to over 2000 ads a day, constituting perhaps the most powerful educational force in society. The average American will spend one and one-half years of his or her life watching television commercials. The ads sell a great deal more than products. They sell values, images, and concepts of success and worth, love and sexuality, popularity and normalcy. They tell us who we are and who we should be. Sometimes they sell addictions." Bagdikian writes, "Large media corporations have shared values. Those values are reflected in the emphasis of their news and popular culture. They are the primary shapers of American public opinion about events and their meaning. And through that, and their organization in large powerful corporate units, they are a major influence on government."

THE BIG 5—DOMINANT MEDIA CORPORATIONS (U.S. AND GLOBAL)

U.S. media, including television, film, music, and publishing, are dominated by just five corporations. In other words, just five companies own and transmit the vast majority of the content you receive on television and in the movies, the music you hear, and the books, magazines, and newspapers you read. The control of our mediasphere has become more concentrated, further dominated by large multi-national corporations, over the past several decades. In the early 1980s, 50 corporations dominated U.S. media. By 1990, that number dropped to 23. In 1997, just ten; and today, five.

As this book went to press, the Federal Communication Commission (the branch of government responsible for overseeing America's media system) was quietly considering even further relaxation of media ownership, leading to further consolidation. According to *Advertising Age*, the leading magazine serving the advertising business, the FCC "is proposing loosening the newspaper/TV station cross-ownership ban in the top 20 markets, and lifting restrictions entirely on newspaper/radio cross-ownership." Earlier attempts during the Bush Administration to lift existing ownership caps were blocked due to the anticipated adverse effects on minority and women ownership of media properties—already described as "slim" according to media watch groups. Democrat member of the FCC Michael Copps questioned the Democrat chairman

Former FCC Commissioner:
Big Media Dumbs Down Democracy

This week, we're focusing on the Federal Communications Commission's proposal to relax the rules that prevent one company from owning radio stations, television stations and newspapers all in the same city—a move activists say would hurt diversity and be a boon for the Rupert Murdochs of the world.

It's déjà vu for Michael Copps, who served on the commission from 2001-2011 and was acting chairman from January to June 2009—a tenure marked by his concern for diversity and opposition to media consolidation. Copps is now the senior advisor for media and democracy reform at Common Cause. He stopped by our office Monday to share his concerns about the FCC's latest proposal.

Bill Moyers: After all the conversations we've had over the years, why are we still talking about media concentration today?

Michael Copps: Because media concentration is still very much a reality today. If you opened up the papers last week, you'll see Rupert Murdoch is maybe thinking about buying the *Los Angeles Times or the Chicago Tribune*. Every time you have one of these consolidation transactions, they look around for all of these wonderful economies and efficiencies that they're supposed to harvest from becoming big conglomerates. The first thing they think is, "How do we impress Wall Street now? Where do we cut?" And the first place they cut is the newsroom. We've had, across this country, hundreds of newsrooms shuttered, thousands of reporters who are walking the streets in search of a job, rather than walking the beats in search of stories. And the consequence of that is, I think, a dramatically dumbed down civic dialogue that is probably—and I don't think I'm exaggerating—insufficient to sustain self-government as we would like to have it.

There's this wonderful story about Bill Paley, who I never knew, but—

Moyers:—founder and chairman of the board of CBS—

Copps: Right. Getting his news folks together back in the '50s or '60s, whenever it was, and saying, "I want you folks to go out and get the news. And don't worry where the money's coming from. I got Jack Benny. He'll provide the money and you go get the news." Can you imagine any of the current CEOs of the media companies here, Les Moonves or anybody like that, telling their news people, "You just go and get the news and don't worry where the money's coming from"?

Bill Moyers (left) and Michael Copps (right)

Moyers: The argument we hear in rebuttal is "Well look, we don't have to worry about monopoly today, we don't have to worry about cartels today, because we have the Internet, which is the most democratic source of opinion, expression and free speech that's available to us. You and Moyers are outdated because of your concerns about broadcasting and newspapers and all of this."

Copps: I don't buy that argument at all. The Internet has the potential for all of that. The Internet has the potential for a new town square of democracy, paved with broadband bricks. But it's very, very far from being the reality. The reality is—and you don't have to really look too closely—throughout history, we've seen every means of communication go down this road toward more and more consolidation. Wouldn't it be a tragedy if you took this potential of this open and dynamic technology, capable of addressing just about every problem that the country has—no problem that we have doesn't have a broadband component to its solution somewhere along the line—and let the biggest invention since the printing press probably as communication goes, morph into a cable-ized Internet? That's what I think is happening. Most of the news generated on the Internet, is still coming from the newspaper newsroom, or the TV newsroom. It's just there's so damn much less of it because of the consolidation that we've been through, because of the downsizing, and because of a government that has been absent without leave from its public interest responsibilities for many, many years—a better part of a generation now.

Moyers: You came to the commission advocating more ownership, more diversity, more participation by minorities and women—where does that stand now? Have they made gains?

Copps: It stands pretty much where it stood when the new commissioner came through the door in 2009. We have pending before the commission dozens and dozens of recommendations to incentivize minority and female ownership. It can't right now be truly a race-conscious policy—I hope it will be some day—because we don't have the legal justification, and that's due to the FCC's not doing its homework. But they have something called overcoming disadvantage, sort of like the University of Texas and all that, where you can take into consideration a number criteria, and one of those would be minority status.

I wrote a piece on Benton's blog that came out today, and I go back and quote from Barack Obama in previous years. This is Barack Obama at an FCC hearing, he submitted this statement, 2007, September 20th: "I believe that the nation's media ownership rules remain necessary and are critical to the public interest. We should be doing much more to encourage diversity in the ownership of broadcast media, promote the development of new media outlets for expression of diverse viewpoints, and establish greater clarity in public interest obligations of broadcasters occupying the nation's spectrum." Seven months later, in February, he and Dick Durbin wrote the commission: "The broadcast ownership rules directly implicate core American values such as diversity, localism, representation and a competitive marketplace of ideas." And listen to this: "I object"—this is Obama, as candidate, October 22, 2007: "I object to the agency moving forward to allow greater consolidation in the media market without first fully understanding how that would limit opportunities for minority, small business and women-owned firms."

Moyers: But, to the contrary, we hear these reports that the man President Obama put on the commission as the chairman is considering further relaxation of the rules prohibiting concentration. How do you explain that?

Copps: Well, first of all, they definitely are considering it. Nobody has seen the document yet except the commissioners, but in point of fact, they are going to liberalize—that's the wrong term—they're going to loosen the newspaper/broadcast cross-ownership [rules] and loosen the constraints on radio and TV stations owning each other.

How do you explain that? I don't know if it's a question of less interest than there should be in the media issues, because people maybe deem them to be an older issue, and let's talk about new media and wireless and spectrum and all of that. And all of that is important, but here's my take. You know, you really have to get people away from this idea of thinking old media versus new media. We have in this country one media ecosystem, and it is partly composed of traditional media—newspapers, radio, television, cable. It's partly composed of new media—broadband and the Internet. And it's going to stay that way, for years yet. I mean there'll be evolution, but we're going to have both of these things to contend with. And neither one of them is operating, at either extreme, where they should. The traditional media is a shell of its former self, as I talked about before, really as hollowed out as Midwestern steel mill, a rust belt steel mill. But the new media—there's wonderful entrepreneurship and experimentation taking place in the new media, but there's no business plan to support expensive investigative journalism. How does a little website run by one or two people, how does somebody say, "Well, you take off six or eight months and go dig out this story in the state capital, would you please?" Or, "Go look at this insurance company and how it's operating," or the city council. You don't get that anymore. You just wonder how many stories are going untold, how many of the powerful are being held completely unaccountable for what they did.

So the new media, for all the good things it has done—and it has done a lot of cool things, with the instant pictures and instant stories and the Arab Spring and all that stuff, but it hasn't replaced what we've lost in traditional media, from the standpoint of serious and sustained investigative accountability, hold-the-powerful-accountable journalism. Until we address both parts of that equation, we will not have a media system that is worthy of the government.

You can go back to the beginnings of our country and find the founding fathers were vitally interested in our news and information ecosystem, or infrastructure, whatever they called it. So important that they subsidized postal roads, subsidized post offices. They said "Let all the newspapers in the country get out. We've got this daring new experiment in self-government. We don't know if it can work or not. Maybe it will, maybe it won't, but the only way it will work is if citizens have information so they can vote and be a part of self-government." Fast forward to the beginning of the broadcast era. I think that was the same kind of mentality then. We've got this public resource here. It can help the news and information infrastructure, so if we're going to license broadcasters to use this spectrum, we can expect them to serve the public interest in return. I think broadcasters took that seriously for a while, until they discovered, 20 or 30 years later, that the FCC wasn't really serious about it in the first place. Now that's all gone, from inattention, and also from the fact that FCC, beginning in the late '70s and coming up with a vengeance after Ronald Reagan, eviscerated all the public interest guidelines that we used to have.

Moyers: On this particular decision now under consideration, the relaxation of some rules prohibiting further concentration, what can ordinary people do?

Copps: Well, they can get involved. It can become a grassroots movement. I spent 40 years in Washington, working on policy with the belief that you can do some good things from the top down, and I still believe that. But the real systemic reforms and the substantive reforms in this country, from abolition to women's rights and civil rights, and labor rights and all that, came from the bottom up. And I think there's enough frustration out there that it's possible to build on that right now.

Julius Genachowski, on moving the proposal forward. According to *Broadcasting & Cable* magazine, Copps said, "Instead of hurrying in the wrong direction, wouldn't the Commission's time be better utilized by considering (and actually voting on) some of the dozens of recommendations that have been put before it by civil rights and public interest groups to establish programs and incentives to encourage minority and female ownership?" he said. "It is time for the FCC to take a deep breath, change direction, and get on with the huge challenge of encouraging a diverse media environment that serves all of our citizens and that nourishes a thriving civic dialogue."

SO, WHO ARE THE BIG 5?

Not only are "51 of the largest 100 economies in the world ... corporations," but the U.S. media is dominated by fewer than ten conglomerates, whose annual sales range from $10 to $170 billion. General Electric, Time Warner, Disney, Viacom, News Corp., and Bertelsmann AG together control approximately 90 percent of the media holdings in the United States. —Henry A. Giroux, The Mouse That Roared Expanded Edition 2e: Disney and the End of Innocence.

American media, including television, film, music, and publishing, are dominated by just five corporate entities. These include:

1. NBCUniversal by Comcast (recently sold by General Electric)
2. Time Warner
3. Walt Disney Corporation (and ABC)
4. News Corporation (Fox)
5. Viacom (and CBS)

Together, these five behemoths control the vast majority of content and ad revenues in the American mediasphere. In this section, we will learn more about the companies that dominate television, film, music, and publishing (newspapers, books, and magazines).

NBCUniversal (Comcast after purchasing from General Electric)

NBC (NBCUniversal) was jointly owned by General Electric (GE) and Comcast, but in 2013 Comcast purchased GE's share of the company. GE had owned NBC since the 1980s and will continue to affect NBCUniversal culture for years to come. GE, with 2011

NBCUniversal

Figure 2.6

revenues of $147 billion, is the sixth-largest company in the United States. The multinational conglomerate operates energy, technology infrastructure, capital finance, industrial, and consumer businesses. While GE is highly regarded for its size, managerial flare, and innovation, it is also identified, by environmentalists, as a significant air and water polluter. In 2000, the Political Economy Research Institute listed the corporation as the fourth-largest corporate producer of air pollution in the United States, with more than 4.4 million pounds of toxic chemicals released into the air per year. The firm is also a significant toxic waste producer. The U.S. Environmental Protection Agency reports that only the United States government, Honeywell, and Chevron Corporation are responsible for more Superfund toxic waste sites. Currently, GE owns 49% of NBCUniversal.

Comcast, the U.S.'s largest cable television operator with 2011 revenues of $56 billion, owns 51% of NBCUniversal. Comcast, with 23 million cable customers, 17 million high-speed Internet customers, and 8 million voice customers, was named using a combination of the words "communication" and "broadcast." The company was founded in June 1963, and is currently headed by CEO Brian Roberts. The company grew rapidly, primarily through the acquisition of cable, Internet, and television production and programming companies, between 2000 and 2010. In 2009, it was announced that Comcast would take a controlling 51% stake in NBCUniversal. The FCC approved the deal by a vote of 4 to 1 and the sale was completed in early 2011.

NBCUniversal, with 2011 revenues of $21 billion, owns and operates the NBC television network and Telemundo (Spanish-language network) along with cable networks CNBC, MSNBC, Bravo, Syfy, USA, Chiller, G4, Style, ShopNBC, and The Weather Channel. Online properties include Weather.com and Hulu. In the film industry, NBCUniversal owns Universal Pictures and Focus Features. In the music industry, NBCUniversal owns the Universal Music Group (see listing of labels on the following page).

Figure 2.7

UNIVERSAL MUSIC GROUP LABELS (NBCUNIVERSAL)

1 Interscope-Geffen-A&M
      1.1 Interscope Records
      1.2 Geffen Records
      1.3 A&M Records
      1.4 A&M/Octone Records
      1.5 DGC Records

2 The Island Def Jam Music Group
      2.1 Island Records
      2.2 Def Jam Recordings
      2.3 Mercury Records
      2.4 Motown Records

3 Republic Records

4 Capitol Music Group
      4.1 Capitol Records
      4.2 Virgin Records
      4.3 Blue Note Records
      4.4 EMI Christian Music Group
      4.5 Caroline Distribution

5 Universal Music Group Nashville
      5.1 MCA Nashville Records
      5.2 Mercury Nashville Records
      5.3 Lost Highway Records
      5.4 Capitol Records Nashville

6 Universal Music Latin Entertainment
      6.1 Universal Music Latino
      6.2 Fonovisa Records
      6.3 Disa Records
      6.4 Machete Music
      6.5 Capitol Latin

7 The Verve Music Group
      7.1 Verve Records

7.2 GRP Records
7.3 Impulse! Records
7.4 Verve Forecast Records

8 Decca Label Group
    8.1 Decca Records
    8.2 Universal Music Classical

9 Deutsche Grammophon

10 Universal Music Enterprises

11 V2/Co-Operative Music

12 Show Dog-Universal Music
13 Universal Music UK
    13.1 Polydor Records
    13.2 Mercury Music Group
    13.3 Island Records Group
    13.4 Universal Music TV (UMTV)
    13.5 Decca Records
    13.6 Geffen UK
    13.7 London Records

GE, according to *Bloomberg/Business Week*, manufactures electric generators, including nuclear reactors, oil drilling production systems, and pipelines for energy companies; aircraft engines and other equipment for use in military and commercial aircraft; equipment used in healthcare, including pharmaceutical manufacturing equipment; appliances for home and business use; and financial services including loans, lines of credit, and credit cards.

Bloomberg/Business Week describes 'General Electric Company operates as a technology and financial services company worldwide. The company's Energy Infrastructure segment offers wind turbines; gas and steam turbines and generators; integrated gasification combined cycle systems; aircraft engine derivatives; nuclear reactors, fuel, and support services; oil and gas extraction and mining motors and control

Figure 2.8 General Electric CEO Jeff Immelt.

systems; aftermarket services; water treatment solutions; power conversion infrastructure technology and services; and integrated electrical equipment and systems. This segment also provides surface and subsea drilling and production systems, equipment for floating production platforms, compressors, turbines, turboexpanders, high pressure reactors, and industrial power generation and auxiliary equipment, as well as pipeline integrity, measurement, inspection, monitoring, and radiation measurement solutions to the oil and gas industry. Its Aviation segment offers jet engines, turboprop and turbo shaft engines, related replacement parts, and aerospace systems and equipment for use in military and commercial aircraft; and maintenance, component repair, and overhaul services. The company's Healthcare segment provides medical imaging and information technologies, medical diagnostics, patient monitoring systems, disease research, drug discovery, biopharmaceutical manufacturing technologies, and remote diagnostic and repair services. Its Transportation segment provides drive technology solutions to various industries, including railroad, transit, mining, oil and gas, power generation, and marine. The company's Home and Business Solutions segment provides home appliances; lighting products; and plant automation, hardware, software, and embedded computing systems. Its GE Capital segment offers commercial loans and leases, fleet management, financial programs, home loans, credit cards, personal loans, and other financial services. The company was founded in 1892 and is headquartered in Fairfield, Connecticut.'

GE Shifts NBC to the Right

Evans (2007) writes that GE transformed former President Ronald Reagan from a New Deal Democrat to a conservative Republican. After WWII, movie actor Reagan returned to Hollywood where he became president of Screen Actors Guild (SAG). He assisted other AFL-CIO unions in opposition to Republican "Right to Work" legislation and headed the California Labor Committee for Democratic candidate Harry Truman in 1948. "He considered himself a liberal democrat and New Dealer to the core" (p. 6).

But in 1954, Mr. Reagan signed a contract with GE to host General Electric Theater, a Sunday evening television broadcast, on CBS, which reached the top 10 in the Neilsen ratings within a few months. "The show made the already well-known Reagan, who had appeared in many films as a 'second lead' throughout his career, wealthy, due to his part ownership of the show. After eight years as host, Reagan estimated he had visited 135 GE research and manufacturing facilities, and met over a quarter-million people. During that time he would also speak at other forums such as Rotary clubs and Moose lodges, presenting views on economic progress that in form and content were often similar to what he said in introductions, segues and closing comments on the show as a spokesman for GE. Reagan, who would later be known as 'The Great Communicator' because of his oratorical prowess, often credited these engagements as helping him develop his public speaking abilities." (Wikipedia)

Evans (2007) suggests Reagan's abrupt shift toward Conservatism, capped by his televised endorsement on behalf of GE for Neo-Conservative Presidential candidate Barry Goldwater in 1964, resulted from his relationship with GE boss Lemuel Boulware. Boulware's worldview was staunchly anti-Union and, as vice president of employee and public relations, encouraged employees to become grassroots communicators encouraging policies and legislation that "establish a better business climate" (p. 4). From GE spokesperson, Reagan was encourage to pursue his political future as governor of California and ultimately as 40th President of the United States. The author concludes, "And yet, for all the recent interest in the Reagan presidency, little has been written about how his change from liberal to conservative, from actor to politician, came about. A veil of secrecy has been drawn over this crucial period of Ronald Reagan's education. Part of the reason for this was Boulware's concern that GE's political efforts might come under attack as violating federal and state statutes that make partisan corporate political activity a crime".

Bagdikian (2004) says that GE had "launched Ronald Reagan as a national political spokesman by paying him to make nationwide public speeches against Communism, labor unions, Social Security, public housing, the income tax, and to augment the corporation's support of right-wing political movements."

Brock (2004) states that when NBC was purchased by GE in 1986, then President Ronald Reagan convened a meeting between the conservative movement's John McLaughlin (The McLaughlin Group) and GE chairman Jack Welch who, even 30 years later, pumped money into the program. Brock concluded that "Welch's role in promoting McLaughlin was an example of how the Right was able to steer the political debate with eh approval of top-ranked media executives" (p. 228).

GE, and NBC, was later charged by California Congressman Henry Waxman with calling the 2000 Presidential election for George W. Bush under pressure by Welch. While requesting videotapes of Mr. Welsh arguing with news directors in the control room during election night coverage, GE refused to furnish them. Mr. Waxman believes that "Welch had distinct interest in Bush attaining the nation's top post and influenced the network staff in its decision to call the race in Bush's favor" (*The News Media & The Law*, Fall 2001, p. 33).

Later recounts by news organizations state that Gore won the state of Florida, and the Presidential election, by approximately 170 votes. The *New York Times* did its own analysis of how mistaken overvotes might have been caused by confusing ballot designs. It found that the butterfly ballot in heavily Democratic Palm Beach County may have cost Gore over 6,000 votes, and the two page ballot in similarly Democratic Duval County may have cost him a approximately 2,000 votes, each of which would have made the difference by itself.

Politically, the company is considered to be highly conservative. According to Opensecrets.org, the company made $3.5 billion in political contributions, mainly to Republicans, and spent $15.5 billion lobbying Congress and regulatory agencies on legislation and regulations regarding taxes, defense, the federal budget and appropriations, transportation, and finance. Although the firm made $14 billion in profits, it paid nothing ($0) in federal taxes in 2011. When GE CEO Jeff Immelt was appointed to President Obama's Council on Jobs and Competitiveness, liberal groups and progressives called for his resignation. Among their concerns were GE's reliance on federal appropriations and contracts while failing to pay taxes. In addition, GE outsourced 20% of its workforce to other countries. Former Senator Russ Feingold, according to CBSNews.com, asked, "How can someone like Immelt be given the responsibility of heading a jobs creation task force when his company has been creating more jobs overseas while reducing its American workforce?" Sen. Feingold continued, "And under Immelt's direction, GE spends hundreds of millions of dollars hiring lawyers and lobbyists to evade taxes." ("Liberals Want G.E. CEO Jeff Immelt out of Obama Administration," March 30, 2011, <www.cbsnews.com>.)

Recently GE released a glowing video describing Ronald Reagan's tenure at GE, which referenced his 1964 nomination speech of Barry Goldwater, a highly conservative pro-war and anti-civil-rights firebrand, as one of his best. In 2007, Thomas Evans published *The Education of Ronald Reagan: His General Electric Years and the Untold Story of His Conversion to Conservatism* that describes the corporate culture that changed Reagan's political perspectives (see below).

Watch GE's video on Ronald Reagan: <http://www.ge.com/reagan/video.html>.

CallToons TCM & Cartoon Network/Asia Pacific Headline News en Español Radio

NASCAR Races Space Headline News CNN TÜRK Toonami Jetstream

NBC/Turner Court TV Radio Productions CNN International Play On! Powered by ACC Select

Adult Swim Video Cartoonito Cartoon Network Court TB Original Productions CETV n-tv NBA.com

Super Deluxe CNN Originals Williams Street Chilevision TCM TNT Latin America CNN Pipeline

Crime Library TNT HD CNN/US Adult Swim TBS Productions CNN.de (German)

Cartoon Network Video Bamzu.com **Turner Broadcasting** Bleacher Report Pogo TBS HD TNT Overtime

GameTap TCM Europe TCM Productions HTV Boomerang truTV

CNN en Español TNT Originals BOING TNT Cartoon Network Studios SI.com CNN+

DramaVision CNN HD HLN Cartoon Network Cartoon Network HD NASCAR.com

CNN.com CNN Chile I.Sat Retro Adult Swim HD CNN-IBN CNN to Go Cartoon Network Japan (Via Japan Entertainment Network, a joint venture with Itochu)

TheFrisky.com Accent Health MuchMusic Latin America CNN Radio NBA TV

CNN en Español Radio CNNj WPCH TBS

The Smoking Gun Zee Turner Ltd (India) Headline News Radio CNNStudentNews.com

CNN.co.jp (Japanese) Infinito Airport Network Very Funny Ads Court TV Extra

The Checking Network CNN Mobile CNN Newsource Dealer Entertainment Network

CNNMoney.com PGA Tour.com and PGA.com

Fashion TV Latin America

Cinemax HD Picturehouse (co-owned by New Line Cinema) E! Latin America

HBO on Demand HBO HBO India HBO Independent Productions

Cibnemax Multiplexes HBO Video

HBO Poland HBO Asia **HBO** Cinemax HBO Czech Warner Channel

HBO Multiplexes HBO Films HBO Hungary HBO Brazil

HBO HD Cinemax on Demand

HBO Latin America Cinemax Latin America

HBO Domestic and International Program Distribution HBO Romania

New Line Merchandising/Licensing Warner Bros. Technical Operations

QDE Entertainment (50%, with Warner Bros. Pictures International

Quincy Jones and David Salzman) (Affiliate) Warner Bros. Theatrical New Line Cinema

Warner Bros. Animation Turner Entertainment New Line Distribution Rocksteady Studios

Warner Bros. Consumer Products Witt/Thomas Productions Warner Bros. Television Group

Warner Bros. Online Warner Independent Pictures Surreal Software Snowblind Studios

Hanna Barbera

New Line Theatricals Mad Magazine New Line Television Warner Bros. Family Entertainment

The WB

Picturehouse (co-owned by HBO) **Warner Bros. Entertainment** NetherRealm Studios

New Line International Releasing Turbine, Inc. CW Now Looney Tunes

New Line Home Entertainment New Line Music Warner Bros. Consumer Products TT Games

DC Comics Warner Bros. Anti-Piracy Operations

Warner Horizon Television Wildstorm Castle Rock Entertainment Vertigo Warner Home Video

The CW Television Network

Warner Premiere Warner Bros. Television Monolith Productions (50% with CBS Corporation)

WB Games The CW Daytime Kids' WB! Telepictures Productions Warner Bros. Studios

Warner Bros. Digital Entertainment

Warner Bros. International Cinemas Warner Bros. Television Distribution

Warner Bros. Pictures New Line New Media Warner Bros. International Television

Warner Bros. Domestic Cable Distribution Warner Bros. Home Entertainment Group

Warner Bros. Interactive Entertainment

Homes & Gardens Sports Illustrated Housetohome.co.uk

25 Beautiful Kitchens Woman & Home Amateur Photographer Fortune Marie Claire

This Old House Ventures, Inc. Time Atlantic Country Life Park Home & Holiday Caravan

Maghound

Model Collector Leisure Arts Better Digital Photography Shooting Gazette Time Analytics Services The Field

Practical Parenting International Boat Industry Now Style Series Woman's Weekly Fiction Series

Synapse Group, Inc. Motor Boats Monthly Southern Living Hi-Fi News Life TV & Satellite Week

NME Time Canada Cooking Light

Time Latin America Woman's Feelgood Series Wallpaper Warner Publishing Services Freeze World Soccer

Prediction

Woman & Golf Shooting Times Media Networks, Inc. Now Woman Decanter BMX Business News

Bird Keeper Money Wedding & Home Caravan Essence 25 Beautiful Gardens Targeted Media, Inc.

Chat Golf magazine Cycling Weekly Mizz Who Weekly Sporting Gun Time Asia Health

Woman's Own Lifestyle Series **Time, Inc.** Wallpaper Navigator Practical Boat Owner

In Style Germany Look Magazine UK Woman's Weekly Fiction Special Eventing What Digital Camera Aeroplane

What's On TV Ideal Home MiniWorld

Farm Holiday Guides The Railway Magazine In Style UK Hair MBR-Mountain Bike Rider European Boat Builder

The Golf For the Love of Quilting Time Inc. Home Entertainment Uncut Time for Kids

TV Times Yachting Monthly What Camera Nuts magazine Land Rover World

Woman's Own Horse & Hound Ships Monthly VolksWorld Chat Passion Series Woman's Weekly Sunset

Cycle Sport Woman's Weekly Home Series In Style Australia Superbike

Entertainment Weekly

Angler's Mail First Moments 4x4 For the Love of Cross Stitch Time Europe

People en Español Time South Pacific Yachting World TV Easy Motor Boat & Yachting

Country Homes & Interiors Horse In Style 25 Beautiful Homes Sports Illustrated for Kids

Time Distribution Services All You Time Inc. Custom Publishing Essentials Oxmoor House

Coastal Living Mizz Specials

Motor Caravan Real Simple Golf Monthly Stamp Magazine

Soaplife Livingetc Bulfinch Press Amateur Gardening This Old House

Rugby World Shoot Monthly People

TimeWarner

Figure 2.9
_____

Time Warner

Time Warner is the world's largest media conglomerate with $29 billion in 2011 revenues. Time Warner is not a subsidiary of a larger conglomerate like GE/Comcast NBCUniversal, but rather, is a "pure play" media company. The company is a combination of three earlier media giants (Time Inc., Warner Communications, Inc., and Turner Broadcasting System, Inc.) and has major film production, television, and publishing assets. MSNBC reported, "Between 2001 and 2003, Time Warner claimed tax breaks that cut its taxes by 121 percent—and allowed the company to pay nothing at all in (federal income) taxes for at least two years."

Time Warner's television, film, and publishing assets include:

Since its founding in 1923 under Henry Luce, Time (now Time Warner) was considered, politically, as a conservative firm. Luce promoted interventionism, attacked the New Deal, attacked Communism, and encouraged Americans to vote Republican. According to Munk (2004) "some people said he was single-handedly responsible for the cold war" (p. 6).

In November 1963, immediately after the assassination of President John F. Kennedy, Time, Inc. purchased the original copy of the now famous Zapruder film, which documents the several shots, including the fatal head wound, that struck the president during his motorcade through Dallas, Texas. Rather than releasing the film, as a news organization operating in the public interest, it locked the film in a vault in its New York headquarters—although several senior executives made copies for themselves. The film would not be seen by American citizens for years until it was subpoenaed by Jim Garrison, New Orleans District Attorney, who prosecuted the only case against the conspirators involved in the assassination. In 1966, even *Life* magazine (a Time publication) questioned the Warren Commission, the official government investigation into the assassination, after publishing frame 230 from the film, showing that the fatal head shot originated from in front of

Figure 2.10 Time founder Henry Luce with wife Clare Booth Luce, Ambassador to Italy and author best known for her 1936 hit play *The Women*, in 1954 New York World-Telegram photo.

and not behind President Kennedy where Lee Harvey Oswald, the presumed assassin, was located at the time.

Conspiracy theorists believe President Kennedy was killed because he had established a relationship with Russian Party Chairman Nikita Khrushchev to end the Cold War, pull American soldiers out of Vietnam, and pass Civil Rights legislation during his second term. These prospects threatened conservative establishment thinking at the time.

Time founder Luce once stated, "I am a Protestant, a Republican and a free enterpriser. I am biased in favor of God, Eisenhower and the stock holders of Time, Inc.—and if anybody who objects doesn't know this by now, why the hell are they still spending 35 cents for the magazine?" During the 1960s, *Time*, according to Monk, "was a staple of the (not entirely informed) American middle class" (p. 7). Of every advertising dollar spent on consumer magazines, 30 cents went to Time Inc. publications. President Kennedy requested a copy delivered by special messenger to the White House. Time Inc. was reportedly dominated by Yale and Harvard WASPs until the late 1970s. Others who worked there felt threatened and ostracized. An African American interviewed by Monk at the time carried a knife to work out of fear of his surroundings.

In 2011, Time Warner made $2.2 billion in political contributions, mainly toward Democrats. However, it also paid lobbyists $2.6 billion to influence copyright, patent, and trademark legislation; media rights, advertising, and postal regulations that favor big media companies. Most of these lobbyists, according to opensecrets.org, previously held government positions.

In 2013, *The Nation* reported that Time Warner rejected a move by Al Jazeera (Qatar's independent news agency covering the Middle East) to broadcast on Time Warner Cable. After an outcry by an MSNBC host, Chris Hayes, who called the move "cowardly and offensive," Time Warner stated that it may be "open" to the possibility of carrying the new channel. During the second Gulf War, Al Jazeera broadcast images of "collateral damage," civilians killed by U.S. cruise missiles, which prompted the Bush Administration to label Al Jazeera "Osama bin Laden's personal news agency."

Walt Disney Company (and ABC)

If we are interested in the political circumstances which oppress us then we can never know too much about Disney—Eleanor Byrne and Martin McQuillan, Deconstructing Disney.

In 1995, more than 200 million people a year watch[ed] a Disney film or home video, 395 million watch[ed] a Disney TV show every week; 212 million listen[ed] or dance[d] to Disney music, records, tapes or compact discs.... More than

The ᏔᗩᏞᎢ ᗪᎥᏕᏁᏋᎩ Company

Figure 2.11 and Figure 2.12.

50 million people a year from all lands pass[ed] through the turnstiles of Disney theme parks.— Henry A. Giroux, The Mouse That Roared Expanded Edition 2e: Disney and the End of Innocence.

Marketing analysts now report that consumers around the world spend about 13 billion "person hours" per year in contact with Disney's various brands.— Henry A. Giroux, The Mouse That Roared Expanded Edition 2e: Disney and the End of Innocence.

Walt Disney Company is the world's largest media conglomerate with over $40 billion in revenues (2011). The multinational corporation operates movie studios, ABC television network, publishing, merchandizing, cable television channels, and theme parks. Disney was founded in 1923 by Walt and Roy Disney as The Disney Brothers Cartoon Studio. Mickey Mouse is the company's official mascot.

Disney established itself as a major studio after the release of *Snow White and the Seven Dwarfs* in 1937. The revenues from the film were used to build the 50-acre Walt Disney Studios in Burbank, California. In December 1950, Walt Disney Productions teamed up with The Coca-Cola Company for Disney's first venture into television, *An Hour in Wonderland* on NBC television. In 1954, ABC ran Disney's first regular television series, *Disneyland*,

Disney-ABC Television Group

Disney-ABC Domestic Television—formerly Buena Vista Television
ABC Owned Television Stations Group   Walt Disney Television
Disney Television Animation   Disney Channel Worldwide   Lucasfilm
Disney/ABC Television Group Digital Media
Touchstone Pictures   Disneynature   ABC Television Network   Marvel Studios
Times Square Studios (division) Radio Disney   Disney Cinemagic   Disney XD   ABC News
Hyperion Books   **Disney Media Networks**   DisneyToon Studios   ABC Entertainment
Hungama   Live Well Network   ESPN Books   DreamWorks Studios
                         ESPN Inc. (80%)   Disney-ABC International Television—formerly
Walt Disney Pictures   Buena Vista International Television
       ABC Spark—with Corus Entertainment
ABC Entertainment Group   ABC National Television Sales   VOICE   Disney Junior
   Pixar Animation Studios   ABC Daytime Press
      ABC Family   Walt Disney Animation Studios
            ABC Regional Sports and Entertainment Sales[29]
ABC Studios—formerly Touchstone Television & ABC Television Studios

Disney media networks.

which became one of the longest-running primetime television programs of all time. In 1954, Disney used profits from its *Disneyland* series to announce Disneyland the park, an idea conceived out of a desire for a place where parents and children alike could have fun at the same time. In 1955, Disney opened Disneyland to the general public after it was previewed with a live television broadcast hosted by Art Linkletter and Ronald Reagan. Walt Disney World was opened in Orlando, Florida in 1971.

Today, Disney Company is made up of five major units—Disney Media Networks (television, cable), Walt Disney Parks and Resorts, Walt Disney Studio Entertainment (films), Disney Consumer Products, and Walt Disney Interactive/Disney Interactive Group. Most of the company's revenues come from the Disney Media Networks and Disney Parks and Resorts segments. See graphic "Disney media networks" for a summary of Disney media holdings.

Criticism of Disney, according to *Deconstructing Disney* authors Eleanor Byrne and Martin McQuillan, focus on "the right wing agenda more or less implicit in Disney films. The most frequent criticisms include sexism, racism, conservatism, heterosexism, andro-centrism, imperialism (cultural and economic), literary vandalism, jingoism, aberrant sexuality, censorship, propaganda, paranoia, homophobia, exploitation, ecological devastation, anti-union repression, FBI collaboration, corporate raiding, and stereotyping." They also state that, "Disney's powerful hegemonic hold over children's literature, family entertainment, mainstream taste, and Western popular culture remains intact and continues to grow."

Disney fairy tales and love stories are predicated on classic American values. Disney's characters and plots are thought to include racist elements. For example, *Aladdin* features negative Arab stereotypes and lyrics. In *The Lion*

Figure 2.13 Walt Disney (1901–1966), the American film producer, director, screenwriter, voice actor, animator, and entrepreneur, was best known for creating such iconic characters as Donald Duck and Mickey Mouse, for whom Disney himself was the original voice. In the 1930s and 1940s, he produced full-length animated films that included *Snow White and the Seven Dwarfs* (1937), *Pinocchio* (1940), and *Bambi* (1942). In 1955, Disney opened Disneyland, a theme park located in Anaheim, California, that featured many attractions based on Disney film characters. This 1965 photograph shows Disney and his brother Roy (1873–1971) with Florida's Governor W. Haydon Burns (1912–1987), announcing plans to create a Disney theme park in the state. Walt Disney World opened in 1971. Located just southwest of Orlando, Florida, the attraction grew to become the largest resort in the world, covering 47 square miles (122 square kilometers) and encompassing four theme parks, two water parks, a wilderness preserve, and numerous hotels.

King, jive-talking hyenas are portrayed as similar to blacks living in an American inner-city ghetto. In the movie *Aladdin*, the opening song "Arabian Nights" contained offensive lyrics:

1. "Oh, I come from a land
2. From a faraway place
3. Where the caravan camels roam.
4. Where they cut off your ear
5. If they don't like your face
6. It's barbaric, but hey, it's home."

The American Arab Anti-Discrimination Committee protested. After several months, Disney altered lines four and five in the film to:

4. "Where it's flat and immense
5. And the heat is intense"

Figure 2.14 U.S. Senator James Abourezk (South Dakota) is founder of the American Arab Anti-Discrimination Committee, which protested Disney's *Aladdin*, leading to changes in the film.

Critics, going as far back as the 1960s, have questioned Disney's cultural politics and its impact on America's political and social landscape. While student demonstrations, political assassinations, and radical social reform were underway, Richard Schickel accused Disney of fostering "unquestioning patriotism, bourgeois moral nostrums, gauche middle-class taste, racist exclusion, corporate profit mongering, [and] bland stands of social conformity." Disney critic Henry Giroux writes that if these perspectives were appropriate in the 1960s, "they became even apter as Disney grew more powerful under the control of Michael Eisner and Robert Iger."

Giroux questions why Americans love Disney. But he suggests that certain political conditions make Disney's messages more resonant and salient. "The reason millions of people say they love Disney is not nearly as significant as posing the larger questions of how some ideas, meanings, and messages under certain political conditions become more credible as representations of reality than others and how these representations assume the force of ideology by making an appeal to common sense while at the same time shaping political policies and programs that serve specific interests, such as the Telecommunications Act of 1996, the forging of school-business partnerships, and the U.S. invasion of Iraq as a post-9/11 response to terrorism."

Disney's Racism and Sexism

What girl hasn't wanted to be a Disney princess? There are few who haven't fantasized about flying over Arabia on a magic carpet or rescuing Prince Charming from a burning shipwreck as a red-haired mermaid. How about falling in love with a handsome prince in disguise as a beast before the last petal of a magic rose falls?

Since not everyone is as creeped out by Disneyland—the hyperreal land of artificial trees and fuzzy mascots—as I am, I owe you an explanation as to why I'm so anti-fairy tale happiness. Now that we are older, wiser and not so easily swayed by bright colors, sappy theme music and predictable endings, a closer look at the Disney company is necessary. There are two problems within Disney's history: sexism and racism.

Sexist implications are brought up with the way gender is portrayed in Disney movies. Disney princesses have high-pitched voices and disproportionately skinny waists. They each have a picturesque home, whether in a castle or under the sea. Their frames could be mixed and matched by switching hair color and clothing. In other words, they are cinematic Barbie dolls. Disney movies provide unrealistic expectations for girls, whether they are about body image, romance, race or even hair. Disney's gender stereotyping has become a flawed template for what men, women and romance are supposed to be like in modern perceptions.

The gender discrimination and stereotyping goes both ways. Prince Charming is nothing but a two-dimensional, recycled character who exists in every Disney movie. His role is to save the damsel from whatever type of distress she may be in, and to propel a highly unrealistic and hyper-masculine image of what men "should" be like. These sexist ideals are just one facet of Disney's skewed agenda.

Throughout the Disney company, racist implications are consistently instilled in consumers, even simply through the viewing of Disney movies. Aladdin's "Arabian Nights" theme is "Oh I come from a land, from a faraway place/Where the caravan camels roam/Where they cut off your ear/If they don't like your face/It's barbaric, but hey, it's home." These examples of evil and violence are being associated with people of color. This becomes especially evident when they are juxtaposed with other Disney movies that feature white princes with shiny smiles who are always the heroes.

If the representations of minorities are not racist, they are wildly inaccurate in a historical sense, such as the basic plot of Pocahontas (Last time I checked, the 17th century Native American tribes did not solve their differences with the English settlers. Most of them were killed mercilessly through genocide and infectious disease. Nor did they condone the marriage of a pug and a raccoon). In this case, Disney has changed a gruesome history into a visually pleasing story of romance and peace—two ideals that did not exist anywhere in the real historical narrative of Pocahontas. Disney has projected unrealistic concepts and characters that adhere to negative stereotypes. Despite these obvious evils, Disney is a high-profiting company. According to marketwatch.com, the Walt Disney Company's gross income for the year of 2011 was $7.97 billion.

An article by Sara Holmes called "Everything is Not What it Seems: Ideologies of Racial and Ethnic Identity in Disney's Wizards of Waverly Place" published in 2009 by the National Communication Association explains: "Racism is not grounded in irrational thought; rather, the source of racism is economic, psychological, social and political advantages that the white population defends as logical and natural." Disney is an example of a company that defends the white population through its child-approved, colorful and musical rhetoric. Although the movies that primarily contain this sexism and racism are from the 1950s, Disney is a company that contributes to the continuation of racism by marketing minorities as evil or in opposition to the protagonist, and defending itself through its façade as "the happiest place on earth": a magical, child-friendly organization.

Disney has attempted and failed to correct racial stereotypes with more recent movies such as "The Princess and the Frog," which stars a black princess and a racially ambiguous frog-prince. However according to the Internet Movie Database (IMDB), this movie grossed $207,075,765, whereas "Tangled," a Disney movie with a white hero and heroine, was more than twice as successful, grossing $590,721,936. The allotted budget for "The Princess and the Frog" was less than half the budget of "Tangled" as well.

Disney is not just another monopolizing corporation in the U.S. It seems as though the company is primarily focused on money and has proven that it will go to any extent of hegemonial action to profit and stay in charge, even if that means using rhetoric that enforces racism and gender stereotyping into impressionable minds. All the while, Disney puts on the mask of friendliness and warms our hearts through fairy tales and childhood nostalgia.

What it comes down to is whether you want to be blissfully ignorant about where the money you spend is going or actively think about the kinds of companies you choose to support. By purchasing Disneyland tickets or Disney products, we are doing their advertising for them. We are supporting a company that upholds ultra-capitalistic strategies and enforces racist and sexist propaganda. Consider these points before purchasing your next season pass.

Backlash for Disney's First Latina Princess

Move over Pocahontas and Mulan. Sofia está aquí. Disney's first Latina princess, featured in the movie "Sofia the First: Once Upon A Princess," has received backlash as well as support from media outlets, especially the Latino community. Is Disney's new princess a milestone for Latinos or a culturally irrelevant character?

To continue reading visit: http://www.cnn.com/2012/10/19/showbiz/disneys-first-latina-princess

Giroux argues that Disney, regardless of its claims of being an entertainment company, endorse and vigorously support partisan neo-conservative political issues including the "war on terror" and resultant culture of security. The author points to ABC/Disney's *The Path to 9/11* (2006) and Disney/Pixar *The Incredibles* (2004) as examples of this relationship along with Disney's production of films for the military during WWII. The more recent films "present a reactionary politics, which not only justifies U.S. military power abroad but also suggests deeply authoritarian ideas and practices are the best way to secure the ongoing domination of American cultural identity at home."

Giroux concludes, "Corporate culture uses its power as an educational force to redefine the relationships between childhood and innocence, citizenship and consumption, civic values and commercial values."

News Corp.

Fox News began with a simple concept: build a network based on the triumph of conservative talk radio. This model was successful at the tail end of the Clinton administration and was even better suited to cheerlead for George W. Bush. In less than a decade, Fox News president Roger Ailes created for Rupert Murdoch a network with a built-in audience driven by conservative ideology—David Brock and Ari Rabin-Havt, *The Fox Effect: How Roger Ailes Turned a Network into a Propaganda Machine* (2012).

Misinformation has consequences, especially in a democracy. "In general, you end up with citizens who are acting on bad information when they carry out their civic duties," says Kelly McBride, an expert on media ethics at the Poynter Institute, speaking about the media in general. "It affects the governing of a nation. It inspires people to make their voting decisions on fear or lies."—David Brock and Ari Rabin-Havt, *The Fox Effect: How Roger Ailes Turned a Network into a Propaganda Machine* (2012).

Following the 2010 election, the University of Maryland released a study finding that Fox News viewers were the most misinformed audience of any major news

Figure 2.15 Rupert Murdoch, Chairman and Chief Executive Officer, News Corporation, USA; Co-Chair of the World Economic Forum Annual Meeting 2009 captured during the session "Advice to the U.S. President on Competitiveness" at the Annual Meeting 2009 of the World Economic Forum in Davos, Switzerland.

⊞ News Corporation

network—David Brock and Ari Rabin-Havt, *The Fox Effect: How Roger Ailes Turned a Network into a Propaganda Machine* (2012).

Figure 2.16

News Corporation is the holding company for media and other holdings managed by Australian businessman Rupert Murdoch. It is one of the five largest media conglomerates in the world with $34 billion in revenues (2012). News Corporation includes businesses in filmed entertainment, television, satellite and cable network programming, newspapers, magazines, book publishing, music, digital television technology, and online programming. News Corp. also owns 85 percent of the Fox Entertainment Group, 40 percent of the STAPLES Center—the home of the Los Angeles Lakers basketball team and the Los Angeles Kings ice hockey team—and major league baseball team the Los Angeles Dodgers. Nearly 75 percent of the firm's revenues stem from its U.S. operations, while Canada, Europe, the United Kingdom, Australia, Latin America, and the Pacific Basin region account for the remaining 25 percent.

Murdoch built Fox into the fourth major television broadcast network in the U.S. (after ABC, CBS, and NBC). The feat was particularly noteworthy, considering U.S. law requires

20th Century Fox Television
Vogue Entertaining + Travel   BSkyB [United Kingdom] (39.1%)   Two Wheels Scooter
Fox College Sports   Fox Soccer Channel   The Corning Leader   Speed Channel
20th Century Fox Home Entertainment   Lifestyle Pools + outdoor design   STAR TV   Over 100 daily, weekly, and community newspapers,
New York Post   Fox Searchlight Pictures   Fox International Channels Philippines   predominantly in Australia.
Fox Business Network   Zondervan Publishing: Christian publishing   Foxtel [Australia] (25%)
20th Century Fox Television   company taken over by HarperCollins in 1988   Truckin' Life   Big Ten Network (51%)
HarperCollins   National Geographic Channel (International) (50%)   Country Style GQ Australia
Fox Sports Net   FX Networks   Foxtel   Tata Sky [India] (20%)   SportSouth   Fox Sports en Español
SmartSource Magazine   Fox Channels Benelux   Overlander 4WD   Shine Group
Fox Sports Australia   Truck & Trailer Australia
SKY Network Television [New York] (43.65%)   MyNetworkTV
Two Wheels   The Brooklyn Paper   Tattoo   Fox Reality Channel   Fox Sports Enterprises   20th Century Fox
Fox Studios LA   **News Corp Assets**   Inside Out   Australian Football Weekly   Fox Telecolombia
Fox Television Studios   MasterChef Magazine   Australian Parents (with Woolworths)   Fox Movie Channel   Big League
Chopper   Super Food Ideas   20th Television
Vogue Australia   Fox Television Stations   Inspirio—religious gift production   Alpha
Sky Deutschland [Germany] (49.90%)   Modern Boating
Telecine (Brazil—co-owned with Globosat Canais,   Imedi Media Holding
Courier-Life Publications   Paramount Pictures, MGM, Universal Studios, and
Community Newspaper Group   DreamWorks)   Blue Sky Studios   TimesLedger Newspapers
Foxtel (50%)   Australian Good Taste (with Woolworths)   Fox News Channel   20th Century Fox International
Fox International Channels Italy   Live to Ride   Fox International Channels Portugal   FUEL TV
Modern Fishing   LAPTV (Latin America—co-owned   Fox International Channels Portugal
Fox Television Studios   with Paramount Pictures/Viacom,   National Geographic Channel (US) (67%)
Fox Studios Australia   Metro-Goldwyn-Mayer/MGM Holdings   Latvijas Neatkarīgā Televīzija   TV5 Rīga
SKY Italia [Italy] (100%)   and Universal Studios/NBCUniversal)
Fox International Channels   Fox Broadcasting Company   Wall Street Journal
Star TV [India and Greater China] (100%)   20th Century Fox Español
Best of the Gold Coast Magazine   Australian Golf Digest   Bronx Times Reporter Inc.

News Corp Assets.

station owners to be American citizens with corporate headquarters in the United States. At the time, Murdoch was an Australian citizen, with News Corporation headquartered in Adelaide, Australia. Since then, Murdoch has become an American citizen and News Corp. is now headquartered in New York City. And, while the company presents itself as patriotic (i.e., consider the American flag that waves in the background on Fox News), alternet.org states that the Government Accountability Office issued an analysis concluding that one of the companies with the greatest number of subsidiaries in offshore tax havens was none other than News Corp., which then had more than 150 of them scattered across the world in 2008.

News Corporation acquired television stations, launched cable television channels, and for several years, was majority owner of DirecTV. In 1985, News Corporation purchased six independent television stations in major U.S. cities from earlier station group owner, Metromedia. Later that year, 20th Century Fox announced its intention to create a major television network and then 20th Century Fox studios merged with Metromedia to both produce and distribute programming.

The Fox network officially launched in 1986 with 88 affiliates. By 1988, the network was still struggling, and Murdoch considered shutting it down. But in 1990, Fox hit the ratings with *The Simpsons*, the first series from a fourth network to reach the top 30 programs viewed on U.S. television. The network became profitable by the early 1990s, and in 1994, was able to lure major independently owned television stations

Figure 2.17 Roger Ailes. Former media advisor to President Richard Nixon proposed a plan during the Watergate scandal to neutralize the "liberal media" in the United States. In the Watergate tapes, he discusses plan to infiltrate the media system by creating conservative think tanks to counter those more liberal leaning, and, to create a news station to contradict objectivist journalism.

away from CBS by purchasing the rights to air NFL football. In 2008, Fox became the most-watched network in the U.S.

News Corporation is most widely known as the network that brings Fox News Channel to American and international viewers. The channel, launched in 1996, was created by Rupert Murdoch, who hired former NBC executive and Republican Party operative Roger Ailes as its founding CEO. It grew between 2000 and 2009 to become the predominant cable news network in the United States. By 2010, Fox News took the top ten spot for most-watched cable news programs in the coveted 25–54 age segment.

While critics say that Fox News Channel promotes conservative political positions and biased reporting, reporters and anchors at Fox News Channel say news reporting and political commentary operate independently of each other, and deny any bias in news coverage. Fox News' first, and current, news director is Roger Ailes, a highly conservative Republican who served in the Nixon, Reagan, and Bush administrations. Afterward, he went to work with TVN, an earlier news channel founded by neo-Conservative Adolf Coors (head of Coors Brewing). According to Brock and Rabin-Havt (2012), after doing some public relations consulting work for TVN, Roger Ailes transitioned to become the network's news director. The reason for his appointment was clear, according to a TVN staffer. "The Coors people trust Ailes because of his affiliation with the Republicans, and because he's not a newsman. They don't trust newsmen."

Roger Ailes began his tenure at Fox News in 1996. When the station debuted, about 10 million households were able to watch but it was not in New York City and Los Angeles. To gain viewers, Fox News paid cable television systems up to $11 per subscriber to distribute the channel. This was a successful strategy. Following Ailes' philosophy, Fox News places heavy emphasis on visual presentation. Graphics are colorful and attention-getting, which steer viewers to comprehend the key points of what is being reported. "Fair & Balanced" is a trademarked slogan used by Fox News, originally used in conjunction with the phrase "Real Journalism." However, polls consistently find Fox News viewers the most ignorant and misinformed among television news viewers. For instance, Mediamatters.org reports that a 2003 University of Maryland poll found significant misperceptions about the Iraq war. A 2013 study conducted by Farleigh Dickenson University revealed that Fox News viewers were significantly less likely to know that Egyptians overthrew their government than people who don't watch television news at all. In 2010, Stanford University released a study showing that Fox News viewers reject scientists claims about global warming, believing that measures to remedy the situation will ruin America's economy. Most serious media scholars simply regard Fox News as the propaganda organism of the Republican National Committee (RNC), which manages Republican presidential and congressional campaigns, and the "talking points" or rhetoric stated by Republican politicians. These points resonate among conservative viewers because they are also echoed daily on Fox News.

Fox News is now available in the following countries:

- Australia
- Brazil
- Canada
- France
- Ireland

- Israel
- Netherlands
- Pakistan
- Philippines
- Scandinavia
- Singapore
- South Africa
- United Kingdom
- United States
- Fox News Channel is carried in more than 40 other countries.

Polls consistently find Fox News viewers among the most ignorant on a variety of issues. For example, NBC News's online publication *First Read* reported in April 2009 that "72% of self-identified FOX News viewers believe the health-care plan will give coverage to illegal immigrants, 79% of them say it will lead to a government takeover, 69% of them say it will use taxpayer dollars to pay for abortions, and 75% believe that it will allow the government to make decisions about when to stop providing care to the elderly." As First Read pointed out, this was rampant misinformation that large numbers of Fox viewers believed.

Viacom/CBS

Viacom, which is short for video and audio communications, is the world's fourth-largest media conglomerate, behind The Walt Disney Company, Time Warner, and News Corporation. Remember that the vast majority of GE's (owner of NBCUniversal) revenues arise from non-media sources. Viacom is owned by National Amusements, Inc., a Dedham, Massachusetts, movie-theater company owned by Sumner Redstone (and members of the Redstone family) who also owns a controlling stake in CBS Corporation. National Amusements was founded in 1936 as a movie-theater chain called Northeast Theatre Corporation.

Viacom, a cable television company, was purchased in 1987 by Sumner Redstone, who was 64 at the time. The innovative and litigious Redstone, according to the *New York Times*, "acquired Viacom by going deep into debt and putting up his

Figure 2.18 and Figure 2.19

movie-chain business as collateral" (*New York Times*, "Times Topics," Sumner Redstone). Through acquisitions, Redstone turned the company into a major production and broadcast company in the 1990s by purchasing Paramount Pictures, the United Paramount Network (UPN), and finally CBS itself. The companies split in 2005. But while, on paper, the companies appear as separate entities, they are largely owned and managed by Viacom CEO Sumner Redstone and his daughter Shari (National Amusements). The company also acquired the major Hollywood studio DreamWorks in 2005.

In 2011, Viacom and CBS had combined revenues of $29 billion (Viacom $15 billion and CBS $14 billion). In 2012, according to Forbes.com, Sumner Redstone's net worth was estimated at $4.1 billion, placing him 91st in the Forbes 400 richest people in America. In general, CBS holds the combined firm's broadcasting and publishing units while Viacom owns cable and movie units. These include:

Broadcast television networks
- CBS television network
- The CW (co-owned with Time Warner)

Broadcast television stations
- Thirty-nine television stations in more than 25 cities including New York, Los Angeles, Chicago, San Francisco, and Philadelphia
- Radio stations
- CBS radio owns and operates 147 stations
- Westwood One (radio syndication)—part owner

Cable television networks
- MTV Networks (17 channels including MTV, VH1, Nickelodeon)
- BET
- Home Team Sports
- Showtime
- Country Music Television
- Comedy Central

Movie Studios
- Paramount Pictures
- DreamWorks

Book Publishing
- Simon & Schuster

The U.S. Senate Subcommittee on Antitrust, Business Rights, and Competition (Committee of the Judiciary) explored the Viacom/CBS Merger in October, 1999. On the next page are excerpted comments from subcommittee member the late Senator Paul Wellstone of Minnesota (who died in a plane crash in 2002 while campaigning for re-election in his home state) during the hearings.

Senator Paul Wellstone's Statement During the Viacom/CBS Merger Hearings

"Mr. Chairman, I think the recent wave of mergers among media companies, including the proposed acquisition of CBS by Viacom, raises some very troubling questions for our system of representative democracy. These media mergers warrant the highest level of scrutiny by our antitrust agencies and by the Federal Communication Commission. They may also require Congress to consider a new legislative framework to address the growing problem of media concentration."

"The media is not just any ordinary industry. It is the lifeblood of American democracy. We depend on the media for the free flow of information that enables citizens to participate in the democratic process. As James Madison wrote in 1822, 'A popular government without popular information of the means of acquiring it is but a prologue to farce or a tragedy, or perhaps both.' … We depend on the media to do two things. We depend on them to provide citizens with access to a wide and diverse range of opinions, analyses, and perspectives, and we depend on the media to hold concentrated power, whether it is public or private power, accountable to the people. The greater the diversity of ownership and control, the better they will be able to perform those functions."

"Some have argued…that the recent round of consolidation in the media and entertainment industries, especially the trend toward vertical integration, will offer consumers a more diverse array of choices. But it is important to distinguish between outlets and content. It is a very important distinction. A proliferation of new media does not guarantee any greater diversity of viewpoint. After all, one corporate conglomerate can still exercise control over the content of the media that reaches citizens through many different outlets. The safest and best way to ensure diversity of viewpoints is through diverse ownership."

"These concerns about media concentration need to be addressed by both the FCC and our antitrust agencies. Congress has directed the FCC to uphold a 'public interest' standard in approving media mergers, though that standard has been severely weakened in recent years. Last month, (FCC) Chairman Kennard said in a speech, and I think this is what is at issue, 'Broadcast ownership rules serve principles that we still cherish, principles like competition, localism, and a diversity of voices. We can and must do more to make sure that there are a multitude of voices and opinions on the airwaves.'"

"Undoubtedly, and I conclude this way with a sense of irony, such an effort would meet considerable resistance, not the least from media corporations themselves. Progress in the area of antitrust has almost always come in response to public pressure. Yet, this is the quandary of democratic, with a small 'd', I say to the chairman (Sumner Redstone) seeking media reform. Involvement of the public in this debate depends on coverage and attention by the major media. Unfortunately, the record to date has not been encouraging. There has been virtually no public awareness or public discussion of the rapid concentration of media that has occurred over the last 15 years."

Paul Wellstone, from *The Viacom/CBS Merger: Media Competition and Consolidation in the New Millenium*, pp. 4-6. Copyright in the Public Domain.

THE BIG 5 ARE LIKE OPEC

Bagdikian likens the big five to OPEC (Organization of the Petroleum Exporting Countries), the intergovernmental organization of twelve oil-producing countries including Algeria, Angola, Ecuador, Iran, Iraq, Kuwait, Libya, Nigeria, Qatar, Saudi Arabia, the United Arab Emirates, and Venezuela. OPEC significantly increases oil production power as it negotiates oil prices and regulates production among these petroleum-rich nations. In turn, OPEC can maximize revenues while they deal with oil companies in other countries, like the U.S. While making the analogy, Bagdikian states, "Technically, the dominant media (the Big 5) are an oligopoly, the rule of a few in which any one of those few, acting alone, can alter market conditions" (*New Media Monopoly*, p. 5). According to a study by Aaron Moore in the March/April 2003 *Columbia Journalism Review*, News Corporation, Disney, Viacom, and Time Warner have forty-five "interlocking" board members. This is when the same board member sits on the board of more than one corporation. The Big 5 also participate in over 100 joint ventures—including production companies and cable channels.

The Big 5 are also dominant participants in the National Association of Broadcasters (NAB). The NAB is among the top 20 lobbying groups in the U.S. In 2011, they spent over $11 million lobbying Congress, the White House, and Federal Communication Commission (FCC) on communication issues, according to opensecrets.org. The NAB made 64% of its campaign contributions to Republican and 36% to Democrat candidates for office. Bagdikian states, "The Big Five have become major players in altering the politics of the country. They have been able to promote laws that increase their corporate domination and that permit them to abolish regulations that inhibit their control" (p. 10). The current environment isn't the first time we've seen this. When FDR launched the New Deal, which provided tangible jobs and benefits for the American people, the traditional newspapers of the time that promoted corporate approaches to solving problems lost their credibility. "They had glorified the policies that produced the stock market crash of 1929. Roosevelt created 'radical reforms,' like the SEC (Security Exchange Commission) to monitor stock sales, Social Security to create old age pensions, and laws that prevented banks from speculating on depositors' money."

WAIT A MINUTE: I THOUGHT THE MEDIA WAS LIBERALLY BIASED?

Talk to your family, relatives, and friends and you will undoubtedly hear someone say, "The media are too liberal." This is a popular perspective. A 2011 Gallup Poll found that

60% of Americans believe the media are biased—47% believe the media are too liberal and 13% say the media are too conservative.

Considering the consolidated ownership structure of the media and their reliance on corporate sponsorships and advertising for revenues, many academics and others studying the U.S. media system believe the media are conservative enterprises. If there is a bias, it's certain to slant toward conservative perspectives.

Media scholar Robert McChesney estimates that, through the work of conservative foundations and think tanks, conservatives spent close to $1 billion in public relations since the 1970s to change public opinion about the media. Seth Ackerman, at Fairness and Accuracy in Reporting, states, "Years ago, Republican party chair Rich Bond explained that conservatives' frequent denunciations of 'liberal bias' in the media were part of 'a strategy' (*Washington Post*, 8/20/92). Comparing journalists to referees in a sports match, Bond explained: 'If you watch any great coach, what they try to do is "work the refs." Maybe the ref will cut you a little slack next time.'"

Author Eric Alterman, in *The Nation*, wrote, "Bill Kristol, perhaps the most honest and intelligent conservatives in Washington (excluding, of course, that funny, friendly, charming McCain fellow). 'The press isn't quite as biased and liberal. They're actually conservative sometimes,' Kristol said recently on CNN. If Chris missed that one, he might have come across a similar admission by Kristol offered up in the spring of 1995. 'I admit it,' Kristol told *The New Yorker*. 'The whole idea of the "liberal media" was often used as an excuse by conservatives for conservative failures.'" And, while Time Warner picked up Al Gore's Current TV, they dropped the channel in 2013, leading many Liberals to wonder why. According to *The Nation*, Gore sold Current TV to Al Jazeera, which has, for a long time, been trying to establish itself in the United States. Time Warner refused to broadcast Al Jazeera, the award-winning international news organization headquartered in Qatar. During the Gulf War, the neo-Conservative Bush Administration accused Al Jazeera of being the mouthpiece of Osama bin Laden. Since this time, Americans have learned that the network is an independent news source dedicated to the welfare of Middle Easterners and others around the world. After an outcry by MSNBC host and *Nation* editor Chris Hayes, Time Warner reported that it may be "open" to carrying the new channel.

What follows are some observations made by students after learning about the concentration of media ownership in the US.

Media Ownership

The discussion that has had a major impact on how I consume media was the series of classes in which we looked at information on the backgrounds of the major 5 media companies. While each company had a series of skeletons in their closets, researching the background of General Electric, a company which maintains a positive image in the face of the media, revealed the scope of issues which these companies are able to cover up. For example, reading that the media networks restricted the flow of information regarding the recent Fukushima nuclear disaster in order to censor the fact that GE designed the reactors which failed, thereby shielding GE's image from any public scrutiny. Like the criticism of Fox, the lesson behind GE's deep manipulative maintenance of their image was more important than the analysis of the company itself. Each of these major companies has the power to shape their appearance in the eye of the public by covering their missteps and presenting a limited positive perspective of themselves to the public.

—Ben Nola

In the 2004 documentary, "Outfoxed: Rupert Murdoch's War on Journalism", director Robert Greenwald fully exposes Fox News Network, a media empire led by Rupert Murdoch, for going against legitimate and fair journalism, and instead basing their reporting on opinion, misinformation and right-wing propaganda. A few of the allegations showcased in the film, were that the network politicized coverage to support the war in Iraq and that they tipped election projections in favor of Bush for the 2000 election, even though they affirm that they're news reports are unbiased and fair to both sides of the political party. In defense of the controversy surrounding his media empire, Murdoch once argued, "I challenge anybody to show me an example of bias in Fox News Channel" (Ackerman). In addition, The claims of former Fox employees who reveal that they were forced to push a "right-wing" point of view when reporting stories, whether it was right or wrong, or they believed in it or not, in order to keep their jobs, was plain despicable, in my opinion. While I personally have used Fox news as one of the main outlets for receiving the latest news on the current happenings in our nation for years, this documentary has completely changed my outlook on the Fox News Network's ability to report the truth. I've always believed in the act of fair and factual journalism, and that the use of propaganda is bad for all of us.

It's clear as day to me, after watching this documentary in class a few weeks ago, that this network is not a legitimate news organization. Although, many have reported that since the release of one of the first outspoken critiques of this controversial news network, both the political landscape and

Fox News have positively changed, and that the network has strived to alter the way they report and research stories. Thus, we should be hopeful that they will continue to do so, I, on the other hand, am still left questioning the network's methods and practices for developing and reporting fair and unbiased news. Since watching this documentary in class, I no longer turn to Fox News for the latest happenings, and even have stopped visiting their website, because I refuse to support a news network, as both a consumer and possible future reporter, that for so long, has fully controlled the public's right to know the truth, form their own opinions and beliefs, and make their own decisions. However, I'm open to the possibility for change, and only time will tell, whether Fox News will continue to positively revamp their methods for reporting news, and practice what they so heavily preach to viewers with their most recognized slogans: "Fair and Balanced" or "We Report, You Decide."

—Jessica Fernandez

First, learning about the big five corporations has affected my attitude as a consumer. We discussed what these corporations own and how in control they are. Prior to gaining this knowledge, I was aware of the companies including Time Warner, Disney, News Corporation, Viacom, and General Electric, however not to the extent that we have studied. I have always heard these names without really knowing their meaning or what they were truly represent. I have learned that they control a large portion of all production and what is created for consumption of consumers. Knowing this has altered the way I obtain much of my information. For instance, I now know how these companies control the content of what is presented as news. Instead of relying solely on broadcast television news, I know to find other sources such as NPR to broaden my knowledge and obtain more information.

In addition to the knowledge of the big five, learning about advertising has affected the way in which I consume media. Seemingly short, simple advertisements such as commercials on television actually have so much more work put into them than I had imagined. Advertisers have to look at many aspects such as the audience as well as the speaker. In addition, in class it was brought to my attention how certain people are chosen for specific ads. The creators try so hard to appeal to the audience and draw them in. They also target products for specific demographic groups. All of this has made me aware that companies are constantly trying to get my attention. If one is able to see beyond the advertisements and be aware of their true purpose, one can understand the media much better. Personally, after learning this I have been able to recognize that advertisements attack vulnerabilities to accomplish their goals. Being aware of this has made me able to resist certain traps. Most people would benefit from this type of awareness.

—Corinna Kaufman

THE EFFECTS OF MEDIA EXPOSURE

Over the years, it has become clear that media has significant cognitive, psychological, and behavioral effects on audiences. Likewise, each medium we attend to, regardless of its content, seems to change the perspective and sensibilities of audiences. And clearly, based on the last section of this textbook, ownership effects—that is, the effects on message development due to the worldview of the owners and their customers: corporate advertisers—are apparent and well documented by academics and industry watch-dog groups. According to Sonia Livingstone (1998), "Researchers are now reconceptualizing media effects as gradual, symbolic, and cognitive, affecting people's frameworks for thinking as well as the content of their thoughts." Livingstone, a media communications and social psychology expert, contends that the repetition in programs and genres increases the importance of certain ideas and values on the part of viewers. In addition, the redundancy in the narrative requirements for television programs and films may "organize people's beliefs and frames of thinking in specific, robust, and often simplified ways" (p. 20).

THE FRANKFURT SCHOOL

With the rise of the industrial revolution and the advent of mass media (newspapers, magazines, and books), sociologists and philosophers—like the Frankfurt School in the 1930s—raised concerns about the alienation and isolation of people working as interchangeable agents in production at work and as a mass audience of consumers when not at work. With the advent of radio and television during the 20th century, sociologists

Figure 3.1 Max Horkheimer reunites with Theodor Adorno in 1964 photograph by Jeremy J. Shapiro.

began to note mass media as replacing the community, church, and family as principle shapers of culture and opinion.

The Frankfurt School of neo-Marxist interdisciplinary social theorists was located at the Institute for Social Research at the University of Frankfurt am Main. The school's philosophical perspectives are generally attributed to Max Horkheimer (philosopher, sociologist, and social psychologist) who took over as the institute's director in 1930. He recruited other important theorists, like Theodor W. Adorno (philosopher, sociologist, musicologist), Erich Fromm (psychoanalyst), and Herbert Marcuse (philosopher).

THE CULTURE INDUSTRY: ENLIGHTENMENT AS MASS DECEPTION

"Yet the city housing projects designed to perpetuate the individual as a supposedly independent unit in a small hygienic dwelling make him all the more subservient to his adversary—the absolute power of capitalism. Because the inhabitants, as producers and as consumers, are drawn into the center in search of work and pleasure, all the living units crystallise into well-organised complexes. The striking unity of microcosm and macrocosm presents men with a model of their culture: the false identity of the general and the particular. Under monopoly all mass culture is identical, and the lines of its artificial framework begin to show through."

"No mention is made of the fact that the basis on which technology acquires power over society is the power of those whose economic hold over society is greatest."

"The need which might resist central control has already been suppressed by the control of the individual consciousness. The step from the telephone to the radio has clearly distinguished the roles. The former still allowed the subscriber to play the role of subject, and was liberal. The latter is democratic: it turns all participants into listeners and authoritatively subjects them to broadcast programs which are all exactly the same. No machinery of rejoinder has been devised, and private broadcasters are denied any freedom. They are confined to the apocryphal field of the 'amateur,' and also have to accept organisation from above."

"We are closer to the facts if we explain these phenomena as inherent in the technical and personnel apparatus which, down to its last cog, itself forms part of the economic mechanism of selection. In addition there is the agreement—or at least the determination—of all executive authorities not to produce or sanction anything that in any way differs from their own rules, their own ideas about consumers, or above all themselves."

"In our age the objective social tendency is incarnate in the hidden subjective purposes of company directors, the foremost among whom are in the most powerful sectors of industry - steel, petroleum, electricity, and chemicals. Culture monopolies are weak and dependent in comparison. They cannot afford to neglect their appeasement of the real holders of power if their sphere of activity in mass society (a sphere producing a specific type of commodity which anyhow is still too closely bound up with easy-going liberalism and Jewish intellectuals) is not to undergo a series of purges. The dependence of the most powerful broadcasting company on the electrical industry, or of the motion picture industry on the banks, is characteristic of the whole sphere, whose individual branches are themselves economically interwoven. All are in such close contact that the extreme concentration of mental forces allows demarcation lines between different firms and technical branches to be ignored."

On film: "It is the triumph of invested capital, whose title as absolute master is etched deep into the hearts of the dispossessed in the employment line; it is the meaningful content of every film, whatever plot the production team may have selected."

"There is nothing left for the consumer to classify. Producers have done it for him. Art for the masses has destroyed the dream but still conforms to the tenets of that dreaming idealism which critical idealism baulked at. Everything derives from consciousness: for Malebranche and Berkeley, from the consciousness of God; in mass art, from the consciousness of the production team. Not only are the hit songs, stars, and soap operas cyclically recurrent and rigidly invariable types, but the specific content of the entertainment itself is derived from them and only appears to change. The details are interchangeable. The short interval sequence which was effective in a hit song, the hero's momentary fall from grace (which he accepts as good sport), the rough treatment which the beloved gets from the male star, the latter's rugged defiance of the spoilt heiress, are, like all the other details, ready-made clichés to be slotted in anywhere; they never do anything more than fulfil the purpose allotted them in the overall plan. Their whole raison d'être is to confirm it by being its constituent parts. As soon as the film begins, it is quite clear how it will end, and who will be rewarded, punished, or forgotten. In light music, once the trained ear has heard the first notes of the hit song, it can guess what is coming and feel flattered when it does come. The average length of the short story has to be rigidly adhered to. Even gags, effects, and jokes are calculated like the setting in which they are placed. They are the responsibility of special experts and their narrow range makes it easy for them to be apportioned in the office."

"Real life is becoming indistinguishable from the movies. The sound film, far surpassing the theatre of illusion, leaves no room for imagination or reflection on the part of the audience, who is unable to respond within the structure of the film, yet deviate from its precise detail without losing the thread of the story; hence the film forces its victims to equate it directly with reality. The stunting of the mass-media consumer's powers of imagination and spontaneity does not have to be traced back to any psychological mechanisms; he must ascribe the loss of those attributes to the objective nature of the products themselves, especially to the most characteristic of them, the sound film. They are so designed that quickness, powers of observation, and experience are undeniably needed to apprehend them at all; yet sustained thought is out of the question if the spectator is not to miss the relentless rush of facts."

"The might of industrial society is lodged in men's minds. The entertainments manufacturers know that their products will be consumed with alertness even when the customer is distraught, for each of them is a model of the huge economic machinery which has always sustained the masses, whether at work or at leisure—which is akin to work. From every sound film and every broadcast program the social effect can be inferred which is exclusive to none but is shared by all alike. The culture industry as a whole has moulded men as a type unfailingly reproduced in every product. All the agents of this process, from the producer to the women's clubs, take good care that the simple reproduction of this mental state is not nuanced or extended in any way."

"The most intimate reactions of human beings have been so thoroughly reified that the idea of anything specific to themselves now persists only as an utterly abstract notion: personality scarcely signifies anything more than shining white teeth and freedom from body odour and emotions. The triumph of advertising in the culture industry is that consumers feel compelled to buy and use its products even though they see through them."

Max Horkheimer and Theodor W. Adorno, from *Dialectic of Enlightenment*, pp. 120-126, 158, 167. Copyright © 1972 by Verso Books. Reprinted with permission.

FROM THE CRITICAL PERSPECTIVE TO THE DIRECT-EFFECTS SCHOOL

The Frankfurt School represents a *critical or cultural perspective* on the rise of mass society and the mass mediums used to develop them. We will turn to a more recent form of the critical/cultural perspective years later, but historically and chronologically, research on media effects shifted during the 1930s. Research sought to better understand the persuasiveness of propaganda in the media during World War I. Most of these studies relied on a *direct-effects* approach that presumed audiences to be passive targets of media messages. Some researchers refer to this as the *hypodermic model*, where audiences are "injected" with a media message that leads to predictable attitudes and behaviors. The direct-effects perspective is still a popular one that drives research to this day—into issues like media violence and violence in society, media messages that promote conspicuous consumerism, and gender-role specificity.

The direct-effects school gained a great deal of credence as a result of the October 30, 1938 CBS radio broadcast of H. G. Wells' *The War of the Worlds*, performed by Orson

Welles and the Mercury Theatre on the Air. The first hour of the broadcast featured a series of news bulletins, including "We interrupt this story…," stating that an invasion by Martians was underway. The invasion was reported to be taking place in Grover's Mills in West Windsor Township, New Jersey (rather than 19th century England, as in Wells' novel). According to newspapers, many people panicked when they heard the broadcast (a direct effect). In the northeastern United States and Canada, people fled their homes. Things got really scary in Concrete, Washington, where, coincidently, a power company substation went down, leaving residents with no power or phone. Within a month, 12,500 articles appeared in U.S. newspapers about the panic although it was later thought to be less widespread than originally reported.

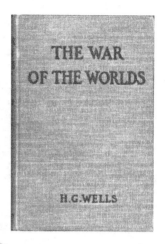

Figure 3.2 First edition of HG Wells' *The War of the Worlds* published in 1898.

In the 1940s and 1950s, especially after the work of Paul Lazarsfeld in his *The People's Choice* study, researchers began to think that the media may have less-immediate and -profound effects on its audiences than initially thought. The *People's Choice* study, which tracked the media's effect on voting during the U.S. presidential election campaign between Democrat Franklin D. Roosevelt and Republican Wendell Willkie, suggested the following:

- Voters with strong opinions are not likely to change them based on media messages
- Voters who pay the most attention to media's coverage of a campaign have strong opinions
- The most persuadable voters are not influenced by campaigns because they do not pay much attention to campaign media coverage
- The most persuadable voters are most influenced by opinion leaders—other people these persuadable voters know personally who hold strong opinions on candidates before the election.

Figure 3.3 Orson Welles who recreated the HG Wells' book on radio and scared a great many of his listeners as a result.

The limited effects school of research established a tension with those conducting research on direct effects of media exposure. According to communication scholar and Professor Justin Lewis, "at the heart of this debate is a tension between the viewer and the viewed. Where does the power to create and solidify meanings—really lie? Does it rest in the hands of the TV producer or TV consumer? Do we create our own meanings, or are they passed on to us, pre-wrapped in an attractive, well designed package?"

With the advent of television in the 1940s, direct- and limited-effects researchers focused on audience studies. During the 1950s and 1960s, these studies tended to cover two questions: Does violence on television lead to aggressive behavior among viewers? Does television affect viewers' political perspectives? Professor Lewis describes the findings from these studies, which numbered in the hundreds, as "inconclusive or confusing." Unlike other psychological and sociological studies of the era, measuring effects of television viewing introduced a number of difficult variables into the equation of understanding cause and effect. While psychological studies, in particular, in the U.S. followed the expectations and conventions

Figure 3.4 President Franklin D. Roosevelt during one of his "Fireside Chats" where he used radio to speak directly to the American people. Paul Lazarfeld's The People's Choice study questioned the direct effects of radio and television political coverage on American's voting patterns.

of the *behaviorist school*, where the best or most reliable measure of an effect was thought to be peoples' behaviors (rather than their thought processes, attitudes, or emotional responses to stimuli), it's also important to note that most of these studies of behavior were conducted with lab rats or pigeons. People are a little more complex.

Researchers during the period confronted lots of complications that their behaviorist and direct (or even limited effects) schools' counterparts didn't have to deal with. Professor Lewis summarizes these as follows:

Figure 3.5 John Watson is considered the father of the behaviorist school of psychology. The school rejected the study of cognition (thoughts), emotions, or instincts but believed psychology should instead focus on behavioral responses to stimuli. Behaviorism dominated the field of psychological research in the United States from the 1920s until the 1970s. Here he is pictured while professor at Johns Hopkins University in Baltimore.

- Television may not affect the way we behave, but the way we think.
- With traditional experimental designs, researchers need to develop a hypothesis and then determine whether the hypothesis is correct (based on the research findings). While hypotheses may be wrong, it may look like TV had no effect.
- Television is difficult to measure in controlled settings because we watch television differently depending

on the program being aired and what it is we're doing while watching. Sometimes it is a primary activity. In other times it is a secondary activity (for instance, watching while doing homework or laundry).

• Television viewers are not passive.

Joseph Klapper's *The Effects of Mass Communication* (1960) is often cited as the text that closed the curtain on the direct- and indirect-effects approaches to assessing mass media's influence on its audience. He concluded, "Mass communication does not ordinarily serve as a necessary or sufficient cause of audience effects, but rather functions through a nexis of mediating factors" (p. 8).

Figure 3.6 From a uses and gratifications perspective, viewers may watch NBC News for surveillance of their environment, to relax, or to gather information to use during conversations with people the next day. Many also tune-in because they have established a parasocial relationship with anchor Tom Brokaw (above) which is a relationship between users of mass media and "representations of humans appearing in the media (media figures such as presenters, actors, and celebrities)" (Giles, 2009). Parasocial relationships are a prime motivator of viewing many forms and genres of media, including movies, television dramas, newscasts, and reality television programs. Such findings emerged from uses and gratification studies.

USES AND GRATIFICATIONS

From the late 1950s to the 1970s, a new school of audience analysis emerged with a whole new set of ideas. Similar to the realm of psychological research, where the behaviorist school emerged from the structuralist school, the new ideas are revolutionary but may not (in retrospect) get to the heart of the matter. The Uses and Gratifications school is a framework that does not ask "what do the media do to people," but, "what do people do with the media?" (Katz, 1959, p. 20). This represented a huge shift in research away from the television set and its influence on people to an understanding of why people tune in to television in the first place. The basic assumptions of the Uses and Gratifications approach are (McQuail, Mass Communication Theory, 2000, p. 387–8):

• Media and content choice result from a generally rational decision (by the user) and directed toward specific goals and satisfactions

• Audience members are conscious of these needs and can voice these in terms of motivations

- In general, personal utility has a greater influence on audience formation than aesthetic or cultural factors
- The essential factors explaining audience formation (for a particular television program, for instance) can be measured.

While many researchers in the Uses and Gratifications school believed viewers held all of the cards when it came to media effects, others conducted research from the perspective that "the power of the television message was not negated but mediated by active, socially constructed viewers" (Lewis, 1991, p. 14). In other words, they sought to discover how viewer-related variables, such as the goals they hoped to achieve by watching a program, or perhaps, their perspectives on life in general, influenced the effect of specific media messages on their thoughts, attitudes, beliefs, or behaviors. While this was progressive thinking for the time that helped to move audience research and the quest to understand media's effects on audiences forward, it also opened up a methodological can of worms. Where does the researcher begin, and end, her measuring of the viewer-related variables?

One interesting set of findings to fall out from the Uses and Gratifications school of research is the notion of *Parasocial Interactions* or *Relationships*. Giles (2009) describes the concept of parasocial relationships as the interaction between "users of mass media and representations of humans appearing in the media (media figures such as presenters, actors, and celebrities) which can produce a form of parasocial relationship, to which the user responds as though in a typical social relationship" (p. 279). West and Turner (2010) define parasocial interaction as "the relationship we feel we have with people we know only through the media" (p. 396). Parasocial relationships are a prime motivator of viewing of many forms and genres of media, including movies, television dramas, newscasts, and reality television programs (Giles, 2009; Nabi, Biely, Morgan, and Stitt, 2009).

While communication researchers have explored parasocial relationships since psychiatrists Horton and Wohl (1956) first introduced the theory, Giles (2009) states that the concept has not yet been developed to the point that it can be taken up by practicing psychologists. Unanswered questions include how parasocial relationships integrate within normal social activity, how these relationships vary based on the media figures included, and finally, "what processes over time and media use bind user and figure into a parasocial relationship" (p. 279).

Giles' (2009) literature review on the parasocial relationships concludes with a call for the use of qualitative methodologies to explore parasocial interactions to gain a richer understanding of its psychological implications with an emphasis on discovering the information obtained during the parasocial relationship and exploring the "meaning of parasocial relationships" among media users (p. 298). Potential applications for findings from this research may include the development of quantitative studies in the communication and psychology fields, new insights for social psychologists exploring media-based social learning theory applications, the use of media figures in the clinical field acting as social models or "providing a cathartic or escapist function" (p. 299), and, from a psychopathological perspective, perspectives that may assist in the potential identification of erotomania, which Colman (2006) defines as "a delusion of being loved by another person, often a famous person" (p. 258).

Uses and Gratifications researchers also developed typologies regarding why people use media. These include connecting with others (e.g., parasocially or comparing reactions to viewing a program), separation from others, surveillance (i.e., understanding what's happening in the environment), diversion, development of personal identity, relaxation, enjoyment, escape, excitement, companionship, and passing time (Katz, 1973; McQuail, 1972; Rubin, 1981).

CULTIVATION ANALYSIS

During the period that Uses and Gratifications research made headway (1960s–1980s), some researchers rejected it while attempting to improve upon the direct-effects approach. One of the most important of these efforts became known as "cultivation analy-

sis." The approach has its roots in George Gerbner's Violence Index, a yearly content analysis of television network primetime programs that numerated the amount of violence presented. His work was the result of President Lyndon Johnson's call for the creation of a National Commission on the Causes and Prevention of Violence (1967) and in 1972 the surgeon general's Scientific Advisory Committee on Television and Social Behavior. Both bodies required a frequency report on acts of televised violence. Beyond these efforts, Gerbner and his colleagues conducted large nationwide studies of television viewers to understand their perspectives about life in their communities. What they discovered is that heavy viewers of television (4 or more hours per day) believe that their likelihood of being a victim of an actual crime was as high as depicted on television (i.e., ten times more rampant than in real life). Lighter viewers tended to report the incidence of becoming a victim more in line with local crime statistics.

Figure 3.7 George Gerbner (right), father of Cultivation Analysis and director of the Cultural Indicators Project, seated with Michael Morgan who has moved the research tradition forward. Photo was taken in 1979 at the Annenberg School of Communicaton at the University of Pennsylvania, where the project was conducted. Professor Morgan is now Professor of Communication at the University of Massachusetts—Amherst.

Figure 3.8 George Gerbner and the Cultural Indicators team (1976). In background, students code, or develop computer readable categories that representing the content of television programs for the purposes of developing statistics including the number of acts of violence broadcast per hour.

Cultivation analysis, according to West and Turner (2010), suggests that:

Television and other media play an extremely important role in how people view their world. In today's society, most people get their information from mediated sources rather than through direct experience. Therefore, mediated sources can shape a person's sense of reality. This is especially the case with regards to violence. Heavy television viewing cultivates a sense of the world as a violent place, and heavy television viewers perceive that there is more violence in the world than there actually is or than lighter viewers perceive.

Put differently, Cultivation Analysis explores television's contributions to viewers' conceptions of social reality. Television drives our symbolic environment—our creating of meanings transmitted through the use of symbols including words, gestures, actions, expectations, norms, and values. McQuail (2000) states that Cultivation Analysis "holds that television, among modern media, has acquired such a central place in daily life that it dominates our 'symbolic environment,' substituting its (distorted) message about reality for personal experience and other means of knowing about the world." Gerbner and Joyce (1972) state that "the substance of the consciousness cultivated by TV is not so much specific attitudes and opinions as more basic assumptions about the 'facts' of life and standards of judgment on which conclusions are based" (p. 175). Morgan and Shanahan (2010) state that "those who spend more time watching television are more likely to perceive the real world in ways that reflect the most common and recurrent messages of the world of fictional television" (p. 337).

Television develops, among its audience—particularly among its heaviest viewers—a "mainstreaming" of various perspectives, above and beyond fear and distrustful attitudes toward the outside world. These include more conservative political views on social and political issues, and an inert, withdrawn, and more depoliticized view of the world. According to Morgan (1989), television develops, in the minds of heavy viewers, a world in which the voting booth is more and more irrelevant. Morgan and Shanahan (2010), in their analysis of cultivation studies conducted since 2000, state that television viewers who watch talk shows (e.g., Oprah Winfrey) believe that the rate of marital infidelity, premarital sex, and the incidence of running away are much higher than the true incidence among the U.S. population at large. Those who watch "makeover" programs report lower self-esteem, body image, and a higher incidence of suffering from perfectionism schema than their counterparts who watch other shows.

Across the board, heavy viewers of television, according to Morgan and Shanahan (2010), believe that people

Just a Third of Young People Watched Any TV News Yesterday

Watched news on television yesterday ...	2006 %	2012 %	Change
Total	57	55	-2
18-29	49	34	-15
30-49	53	52	-1
50-64	63	65	+2
65+	69	73	+4

PEW RESEARCH CENTER 2012 News Consumption Survey. Q13.

with mental illnesses are dangerous, that traditional gender and family roles are more pervasive than they actually are (e.g., just 14% of households are comprised of a married couple with children), and they are more accepting of sexual stereotypes, and the assumption that peers are sexually active.

In recent research on science, heavy television viewing leads to a sense that "scientists are strange, and that science is potentially dangerous and always on the verge of running out of control" (p. 347). Interestingly, the higher the number of hours of viewing television, the lower the science-knowledge level of the viewer. In general, television viewing is linked with environmental apathy, which is "explained by television's cultivation of materialism and distorted perceptions of affluence, rather than solely by the invisibility of the environment as an issue" (p. 347). In fact, other studies found that viewing of nature documentaries and the news was positively correlated to environmental concern.

Among those who rely on television as their sole or main source of news (estimated at 55% of Americans according to Pew Research, in 2012), there is a heightened belief that crime is rampant both locally and nationally. Television news viewers, according to Morgan and Shanahan, share "exaggerated perceptions of juvenile crime rates, and with holding the erroneous belief that imprisonment is more effective than rehabilitation" (p. 342). Television news viewers are also more likely to believe that crime rates are higher than they actually are and, as a result, are much more likely to support capital punishment and handgun ownership. Similar results are found among viewers of reality police shows.

Gross (1977) described television as "the cultural arm of the established industrial order (which) serves primarily to maintain, rather than to alter, threaten, or weaken conventional beliefs or behaviors."

MEDIA ECOLOGY

Figure 3.9 Marshall McLuhan, father of the media ecology movement.

Most of the media effects described up to this point result from the exploration of media-delivered content on a passive or active audience over a short or long period of time. These effects result from the human (audience) processing of messages delivered over mass media systems. Central to the media effect is the content itself—the television programs, films, songs, news stories, and other forms of information delivered to audiences. Unlike traditional effects research, media ecology explores the effects of the mediums themselves, regardless of content, on users of these mediums. In other words, media ecologists explore the way our attending to a specific medium (e.g., print, radio, television, film) alters the way we process information and otherwise make sense of the world.

The media ecology movement resulted, in large part, on the innovative thinking of Canadian scholar Marshall McLuhan who coined two poetic and prophetic phrases in the annals of communication thinking:

Figure 3.10 Story telling at Ancient Technology Centre in Cranborne, UK. Gayle Ross, visiting from the USA, tells traditional stories of the Cherokee people in the Earth House.

The Medium Is the Message and the Global Village

"The medium is the message" holds as the mantra of media ecologists who study how the mediums we attend to "influence human perception, feeling, understanding, and value" (Parameswaran, 2008, "Interactive Television Programs: A Study in Media Ecology." *Language in India*, 8, 2). McLuhan postulated that humans maintain a symbiotic relationship with technology, describing humans as "the sex organs of technology," where, according to West and Turner (2010), "we create technology, and technology in turn re-creates who we are" (p. 429). McLuhan's mentor, Harold Innis, a political

economist and author of *The Bias of Communication* (1951), had a strong influence on his thinking. Innis' contention was that, throughout history, the great empires (Rome, Greece, Egypt) were built by those in control of their media systems (in the cases listed, the written word) while today's empires are built by those in control of today's media systems (television, film, radio, print). The power to shape a society or culture using technology is the bias of communication.

But McLuhan transcended the thinking of his mentor by arguing that a medium's content itself falls prey to the medium used to deliver it. Each medium uses its audience in a way that biases message interpretation. The predominant medium of the time changes the sensibilities of the society as a whole. This occurs because: 1) media is all-pervasive—we live in a mediasphere, where (today) sound, pictures, and words surround us almost every hour that we're awake; 2) mediated communication (print, video, audio) fixes our perceptions and organizes experience; 3) mediated communication dissolves time and space, thus creating a "global village."

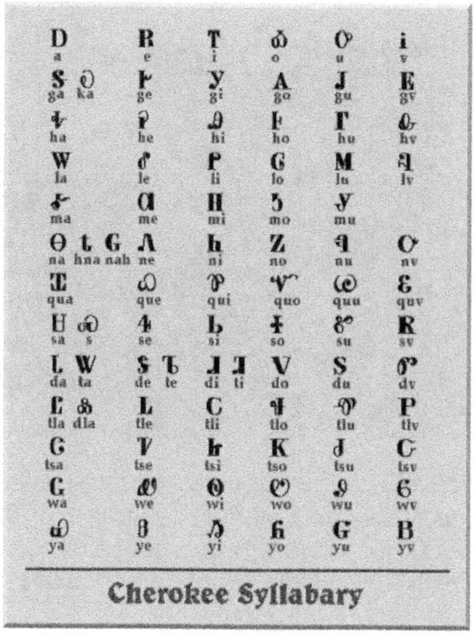

Media ecologists have examined the effects that predominant mediums during various epochs in history have had on the sensibilities of the people of the time. McLuhan identified at least four: the tribal era, the literate era, the print era, and electronic era.

Cherokee Syllabary

Figure 3.11 Syllabic script used symbols to capture verbal sounds. Syllabaries, like this one from the Cherokee Nation in North America, were symbols that captured the essence of the spoken word. These scripts simply offered a representation of the spoken word. It wasn't until much later that written text became standardized to include spelling, punctuation, syntax, etc.

The tribal era, which relied upon interpersonal contact and listening, honored the notion of stability and predictability, and probably assessed human intelligence based on one's ability to memorize orations—perhaps lasting several hours. The more specific passages one could recall, the better. Rhymes, mnemonics, and narratives were just three of the techniques used to bolster recall. These cultures, according to McLuhan, were "ear-centered" (i.e., hearing is believing), with culture (values, rituals, and traditions) communicated verbally.

The literate era, which relied upon the written word, emphasized the sense of sight and encouraged people to look at the world with a bias toward the visual and spatial. Knowledge became more available and reduced the power of tribal leaders. Using the written word, social structures changed to emphasize rational thinking. The written word requires users to encode experiences into logic statements (i.e., subject, verb, predicate) without the benefit of non-verbal communication (i.e., tone of voice, gestures, eye contact, facial expressions, etc.), which is processed in the limbic system (i.e., emotion

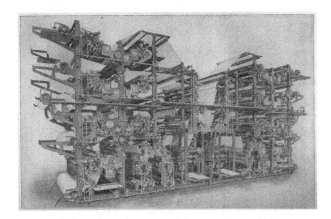

Figure 3.12 The Double Octuple Newspaper Press. This press, the largest in use in the 1910s produced 96,000 16-page newspapers per hour, folded to half size (like the *New York Times* or *USA Today*) and counted.

center) of the brain. McLuhan postulated that this era led to increased individualism and reduced collectivism. People could obtain information without the help from people in their community.

The print era, which relied upon the mass production of the written word, led to the development of mass culture and mass production. The era begins shortly after German Johannes Gutenberg develops the printing press with moveable type in 1450. The printed, rather than scribed, word intensifies the "reading is believing" perspective and increases the significance of noninvolvement and detachment in culture. McLuhan called printed texts "the first teaching machine" and, to this day, students would be hard-pressed to find a course that doesn't include a textbook. The mass production of text, according to McLuhan, leads to the production of people who are very similar to one another. As West and Turner (2010) state, "The same content is delivered over and over again by the same means. This visual-dependent era, however, produced a fragmented population because people could remain in isolation reading their mass produced media" (p 434). The era continued to emphasize logical and linear thinking leading to The Enlightenment and The Age of Reason where ideas and knowledge, predominantly based on science, began to overtake religion as a way of life.

The electronic era, which relies upon the visual and aural senses, is characterized by the break-neck development of technologies in the 19th and 20th centuries, including the telegraph, telephone, radio, television, and computer. These technologies, in many respects, returned us to the *tribal era,* with its emphasis on rhetoric and oral communication. They also overcame time and space by providing nearly instantaneous transmission of content leading to

Figure 3.13 Geosynchronous communication satellites like this one transmit television, radio, and data from a position 22,300 miles from Earth. The high orbit allowes the satellites' orbital speed to match the rotation speed of Earth and therefore remain essentially stable over the same spot.

the development of time zones, which were not at all necessary before the advent of the telegraph. Today, near-instantaneous and pervasive electronic digital media have led to the realization of Marshall McLuhan's vision of a "global village."

While messages attract our attention, media ecologists believe that mediums change the way we perceive the world. According to West and Turner (2010), "McLuhan thinks that although a message affects our conscious state, it is the medium that largely affects our unconscious state" (p. 436). Interestingly, current brain science, relying on fMRI brain scans, seems to be confirming McLuhan's hypothesis. Of special importance is work being done on users of the web for reading, research, and entertainment. In 2009, Nicholas Carr authored a book summarizing key findings on mediums and the mind in *The Shallows: What the Internet Is Doing to Our Brains*. Among the key findings:

- In one fascinating study, conducted at Washington University's Dynamic Cognition Laboratory and published in the journal Psychological Science in 2009, researchers used brain scans to examine what happens inside people's heads as they read fiction. They found that "readers mentally simulate each new situation encountered in a narrative. Details about actions and sensation are captured from the text and integrated with personal knowledge from past experiences." The brain regions that are activated often "mirror those involved when people perform, imagine, or observe similar real-world activities." Deep reading, says the study's lead researcher, Nicole Speer, is by no means a passive exercise. The reader becomes the book.

- After 550 years, the printing press and its products are being pushed from the center of our intellectual life to its edges. The shift began during the middle years of the twentieth century, when we started devoting more and more of our time and attention to the cheap, copious, and endlessly entertaining products of the first wave of electric and electronic media: radio, cinema, phonograph, television. But those technologies were always limited by their inability to transmit the written word. They could displace but not replace the book. Culture's mainstream still ran through the printing press. Now the mainstream is being diverted, quickly and decisively, into a new channel. The electronic revolution is approaching its culmination as the computer—desktop, laptop, handheld—becomes our constant companion and the Internet becomes our medium of choice for storing, processing, and sharing information in all forms, including text. The new world will remain, of course, a literate world, packed with the familiar symbols of the alphabet. We cannot go back to the lost oral world, any more than we can turn the clock back to a time before the clock existed. (40) "Writing and print and the computer," writes Walter Ong, "are all ways of technologizing the word" and once technologized, the word cannot be de-technologized. (41) But the world of the screen, as we're already coming to understand, is a very different place from the world of the page. A new intellectual ethic is taking hold. The pathways in our brains are once again being rerouted.

- A search engine often draws our attention to a particular snippet of text, a few words or sentences that have strong relevance to whatever we're searching for at the moment, while providing little incentive for taking in the work as a whole. We don't see the forest when we search the Web. We don't even see the trees. We see twigs and leaves. As companies like Google and Microsoft perfect search engines for video and audio content, more products are undergoing the fragmentation that already characterizes written works.

- The news is even more disturbing than I had suspected. Dozens of studies by psychologists, neurobiologists, educators, and Web designers point to the same conclusion: when we go online, we enter an environment that promotes cursory reading, hurried and distracted thinking, and superficial learning. It's possible to think deeply while surfing the Net, just as it's possible to think shallowly while reading a book, but that's not the type of thinking the technology encourages and rewards.

- The Net's interactivity gives us powerful new tools for finding information, expressing ourselves, and conversing with others. It also turns us into lab rats constantly pressing levers to get tiny pellets of social or intellectual nourishment.

- But Dijksterhuis's work also shows that our unconscious thought processes don't engage with a problem until we've clearly and consciously defined the problem.3 If we don't have a particular intellectual goal in mind, Dijksterhuis writes, "unconscious thought does not occur."4 The constant distractedness that the Net encourages—the state of being, to borrow another phrase from Eliot's Four Quartets, "distracted from distraction by distraction"—is very different from the kind of temporary, purposeful diversion of our mind that refreshes our thinking when we're weighing a decision. The Net's cacophony of stimuli short-circuits both conscious and unconscious thought, preventing our minds from thinking either deeply or creatively. Our brains turn into simple signal-processing units, quickly shepherding information into consciousness and then back out again.

- In particular, "the computer-savvy subjects used a specific network in the left front part of the brain, known as the dorsolateral prefrontal cortex, [while] the Internet-naïve subjects showed minimal, if any, activity in this area." As a control for the test, the researchers also had the subjects read straight text in a simulation of book reading; in this case, scans revealed no significant difference in brain activity between the two groups.

- "After just five days of practice, the exact same neural circuitry in the front part of the brain became active in the Internet-naïve subjects," reports Small. "Five hours on the Internet, and the naïve subjects had already rewired their brains." He goes on to ask, "If our brains are so sensitive to just an hour a day of computer exposure, what happens when we spend more time [online]?"

- The information flowing into our working memory at any given moment is called our "cognitive load." When the load exceeds our mind's ability to store and process the information—when the water overflows the thimble—we're unable to retain the information or to draw connections with the information already stored in our long-term memory. We can't translate the new information into schemas. Our ability to learn suffers, and our understanding remains shallow. Because our ability to maintain our attention also depends on our working memory—"we have to remember what it is we are to concentrate on," as Torkel Klingberg says—a high cognitive load amplifies the distractedness we experience. When our brain is overtaxed, we find "distractions more distracting." (17)

- The division of attention demanded by multimedia further strains our cognitive abilities, diminishing our learning and weakening our understanding. When it comes to supplying the mind with the stuff of thought, more can be less.

Nicholas Carr, from *The Shallows: What the Internet is Doing to Our Brains*, pp. 74, 77, 94, 115-117, 119, 121, 125, 129. Copyright © 2011 by W. W. Norton & Company, Inc. Reprinted with permission.

CULTURAL STUDIES—A RETURN TO CRITICAL ANALYSIS

In the 1970s, the Centre for Contemporary Studies in Britain drew from history, feminism, Marxism, literary criticism, and other traditions to better understand how culture evolves. These studies focused on the notion of "hegemony," or the concentration and distribution of power in a large society, and the creation of a nucleus, or central point, in the creation of a culture's worldview. For instance, according to Lewis (1991), "the semiotic environment for the support of free market capitalism or patriarchy takes place in all sorts of places, from the supermarket to the cinema" (p. 41). Hegemony, one might say, is the battleground of meaning. He continues:

> As TV viewers, we are usually innocent of our inevitable struggle for meaning. As we put our feet up in front of the television, our mood is more likely to be relaxed than combative. And yet, like it or not, our regular encounters with the kaleidoscope of words and images that flow in to our living rooms form an inexorable part of our semiotic universe (p. 42).

According to Hall, Lowe, Hobson, and Willis (*Culture, Media, Language: Working Papers in Cultural Studies, 1972–79*; Roetledge, 1980), popular culture is seen as a significant instrument of social and political control. To create a template for understanding this relationship, the Centre turned to the work of Antonio Gramsci, a 1930s intellectual, who sought to understand why the Italian underclass voted heavily for the fascist party, which supported the expansion of corporate interests at the expense of their own. The Centre later learned that, in capitalist societies (like the United States), class alliances

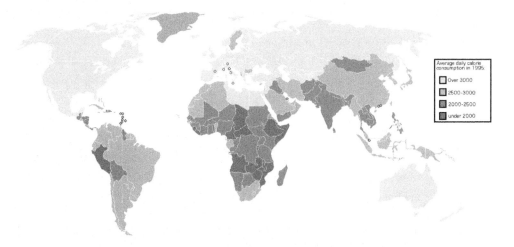

Figure 3.14 Global consumption of calories. A map showing the average daily calorie consumption in countries all over the world. Countries with high caloric consumption are also those with more sophisticated media systems.

are developed and reinforced through cultural norms and expectations that are codified through media systems. Not only is force (police, jail, repression, war) a tool of the social (and corporate) elite, but so is popular culture.

Stuart Hall, who headed the Centre, contends that mainstream media in the United States suggests an appearance of egalitarianism, or class equality, including the respect for diversity, individual rights, and equal opportunity, but fails to provide insights and perspectives from marginalized populations such as the elderly, many minorities, the poor, and women, among others. Hall's research attempts to transcend the *content* of information presented in the media to include an understanding of *who* is creating and sending these messages. Ultimately, cultural studies call for the American mass communication system to provide more voices (i.e., programs, perspectives regarding news and politics) to these marginalized populations who currently have no voice.

There is little doubt that consumerism is a significant part of the American culture as promulgated by its media system from the time of the penny press when manufacturers and retailers conspired to create a culture of mass consumption. With the advent of other advertising-supported media including magazines, radio, and television, this cultural attribute has solidified and increased in power. According to cultural analyst Jeremy Gilbert, "We now live in an era when, throughout the capitalist world, where the overriding aim of government economic policy is to maintain consumer spending levels. This is an era when 'consumer confidence' is treated as the key indicator and cause of economic effectiveness." Critical studies treat consumerism as a major problem, especially from an environmental perspective. With accelerating rates of consumption, we've reached a level of non-sustainability that threatens the very health of the planet and human survival. But with increased exposure to advertisements, consumption will fail to slow. Since the American media system relies on corporate advertising to increase sales and consumption, this system downplays or even fails to discuss, in a meaningful way, the dangers inherent in the ever-increasing production and consumption of products. Americans continue to maintain a cultural outlook that covets possessions. In fact, we tend to characterize and categorize both the relative success and values of people based upon their acquisition of material goods including homes, cars, technology, jewelry, clothes—and even the brands of foods served during social events. Indeed, we tend to consider our culture's preference for and belief in free market capitalism as a "natural system" while there are many other similar systems. While cultural studies are critical of conspicuous consumerism, most do not call for a significant change. Rather, they call for the acculturation of alternative perspectives, and voices, that speak to reverse the damage we've done to our planet, and to the overall improvement of human health.

When we actively or critically view television programs, films, and printed media from a critical or cultural perspective, we become more aware of the cultural influence our media system has on our values, beliefs, and perspectives. We need to become more acutely aware of the power relations (i.e., that advertising media attract audiences via their content in order to sell us to corporate advertisers) that result in the messages transmitted by our media system. Try to keep this in mind while watching TV, listening to the radio, or surfing the net.

SEMIOLOGY AND POST-POSITIVIST PERSPECTIVES

Semiology, the study of meaning, began to take hold in the analysis of popular culture in the 1970s thanks to the works of Umberto Eco, Roland Barthes, and others. Many believe that semiology is a simple restatement of George Herbert Meade's symbolic interaction theory that suggests meanings are created through interactions between people and codified using symbols (i.e., words, images, signs, gestures). Even our sense of self and

Figure 3.15 What we experience through television is simply a symbolic representation of an experience. Meaning is made by the each viewer by processing symbols into meanings. This is an important part of the process for semiologists and symbolic interactionists who are working to understand how meanings are created by people.

our perspective of "reality" emerge from these symbols and meanings. According to Meade, we socially construct our realities.

Semiology, and Symbolic Interactionism, had profound significance on the analysis of media effects from the 1990s to today. The general principle of semiology can be shown through a simple formula:

the signifier + the signified = the sign.

We experience the signifier through our sense organs (sight, sound, smell, taste, touch). It is the "thing" that we "see," be it a word, action, image, or sound. It is a stimulus that enters our sense organs and sensory stores before the cerebral cortex tags a meaning to it.

The signified is the concept or meaning that we associate with the signifier. The signified is not material, rather, it is what we think (and feel) in response to the signifier. The signified has a quality that makes it difficult to put into words, but is thought and felt in conjunction with the signifier. Because our brains process symbols (the signifier) and meanings (the signified) so quickly, it is difficult for us to separate the two. This is why they are tied together with the third term, the sign. The sign incorporates both the symbol and the meaning. As Lewis (1991) states, "It is the material entity made meaningful" (p. 27).

The implications of semiology on the study of media effects are significant. Media studies may now explore the relationship between the viewer (source of the signified) and what's on the screen (the signifier). According to Lewis, "The meaning of the television message is not fixed, but neither is it arbitrary. It will be determined by the viewers' semiotic environment—which includes their history, their neighborhood, their class, and, of course, television itself. It takes us beyond the confines of 'effects' and 'uses and gratifications,' allowing us to evaluate the process whereby television signifiers become television signs. These signs can be taken apart in order to see what binds them together" (p. 31).

Semiology also got researchers to consider an important question—how can we identify and isolate cause and effect factors in media research when the source (the media) was instrumental in defining the symbols not only associated with the cause but also the effect?

McQuail (2002) states that semiology "has a special advantage of being applicable to 'texts' that involve more than

Figure 3.16 Lady Gaga performing "Beautiful, Dirty, Rich" on the Fame Ball tour. Semiologists like Judith Williamson believe we form our identities, our selves, through the things we purchase, display, and consume.

one sign system (such as visual images and sounds) for which there is no established 'grammar' and no available dictionary" (p. 314). McQuail further states:

> This body of theory supplies with an approach, if not exactly a method, for helping to establish the 'cultural meaning' of media content. It certainly offers a way of describing the content; it can shed light on those who produce and transmit a set of messages; it has special application in opening up layers of meaning which lie beneath the surface of texts and deny simple description at the 'first level' of signification. It is also useful in certain kinds of evaluative research, especially as directed at uncovering the latent ideology and 'bias' of media content.

The research and analysis by Judith Williamson in *Decoding Advertising: Ideology and Meaning in Advertising* (2010) is made possible through semiological analysis. Among her findings, people tend to form their identities through the things they purchase and relate with one another "through the language of our possessions" (p. 8).

> In our society, while the real distinctions between people are created by their role in the process of production, as workers, it is the products of their own work that are used, in the false categories invoked by advertising, to obscure the real structure of society by replacing class with the distinctions made by the consumption of particular goods. Thus instead of being identified by what they produce, people are made to identify themselves with what they consume (p. 13).

> Ultimately, advertising works in a circular movement which once set into motion is self-perpetuating. It works because it feeds off of a genuine use-value; besides needing social meaning we obviously do need material goods. Advertising gives those goods a social meaning so that two needs are crossed, and neither is adequately fulfilled. Material things that we need are made to represent the other, non-material things we need; the point of exchange between the two is where meaning is created. (p. 14)

University of Wisconsin media scholar John Fiske, who authored *Television Culture* (1997), states, "The point is that 'reality' is already encoded, or rather the only way we can perceive and makes sense of reality is by the codes of our culture. There may be an objective, empiricist reality out there, but there is no universal, objective way of perceiving and making sense of it. What passes for reality in any culture is the product of that culture's codes, so 'reality' is always already television culture."

The implications of semiology on the study of media effects are profound. Rather than thinking about media as effecting certain social or anti-social behaviors, or, considering certain re-occurring themes and messages from a power elite as being consonant with our own, semiology and other post-positivist studies suggest that media inject us with an operating system of sorts. It's an entertainment-based means for programming the meaning of symbols, be they words, actions, the visual appearance of people, music, or sounds, into our collective frame of reference. These symbol-to-object associations drive our perspectives of reality itself.

SOCIAL PSYCHOLOGY

Explorations into how media affects audiences are also being conducted by social psychologists who explore how people make sense of their everyday lives. How one interprets the environment by way of one's set of "knowledge representations" is a central focus of research. While we tend to differentiate reality from the content of television, social psychologists are learning that we have a difficult time distinguishing what we learn first-hand from that which we learn watching television when it comes to constructing, and relying upon, our knowledge representation to perceive the world and solve problems.

Based on social psychological studies on how people learn about factors that contribute to the construction of their realities, factors like recency (how recently we've learned something), frequency (how often we've learned a similar lesson), and referentiality (frequency of outside events and ideas) come into play. The more recent, frequent, and referential a meaning—the more it seems real.

Social Learning Theory (or Observational Learning), put forward by Albert Bandura, suggests that people also learn from and are influenced by exposure to role models, typically found in the media. Role models who achieve their goals through the use of aggressive behaviors, including violence, and are not punished—mainly due to their status as "hero"—are the most likely to elicit aggressive behaviors among viewers. This is because, over time, these viewers hold more positive attitudes and beliefs about aggression leading to the construction of scripts, or guides for behavior, that are used when forced to solve a social issue or conflict. The key is the viewer's repeated exposure to the outcome of the behavior—rewards and punishments—as depicted in the media. The central tenet of the theory is that people tend to observe others' behaviors and assess the outcomes of their behaviors to develop a template for their own future behavior. Television is thought to provide pro-social and anti-social learning outcomes. For example, a calm, non-aggressive hero can spawn similar behaviors among fans.

Think about the role models you encounter in the media. Who are they? Are their actions rewarded or punished? What actions lead to achieving goals while avoiding punishment?

MISINFORMATION EFFECT

Elizabeth Loftus conducted groundbreaking research in the 1970s on the memories of eyewitnesses to crimes being altered after being exposed to incorrect information about the event. Loftus learned that memory is easily influenced and open to suggestion. The misinformation effect became one of the most influential and widely known effects in social psychology and her work resulted in hundreds of follow-up studies examining factors that improve or worsen the accuracy of our perspectives of reality.

Figure 3.17 Social psychologists believe that our perspectives on groups that we don't spend much time with, such as the elderly, manifest through our exposure to the elderly on television, film, and other mediated sources.

The theory highlights two weaknesses of human memory: suggestibility, or the influence of others' expectations on our memory; and misattribution, or information attributed to an incorrect source. With suggestibility, Loftus learned that recency, frequency, and referentiality play on and distort our memory of events that we may have witnessed first-hand. For example, if we witnessed a crime but then learned new (updated) information on the crime during repeated news broadcasts, we would begin to incorporate these repeated updates into our own first-hand recollection of the event. With referentiality, Loftus learned that while human memory of people, actions, information, and meanings is good, our memories are average or poor at recollecting their *source*.

Most of Loftus' work centered upon the contamination of eyewitnesses' memories (called "false memories"), mostly by interrogators, of the crimes they've observed but other researchers used her theoretical framework to explore the impact of the media. For example, Cowley and Janus (2004) describe an experiment that demonstrated the effectiveness of television advertisements on the creation of false memories among consumers. After drinking a brand of orange juice that was tainted with lemon juice and other ingredients to make it taste bad, respondents were exposed to a series of advertisements that described how good it tasted. Later surveys revealed that the respondents believed that the orange juice actually tasted great—significantly better than they first reported after consuming it.

Figure 3.18 American cognitive psychologist and human memory expert Elizabeth Loftus. Her theory of misinformation effect states that humans have wonderful memories—however, we tend to not recall the source of our memories. Resultantly, a great number of our "memories" are actually mediated memories.

Social psychologist and media scholar Sonia Livingstone confirmed this idea that people blend real experiences from media messages suggesting that "television has become inextricably a part of, and often indistinguishable from everyday life. We often do not remember whether we learned of a certain fact from a friend or television, we fail to notice that our images of the elderly, for example, derive more from television than everyday interactions, and when we recount an anecdote or interesting observation, does it matter if it came from watching television or a personal experience?" (p. 5). Psychologically, she contends, it is not plausible to segregate knowledge gained from television from real life.

The misinformation effect and creation of false memories are important to keep in mind while evaluating what you know about life, about current events, and your experiences with products and services.

TELEVISION'S EFFECT ON BRAIN FUNCTION

In less than a minute after turning on the television, our brain waves switch from predominantly beta waves, which represent active or critical thinking, to mostly alpha waves indicating receptive and unfocused attention. Very similar changes occur when we are placed under hypnosis. According to Dr. Aric Sigman, author of *Remotely Controlled: How Television Is Damaging Our Lives* (2005), activity in the brain's left hemisphere tends to quiet down, while our right hemisphere functions as usual. Generally speaking, the left hemisphere manages information analytically and logically. It is the problem-solving region of our brains and is also responsible for our ability to sustain attention. The right brain processes information uncritically and emotionally. Sigman's

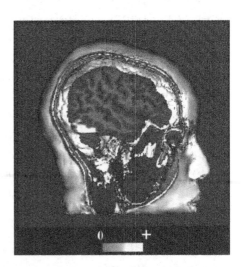

Figure 3.19 This is a computer-enhanced fMRI scan of a person who has been asked to look at faces. The image shows increased blood flow in the part of the visual cortex that recognizes faces.

conclusion is that television transmits very large quantities of information that are not critically analyzed or decoded while being received by audience members.

Under hypnosis, we are focused but highly responsive to suggestion. Brainwave research indicates that our frontal lobes, responsible for linking our emotional right brains to the analytic oversight of our left brains, shut down. In addition, the frontal lobe monitors the passing of time and supports self-awareness. While watching television, the brain's organization is altered with dramatic shifts from left-brain activity to right-brain activity, leaving us highly suggestible to the messages and meanings we receive. A study, reported by Dr. Sigman, conducted in a remote British Columbia community that previously had no access to television, amplified these effects. After a cable television system was installed, researchers learned that, over time, both adults and children became less creative in problem solving and were less able to stay focused on tasks.

The frontal lobes, which appear to shut down shortly after beginning a television-viewing session, "are the brain's executive control system, responsible for planning, organizing, and sequencing behavior for self-control, moral judgment and attention. Again, both hypnosis and television reduce our ability to analyze critically what we are being told or what we see" (p. 95).

Operation Frontal Lobes (1956)

For the past four months, NBC has been engaged in an earnest conspiracy directed at U.S. televiewers. Its commendable purpose, as explained by NBC's dedicated Vice President Davidson Taylor: to smuggle cultural and educational tidbits into the network's TV schedule.

To continue reading visit: http://www.time.com/time/magazine/article/0,9171,815872,00.html#ixzz2LfMawWlz

Pro-Social Effects of Media Exposure to Body Image

The article "More than just Anorexia and Steroid Abuse: Effects of Media exposure on Attitudes toward Body Image and Self-Efficacy" written by Xiao Wang talks about the effects that the Mass Media has on the individual. Mass Media can influence how people perceive the world. Researchers argue that the effect can have negative but also positive effects on the individuals. Studies have shown that women's body image is influenced by fashion and entertainment as well as by sports and health magazine reading, whereas males are influenced by their sports and health magazine reading. The results showed that neither of the groups were influenced by viewing a popular television show. The women have been represented as ultrathin and men as ultra muscular in the US media. Whereas women focus on losing weight while dieting, men are more concerned about increasing their body mass and may rely on the use of steroids. Researchers argue that the body image exposure leads to positive outcomes, because more and more people are physically active (Wang). The study that Wang is talking about in his article is trying to find out, if there are any positive effects regarding media exposure.

The article talks about what effects the media exposure has on the individual. In Wang's article he talks about one of the first studies that is trying to find out if there are positive media effects or if it's all bad, because most studies only focus on the negative impact of media exposure. In my opinion it is interesting to see that Wang is trying to find out if mass media has a positive impact on the individual. But when you really think about it, it actually might have a positive impact on people. A lot of people in America are overweight due to eating too much fast food, which is bad for the body. On the contrary a lot of young girls starve themselves to death just because they want to look like the skinny model that they saw in their fashion magazine.

These are examples of the two extremes but no one ever thinks about the option in the middle. People do not have to become obese or starve themselves to death. The healthy way would be to eat the right nutrition and exercise to keep your body healthy. Fitness magazines as well as Fitness TV shows or even if it is your favorite TV character in your favorite soap opera can all show you how you can look and live healthy. In addition the article was saying that it depends on how the individual is perceiving the message that is being transferred to the individual. For example two people are watching the same show and the one person ends up being anorexic, but the other person is perfectly fine. It depends on your self-esteem and confidence I would say. For example I would like to look like a Victoria's Secret Model but I know I will never look like one, because first of all they are all super tall and I am not. Furthermore they probably do not eat that much food, and I love to eat, so I could never not eat. But on the other hand I also want to be healthy and exercise to maintain a healthy body. But then there are girls that starve themselves, because they want to look exactly like those models and bring themselves in danger. This example shows that it depends on how you work with these images in your head. If you have a low self-esteem and think you are going to be rejected if you do not look like one of those models, you are more likely do end up being anorexic. But if you have a high self-esteem, you are more likely to either ignore the message that is being transferred or you notice it but it does not have an effect on you.

All in all you can say that it is interesting to see that someone is actually trying to find out what the positive effects of mass media are, since most researchers focus on negative effects. I never thought about if there are any positive effects of Mass Media, because you always hear stories about young girls that starved themselves to death, because they wanted to look like the model on the cover of Vogue. No one ever reports about the positive effects, which makes you not aware that there actually might some. The information you get in this article makes you think about what the positive effects of media might be.

—Joelle Regh

Reviewed: Xiao, W. (2010). "More Than Just Anorexia and Steroid Abuse: Effects of Media Exposure on Attitudes Toward Body Image and Self-Efficacy." *Atlantic Journal of Communication*, 18(1), 50–62. doi:10.1080/15456870903210089

Body Image and Eating Disorders

The influence of mass media on body image and eating disorder behaviors in many adult and adolescent females has always been a primary fixture on the perception of what the "beauty and thin ordeal" should be. "The average amount of time spent watching television content among all 8-18 year olds is 4.29 hours in a typical day" (Rideout, Foehr, & Roberts, 2010, p. 388). This average totals to about 30 hours a week in which vulnerable children and young adults are subjected to just one form of media—television.It has long been a fact, that constant exposure to television programming, advertising, radio, movies, and magazines where a distorted vision of unhealthy and/or unrealistic body images are displayed, has a great influence on how females as young as 8-years old feel about their own bodies. As studies discussed in the article have proven, the effects are greater on those who are already struggling with low self-esteem, and self-worth issues. Thus, these young girls are at a higher risk of developing eating disorders and/or making poor, unhealthy, personal choices in their lives, as they grow older.

I chose this journal article for this assignment, because as a single mother of a now 9-year old girl, I constantly struggle with limiting her exposure to the amount of appearance-focused media that could in some way encourage actions that could lead to body dissatisfaction. Growing-up, in a household with two full-time working parents, and the oldest of three siblings, television & movies was always one of the primary outlets for entertainment in our household. As a Hispanic American, living in a community where most of my peers were white, middle to upper class families, it was very difficult for me growing-up at times. I constantly struggled with low self-esteem issues, and never felt like I belonged, because I looked different from those around me. I was naturally thin, but curvy, tan skin with dark, frizzy, curly, thick hair that was most times unmanageable. My friends were mostly thin, light-skin, and had beautiful hair that always seemed to look perfect. Looking back, it certainly didn't help that most of the television programming I watched constantly, and teen magazines I read, depicted girls my age, who looked more like my peers, than me. It was a struggle to fight the urge of not wanting to look like the character on my favorite TV show, or favorite music star. It was a heavy influence on how I felt about myself all the way through my late teens. In fact, it wasn't until I was in my early 20s that I fully understood the obsession with thinness in media, and the distorted, unrealistic images that was portrayed as the ideal way to look in order to feel beautiful, and/or be accepted socially.

These days, being a parent presents a greater challenge than ever, because our children are being raised in an era where the influence of mass media is much greater on young adolescents than it was two decades ago. As parents, we can certainly limit our children's exposure to media in our homes, but unfortunately, we can't control the influences of their friends and peers at school or when they're outside their homes. Especially, as they get older, and become more independent, and widely aware of the easy access to information via the internet. On another note, one of the things I found most interesting, while reading the article, is that the level of impact of mass media in regards to the internalization of the "thin beauty ideal" in vulnerable adolescents and young teens depends on the positive influences and support that surrounds them in and outside their homes.

As Stice et al. suggests in the article (2001), "Perhaps exposure to thin ideal images does not produce negative effects for adolescents who feel accepted in their immediate social environment" (p. 395). I'm in full agreement when the article's author suggests that having a healthy level of social and emotional support from family and friends can make a huge difference in how much influence media exposure can have on females who are at high-risk in body dissatisfaction, negative eating behaviors and beliefs. "The messages transmitted by parents (especially mothers) and by friends (primarily same-sex friends) have more influence on awareness and internalization of the thin beauty ideal and on body dissatisfaction and unhealthy weight-control behaviors than do mass media" (McCabe & Ricciardelli, 2005; Presnell, Bearman, & Stice, 2004; Stice, 1998, p. 400). Young girls who are positively influenced directly and indirectly by people who are important to them (e.g., mothers, fathers, aunts, uncles, grandparents, older siblings, teachers, and friends) plays a major role in how these innocent girls portray the images and messages they see, hear and read on television, in movies, radio, books, magazines and the internet.

In reading the journal articles content on media influences, along with the supported results from numerous studies conducted at various times, it further enforces my own beliefs on the importance of communication with our children. My own experience as a young adolescent, Hispanic American female, who struggled with self-acceptance growing-up, and felt there was a lack of support and understanding at home, taught me the importance of ensuring that my own daughter grows up feeling she can openly have discussions with me about anything, without the fear of judgment or misunderstanding. As quoted from a reference in the journal article, A considerable amount of data indicated that the negative impact of media images depends on the conscious and, in many instances, cumulative processing of unambiguous direct, and "attractive" social messages (Harrison & Heffner, 2008; Levine & Harrison, 2009, p. 401) This statement in the article further confirms my beliefs that the way young girls learn to portray the images and messages in media, whether positive or negative, all depends on the influences they've been subjected to in their homes since birth.

The media effect also highlighted in the article is the process of social comparison. It refers to people's tendency to compare themselves to others, especially with characteristics involving beauty, talent or sexiness. The article's author, Guimera-Lopez, Gemma writes that, "Applied to the context of media, self-perception of attractiveness, and body image, social comparison denotes the process in which women compare themselves with the idealized, symbolic images, and on finding they "fail" to meet the social and cultural standards, show increased body dissatisfaction." (p. 403–404) Having a negative body image not only leads to body dissatisfaction, and self-esteem issues, it also leads to the participation of social comparison among their peers, family, and the beauty ideas represented in the media as people whom society might consider to be more attractive. The article goes on to further explain that females who struggle with these issues convince themselves that in order to be accepted, and feel beautiful, they have to look like these media endorsed images of what acceptable beauty is.

In conclusion, it's evident that mass media is the primary source of information and reinforcement in relation to the distorted vision of beauty portrayed in television, magazines, films, commercials and billboard advertisements. In my sole opinion, as powerful as the impact and influence of media on females' perception of "the perfect body image" can be, it won't ever be the primary source of distorted body image, increased eating disorder behaviors and beliefs. It may play a major role, but the real factor is the influences and support system that surround these females throughout their daily lives. Having a strong, female role model growing-up (e.g., mother, older sister, aunt, grandmother, mentor, etc) can really positively influence adolescent females, because they all have the one powerful source that the media will never have—unconditional love. They can provide encouragement in the importance of self-acceptance, self-awareness of what's real and what's not in regards to media, and making healthy lifestyle choices. Thus, minimizing the negative adverse effects the media can have on females, especially adolescents.

The information in the article has been a great educational source in learning more about the effects behind mass media influences. I also feel that it's important to note here that a few of the case study's discussed in the article, are ones I could personally relate to, because of my past issues with body dissatisfaction and self-acceptance. In fact, it was the primary reason I decided to use the chosen article for this assignment. I felt that being able to emotionally connect to the topic discussed, would lead to a more powerful and effective summary analysis for the class assignment.

—Jessica Fernandez

Reviewed: Guimera-Lopez, Gemma, Levine, Michael P., Carracedo-Sanchez, David, Fauquet, Jordi (2010). "Influence of Mass Media on Body Image and Eating Disordered Attitudes and Behaviors in Females: A Review of Effects and Processes." *Media Psychology*, 13, 387–416. Retrieved from DOI: 10.1080/15213269.2010.525737

Adolescents and Sex

The media. Most often its connotation precedes itself, but it is to be characterized accordingly based on each individual's level of engagement, cognitive reasoning, and even the deep down subconscious. The problem is an underage individual with surging hormones and emotions and a lack thereof in the life experience department is vulnerable to the images being constantly burned into their minds.

Television, magazines, even the news these days seem to be rather consumed in explicit, often vulgar, portrayals of sex. Those include but are not limited to rape and murder on CSI, over-indulgence in alcohol, partying, abuse and even less intensive Disney Channel relationships being formed before the age of 12. Nobody ever said sex was bad, dirty, or mischievous … but I am saying the images they're displaying attract that kind of raunchy attention that maybe someone who is not feeling so loved otherwise might find attractive?

The United States has the highest rates of teenage pregnancy and birth in the Western industrialized world, and research indicates that television and other mass media are important sources of sexual information for young people. (Effects of a Peer-Led Media Literacy Curriculum on Adolescents' Knowledge and Attitudes Toward Sexual Behavior and Media Portrayals of Sex) The very same journal mentioned discusses the idea that the media holds some of the blame, while also being an educator. It held some great statistics and factual information to support that very idea.

Research indicates that sexual content and related portrayals dominate television programming content, including those programs popular with adolescents (Kunkel et al., 2003). It just goes to show, sex sells! But that's always been the case. My question is, why shock the public so forcefully? Why incorporate something into the mainstream that was once taboo, stare at the numbers of teen pregnancies sky rocket, then scratch our heads and continue on with our lives? The journal discussed the media as a significant role in the adolescents life when it comes to deciphering how to act, look behave. It mentioned that sexual media can sometimes be an educator, and while I agree with that, at the same time I'll always get that icky feeling when I'm watching friends and my 3 year old niece hears the word "twat" (I'll never live that one down.)

I think the fact of the matter is the portrayals of sex in the media have become not only assumed, but outright exploited (for lack of better words!). If it is necessary for this industry to slip it in, then I feel teens should be given the tools public schools, the home, and other trusted sources. It's not an answer to the problem, but a step in fixing the issue slowly as the media continues to bombard us with these innuendos.

—**Sara Popa**

Reviewed: Pinkleton, B. E., Austin, E., Cohen, M., Chen, Y., & Fitzgerald, E. (2008). "Effects of a Peer-Led Media Literacy Curriculum on Adolescents' Knowledge and Attitudes Toward Sexual Behavior and Media Portrayals of Sex." *Health Communication*, 23(5), 462–472. doi:10.1080/10410230802342135

Mass Media and Fear Mongering After 9/11

The Mass Media played a pivotal role it in selling the misconception that Saddam Hussein and his regime were somehow involved in the attacks of 9/11 and that they had WMDs. In hindsight we all know that this is not true. But the fact of the matter is that at the time when decisions were made the people were not informed. Americans fell into line when they followed blindly with "if you're not with us, you're against us."

Media and government were stirring the pot of false patriotism that allowed them to take any means necessary to fight terrorism. The American people were shaking in their boots at the thought of a terrorist allowing the government to pass the Patriot Bill. Allowing the government to break all liberties and rights to hunt supposed "terrorists". Not only did it take the rights away from terrorists it also took the rights of American citizens. The Media did little to nothing to inform their viewers of all the rights that were lost, almost selling it as if it were to really fight terrorists. It is the roll of the American Media industry to inform the people, keep the government in check and always remain unbiased thus to ensure the legitimacy of the context of your information. Post 9/11 it became more and more apparent that the media successfully legitimized fears before the threat of fear ever existed.

— **Frank Pinheiro**

Reviewed: Abdalla Salih, A. (2009). "The Media and American Invasion of Iraq: A Tale of Two Wars." *Journal of Arab & Muslim Media Research*, 2(1/2), 81–90.

Why We Seek Out Fear-Based Programs

This article first published in Vol. 1 Issue 4 of *Media Psychology* (1999) explained in detail the need for and findings of an experiment conducted to find out not only why people enjoy forms of entertainment that involve tragedy or death, but why it is specifically sought out as a preferred form of entertainment. As noted in this article, "…in general people want to feel good and will avoid painful situations whenever possible (e.g. Freud, 1960); they will even distort their perceptions and beliefs in order to feel good about themselves… (Goldenberg et al., p. 2)." With this in mind, it is easy to see how it would seem counter intuitive for people to not only get pleasure out of witnessing tragedy but to actively pursue tragic stories as a preferred form of entertainment. The studies conducted by Goldenberg et al. attempted to further develop, build upon, and explain past psychological and physiological theories pertaining to the seemingly natural affinity humans have towards forms of entertainment that are tragic in nature.

As stated in the foreword of the article, humanities questioning of the appeal of tragedy dates back to Plato, Aristotle, and the origins of Ancient Philosophy. Still today, there is no universally accepted theory for the, "seemingly paradoxical appeal of tragedy (Goldenberg et al., p. 2)." As stated before, most people tend to agree that the general population want to feel good. Some people will even alter memories (be it consciously or subconsciously) in a more favorable way, than what was the true reality of what took place, in an attempt to protect their mental well-being from reliving traumatizing events. In 1980, Lerner published The Belief in a Just World: A Fundamental Decision, where he presented considerable empirical evidence that the general population believes that, "the world is fair and just (i.e. good things happen to good people and bad things to bad people) and that people employ a broad range of strategies to enable themselves to maintain such beliefs in the face of contradictory evidence (Goldenberg et al., p. 2)." But with all these findings, we seem to be left with more questions than answers. And the most prominent of which seems like it has yet to be formally addressed; "Why, then, would people seek out and enjoy a genre of entertainment in which death is such a prominent outcome (Goldenberg et al., p. 2)?"

In 1997, Efran and Sprangler proposed a physiological theory which focused on the effects crying had on the human body. Their theory suggested that crying is an effect on the body that occurs to the body during a recovery phase following stimulation. Goldenberg et al. state, "From their prespective, 'All tears can be thought of as "tears of joy"' (p. 63) because crying functions to provide relief (Goldenberg et al., p. 3)." However in 1988, multiple studies began that provided significant evidence that crying actually increases one's level of arousal. Further investigation into the subject came in 1994 when de Weild, Zillmann, & Ordman found that, "purely physiological explanations for the appeal of tragedy are inadequate because they imply that arousal in the autonomic nervous system decays sharply, [when evidence shows] recovery is, in fact, a gradual process (Goldenberg et al., p. 3)." In addition to this, the purely physiological theory implies that one must physically shed tears in order to enjoy tragedy which has demonstrated to be false. Other physiological theories have been suggested such as Zillmann's excitation-transfer theory which takes into account the gradual decay of human arousal. Furthermore it states that if a story of tragedy ends with an uplifting conclusion, audiences will experience, "residual arousal from the tragic stimuli [which] will intensify the positive evaluation (Goldenberg et al., p. 3)." Haskins found evidence supporting the fact that, "...people preferred violent news stories that suggested an optimistic outlook compared to those that were entirely pessimistic (Goldenberg et al., p. 3)." And although there may be physiological evidence to support this, it does not fully explain why people have an affinity for tragic stories, considering not all tragic stories end with the traditional "Hollywood-istic" happy ending; such is the case with Macbeth.

One cognitive perspective suggests a theory that is based on social norms and expectations. It states that if someone believes they should be sad when they hear of tragic news, then there is a positive justification associated with feelings or expressions of sadness when faced with stories of tragedy. Mills explains that, "holding the attitude that it is good to empathize with suffering is positively correlated with enjoyment of tragedy (Goldenberg et al., p. 3)." But still this fails to explain why tragedy is sought after.

Taylor and colleagues further investigated Festinger's 1954 social-comparison theory, which was originally only applied to dealing with stress and illness. They revisited this theory thinking that it could possibly be used to help explain the, "seemingly paradoxical appeal of tragedy (Goldenberg et al., p. 4)." Taylor and colleagues explain, "In short, people may find tragedy appealing because they compare their own lives to the tragic characters and conclude that in comparison their situation is not so bad (Goldenberg et al., p. 4)." By combining some of these theories we begin to set the framework for how it is possible for people to get enjoyment out of seemingly unpleasant situations they themselves would desperately try to avoid. But yet again, the question as to why people seek these stories for entertainment has not been addressed.

Goldenberg et al. propose the terror management theory based on research conducted at an unmentioned university, involving undergraduate students. This experiment based was based loosely on the previous theories as well as Aristotle's catharsis theory which suggested that, "...expression of negative emotions provides relief by purging these feelings from one's system (Goldenberg et al., p. 4)." Their theory suggests that, "Aversive emotions can produce a drive toward safe expression... people may desire and seek out vicarious expression of feelings that they would rather not experience in a direct and self-relevant way (Goldenberg et al., p. 4)." As suggested before that people will use different tactics to maintain favorable mental adaptations of reality. Stories of tragedy work as an outlet for people to indirectly experience their own mortal fears without facing any real physical danger. Furthermore, actively seeking tragic entertainment is a conscious decision, one that a person's mind tends to do subconsciously to its memories in an effort to protect them.

Students who participated in this study were given a packet of materials to answer in a classroom setting. The packet included questions related to mortality salience as well as filler personality questions. The participants were then asked to answer two open-ended questions either related to their own mortality or a control subject. Students were then asked to read two excerpts from different Hemmingway novels; both of which were the same length, had similar characters, romantic undertones, but one of the excerpts ended with tragedy and the other did not. After reading the passages, the participants were asked to answer eight questions regarding how much they liked certain things about the passages as well as how they reacted to the passages emotionally.

The results suggested that, "After thinking about their own death, participants responded more emotionally to and were more touched by the tragic literary portrayal... the findings suggest that mortality salience increased the relative appeal of tragedy by leading participants to find the nontragic excerpts less enjoyable and to care less for the [character] in the nontragic excerpt (Goldenberg et al., p. 8)." This finding helps to bridge some of the gaps between the previously addressed theories by incorporating reflection on one's own mortality. However, even when participants were asked the control questions they still rated the tragic passage more favorably than the control passage. But the rating of the preferences between the two stories was more drastic with the participants who were initially asked questions pertaining to their own mortality. Although Goldenberg et al. admit that this does not fully explain the reason behind people's affinity for tragic stories, in fact they admit it needs more research, it does bridge the gap of many previous theories. Goldenberg et al. say, "...the present findings indicate that when death is on the fringes of consciousness the appeal of tragedy is actually heightened... individuals attempt to cope with [thoughts of one's death] through safe vicarious emotional expression (Goldenberg et al., p. 10)." Their research is not complete and has not produced a universally accepted answer; however it has laid down a significant framework for future research. Goldenberg et al. concluded, "... the current findings suggest that the terror management perspective may help explain why people seek out tragedy and other symbolic representations of death: They help people grapple with their vulnerabilities and inevitable demise (Goldenberg et al., p. 10)."

—Pat Fox

Reviewed: Goldenberg, J. L., Pyszczynski, T., Johnson, K. D., Greenberg, J., & Solomon, S. (1999). "The Appeal of Tragedy: A Terror Management Perspective." *Media Psychology*, 1(4), 313.

Gender Roles

The article "Gendered Relationships on Television" is written by Adrienne Ivory, Rhonda Gibson, and James Ivory and focuses on how both heterosexual and homosexual couples are portrayed in television. The article also focuses on how females and males separately are portrayed, and the stereotypes they help reinforce. Males and females on television are almost always portrayed in the same masculine/feminine way. Males are seen as strong, successful, and powerful while women are portrayed as unambitious, emotional, weak, and dependant. They are also stereotyped into the roles of dominant/submissive, with the males almost always being dominant. At the same time, gays and lesbians are also stereotyped. Gay men are usually portrayed as either masculine and athletic, or as "queens" and "fairies". (175, Tropiano) Lesbians are then shown to be butch (very manly) or femme (traditional feminine appearance). All of these stereotypes also transfer into other things for these genders, such as which type of job they have, what car they buy, how they speak, how they dress, ect. All of this stereotyping transfers into then how the relationship is perceived to be.

Research shows that both homosexual and heterosexual relationships on television are usually made up of the same two components; a dominant and a submissive. Whether it be a male and a female or two males, the relationship will be portrayed as heterosexual. This means that with two females in a relationship, one will retain the roll of the submissive (female) and one will fit the dominant (male) role. Even though that is how the media shows it to be, this is not always the case, which then gives the audience a false sense of what a homosexual couple should be (and even a heterosexual).

Television seems to be portraying their characters with a gendered frame of reference. This can be detrimental to all viewers, young and old. Children watching television start to get the idea of how males and females should act, even though television is not an accurate reference to follow, yet unfortunately children to not know this. Young girls may watch television and notice that the male seems to always be swooping down to save the damsel in distress, and on the other hand they may see a wealthy woman living off the success of her husband. Both of these examples can negatively impact child's view of the world. Young girls may start to think that they don't need to do anything because eventually they will have a man to care for them, while young boys may see that men are the protectors of woman because women are weak. This is also an important matter because by showing homosexual relationships on television and giving a certain idea of what gay men and women are like, the audience is fed false information. People who don't really interact much with homosexuals may perceive them wrongly and in a stereotyped way, using only the knowledge they've gathered from watching television.

I have learned quite a few new things from this article, but I will list some of the main ones. I never knew that sex and gender are two different things. Sex is determined by biological factors while gender is determined by different components such as cultural, social, and physiological components. Homosexual couples on television are also become more prevalent, although not necessarily any more accurate. With this information I can look at television in a different light, and also explain to others, such as future children, that you can't always depend on the tv to give you proper details on genders and relationships. Maybe I should develop a show that defies all of the stereotypes are already in place for both males and females and heterosexuals and homosexuals.

—Stephanie Suker

Reviewed: Holz Ivory, Adrienne; Gibson, Rhonda; Ivory, James D. "Gendered Relationships on Television: Portrayals of Same-Sex and Heterosexual Couples." *Mass Communication & Society*; Apr–Jun 2009, Vol. 12 Issue 2, pp. 170–192

Pharmaceutical Advertising

This paper is awfully significant and does a solid job of presenting a general overview of the problem concerning the lack of criticism of "the commodification of pharmaceuticals." The paper essentially calls for the public to adopt a much more skeptical stance towards the practice of drug advertising via the media. The pharmaceutical industry is a $400 billion per-year business, as stated in the abstract. Ever since 1997 the United States "pharmaceutical industry has been allowed to appeal to potential customers via commercial advertising," (Tracey 1). This is otherwise known as direct to consumer advertising. While the industry maintains this practice simply educates the public, the author—among many others—has a quite different view. Drugs are now a commodity, and this is reflected in virtually every aspect of their development, from inception to sales. In fact, the advertising department or agency begins their campaign for a potential new drug as soon as the drug idea is conjured up. Furthermore, and more concerning, is the effects of treating what should be a strictly medical practice left to doctors and other professionals, as a commodity, or thing, to sell and thus make profit. This undermines the integrity of the doctor-patient relationship, as potential consumers frequently assume, they have the power to almost doctor themselves. In other words, people will approach their doctors with a specific drug name in mind and diagnosis already in place so all that needs to happen for the companies and doctors to get paid is for the professional to write the script. This is a distinguishing feature as compared with other commodities as drug advertising impedes on medical authority. Switching gears a bit, one must also look at some of the statistics related to the marketing and advertising of these prescription drugs. In the year 2000, "drug companies spent $15.7 billion on promotion alone," (Tracy 14). This number is atrocious, especially when one considers the significance. One must question why so much money is spent on just promoting a new drug. Another key fact is that the United States is only one of two countries in the entire world that allow such advertising—New Zealand being the other. Why is this the case? Clearly the rest of the world disagrees rather strongly with the stances of the U.S. and New Zealand. Equally concerning is that there is currently no attempt to limit drug advertising nor is the any effective regulatory apparatus in place. As far as the media effects go, these advertisements are everywhere: television, radio, internet, and so on. People do not have much of a chance to avoid these advertisements completely. So what should one do? What can we do?

The public needs to adopt a much more critical method of thinking in regard to these powerful, incessant advertisements. Since, as for now, we cannot simply eliminate all advertisements, something must be done in the meantime. I think we as a people need to take Tracy's suggestions seriously and adopt them into our own minds and modes of thinking. A major problem is people commonly turn on the tube to veg out or relax and thus do not activate their heavy processing arenas of their mind. In other words, although there are a variety of motives as to why one turns on the television, or radio, or other medium, commonly the purpose has something to do with relaxation and thus the individuals are not prepared to do any deeper thinking than the minimum required to stay awake and follow the program. But more specifically in regard to pharmaceuticals, the psychological effects on subliminal yet profound. Commoners feel like they can self-diagnose and even recommend a treatment option simply because they viewed a certain drug advertisement a few times. This clearly undermines the medical authority of doctors who have studied and trained extensively in order to practice real medicine. So in the short term, people need to take a step back and reflect on their media usage habits. They need to think critically about these issues, such as the one mentioned in this article about pharmaceutical advertising directly to potential consumers. What about the long term or future? Nothing short of a mass revolution must occur in order to manifest any sort of fundamental change within the media system. This system is so large and strong it may seem impenetrable, but I still have hope. After all, what would happen if everyone simply turned off the television, or even just cut down on daily usage. This would certainly have visible effects, especially over time. As for me personally, I am going to continue my non-usage plan as far as television goes, and perhaps attempt to educate others. I may even write a few posts on my blog for the world wide web to see. In fact, I already have mentioned some things we have discussed in class on my website and seeing how the media system is such a large factor, I foresee more posts to come, even in the very near future. I am a big proponent of education but I recognize with education comes responsibility. For what good is an unapplied education? In this light, I will try to spread my knowledge when appropriate and whenever I can, to whomever will listen. Who knows, maybe one of my listeners, or readers, will do the same.

—Paul Hopkins

Reviewed: Tracy, J. (2003). "Hearts, Minds, and Maladies: Toward a Critical Theory of the Commodification of Pharmaceuticals." *Conference Papers—International Communication Association*, 1–25. doi:ica_proceeding_12017.PDF

Fox News Network

For my media effects research, I chose to take a look at what the consequences of media slant/bias are on viewing audiences in the article "Slanted Objectivity? Perceived Media Bias, Cable News Exposure and Political Attitudes". This article explores the detrimental effects that the fragmentation and polarization of the news media has had on both sides of the equations, as well as exploring the effect it's had on both partisans and moderates alike. It has been demonstrated in research that where bias is concerned, the same set of information can be presented to partisans on both sides and perceived by both as being biased towards the other. This is because our general perception of the media is one that's skeptical of iits journalistic objectivity, as we've been led to believe in its having an inherent bias one way or the other. This perception is referred to as the "hostile media phenomenon."

Many politicians on the right have painted a perception, one which has no real evidence to support it, that the media has a "liberal bias". Despite the lack of evidence, many republicans believe this to be accurate, and the Fox News network has been able to successfully brand itself as "fair and balanced" to appeal to this notion of a liberal bias, despite an agenda that is less "fair and balanced" and far more slanted towards right-wing politics. During the 2004 presidential election, Fox News was shown to have presented a consistently more flattering portrait of President Bush than did the other cable news networks (CNN, MSNBC, ect.) whilst simultaneously presenting a less flattering portrait of democratic nominee John Kerry than did the other cable news networks.

It has also been shown in an analysis of Fox News viewership that those who received their news from Fox News often had a skewed an inaccurate perception of Bush's foreign policy, for example, they were likely to believe that there was a proven, direct link between the 9/11 attacks by al-Qaida and Iraqi leader Saddam Hussein, which there never was. Fox viewers were also more likely to believe that the US had found weapons of mass destruction in Iraq and that there were fewet casualties in the Iraq war than there were in reality.

The dangers of this kind of partisan media is easily seen in the ignorance of many regular Fox viewers, as well as the enormous popularity of Fox News as the primary or sole source of news for many Americans. As one of the acharts in the article demonstrates, Fox News, along with being the most popularly rated among the news networks, is also the second most popular source of news out of any major news resource, the sole exception being newspapers. The shift towards a polarized and extremely partisan America is detectable even in our daily lives now. It is an issue that stems less from the media's agenda, and far more from our inability to accurately perceive and process bias in the major news networks due to a lack of information.

—Dylan Stump

Reviewed: Morris, J. (2007). "Slanted Objectivity? Perceived Media Bias, Cable News Exposure, and Political Attitudes." *Social Sciences Quarterly*, 88 (3), 707–728.

MEDIA LITERACY

Just as we now try to control atom-bomb fallout, so we will one day try to control media fallout. Education will become recognized as civil defense against media fallout. The only medium for which our education now offers some civil defense is the print medium. The educational establishment, founded in print, does not yet admit any other responsibilities

—Marshall McLuhan, *Understanding Media: The Extensions of Man (1964).*

The theory explaining why people are persuaded by information in fictional stories is called transportation. People reading a book, watching a movie or TV show, or playing a video game become transported, swept up, or lost in the story, even feeling like they themselves are part of the story. This is one of the appealing properties of media: being transported is a state of flow in which the person loses track of time because of deep engagement. When a fictional story transports us, we are persuaded rather uncritically because transportation decreases counterarguing (questioning assertions) and increases connections with the characters and the sense that the story has a reality to it. Engaging with a story means we have suspended our disbelief, and this facilitates our persuasion to points of view embedded in the story. In fact, some theorists believe that we accept beliefs not only uncritically but involuntarily.

—Karen Dill, *How Fantasy Becomes Reality : Seeing Through Media Influence*

Figure 4.1 When we hear the word literacy, we tend to think about reading and writing. And while the primary definition is the ability to write and read, the noun also relates to knowledge and proficiency in a specified area.

Figure 4.2 World travelers watching television on a British Air Boeing 747. Photo by Charlie Brewer.

CRITICAL THINKING AND MEDIA EXPOSURE

When we think of the word *literacy* we typically think about words or the print medium. Our school systems (kindergarten through 12th grades) focus on literacy (i.e., print), math, and science. Each of these mediums requires knowledge and understanding of symbols, systems of expression, along with the theories and philosophies that move their use forward. Missing from elementary, middle school, and high school educations is a focus on the symbols, systems of expression, theories, and philosophies of mediums that have evolved since the 1800s. Specifically, our educational system is woefully inadequate in teaching us how to both consume and produce static images, sound, moving images, film, video, and digital forms of expression.

And while most Americans maintain a 4+ hour per day television diet, along with several more hours attending to music, television, film, and other mass mediums on PCs, iPods, and smartphones, we also spend less than 15 minutes per day reading. In short, there's a significant disconnect between the mediums we've come to master versus those that we simply consume—mainly for the purposes of enjoyment, relaxation, and the passing of time.

The goal of this section is to provide users of visual and aural media with some tools that foster critical thinking about messages being sent by mass communicators and decoded/interpreted by us. Rather than simply succumbing to decreased activity in the prefrontal cortex, and decreased gamma wave activity, which appears to be the physiological response to viewing television according to numerous brainwave studies, beginning with those published by David E. Tupper and Keith D. Cicerone in their book *The Neuropsychology of Everyday Life: Issues in Development and Rehabilitation,* the goal of media literacy is to remain active and critically aware while consuming television shows, films, and video. The goal of media literacy is to better understand what we believe to be the goal, or agenda, of the program. How is the producer, using production elements, the script, characters, conflicts, and resolutions, trying to affect us? What is the producer's aim in sending these messages?

Because we typically watch television without giving a great deal of thought to what we watch, the notion of viewing a program critically may very well feel uncomfortable, counter-intuitive, and just plain difficult. In fact, many of my students who are asked to complete media literacy assessments of television programs report that they simply cannot view a program critically. This may very well be the fall-out from thousands of hours of viewing television for pleasure, for companionship, to relax, become stimulated, or just to be entertained. As we learned in the previous chapter, our critical thinking brains are shut down within a minute of turning on the set.

Recently, a student reported getting headaches trying to analyze a situation comedy from a media literacy/critical thinking perspective. I responded that I have had similar symptoms but that she should watch the program episode a few times in succession simply to allow the entertainment value of the program to subside. After all, what we watch is the culmination of decades refining the genre in the television medium. After several viewings, you will find it easier to analyze the program from the various perspectives that enable critical analysis. This student's question was followed by another's. He asked, "If we are watching to be entertained, does the program have the effect the producer intended on us?"

I responded by describing what's known as the *sleeper effect.* Karen Dill defines it as "persuasion through fictional narratives which increases over time as the source of the information becomes remote." When similar stories and outcomes are told over and over again, we tend to not recollect

Figure 4.3 Television set from the 1950s. Students performing media literacy assessments say that doing older television shows or those from other countries and cultures is a little easier to conduct because we are not immersed in the dominant cultural ideologies being expressed or reinforced.

where we learned them and, but at the same time, our confidence in their meanings is enhanced. In other words, the answer is "yes."

MEDIA LITERACY: AN OVERVIEW

"Media literacy" as a term means different things to different people. In general, it involves developing competencies that allow for the analysis of media messages from both a production and consumer perspective. Being media literate enables people to evaluate and create messages in a wide variety of mediums, genres, and forms. A person who is media literate is liberated by understanding the methods, techniques, grammar, syntax, and metaphors that are used in non-print mediums (i.e., radio, sound recordings, television, film, and digital media) to influence audiences.

While developing an understanding of how media influences our perspectives of our world and our place within it is important, it is also critical to understand how much influence media has on our worldview, sensibilities, and perspective on reality. The great mass of research on the topic suggests that the more we consume, the more we are consumed by it. So, media literacy begins by understanding how much time we spend watching, listening, and reading messages sent by mass communicators.

MEDIA CONSUMPTION

The first step toward becoming media literate is to become aware of one's usage or diet of mediated messages. For how many hours do we watch television on an average day? Listen to music? Watch a movie on Netflix or at a movie theater? For how many hours do we surf the Internet, play videogames, or read and post on Facebook? For many of us, most of our waking hours are consumed by exposure to the media through focused attention, as "background" as in the case of exposure to music while working at a store, or as part of a multi-tasking environment such as while going onto Facebook while watching TV and listening to your iPod.

Students in my classes are asked to record, analyze, and interpret their usage of mediated communication over a five-day period. Their findings tend to fall in line with national averages for young adults in their age groups. Let's take a look at the anecdotal and reflective summaries on media usage submitted by some of my students.

STUDENT PERSPECTIVE

Media Literacy

For this media usage project, my results were as such: I listen to the radio on an average of 45 minutes per day, I read my books/textbooks on an average about 2 hours per day, I watch TV on an average of 5 hours per day, I surf the internet on an average of 3 hours per day and I listen to music on an average of 1 hour 20 minutes per day (or about 12 hours in total). When I saw my results, I was aghast. I couldn't believe how many hours I was wasting away when I really could be studying or spending time with my family or friends. My results truly showed me that I need to get a life, and I need to get out of the house more often or find a hobby that doesn't involve the media in any way. My results indeed surprised me, but to an extent. I am well aware that I spend a lot of time watching TV and on the Internet (mainly for social networking) but I didn't know it would be this bad. I knew for a fact (before this assignment) that I didn't really listen to the radio that often (I listen to the radio when I'm on my way to school) and I thought I listened to it a whole lot less before I saw my results for this assignment. The numbers seen on this assignment show that I'm a homebody in need of a social life; it also shows that I can be bored on many occasions because when I'm bored is when I usually turn to the TV or get on the Internet. I'm surprised how low the number is for my average time spent reading my books; I really should be giving that area more attention rather than wasting my time with mindless activities. I think my grades will reflect my habit, and I don't feel too great about looking at these numbers. I now know what I will have to cut back if I want to succeed in college, and TV and internet won't help me succeed. This project was truly a wake-up call for me, and I'm glad I took part in it.

— Thankin Savidas

After examining my media usage results after a five day period, it became clear how prevalent these mediums are in my everyday life. As soon as I was consciously thinking about whether I was attending to a medium or not, I became aware of how mass media follows you everywhere. I also became aware that it was rare to not be participating in media usage. I assumed from the beginning that the internet and television would be the most used mediums for me and was surprised to discover that I was writing down music related mediums much more frequently. Since I do attend community college, I drive around a lot but never thought to record the amount of music I listen to on my drives. On a daily average I listened to the radio forty five minutes a day. Considering this, it is clear that I am exposing myself to a medium, even if I am not actively listening while driving. The radio consists not only of music, but also commercials which are used to advertise products just like television. Even if I am driving I am still experiencing the influence of mass media.

Additionally, I was being exposed to music in general on a daily basis both intentionally and unintentionally. I would listen to my personal music in the morning while getting ready for school but the bulk of listening to music occurred at work. I work at a children's clothing store which plays preselected songs that come on a new CD every month. Over the five day period I had a daily average of 2 hours of music. I had off of work for three of the five days so my daily average realistically is a lot higher. I found it interesting that even though I was at work and not actively paying attention to the medium I was still exposed to it and therefore it could potentially affect me.

After music, the next mediums that were most prevalent were television and film, which did not surprise me. When I come home from school or work one of the first things I do is check my DVR to see if I have any prerecorded shows that I missed throughout the week. I don't watch a lot of television but I do have particular shows that I follow such as Project Runway and the Big Bang Theory. I watch around an hour and a half of television and film per day. I am also taking a film class at school which also is contributing to my media usage. I also like to go to the movies a lot and stream movies as well. After television and film comes the internet which I spend around an hour a day doing. This makes sense to me since unlike most of my friends and family I do not have a smart phone nor do I use Facebook on a daily basis. The main reason I use the internet is for online shopping and homework purposes. When I was younger and in high school, my internet use would have been well over an hour but seeing as I am not near a computer for most of the day, my daily average is a little lower than most.

The last two mediums which I use on a daily basis both for under an hour are reading and video games. The only time I really play videogames is when I am hanging out with my boyfriend, which often just results in playing for an hour or so. It's not something I do by myself in my free time and it's mostly wii sports or Mario that we play not violent shooting games. I also participate in reading for a little under an hour on a daily basis. This medium is also important since I am a student and most of my classes require reading. Overall, after assessing how much time I spend on each medium on a daily basis, it is clear that I am using some form of mass communication about 8 hours out of my day. Considering I go to school and work, it seems the majority of my day is spent involved in some type of medium.

—April DeFazio

AN OVERVIEW OF MEDIA LITERACY (CRITICAL THINKING ABOUT A TELEVISION SHOW)

To view television actively and critically, we will need a set of tools. These tools will be used to conduct a formal media-literacy assessment. The tools are used in much the same way a doctor uses a stethoscope, tongue depressor, blood pressure gauge, and thermometer to understand the condition of someone's health. To view a program critically, to fully understand the messages producers are trying to send, and how these messages affect us, we will use the following set of tools called "perspectives." These tools, which act as separate lenses through which the program is analyzed, include the producer perspective, the production perspective, the ideological perspective, the cultural perspective, the character perspective, and the worldview perspective. Each perspective may yield similar or different insights into the program's agenda, main messages, and cultural reinforcement (or alternatively, cultural criticism). However, the careful application of each perspective should yield important insights that we typically miss while passively viewing a program.

Here is a brief description of each of the perspectives, including the important questions to consider while analyzing a program:

Executive Producer Perspective

The executive producer of a television program is its guiding force, its creator, its dictator, and its head writer. While movies are a director's medium, television is a producer's medium. The producer has an agenda, story, insight, or perspective that he or she is really trying to tell, which is embedded within the rule-set of a program's genre. The producer makes sure, personally, that his or her vision of the program's purpose is reflected in the final product. Similar to conducting biographical research on an author to prepare for a Literature essay or a director in a film appreciation class, television programs require biographical information on their producers.

Executive producers are typically in charge of the entire production because the show is their idea—they created it. Executive producers work closely with casting directors to ensure the actors are ideal for their roles and are the guiding force in the writer's room, making final decisions on the overall story and what characters will and will not do in each episode.

The producer clearly needs to meet the needs advanced by advertisers and networks, and has an eye on maximizing revenues, but typically he or she also has a social issue, cultural perspective, ideological perspective, or worldview that he/she wants to send. Understanding the producer's perspective requires research. What does the producer say about his or her program in the news media? What agenda is advanced in interviews (youtube.com is a wonderful source of in-depth interviews with creator/producers)? What does the producer say during commentaries in the program's DVDs?

Developing a clear picture of the producer's intent in creating, developing, and producing his or her program will go a long way in guiding your analysis using the next series of analytical perspectives.

Production Perspective

Among the producer's most important tools in communicating intended meanings are production techniques that have a mild to strong impact on how we perceive the action and dialog taking place in the program. Framing, camera angles, lighting, costumes, and sound, among others, play a critical role in how we feel and respond to the dialog, action, or comedy written into a program. The production perspective analysis requires a careful reading of the program for use of:

1. Framing (above midline, below midline, marginalized, foreground, background)
2. Camera angle (tilt down, tilt up, eye level)
3. Camera movement (toward subjects, away from subjects)
4. Laugh track (Who do we laugh with? Who do we laugh at?)

Some Insights into All in the Family by Producer Norman Lear (Campbell, 2007)

Author Sean Campbell says that he learned what's right and what's wrong by watching situation comedies (i.e., similar to social learning theory). By the mid-1970s, more than 50 million Americans watched Norman Lear's All in the Family. Archie Bunker, who headed the household, spoke in malapropisms, aligned Jews with bankers and Asians as "chinkiepuncturists." Archie represented the worldview of World War II veterans. Norman Lear intended the show to become an agent of change with regards to racial prejudice in America. People who watched the show wanted to see America improve as a society. According to Campbell, one-fifth of those interviewed in a national study who were bigoted before watching the show over several seasons, said they had gained many important insights by watching the show. The author provides additional evidence into how male heads of household changed by watching All in the Family which was one of the most effective pro-social television sitcoms in American history.

—Campbell, S. (2007). The Sitcoms of Norman Lear. Jefferson, NC: McFarland & Company.

TO SHAPE AND DIRECT THE AUDIENCE'S POINT OF VIEW: PRODUCTION APPEALS

"The instruments of discourse are increasingly being replaced by the instruments of show business."
—Neil Postman

In 1979 the Journal of Communication published a study entitled "Subtle Sex-Role Cues in Children's Commercials." The authors had taped sixty television commercials. Twenty of them showed little girls playing with toys, twenty showed little boys, and twenty, labeled neutral, showed both. They examined these commercials not for message claims but for "the level of action or movement, pacing, camera techniques such as cuts, zooms, and animation, and auditory features such as music, sound effects, and narration" (Welch et al. 203).

The study's findings illustrate that a critical thinker in today's environment needs to know about more than words. The study found that production techniques "…convey messages about masculine and feminine stereotypes at a level that is not easily recognized and therefore may be more influential than the more obvious content messages" (Welch et al.):

> Male and neutral commercials had higher rates of cuts than did female commercials. … Female commercials contained more fades and dissolves than did male commercials. Male commercials were characterized by more abrupt, instantaneous shifts in view, whereas female commercials contained more slow, smooth transitions or terminations. … Male commercials had more noise than the other types. Background music, however, occurred more often in female commercials, which were characterized by soft music forming a background to dialog or narration. Male commercials contained more loud music and sound effects that were highly salient. … The formal features that were unique to female commercials—fades and background music—convey images of softness, gentleness, predictability, and slow gradual change. At the very subtle level of visual and auditory images, then, the stereotypes of females as quiet, soft, gentle, and inactive are supported. … Messages about what is distinctively "masculine" are conveyed through a high rate of action, aggression, quick shifts from one scene to another, and a jazzed-up sound track. (205–208)

Clearly, if you want to think critically in this media age, you need to know about more than direct arguments and straightforward claims. You need to understand messages conveyed in a new form of language. Almost without exception, messages that reach the largest audiences and thus have the most potential impact are communicated via some mediated channel such as television, print, radio, music or film. Such media do not merely transmit messages in an impartial fashion. Even a situation as basic as one person seated at a desk and speaking directly to a television audience is influenced by camera angles, sound equipment, lighting, editing techniques, and stage setting, elements Rod Whitaker labels film language:

> At the risk of offending literary people, it must be recognized that the language of film is vastly more complicated than the verbal language. After all, words are only one component of the total film message, and not the most important one at that. ... In the film, which operates in time and space simultaneously, spoken words, written words, compositions, angles, lighting, histrionics, music, background sounds, montages—many content elements wash over the viewer, and the message flows on steadily, out of the control of the receiver. (6–7)

Such techniques operate in a variety of media. The most obvious are television and film, but many of the same principles apply to advertising layouts, record album covers, billboards, magazine covers, and so on.

That these techniques operate outside most viewers awareness makes them particularly powerful. Production techniques influence us whether we know it or not. Bernard Timberg describes how he came to realize this power of production elements to escape "our conscious notice while shaping our unconscious response" (135):

> Seeing General Hospital fresh after eighteen months, I realized I had developed a strong point of view about the characters, and I began to wonder how I had come to see them as I did. ... I found my point of view shaped most powerfully not by words but by visual images and sound. I suspect that these nonverbal, nonliterary forms of communication have kept many critics from understanding the rhetoric of soap opera—a rhetoric based on specific camera and sound conventions that structure the viewer's experience of the soap opera world. (133)

He cautions of the danger of not thinking critically about these conventions:

> Like the visibility of the purloined letter in Poe's short story, the very obviousness of the cinematic codes of soap opera keeps people from thinking about them and thus makes them more effective in doing their job: to shape and direct the audience's point of view. (134)

Timberg's warning is echoed by Ronald Primeau in his book *The Rhetoric of Television*:

> Ordinarily the special visual and audio effects of a TV program are not noticeable unless viewers are looking for them. A long series of close-ups will create emotional intensity without calling attention to themselves. Loud noises may make audiences irritable before they are aware of what is causing the irritation. Feelings of urgency or chaos accompany

montage segments, even though audiences may feel little sense of how carefully those segments are selected and manipulated to achieve those effects. (73)

Because the power of production techniques lies to a large extent in the fact that they work outside the realm of consciousness, the best way to begin thinking critically about them is to be able to recognize and identify them. In use, of course, production techniques work in conjunction with one another, each enhancing the other; however, for the sake of clarity here, each technique will be individually described.

The Camera's Viewpoint

"The camera has a point of view; it becomes a viewer" (46), report Kathleen Jamieson and Karlyn Campbell in The Interplay of Influence. The viewer "very readily assumes the camera's viewpoint" (Zettl 227). What that viewpoint is, therefore, is highly significant.

Five dimensions of camera technique generate this influential power: the field of view, the angle at which the camera is aimed, the type of lens on the camera, the focus used, and camera movement.

Field of View

A limited number of basic camera shots form the framework from which visual media tell their story:

1. Establishing shot—the first full shot of the scene; a wide view of the set that lets the viewer know where the scene takes place, what the mood is, what time frame we will operate in. This is the shot that lets us see the almost deserted western town from the viewpoint of the cowboy poised on the ridge. In the foreground to the side we can just see the scrawled sign "Dry Gulch, population 232."

2. Long shot—a full shot of a scene or person whether sitting or standing. Now our view of the western village is limited to the swinging saloon doors and crooked sign "Lucky Lady."

3. Medium shot—an individual shown from head to hips. The saloon doors part and Lance Lobotomy looms before us framed by his gun and his hat.

4. Medium close up—the individual's head and half the torso. The camera closes in on Lance, the frame now being his shirt pocket and hat brim.

5. Close up—an individual's head and shoulders. Now we can see that Lance is frowning and staring at us.

6. Extreme close up—the individual's face fills the screen. At this point we can clearly see Lance's vacant eyes and the frown that dissects his forehead.

Typically a scene moves through these shots like sentences in a paragraph, beginning with the establishing shot or thesis, moving to the medium shot, the medium close-up, then the close-up, in a systematic way reminiscent of grammar. Such a pattern can of course be varied for effect, and often is. Several other shots are also standard patterns:

7. The one shot—close up of one person. Lance suddenly smiles in recognition.
8. The two shot—close up of two people in a scene together. Lance reaches out and grabs Heck Hunnycutt, pulling him into the scene while slapping him on the back and drooling.
9. The over-the-shoulder shot—over one person's shoulder we see another's face, linking the two together. Hunnycutt's shoulder and hat fill the right corner of the screen and beyond them Lance nods and rolls his eyes happily.

Each of these different shots has its own rhetorical impact. To an extent, field of view matches interpersonal distances. When we are far from people, we are less involved with them; when we are intimate, we are generally very close physically as well as emotionally. The way a camera presents a person creates the same effect. Typically, a long shot creates a sense that the subject viewed is distant, merely one small part of the world we are examining; a medium shot is more interactional, conversational; a close-up generates intimacy or, in negative situations, intrusion or threat.

Jamieson and Campbell describe how these principles affect not only drama but news shows as well:
> Reporters and anchors are shown in the medium close-up and medium shot as are nearly all individuals in hard news stories. These distances are considered impartial and detached, the visual counterpart of journalistic objectivity. ... Similarly, news programs rarely show individuals full length in longer shots at what is public distance. Such distances depersonalize and decrease the emotional involvement of the viewer. They destroy the personal and social contact that is the hallmark of television news. (46)

Camera Angle

Camera angles are traditionally discussed in terms of three basic angles—eye level, below eye level and above eye level. Obviously wide variations exist within these three categories; even so, they serve as basic descriptors.

Herbert Zettl in his book *Sight, Sound, and Motion* explained why camera angles may influence:
> For some time, kings, school teachers, preachers, judges, and gods knew that sitting up high had very important effects. Not only could they see better and be seen more easily, but also they could look down on people, and the people had to look up to them.

This physical elevation has strong psychological implications. It immediately distinguishes between inferior and superior, between leader and follower, between those who have power and authority and those who have not.

The camera can do the same thing. When we look up with the camera, the object or event seems more important, more powerful, more authoritative than when we look at it straight on or even look down on it.

When we look down with the camera, the object usually loses somewhat in significance; it becomes less powerful, less important than we we look at it straight on or from below. (227)

To illustrate how camera angle generates emotional response, Haig Manoogian provides an example:

A striking example of the use of such an angle is to be found in Fred Zinnemann's High Noon (1952), in which the sheriff is alone on a street, abandoned by the people of the town, who know full well that he is to be killed by the returning gunmen. The camera pulls back to a full long shot, catching the weakness of the man's position by reducing him in size in relation to the fairly large town, now underscored in its emptiness. If you imagine the same subject, still in a lost situation but seen from a low angle, with the camera looking up, his plight loses its edge. (115)

As well, the camera's angle often determines the picture's background. Upward angles tend to be shot against the sky, cloud banks, walls, windows, all of which are positive; downward angles, on the other hand, show the subject against floors, dirt, litter, feet, and such non-inspiring subjects.

Even inanimate objects are subject to camera angle manipulation. A towering U.S. army tank looks menacing and fearful when shot from below. A harvester in a field of wheat looks powerful and efficient framed against the sky. Even an automobile "seems to be able to go faster when we look up at it." (Zettl 229)

The same camera angle that creates an image of strength can create quite an alternate effect. The camera with a low angle, looking up, can introduce strength, security, and stature. Yet, depending on the emotional qualities of the subject, the same angle can serve to intensify horror, fear, or the feeling of being overpowered. A standard procedure for monster films is the use of this angle. Nothing can be so frightening and bloodcurdling as a horned, smoke-bellowing, scaly creature, towering above on the screen at an extremely close perspective. (Manoogian 116)

What this demonstrates, in essence, is that both Superman and Godzilla can be shot effectively from much the same angle. This is not as inconsistent as it might initially seem. As a child, you craned your neck upward at all adults. A loving grandparent, taking your hand to lead you to the circus, was tall and wonderful, magnified by love and the angle at which you gazed. However, an angry neighbor, standing above you, breathing heavily while veins pulsed on his forehead as he demanded to know why you threw the rock at the window, was the same tall, magnified height seen from the same angle.

Nowhere is the question of camera impact more closely scrutinized than in presidential debates. Leslie K. Davis examined "eye-contact behavior with the camera lens" (432) in the 1976 debates. A straight angle creates the effect of looking the audience in the eye. This effect is enhanced by a medium close-up or close-up shot. Asking what kind of relationship existed between "eye-contact behavior" and the results of the debates as defined by polling measures and/or political analysts, Davis concludes that … "eye-contact behavior is a key ingredient to an evaluation of the televised Presidential Debates of 1976. … The ability to carry out a performance strategy which includes eye-contact technique may have great influence on the effect of a debate series on television" (455).

A final camera angle worthy of discussion here is the tilted angle. The familiar horizontal plane "gives us a feeling of stability" (Zettl 117). By tilting the horizontal plane, however, "We can create an intense feeling of dis-orientation." This can be used to signify "extreme physical or mental stress or simply to make a scene appear more dynamic, more energetic" (Zettl 120). As Alan Armer explains in Directing Television and Film, "The tilted shot … suggests a world that has gone awry, in which normal standards of security have disappeared" (186).

Camera Lens

Camera lenses can be divided into three categories: normal, wide angle, and long. A normal lens corresponds to the perception of the human eye and presents images with a minimum of distortion, creating the impression that the camera perceives what the eye perceives. This, coupled with the notion that seeing is believing, can lead viewers to believe they are observing reality even when they are viewing distorted images. Distortion typically occurs when images are shot through special lenses. Wide angle and long lenses can affect perception of depth. Armer notes:

> One property of the wide angle lens is that it enlarges objects in the immediate foreground and reduces background objects, distorting space, creating the illusion of greater distance than actually exists. Thus, a corridor actually twenty feet long might appear double or triple that length when photographed with a wide angle lens. (190)

Zettl points out that "relative size is greatly exaggerated by the wide angle lens. Objects close to the camera are reduced in image size quite drastically" (189). He demonstrates this in Sight, Sound, Motion with a photo of two men, one behind the other, photographed using a wide angle lens. He notes: "We perceive one man to be farther away from the other than he really is" (189). He then shows the same scene shot with an alternate lens: "When shot with a narrow-angle lens, the image size of the two men becomes more similar. They seem, therefore, to be standing much closer together than they really are" (189). The long telephoto likewise distorts perception as Clark Agnew and Neil O'Brien demonstrate with a familiar example of a horse race:

When a telephoto lens is used, the foreground, middle ground, and background all seem to be on one flat plane. When the horses turn in the backstretch and head toward the camera, they usually appear to be running furiously in the same spot for an interminable length of time. (189)

On occasion special lenses are used to distort images overtly. An Alka Seltzer commercial showed close ups photographed with a wide angle lens of characters with distorted faces, symbolic of the inside of the head in pain. In these cases the distortion is obvious.

Camera Focus

Camera focus sets mood and directs attention. Two common focus styles are the sharp focus, in which every item is clearly visible, and the soft focus, which puts a hazy touch over the picture. Typically the soft focus is used for "tender" cinematic moments, is a cue for memory (flashbacks) or imagination, and sometimes indicates the passage of time. "Reality" is more likely to be sharp and clear.

Shots also vary in terms of how much of the scene is in focus. With a long depth of field, an entire scene may be in focus. With a shallow one, only a segment of the scene is in focus and the rest is hazy. In such cases, as Armer remarks, "Camera focus tends to be needle sharp on some characters and fuzzy on others. This selective focus remains a time-honored device for directing and controlling emphasis" (179).

This can be heightened by using a technique called rack focus, changing the focal point of an image, typically from the foreground to the background or vice versa. Very quickly, certain elements in a picture cease to be in focus and certain others come into focus, forcing viewers' attention where the director wants it. So common is this technique that a spoof of soap operas, Fresno, also spoofed the technique, zooming quickly from Carol Burnett in the back of the car to her chauffeur in the front, then back again repeatedly whenever either would speak.

Frequently camera focus is used in conjunction with editing techniques. A common procedure for ending a scene, for example, is to fade out of focus to black.

Camera Movement

On the screen you see a jet black cat, observing the scene around him. He is the only witness to the family's strange disappearance. Carefully he licks his paws, never taking his eyes away from your face. Suddenly he sits up, leaps from the table and stalks silently down the hall, closer and closer to the bedroom where the furniture has been ravaged, the drawers dumped out, the clothes carefully searched and thrown in ragged heaps onto the floor. You follow him down the long hall, longing to see what he sees, what he has seen. He turns; his ears flatten and he looks directly into the camera lens, directly into your eyes, seems to stalk closer, closer, until his face fills the frame. He hisses and bares his teeth, poised ready to spring into your face, protecting the dark house with its silent secrets. You pull back, leaning away from the video cat.

We can be pulled into a story and emotionally involved by camera movement. Stephen Baker describes how pictures which move away have a "beckoning quality; moving toward the viewer, they make him instinctively draw back" (174). Manoogian elaborated on this in The Film-Maker's Art: Should the camera move forward, the viewer begins to anticipate, seek, hunt, and expect. ... Having the camera retreat de-emphasizes the subject matter and induces isolation, loneliness, and abandonment. Depending on the content, such use of the camera can help to create a shrinking revulsion, a feeling of disgust. (118)

Lighting

Lighting creates mood, directs attention, and, in the way it is angled, changes the picture. It conveys time and place and sets mood:

> Soft, indefinite lighting may suggest romance or peace; strong lighting often is used to convey a feeling of realism; abrupt changes in lighting may be effective in portraying a startling development of any kind, perhaps in emphasizing a product improvement. (Agnew and O'Brien 179)

The film Lenny demonstrated the mood-setting power of lighting, as Peter Klinge and Lee McConkey describe:

> An accident sequence was appropriately dark and wet; a flaky sex scene ... couldn't have been darker and still be recorded on film. ... The ultimate degradation, Lenny Bruce lying dead and naked on a bathroom floor, was appropriately rendered by a grainy, harshly lighted still picture.
>
> The film's few happy moments were properly bright: Honey being released from the hospital; Honey and Lenny making love shortly after they met. The most memorable was a nude Honey, posing like an Esquire calendar girl, surrounded by Lenny's gift of a thousand flowers. That was their happiest moment; it was also the brightest scene of the film. (137)

Lighting is also used to direct attention, often by lighting a subject so that "while it appears completely natural, the product is treated in a way that attracts the eye" (Agnew and O'Brien 180). This is true whether the product is Tide or a politician. Howell Raines reported in the New York Times on Ronald Reagan's use of these tactics during the 1984 presidential campaign:

Before the president's two-hour, 20-minute visit to Grand Rapids, the advance team hired a lighting contractor to make sure the president would be bathed in glowing, shadowless light suitable for a stage play, even when speaking in the dim, cavernous Westinghouse plant (qtd in Sacramento Bee A19).

Like cameras, lights can be angled onto subjects to create certain effects. The killer who leans toward his sleeping victim and pauses with his face above the bedside lamp, shadows jutting upward, has his evil intent conveyed by his lighting. When lighting is angled from below the face, "normally shadowed areas under brows, nose and chin are now fully lit. Strange shadows are seen. ... The eyes become strongly lit, the overall effect being bizarre, uncanny, horrific" (Millerson 126). Lighting from above, on the other hand, makes a subject seem gaunt: "Downward shadows grow, progressively 'aging' the subject. ... Nose and chin shadows lengthen, as do eyebrow, cheek and lip shadows" (Millerson 119). Front lighting creates a flat effect which "may help where it is diplomatic to make the subject look younger, or where a face is very strongly wrinkled" (Millerson 127). Back lighting softens, may even create a halo effect. This lighting is often seen in shampoo commercials, demonstrating highlights and glows in hair that yours never seems to have no matter how many times you wash with Jhirmack. (Perhaps you should try standing in front of a spotlight.)

Editing

Editing is the process of putting individual shots together to create a whole product. The dramatic editor as well as the news editor have great power here in terms of what standard editing devices are used, what information is omitted or included, and how the information is sequenced.

One of the most famous experiments on the impact of editing was conducted during the Twenties by Russian director Lev Kuleshov. A neutral image of actor Ivan Mozhukin was alternated with shots of a bowl of soup, an elderly woman lying in a coffin, and a little girl playing with a teddy bear. The audience was moved by the actor's hunger when looking at the bowl of soup, his sorrow at the death of his mother, his pleasure watching his daughter play. V.I. Pudovkin described the reaction: "The public raved about the acting of the artist, ... the heavy pensiveness of his mood, ... the deep sorrow, ... the light happy smile. ... But in all three cases the face was exactly the same" (Pryluch, Teddlie & Sands 685). This illustrates, asserts Armer, "an audience's ability to project their own thoughts or emotions into what they watch" (173).

Jamieson and Campbell believe audiences are aware that manipulation is possible through editing, but that awareness is rarely conscious. This is because many editing techniques have assumed certain standard meanings: "Slow motion footage is considered tender, even romantic; jumpy images are considered dramatic; extreme close-ups are considered intense and dramatic" (46). Audiences respond to these meanings without really thinking about them. Agnew and O'Brien offer other examples: "When many fairly brief shots are used, a feeling of excitement and tension tends to be created, and, at the other extreme, a long, unbroken shot may be helpful if a leisurely and restful atmosphere is wanted" (202).

Standard editing devices allow directors to create particular effects:

1. Cut—an instantaneous change from one image to another.
2. Dissolve—a slow change from shot to shot, involving a moment when the two images blend.
3. Fade—the picture vanishes gradually to black (fade-out) or appears gradually on the screen from black (fade-in).
4. Wipe—an obvious removal of one image by another by one rolling the other off the screen in one direction or another.
5. Defocus effect—one shot ends out of focus; another begins there.
6. Freeze frame—movement in the sequence is stopped, creating the effect of a photograph.
7. Zoom in and out—a character photographed in a long shot suddenly is zoomed into a close up or vice versa.
8. Slow motion—characters seem to move at an abnormally slow pace.
9. Speeded up motion—characters move very fast in jerky sequences reminiscent of silent movies.
10. Montage—many images are put together to create a single impact; often used with music for poetic or advertising effect.
11. Metric Montage—images change with the music beat.

The director also determines, as part of the editing process, which shots will be used and which will be left on the cutting room floor (or on the unedited tape) and how long the viewer will focus on one scene rather than another. A scene may be prolonged, for instance, by adding reaction cuts, the response of one character to another.

Selectivity is, of course, particularly relevant in news reports. C. Richard Hofstetter and Terry F. Buss examined this problem at some length. What will be included in a news show is based, they assess, on "judgments of relevance" which depends on "the journalists' view of the world" (518):

> A story may describe all policy alternatives and those selected by politicians, or a story may report only the "chosen" alternative while omitting others. Reporting may "legiti-mize" a policy; failing to report a policy might make it suspect. Thus some policies may become "legitimized" not because of intrinsic merit, but because of coverage received." (526–27)

Newsweek offered a clear example of how television coverage of news can vary when they discussed the impact of how news reporters covered the 1982 mideastern crises:

> By training their cameras on the stark rubble and bloody civilian casualties produced by the Israeli assault on Beirut, television reporters did more than anyone else in the media to transmit Israel's international image, once that of an embattled underdog, as something much closer to a brutal aggressor. Practically overnight, the familiar television picture of unarmed Israeli citizens bleeding and screaming after PLO terrorist attacks had been replaced by nearly nightly shots of a smiling Yasir Arafat cradling Palestinian babies in his arms. (Kaiser 58)

Newsweek quoted Zev Chafets of Israel's government press office: "Television greatly exaggerated the amount of destruction and failed to underline the underlying causes of the war" (59).

Television is not alone in its selectivity. The role of minorities in media is one scholars intermittently examine. Susan Miller systematically analyzed the Los Angeles Times and Washington Post for a six month period. Her results: "In the 46 issues sampled … photos of men outnumbered photos of women by 3 to 1 in the Post and 2 to 1 in the Times" (72). Such results no longer even surprise. But they do illustrate the power of media to create a sense of reality by selective editing.

The editor also decides how information will be sequenced. The Kuleshov experiment demonstrated the power of sequencing, but we do not have to turn to drama alone to see sequencing in action:

> A political commercial for presidential contender Howard Baker, aired during the 1980 primaries, used actual news footage showing Senator Baker responding to a question from an Iranian student. In the commercial the audience then rose to its feet in thunderous applause. But people who were in the audience reported that that was not the crowd's reaction. The commercial, through editing, reordered the event to create the illusion that the audience responded eagerly and positively to Baker's answer. (Jamieson and Campbell 49)

Another example of the power of sequencing occurred in the 1976 Presidential debates:

> … the manner in which the debates were televised altered the appearance of the "live" events by exaggerating their confrontational, or "gladiatorial," component. This was done in two ways: (a) by an overemphasis of the extent to which the candidates were interacting with each other; (b) by a corresponding underemphasis of the extent to which each candidate was interacting with members of the panel. (Messaris, Eckman and Gumpert 361)

This emphasis was accomplished by the type of television shots used and frequent cutting from one candidate to another:

> The panelists appear in a mere 11 shots in those portions of the debates in which the candidates are speaking. Since these portions of the debates contained a grand total of

313 shots…, the magnitude of the difference is quite apparent. (Messaris, Eckman and Gumpert 361)

Yet when the candidates' actual nonverbal behavior was coded from 212 shots, researchers found the candidates looking at the panel in 129 of them, at the camera in 87 shots, and in only two cases were the candidates looking at each other (Messaris, Eckman and Gumpert 362).

Visual Composition

How a magazine advertisement is laid out on a page very obviously influences what a viewer sees. What may be less obvious is that images are laid out on television and film screens as well. Harry Hepner describes the power of print layouts in Advertising—Creative Communication with Consumers:

> Eye movements over an advertisement may be directed almost as definitely as an automobile through a city. … The reader's eye must have a starting point. … This is called the "focus" or "focal point," and should, if possible, fall in or near the optical center, that is, slightly above and to the left of the exact center. This is usually a spot that is given considerable emphasis by the eyes. (444–45) … Laboratory studies of eye movements show that successive movement of the eyes following the initial fixation is toward the left and upward. (446)

But these natural eye directions can be diverted. Hepner describes two techniques that help manipulate eye directions. One he calls structural motion:

> Structural motion means that bodies of people, packages, areas, colors, or other elements are arranged to direct the reader's eye to some desired spot, such as the trademark name of the product or the first line of the copy. (446)

Zettl calls these forces vectors, arguing that "probably the strongest forces operating within the screen are directional forces, which lead our eyes from one point to another within, or even outside of, the picture field" (140):

> A vector on the screen indicates a main direction that has been established either by implication, such as arrows, things arranged in a particular line, people looking in a specific direction, or by actual screen motion, such as a man running from screen-left to screen-right or a car traveling from right to left or toward or away from the camera. (140)

The second technique Hepner identifies is called gaze motion: "Gaze motion refers to the tendency of the reader to follow the direction of the gaze of persons or animals pictured in an advertisement" (446). Thus when you see the handsome sailor looking off at the camera with a wistful look in his eye and a cigarette in his mouth, you follow his gaze toward the brand name in his sight and away from the Surgeon General's warning in the bottom corner of the page.

In his classic work Visual Persuasion, Baker presents numerous illustrations of the impact of subtle visual changes on a message's impact. One shows two versions of the same photograph of a car. One photo is cropped to leave a large segment of sky above the auto and little road before or behind it. The impression created is of a car standing still. The second photograph shows the same scene but cropped with little sky and much road stretching before and behind the car. What Baker calls the "horizontal" photograph helps to "create an illusion of the automobile's moving along the road" (83).

The layout of the TV screen is termed **framing**:

> When the television camera frames an image or scene it creates a limited two-dimensional visual field. The arrangement of elements within this defined space, the sequencing or context of the visual images, the dynamics of movement within the frame, and the images themselves all interact to create a visual message which has meaning for the viewer. (Tiemens, "1976 Debates" 363)

If an individual's head is near the top of the screen, he will fill the screen, appearing to the quite large. On the other hand, if his head is near the center of the screen, with his shoulders at the bottom of the screen, he will seem smaller. Thus framing affects image size. Similarly, how two individuals are framed in the same shot can affect how large or small they appear to be in contrast to one another. Robert Tiemens examined how such framing created a particular effect in the 1976 televised debates between Carter and Ford:

> Those shots in which both candidates appeared reveal one of the most marked discrepancies in the visual portrayal of Ford and Carter. Two-shots used in the first and third debates showed a difference in screen height which favored Ford. This is not surprising in light of the fact that Mr. Ford is three to four inches taller than Mr. Carter. ... In the second debate, however, analyses of the two-shots show a marked difference which favored Carter. (368)

After conducting his analysis, Tiemens concluded, "Differences in camera framing and composition, camera angle, screen placement, and reaction shots seemingly favored Mr. Carter" (370). That such production techniques could have an impact on the telecast of Presidential debates indicates clearly that individuals should be able to think critically about visual media.

Color

Four Tonka trucks sit on the toy store shelf—one red, one brown, one blue, and one gold. Tommy, age four, sees only one—it is red, it is shiny, it is surely the most beautiful Tonka truck ever made and, if he is very lucky, it will be his. Asked about the other choices, he voices surprise. Were there other trucks there?

Individuals are drawn to certain colors over and over. Almost everyone can list his or her favorite color without hesitation. You probably also can name certain colors you never wear, shades you prefer for furniture, for automobiles, for baby boys' clothes. If you are served blue mashed potatoes, despite the fact that your hostess assures you they are made from the finest potatoes and and simply have food coloring in them as an experiment, you may have trouble eating them. You may have experienced the feeling of being very uncomfortable in a room and realized after a while you were being influenced by the wall tones or furnishings.

At my own University, I often teach in a classroom that still astounds me. I have a theory that the University obtained paint for this room at an enormous discount because nobody with any choice in the matter would have purchased it. Three walls are battleship gray. The impact is dismal. I am reminded of battered aluminum cooking pots and galvanized garbage cans. Apparently in an effort to counter this, the fourth wall was painted yellow; not, however, a soft banana yellow, which happens to be my favorite color, but a glaring mustard yellow that could have come straight from a French's jar; this covers an entire classroom wall and oppressively dominates whatever is happening. If nothing else, the choice of paint for room 317 at least graphically demonstrates the power of color.

Colors operate somewhat like words: they have the power to influence but at times their meanings can be ambiguous. When you attempt to discern how colors in a message are influencing you, remember that colors both affect perceptions and carry symbolic meanings. The symbolic meanings may vary from culture to culture; the perceptual impacts, however, seem to be properties of the colors, although as Zettl points out, this is an area not as yet fully understood by researchers:

> Certain colors, or color groups, seem to influence our perception and emotions in fairly specific ways. Although we still do not know exactly why, some colors seem warmer than others; some seem closer or farther away. A box painted with a certain color may appear heavier than an identical box painted with another color. Some colors seem to excite us, others to calm us down.
>
> Color influences most strikingly our judgment of temperature, space, time, and weight. (68)

He provides some thought-provoking examples:

> If two identical boxes are painted, one with a cold, light green and the other with a warm, dark brown, the green one will look slightly smaller than the brown one. Under warm light, we tend to overestimate time; under cold light we underestimate time. Red and highly saturated warm colors look closer than cold colors with similar saturation. A baby tends to overreach a blue ball, but underreach a red one. Light, warm-colored areas seem to expand; dark, cold-colored ones seem to contract" (70)....

Some of our perceptions about color are formed by historical links. As Klinge and McConkey put it, "Tradition has associated cliche meaning to the primary colors" (137). They describe red as exciting; green as ambiguously hinting of life, jealousy, immaturity; blue as symbolizing cool, melancholy, calm; and yellow as representing age, disease, cowardice, and joy (137–138). Baker claims, "Gray is noncommital and reduces emotional response" (98).

Sometimes, of course, this faith in the power of colors can be taken to extremes:

> Knute Rockne, the football coach at Notre Dame, had his team's dressing room painted red, the visitors' dressing room blue, because he was convinced the red would keep his team fired up. Blue, he thought, would relax the visitors, causing them to let their guard down." (Nelson 224)

Colors are also used symbolically. While this use of color to carry symbolic messages can be widely documented, Zettl reminds us meanings are not universal: "Such symbolic associations are learned. They are, therefore, subject to habits and traditions of people, which can vary considerably from culture to culture, and from period to period" (87).

In Photographic Seeing Andrea Feininger delineated some symbolic uses of color in the American culture:

> White and lightness suggest happiness, gaiety, youth, virginity, innocence, and brides. Black and darkness symbolize seriousness, power, misery, despair, and death. ... Brown symbolizes earthiness and the soil. ... Red is the warning color par excellence—red traffic stoplights, the red flashers of police cars and ambulances, suggestive of fire, ... violence and blood. As such, red has become a symbol—the symbol of revolution (the red flag of communism), danger (red warning lights, "red alert"), virility (the "red badge of courage," "red-blooded Americans"), forcefulness, and antagonism (the toreador's red cape, he "saw red," a "red-hot temper"). (106–107)

Such symbolism is used widely by advertisers who have but a moment of your time to get a message to you. Hot days of summer, for instance, are often pictured in heavy yellow-gold tones, with hints of fire colors here and there. One air-conditioning ad shows a family sitting on an orange sofa with a deep yellow-gold carpet and similar window curtains, through which ochre rays stream. The family members are sweating, fanning themselves with cardboard fans. Clearly, this is summer without air-conditioning. If a realist were to point out that it is in summer that we have the greatest profusion of blue skies and green leaves and that those would be better symbols of summer, ad executives would laugh. The "reality" of summer is irrelevant to what is portrayed symbolically.

Symbols

In some senses visual symbols are the metaphors of video. They are easily recognized. As Whitaker points out, the film maker "can avail himself of both cultural and literary symbols. ... A shot of the flag, or of the cross, will carry its traditional cultural symbolic value...." (133). Armer explains how symbols influence:

> Often without realizing it, our minds make associations. When a character in a script is named Ethel, that character takes on resonances of everyone we have ever known, seen, or read about named Ethel. We automatically transfer feelings from those earlier associations. Similarly, when a television or movie program is tinted sepia, we recall yellowing tintypes; the program connotes the nineteenth century, which is exactly what its director anticipated. (187)

Thus a cozy fireplace means home and warmth, even in Miami; friends sitting under palm trees send Christmas greetings bedecked with falling snow.

These traditional indicators are used by news media as well as advertisers:

> Ordinary news footage takes advantage of the power of the camera. Correspondents reporting stories are framed against easily recognized locations filled with symbolic significance: the White House, Big Ben, Red Square. A story about New York may be framed against its skyline; a strike is identified by a line of pickets or a silent factory; a murder is indicated by a pool of blood on a sidewalk or a drug bust by a stack of plastic packets. In this way the topics of news stories are instantly identified for the viewer, and the authority of reporters is enhanced; they are there, on the spot. (Jamieson and Campbell 47)

While examining poison control techniques, scientists stumbled across an interesting demonstration of the power of symbols—the fact that children like pirates and are drawn to pictures that represent them. Because of the potential of this discovery, the skull and crossbones is being dropped as a symbol of poison on containers. Replacing it is one of the familiar round faces commonly seen in the form of a happy face; this one has a turned-down mouth and a tongue sticking out, a symbol children readily identify as yukky.

Sound

Hobo Willie strolls along the boulevard. He is ragged, dirty, forlorn. Suddenly he slips on a candy wrapper and begins to fall. He throws out his arms to try to balance himself, but merely throws himself into a spin, twirls along the avenue, finally landing with a thud in the gutter. Why don't you feel concerned for him? The rinky-tink music is happy; the pace is fast, the tune upbeat. You have your clues: this is a comedy.

As early as 1951, describing radio sound effects, soundman Robert Turnbull pinpointed the use of sound to generate desired responses when he wrote, "Psychology has its place in the understanding and use of sound effects. As the human mind develops, it forms definite habits of association. These associative patterns can be utilized to arouse emotional reactions...." (7). He gave multiple examples of standard sound manipulations to illustrate his point. If you consciously attend to the "background" sounds—especially music—the next time you watch your favorite television show, you may identify these in use.

- A steady sustained sound gives a feeling of directness, continuous movement, formality, stability, and, if a quiet sound, one of repose and tranquility.
- An undulating sound, varying in pitch or rhythm, expresses insistence, purposeful movement, or perseverance.
- An intermittent sound expresses informality, indecision, disorder, and lack of purpose or leadership.
- Sounds that suddenly increase in volume express a feeling of climax, intensity, concentration, impatience, and aggressiveness....
- Sounds that gradually increase in volume express a feeling of relentlessness, suspense, progress, patience, pursuit, gathering strength, resolution....
- Sounds that suddenly fade indicate a feeling of cowardice, fear, lack of purpose, loss of strength, or defeat.
- Sounds that gradually fade express a feeling of dejection, temporary defeat, possible regrouping of forces, and suspense.
- Sounds that increase in volume and suddenly stop, or are held to a specific volume level, give a feeling of opposition, conflict, and frustration....
- High-pitched sounds tend to give a lighter feeling, a gayer mood, and sometimes a feeling of tension. Low pitched sounds lean more to the morose and somber mood. (7–8)

The most pervasive of mediated sounds is music. Whitaker describes background music as "so idiomatic that the average filmgoer is unconscious of its presence" (105), adding that "it is precisely because background music operates on a level other than the conscious that it can affect the audience member so subtly and strongly" (105). A clear illustration of this was provided by the 1986 Academy Award presentation when a brief film clip of *Chariots of Fire* without its background music. What had been the key promotional scene from the film became simply a dull clip of men running barefoot on the sand without the musical motif that marked the film. Music's strong impact, according to Patrick Marsh, is emotional: "Since the subject matter of pure music is mood rather than thought, music provides one of the quickest and surest ways of controlling the moods of its listeners" (154).

Music has become so effective and expected a part of dramatic effects that its very absence is now noteworthy. The closing scene from *The Caine Mutiny* illustrates that:

No music was used during that critical moment when Queeg suffered emotional collapse. Two voices, Ferrer's and Bogart's, were those of characters—assassin and victim. Two sound effects, approximately thirteen seconds of silence (one of the longest, most effective, dramatic pauses ever sustained in a theatrical film), followed by the clicking of steel balls, were profoundly telling in their simplicity: a human being's self control had been irrevocably destroyed. (Klinge and McConkey 155)

Research

Message analysts have begun to blend the study of rhetoric and visual messages. Jane Blankenship, Marlene Fine and Leslie Davis wrote, "Sophisticated television events require that 'text' be understood to require simultaneous apprehension of the discursive (verbal texts) and the presentational (visual texts)" (36). Though this is an injunction with which few would disagree, the methodology for complying with it is less certain.

The bulk of critical studies examining the visual texts of public messages have cataloged the use of production techniques in political rhetoric, particularly presidential debates, and have been conducted not by rhetorical critics but by mass media scholars interested in the impact of media production. Consequently, the studies have focused on elements discussed in this paper, such as camera angles, field of vision (especially close-ups), editing, framing, cut-aways, reaction shots, speaker eye contact with the camera, length of time on camera, and so on. (See, for example, Davis; Hoffstetter and Buss; Messaris, Eckman and Gumpert; Morello; Tiemens, "1976 Presidential Debates," "Visual Context of Argument.") In part these studies are a reaction to a recognition voiced by Bob Tiemens about the work of rhetorical critics. He argues that "a review of the research literature on presidential debates reveals that most analyses focus on the verbal texts of the debates, giving little regard to how the visual images might shape the meaning of those texts" despite the fact that "a comprehensive interpretation of the debate's 'text' makes visual and verbal content inseparable" ("Visual Context" 140).

These studies have provided useful insights into the power of production techniques to change the feel of the event. However, initially such studies paid minimal attention to how the techniques interface with what speakers actually say. Tiemens, Sillars, Alexander, and Werling, for instance, showed how Jesse Jackson's 1984 "Rainbow Coalition" speech varied in its message as it was broadcast by NBC, CBS, ABC, CNN, and C-SPAN. They found a great difference in what network cameras showed when directors cut to shots of the audience at the convention; CBS saw a great event for Blacks and televised a strongly disproportionate number of shots of Blacks listening to the speech; ABC saw an emotionally moving speech and cut to shots of people with tears rolling down their cheeks. The study clearly demonstrated the power of editing to create different images. However, at no point did authors correlate the changing shots with the content or emotional development of Jesse Jackson's remarks.

Some recent efforts have been made to consider the two texts together. Tiemens, Hellweg, Kipper and Phillips integratee verbal and visual analyses in their assessment of the 1980 Carter–Reagan debate. Tiemens continued this approach when he examined the September 25, 1988 debate between Bush and Dukakis ("Visual Context").

Hart, Jerome and McComb reported an extensive content analysis of newscasts about the President, identifying formulas through which the news media reported both visually and verbally about presidents in action. This report is illuminating in its discussion of techniques, and does consider content to some degree, though the paper is essentially description of a genre, rather than analytical reasoning about a single message. Barker examined "the relationship between narrative structure and production techniques, as it is manifested in entertainment television" (234). Although the particulars of a given script were irrelevant to his analysis, his findings provided insight into how camera work contributed to the difference between the type of verbal text conveyed by All in the Family as contrasted with M*A*S*H.

Rhetorical critics have certainly not neglected the visual media, especially television and film; however, in most cases their efforts have focused on implications of the values suggested by the subject matter rather than its visual presentation. Rhetorical critical methods are seldom applied to visual texts. The meticulous cataloging generated by scholars of mass media is missing from most rhetorical analyses, and a systematic attempt to apply rhetorical-critical methodologies to the visual text separate from the verbal is rarely attempted.

A notable effort to blend the two is the study of the 1980 Republican Primary Debates conducted by Blankenship, Fine and Davis. Using the Burkean concept of Scene, they detailed both "verbal and visual frames" as they examined how Reagan, especially, was presented on television and what themes his rhetoric developed as he "emerged finally as scenic presence" (35).

A more recent study that examined both visual and verbal texts from a rhetorical-critical perspective is Bormann's analysis of television coverage of the 1981 hostage release as it intertwined with the Reagan Inaugural. Even Bormann's earlier work on "the Eagleton Affair" acknowledged the power of presentational media to impact rhetorical statements, though it does not develop this notion to the extent that his later piece does.

Summary

All of these production elements coordinate much as words and nonverbal expressions do to carry messages to you. They serve to arouse or to minimize your emotions, to generate reactions, to transmit information and to conceal information. Critical thinking in a mediated society demands knowing the hidden influences in information conveyed to you by media.

As you watch your favorite TV show or drool over the new red convertible advertised in People, remember to look carefully for the power of production.

1. Look to see how camera techniques change the message and your response.
   a. Field of view—how close the camera seems to be to the subject shown; which part of the image is in focus. The closer a character's face seems to be, the more intimate the feeling generated. A long shot creates distance between you and the subject.
   b. Camera angle—you assume the camera's view. Looking up at a subject makes it seem more powerful, sometimes even threatening. Looking down makes you feel superior, perhaps even sympathetic. Looking someone "straight in the eye" generates a feeling of trust.
   c. Camera lens—the eye can be deceived by the camera lens. Because we tend to believe that the camera sees what we see, we can be misled into believing the view through a wide angle lens or a telephoto is simply a normal view.
   d. Camera focus—focus helps direct attention and control mood. A sharp focus approximates reality. A soft focus signals softness, memory, hazy thought.
   e. Camera movement—we tend to follow the camera's movement. As it moves forward, we emotionally follow it. However, if the image seems to be coming at us, closer and closer, we tend to draw back. If the camera pulls away from a subject, we become less involved with it.
2. Watch to see how lighting affects the message and your reaction.
   a. Mood lighting—lighting underscores the tone of a scene, emphasizing happiness or depression, excitement or suspense.
   b. Directive lighting—by lighting only part of a scene, a lighting director can force your attention to the product or character the script calls for you to notice. A favorite trick of mystery directors, this technique is also used heavily by advertisers.
   c. Lighting angle—strong upward lighting creates a strange, sometimes horrific impact. Downward lighting ages. Straight lighting flattens details. Typically, people are lighted with multiple fill lights in order to make them look attractive. The impact of lighting angle can be most easily noted on products or special effects.
3. Be aware of the impact of editing.
   a. Standard editing techniques—these let directors create particular effects. These techniques are much more easily identified than camera lens or minimal changes in lighting.
   b. Selectivity—editing can be used to create effects by what information is included and omitted and how long information is shown.
   c. Sequencing—which shots are precede and follow one another can change the impact of messages.
4. Note how the visual composition creates particular effects.
   a. Focul point—the first part of a picture viewers see can influence what they note and what they ignore.
   b. Eye movements—structural motion or vectors and gaze motion encourage viewers to observe one part of a picture and ignore another.

    c.   Framing—how scenes are framed on television not only causes viewers to look in one place rather than another, but also affects their perception of what is shown on screen.

5.   Watch how color influences your preferences and associations.

    a.   Perceptual impact—colors appear to have properties which affect our perceptions of temperature, space, time, and weight.

    b.   Symbolic impact—through the years, certain colors have assumed certain symbolic meaning in our society. These colors can now be used to evoke those meanings.

6.   Identify visual symbols.

7.   Isolate sound effects, particularly the use of music, to determine how these impact mood.

Knowing how production techniques can be used removes you from that area of invisible influence where techniques you don't recognize can move you. You may still be frightened to see the monster tower above you in a sudden jump cut as the background music rises to a feverish pitch; you may still feel sympathy for the lost child the camera looks down on; you may still feel comradery with the friendly newsman who looks you right in the eye from a medium close up distance, like a friend across the dinner table. But at least you can pause and note some of the ways production techniques are helping to arouse those feelings in you, and you can decide for yourself if you would feel the same if the message were framed in some other way.

Works Cited

Agnew, Clark M. and Neil O'Brien. Television Advertising. New York: McGraw-Hill, 1958.

Armer, Alan A. Directing Television and Film. Belmont, California: Wadsworth, 1986.

Baker, Stephen. Visual Persuasion. New York: McGraw-Hill, 1961.

Barker, David. "Television Production Techniques as Communication." Critical Studies in Mass Communication 2 (1985): 234–46.

Benderson, Albert. "Critical Thinking." Focus. Princeton, N.J.: Educational Testing Service, 1984.

Blankenship, Jane, Marlene G. Fine, and Leslie K. Davis. "The 1980 Republican Primary Debates: The Transformation of Actor to Scene." Quarterly Journal of Speech 69 (1983): 25–36.

Bormann, Ernest G. "A Fantasy Theme Analysis of the Television Coverage of the Hostage Release and the Reagan Inaugural." Quarterly Journal of Speech 68 (1982): 133–45.

---. "The Eagleton Affair: A Fantasy Theme Analysis." Quarterly Journal of Speech 59 (1973): 143–59.

Davis, Leslie K. "Camera Eye-Contact by the Candidates in the Presidential Debates of 1976." Journalism Quarterly 55 (1978): 431–37+.

Feininger, Andreas. Photographic Seeing. Englewood Cliffs, N.J.: Prentice-Hall, 1973.

Hart, Roderick P., Patrick Jerome and Karen McComb. "Rhetorical Features of Newscasts About the President." Critical Studies in Mass Communication 1 (1984): 260–84.

Hepner, Harry. Advertising—Creative Communication with Consumers. 4th ed. New York: McGraw-Hill, 1964.

Hofstetter, C. Richard & Terry F. Buss. "Bias in Television News Coverage of Political Events: A Methodological Analysis." Journal of Broadcasting 22 (1978): 517–530.

Jamieson, Kathleen Hall and Karlyn Kohrs Campbell. The Interplay of Influence. Belmont, Ca.: Wadsworth, 1983.

Kaiser, Charles with Theodore Stranger. "The Battle Israel Lost." Newsweek. 13 Sep. 1982: 58–59.

Klinge, Peter and Lee McConkey. Introduction to Film Structure. Lanham, Maryland: University Press of America, 1982.

Manoogian, Haig P. The Film-Maker's Art. New York: Basic, 1966.

Marsh, Patrick O. Messages That Work: A Guide to Communication Design. Englewood Cliffs, New Jersey: Educational Technology Publications, 1983.

Messaris, Paul, Bruce Eckman and Gary Gumpert. "Editing Structure in the Televised Versions of the 1976 Presidential Debates." Journal of Broadcasting 23 (1979): 359–69.

Meyrowitz, Joshua. "Television and Interpersonal Behavior; Codes of Perception and Response." Inter/Media. Ed. Gary Gumpert and Robert Cathcart. New York: Oxford, 1979. 56–76.

Miller, Susan H. "The Content of News Photos: Women's and Men's Roles." Journalism Quarterly 52 (1975): 70–75.

Millerson, Gerald. The Technique of Lighting for Television and Motion Pictures. New York: Hastings House, 1972.

Morello, J.T. "Argument and Visual Structuring in the 1984 Mondale–Reagan Debates: The Medium's Influence on the Perception of Clash." Western Journal of Speech Communication 52 (1988): 277–90.

Nelson, Roy Paul. The Design of Advertising. Dubuque, Iowa: Wm. C. Brown:

Primeau, Ronald. The Rhetoric of Television. New York: Longman, 1979.

Pryluck, Calvin, Charles Teddlie and Richard Sands. "Meaning in Film/Video: Order, Time and Ambiguity." Journal of Broadcasting 26 (1982): 685–95.

Raines, Howell. New York Times 23 Sep. 1984; quoted in Sacramento Bee 23 Sep 1984, late ed.: A 19.

Tiemens, Robert K. "Television's Portrayal of the 1976 Presidential Debates: An Analysis of Visual Content." Communication Monographs 45 (1978): 362–70.

---. "The Visual Context of Argument: An Analysis of the September 25, 1988 Presidential Debate." Spheres of Argument: Procedings of the Sixth SCA/AFA Conference on Argumentation. Ed. Bruce E. Gronbeck. Annandale,Va: SCA, 1989.

Tiemens, Robert K., Susan A. Hellweg, Philip Kipper, and Steven L. Phillips. "An Integrative Verbal and Visual Analysis of the Carter–Reagan Debate." Communication Quarterly 33 (1985): 34–42.

Tiemens, Robert K., Malcolm O. Sillars, Dennis C. Alexander, David W.Erling. "Television's Coverage of Jesse Jackson's Speech to the 1984 Democratic National Convention." Journal of Broadcasting and Electronic Media. 32 (1988): 1–22.

Timberg, Bernard. "The Rhetoric of the Camera in Television Soap Opera." Television: The Critical View. Ed. Horace Newcomb. 3rd ed. New York: Oxford, 1982.

Turnbull, Robert B. Radio and Television Sound Effects. New York: Rinehart, 1951.

Welch, Renate L., Aletha Huston-Stein, John C. Wright, and Robert Plehal. "Subtle Sex-Role Cues in Children's Commercials." Journal of Communication 29 (1979): 202–09.

Whitaker, Ron. The Language of Film. Englewood Cliffs, New Jersey: Prentice-Hall, 1970.

Zettl, Herbert. Sight, Sound, Motion: Applied Media Aesthetics. Belmont, California: Wadworth, 1973.

Ideological Perspective

From *The Dictionary of Media Literacy*, Silverblatt and Elicieri define the ideological perspective as, "A media literacy technique designed to sensitize students to the prevailing ideology in media presentation. Ideology refers to the manner or content of thinking characteristic of an individual group or culture. Critical theorists argue that the media largely present the ideology of the dominant culture as a means of maintaining control. As a result, the media generally reflect the predominant ideology within a culture. This ideology is presented repeatedly in media programming. To illustrate, television most often presents a worldview reflecting a male-dominated ideology. In that sense, the media can create (or re-create) representations of reality that reflect the dominant ideology" (p. 94).

In *Media Literacy: Keys to Interpreting Media Messages*, 3rd ed., 2008, Art Silverblatt states, "Ideology refers to the system of beliefs characteristic of an individual, group, or culture." An ideology contains assumptions about how the world should operate, who should oversee this world, and the proper and appropriate relationships among its inhabitants. A significant branch of audience research and its effects, Critical and Cultural Studies, focuses "on the role of the media as a principal means by which ideology is introduced and reinforced within contemporary culture" (p. 98). These studies demonstrate that media "promote the dominant Ideology" of the culture being explored (e.g., American, Swedish, Japanese, etc.). "The media industry is owned by those people, groups, and interests that maintain economic and social control of the culture" (p. 98). In *Culture and Communication* (1990), Alan O'Conner states that the media serve as "...processes of persuasion in which we are invited to understand the world in certain ways and not others." In this regard, media develop and transmit "representations of reality that support the dominant ideology as a means of maintaining cultural control."

QUESTIONS TO ASK YOURSELF AS YOU ANALYZE YOUR PROGRAM ARE:

What is the system of beliefs, or ideology, which drives the thinking and behavior of the characters? This perspective is typically noted at the sub-text level and reinforced, or signaled, through body language, tone of voice, and production techniques—especially audience reaction (see production perspective). Other times, the ideology may be expressed overtly. For example, consider who is victimized by violence (drama) or emerges as the "butt" of the humor (at whose expense we laugh) in comedy? An analysis by Gerbner and Signorielli (1990) reveals this would be, across all primetime programming, in order: women of all ages, young boys, non-whites, foreigners, and members of the lower and upper class. From a gender-based perspective, what happens when women become assertive? Are they rewarded when they submit to a male's control? Do they become more "desirable" as a result? From whose point of view am I viewing the story? Who is the protagonist? The villain? The victim?

Other questions to answer while analyzing the program include:

1. What is valued in the episode? What is important? What are the characters hoping to achieve?
2. Is the program reinforcing a dominant ideology? How about subcultures? How do the two interact?
3. Is the program critical of the dominant ideology? What aspects of the dominant ideology are challenged?

POLITICAL IDEOLOGIES

Even situation comedies contain references to and present as "natural" or "presumed" certain beliefs and attitudes relative to the political ideology, or belief system, that underlies the story line, conflicts, resolution, and laugh lines. The following article identifies the range of political ideologies that exist in our and other cultures' belief systems. What can you learn by reading this? Which are over-represented? Under-represented? Ignored?

Presenting HUMANISM

by Jende Huang

Whether we use terms like religious liberal, spiritual progressive, or simply the religious left, believers of a more moderate stripe can be a bit of an enigma to humanists.

In contrast with the better known religious right, religious liberals generally employ less literal interpretations of their holy texts, are more focused on social justice issues (ending poverty, protecting the environment), and are less intent on imposing their own personal morality on others in terms of reproductive rights and gay marriage. Though it's always heartening to hear support from any and all quarters on these and other issues of importance to humanists–from church-state separation to stem cell research to support for global institutions such as the International Criminal Court–when it's wrapped in religious language or based on religious text, it can and should give humanists pause. They may even scoff at the theistic justifications of a religious liberal, perhaps going so far as to prefer the "consistency" of a fundamentalist believer to the "wishy-washiness" of a liberal one.

Still, the confluence of views on social issues is vital to coalition-building. Moreover, religious liberals' interpretation of matters such as abortion, gay rights, and the establishment clause raise interesting questions about the thought processes by which we all reach similar conclusions. And an analysis of these processes offers an opportunity for the humanist movement to reach out to religious liberals and draw them away from their theistic foundations toward a humanist worldview.

Humanism is analogous to science in the sense that both are concerned not only with a body of knowledge and the evidence that supports it, but with ensuring the validity of the means and methods used to gain that knowledge. For example, humanist support for the right of gays and lesbians to marry rests on the dual recognition that, 1) there is no justifiable reason to deny a set of rights to a subgroup within a society when that subgroup is harmless and only strives to acquire and maintain the same rights as society as a whole, and, 2) there is no objective evidence that homosexuality is detrimental to the lives of gays and lesbians, the people surrounding them, or society as a whole. This thereby leads to the conclusion that there is no justifiable reason to deny marriage rights to gays and lesbians.

Talk to a religious liberal and you very well could get them to reach the same conclusion. This essentially means that religious liberals, on a moral and ethical level, accept the legitimacy of gays and lesbians and their right to marry, and that religious liberals are willing to codify those rights into law. Not only is their final conclusion a humanist one, the way in which they reached their conclusion mirrors a humanist way of thinking and of understanding of the world. They have seen the lives of their gay and lesbian family members, friends, and coworkers and understand that their aspirations in life are not so different from anyone else's. Even if the religious liberal is simply parroting the views of their church or denomination, it means that at some point, someone sat down and thought through the justification.

> By asking religious liberals to identify their stance on issues and to examine the justification behind their beliefs, we may help them recognize that they have far more in common with humanists than with their conservative brethren.

However, for religious liberals this conclusion isn't enough. It's important for them to place it into the context of religious belief, and even falsely transfer the source of their conclusion to their religious worldview. This arises from a society saturated with the idea that "believing in something" is better than "believing in nothing." So they may add the caveat before or after the fact that pays lip service to their stated beliefs, or cherry pick from their religious text in support of their conclusion. What would be necessary for the dual recognition and conclusion to be reached *without* any reference by the religious liberal to supernatural beliefs or religious texts? The answer to this may actually be found within the humanist worldview.

Ideally, humanists are continually open to new ideas and new information, and refuse to be shackled by beliefs that remain outside the realm of testability. Humanists understand that the human experience, critical thinking, and reason are the best tools available as we seek to interpret our reality. Because of our evolutionary history, the basis for ethics has been hard wired into us, consisting of empathy, compassion, caring, and treating others as we would want them to treat us. And we acknowledge that our evolutionary history has built both good and bad potentials into humans and that we need to encourage those good potentials in people.

None of that last paragraph *precludes* the existence of a supernatural deity, though religious liberals may be vexed that none was mentioned. Despite the fact that God isn't named, can a liberal religionist agree with what was written? Can a liberal religionist say that our ethics must be based in human experience? Can they agree that we as a species generally have a sense of ethics wired into us, which is reinforced by society? That people have the potential to do good and bad, and that we should do what we can to encourage the good?

If they can agree with those statements, it means, in essence, that a personal god plays no day-to-day role in the life of such religious liberals. They may object to this characterization, but their resistance arises more from their need to hold on to the idea of a supreme being than anything else. Our society has been so socialized to accept the idea that believing in God is something that is "good," and even for a religious liberal, there may exist an unconscious desire to hold onto that. The realization that you don't need a god to live your life is a difficult one and one that cannot be easily acknowledged.

Self-realization in these matters is always difficult, if not impossible. According to psychologist Robert F. Morse, cognitive psychotherapy methods and principles, namely those of Rational Emotive

Psychotherapy, offer insights into how a humanist might assist a liberal believer in arriving at such important conclusions. A psychologist must first befriend the patient and gain his or her respect, and he must also avoid angering the patient by challenging or insulting the ideas that he or she might eventually give up, Morse contends. The second step is to discuss matters with the patient on which both agree, and allow the patient to discover the conflicts between what he or she already believes and the ideas that the doctor would like the patient to give up. The third step is to ask questions that will allow the patient to discover that the irrational idea they have held no longer fits in with what is already known or believed.

There are challenges of reaching someone within a clinical setting, and this difficulty is multiplied when simply encountering a religious liberal on a social level. The following are two examples of questions and ideas that can be raised:

- Thousands of years ago, our ancestors blamed gods for everything that we would now attribute to nature (droughts, thunderstorms, floods, earthquakes). Thinking over a longer period of time predisposed humanity to embrace a "god of the gaps" mentality, where everything that couldn't be explained was simply attributed to the supernatural. Could that possibly still apply today in our thinking?
- It seems difficult for religious believers of any stripe to agree on exactly what God wants or commands. Each religion has its own sacred texts, and for religions that share the same text (like the Christian Bible) there are still disagreements about what is being said. Mix this in with the fact that if you accept the Bible as truth, you're agreeing that God spread his message to pre-agricultural desert nomads who couldn't even imagine the evolution of human society over the subsequent thousands of years. Is this the best source to use when dealing with difficult ethical questions in the present day?

Topics such as these provide respectful, powerful ways to raise questions about religious ideas that are no longer credible. And by asking religious liberals to identify their stance on issues and to examine the justification behind their beliefs, we may help them recognize that they have far more in common with humanists than they do with their conservative brethren. From there, we humanists can invite them to work with us to make life on Earth better for all.

Jende Huang is the Programs Manager of the American Humanist Association.

Cultural Perspective

This is a sociological perspective that presumes there is an inequitable distribution of power within a culture, setting, or context (in this case the television program). How is power allocated and demonstrated? Who is dominant and who is submissive? Is the "pecking order" based on gender, class, race, education, sexual preference, or some other obvious demarcation between groups of people (which can be stereotyped and reflected in a single character)?

Figure 4.5 Cowboy herding cattle along Oregon State Highway 31, west of Silver Lake, Oregon in 2004. The cowboy is an American icon or symbol of our staunchly individualistic culture. Photo by Matthew Trump.

INDIVIDUALISTIC VS. COLLECTIVIST CULTURE

Cultures are typically divided into two categories: collectivist and individualist. Individualist cultures, such as those of the United States and Western Europe, emphasize personal achievement at the expense of group goals, resulting in a strong sense of competition. Collectivist cultures, such as those of China, Japan, South America, and elsewhere, emphasize family and work-group goals above individual needs or desires.

Collectivism and individualism deeply pervade cultures. People simply take their culture's stance for granted. In the U.S., things like "self-serve" buffet tables, to the "be all you can be" recruitment ad for the Army, to the staunch individualism expressed in cowboy movies reflect this deeply ingrained culture of individualism. Both ideologies have their failings. People in individualist cultures are susceptible to loneliness, and people in collectivist cultures can harbor strong fears of rejection.

According to the Psychology Wiki (http://psychology.wikia.com), Individualism is a moral, political, and social philosophy, which emphasizes individual liberty, the primary importance of the individual, and the "virtues of self-reliance" and "personal independence." Individualism embraces opposition to authority, and to all manner of controls over the individual, especially when exercised by the political state or "society." It is thus directly opposed to collectivism, which advocates subordination of the individual to the will of the society or community. It is often confused with "egoism," but an individualist need not be an egoist.

Questions to answer while analyzing the program include:

a. How do I list the characters from most to least powerful?
b. What is the source of this power (gender, age, income, knowledge, ideology)?
c. What presumptions can we make about the political ideology of the characters as we rank order them from most to least powerful?
d. Do they proceed from an individualistic or collectivist mind-set? What is the fall-out from "looking out for oneself" versus "looking out for the public good"?

Character Perspective

Each character in a program typically represents an ideology (set of beliefs, perhaps demonstrated in lifestyle) or embodies ideological positions based on the interests they represent. Protagonists typically epitomize characteristics considered admirable by the producer (or dominant culture) while antagonists do not. If you plot the characters in the program along with the ideologies they represent, you can learn some interesting things about what is endorsed and not endorsed by the producer. Questions to answer while analyzing the program include:

a. What does each major character represent from an ideological perspective?
   a. How about the lead or major character?
   b. How about the other major characters?
   c. How about the minor characters (typically stereotyped)?
b. How is each character treated in terms of conformance with or deviation from the dominant ideological perspective?
c. How do representatives of subcultures affect the dominant ideology?

Myths of Romantic Conflict in the Television Situation Comedy

By Aileen L. Buslig
Concordia College, Morrhead

Anthony M. Ocaña
North Dakota State University

Love and fighting have gone hand-in-hand in portrayals of couples' romantic relationships since the earliest days of television. "To the moon, Alice," Ralph Cramden would bellow at his wife on the 1950s sitcom, *The Honeymooners*, as he threatened to punch her "right in the kisser." Yet the message behind the constant bickering between Ralph and Alice was that fighting is really an indicator of the love they felt for each other. Although threats of physical abuse may be used as sources of humor less frequently in today's sitcom relationships, the myth that "bickering and fighting a lot mean that a man and a woman really love each other passionately" (Myth #8; Galician, 2004, p. 185) remains a prominent message in many sitcoms.

The television situation comedy (or sitcom) has been a popular form of entertainment for more than 50 years (Auter, 1990). Defined as a (usually half-hour) episodic series with a small cast of regular characters in a primarily humorous context (Cantor, 1980; Hough, 1981), the sitcom usually centers around a husband and wife and their family in some way, although nondomestic sitcoms also center around themes such as business or working groups, fantasy, or some other "situation" (Hough, 1981). However, it is quite common to find that romantic relationships figure prominently in the story lines of both domestic and nondomestic sitcoms and for conflict to be a source of humor in those relationships. The sitcom's long and lasting presence throughout the history of television and its ever-increasing sophistication and quality (Hough, 1981; Perkinson, 1991), leads one to ask the following question: What are the potential effects of the situation comedy on television audiences, particularly in reference to how people view conflict in romantic relationships? To begin to answer this question, one must first examine a primary component of the sitcom, the element of humor.

Effects of Humor

Although sitcoms may seem relatively benign, research suggests that the use of humor in a message can influence people without their conscious understanding of that influence. For example, as a method of gaining and sustaining attention, humor has been linked to improved memory and recall, because one must attend to a message for learning to occur in the first place (Oppliger, 2003; Schmidt, 1994). Additionally, the pleasurable arousal changes associated with the cognitive contemplation of humor is similarly expected to influence learning of information presented in a humorous way (McGhee, 1979, 1980). Other theorists have argued that humor is effective in reducing stress and tension and can help to put people into a better, more positive, mental state in which information is well received (Freud, 1963; Grotjahn, 1957/1966; McGhee, 1980). Furthermore, the stress reduction facilitated by humor is also likely to increase the persuasiveness of a message because the induced "positive mood" becomes associated with the message favorably (Cantor & Venus, 1980).

So what is to be made of the messages conveyed in sitcoms? More than 20 years ago, after conducting a 30-year evaluation of sitcoms, Hough (1981) bleakly proclaimed that sitcoms tend to be superficial and simplistic and lacking in dramatic depth. He hastened to add, however, that occasionally sitcoms have transcended their genre, undertaking serious topics with sensitivity (albeit generally with a happy ending), and he predicted hopefully that the future would increase this trend in television sitcoms. Certainly, it can be argued that sitcoms have become more sophisticated and realistic in their portrayal of relationships since Hough's research was conducted, as the best of the current sitcoms have regularly addressed real life concerns and recent events intelligently, while still managing to entertain their audiences. However, the question remains whether sitcoms portray the effects of conflict, a serious issue in itself, realistically.

Sitcom Conflicts and Real Life

Although Gottman (1994) suggested that some married couples who seem to "live to fight" (described as *volatiles*) can have successful marriages, he made sure to emphasize that even volatile couples must experience several positive interactions for every negative one they have. Gottman (1994) also warned that the volatile style is the riskiest of the three pure conflict styles that couples might adopt in their marriage, and the potential for excessive and hurtful conflict can cause irreparable damage to a romantic relationship. As Galician (2004) prescribed, "Courtesy counts" (p. 190) in real romantic relationships. Nevertheless, hurtful messages have been shown to be prevalent in sitcoms (Buslig & Ocaña, 2003).

One should also note that two other media myths contribute to conflict situations in real life. The belief that "your true soul mate should KNOW what you're thinking or feeling (without having to tell)" (Myth #3; Galician, 2004, p. 135) leads to less successful conflict management, yet becomes perfect fodder for humor in the television sitcom. Believing that "the love of a good and faithful true woman [or man] can change a man [or woman] from a 'beast' into a 'prince' [or 'princess']" (Myth #7; Galician, 2004, p. 177) has also been the premise of many sitcoms or sitcom episodes, to the detriment of real people everywhere.

As viewers watch sitcom couples engage in conflict, it would seem easy to dismiss the argument that sitcoms, given their frivolous nature, can influence viewers' expectations of romantic relationships. However, one cannot ignore the powerful draw that humor has over large numbers of television viewers or the subtly persuasive effects of humor on memory. To determine whether dysfunctional conflict behaviors are presented as normal in successful romantic relationships, we examine how modern television sitcoms perpetuate myths regarding mind reading (Myth #3), partner transformation (Myth #7), and, most important of all, the belief that conflict is key to loving romantic relationships (Myth #8).

RQ: To what extent do television sitcoms reinforce or counteract media myths about conflict in romantic relationships?

Method

To examine if and, if so, how Myth #8 is reinforced in current sitcoms, we conducted a content analysis. Additionally, examples of dialogue from analyzed sitcoms were used to illustrate the media myths supported or contradicted in the episodes.

Sample

Every sitcom shown during a one-week timeframe (January 511, 2003) on the four major networks (ABC, CBS, FOX, and NBC) was videotaped for coding and analysis. If any given sitcom was shown more than once, only the first episode was analyzed. A total of 25 episodes[1] were collected.

---

1   The shows and couples coded for this study include: (ABC) *8 Simple Rules*, Cate/Paul; *According to Jim*, Cheryl/Jim; *The Drew Carey Show*, Kelly/Drew; *George Lopez*, Angie/George; *Less Than Perfect*, Claude/Charlie; *Life with Bonnie*, Bonnie/Mark, Holly/Nicky*; *My Wife and Kids*, Wanda/Michael; (CBS) *Becker*, (no romantic couple); *Everybody Loves Raymond*, Debra/Ray, Marie/Frank; *King of Queens*, Carrie/ Doug, Kelly/Deacon*; *Still Standing*, Judy/Bill; *Yes, Dear*, Christine/Jimmy, Kim/Greg; (FOX) *Andy Richter Controls the Universe*, Wendy/Keith*; *King of the Hill*, Peggy/Hank; *Malcolm in the Middle*, Allison/ Reese, Nikki/Malcolm, Lois/Hal*, Piama/Francis; *The Simpsons*, Edna/Seymour, Marge/Homer*; *That 70s Show*, -Donna/Eric, Jackie/ Steven, Kitty/Red, Nina/ Fez; (NBC) *Frasier*, Daphne/Niles*; *Friends*, Monica/Chandler, Rachel/Ross; *Good Morning, Miami*, Dylan/Gavin; *Hidden Hills*, Janine/Doug, Sarah/Zack; *The In-laws*, Alex/Matt, Marlene/Victor; *Just Shoot Me*, Maya/Elliot*; *Scrubs*, Carla/Turk, Elliot/JD, Lisa/JD, Mrs./Dr. Kelso; *Will & Grace*, Karen/Milo*. Couples marked with an asterisk (*) engaged in no direct conflict with each other during the show's episode.

Unit of Analysis

The unit of analysis for the study was the *conflict episode*. Based on Wilmot and Hocker's (2001) definition, a conflict episode consisted of an expressed or implied frustration with one's partner and the response it engendered. For the current study only direct conflict between romantic partners in which both partners were present and engaged with one another was coded. Of the 25 sitcom episodes collected for analysis, 20 episodes contained at least one instance of conflict between romantically involved partners, for a total of 123 conflict episodes coded. Of the 5 episodes that did not contain conflict, one show *(Becker)* did not contain a romantic relationship and therefore provided no data for analysis. Another show *(Will & Grace)* contained indirect conflict, in which the couple used avoidance (Wilmot & Hocker, 2001) to deal with the conflict they had with one another, and the relationship was terminated by the end of the show. Three other shows *(Frasier, Just Shoot Me,* and *Andy Richter Controls the Universe)* contained a romantic relationship in which the couples did not engage in conflict during the episode, and all three relationships ended on a positive note by the end of the episode.

Coding Categories

Conflict episodes were analyzed by two coders so that inter-rater reliability could be calculated. Coders practiced together using two sitcom episodes not included in the final report, reporting after each conflict episode how they had evaluated it individually and discussing the episode until they came to consensus. For the actual study, for an episode to be counted as a conflict, both coders had to agree that a conflict had occurred, at which point they coded the event separately. Inter-rater reliabilities were calculated using Cohen's kappa (Cohen, 1960) for nominal-level variables and using Ebel's intraclass correlation (Guilford, 1954) for ratio-level variables. These are reported below.

Character Qualities

Characters involved in a conflict episode were coded for gender, sexual orientation, and character status (major/minor). Characters could be either major or minor to the sitcom, but at least one of those involved in the conflict episode had to be a regular character. Only conflicts involving characters involved in a romantic relationship were coded. Inter-rater reliabilities were calculated using Cohen's kappa (Cohen, 1960): for gender of senders and receivers, 96.7% agreement (k = .93), and for sender and receiver status as a major or minor character, 99.2% agreement (k = .95), with disagreements reflecting different opinions between coders on which partner initiated the conflict. There was 100% agreement between coders for all characters' sexual orientation.

Conflict Qualities

Qualities of the conflict episode itself were also coded, including the target of the conflict, the duration of the conflict, the valence of the conflict outcome, and the media myth or prescription (Galician, 2004) that was illustrated.

Coders determined whether the *target* of a conflict was a partner's behavior (e.g., partner neglected to do a requested chore), a partner's personality (e.g., partner is a "snob"), someone other than the partner (e.g., a family member or co-worker) the situation in which the partners find themselves (e.g., an overdrawn bank account) or some other cause. The length of time (i.e., *duration*) a couple spent engaged in a specific conflict was also recorded. Inter-rater agreement for these qualities of conflict was acceptable: conflict target, 83.6% agreement (k = .73) conflict duration, 99% agreement (k = .99). Additionally, to determine the proportion of time a particular couple engaged in conflict versus nonconflict interaction, the overall amount of time a couple appeared on-screen together or engaged in conversation with one another was measured. Because of the high intercoder reliability for conflict duration, this additional duration measurement was determined by only one coder.

Coders also determined whether the outcome *valence* of the entire conflict episode appeared to be positive and constructive for the relationship or negative and destructive to the relationship. Also coded was whether the conflict involved any of the pertinent media *myths* (Galician, 2004), including mind reading (Myth #3) partner transformation (Myth #7), or simply bickering (Myth #8), or instead illustrated Galician's (2004) corresponding *prescriptions*, "Communicate courageously" (Rx #3; p. 135), "Cease correcting and controlling; you can't change others (only yourself!)" (Rx #7; p. 177), or "Courtesy counts: Constant conflicts create chaos" (Rx #8; p. 185). Inter-rater agreement for these qualities of conflict was also acceptable: conflict outcome valence, 93.4% agreement (k =.83); conflict myth/prescription, 91.8% agreement (k = .83).

Results

A total of 41 different romantic couples were portrayed in 25 sitcoms over a 1-week time frame. Couples represented those who were married (n = 25, 61.0%), engaged (n = 2, 4.9%), dating (n = 12, 29.3%), and ex-daters for whom romantic tension was implied and evident (n = 2, 4-9%). All romantic relationships portrayed were heterosexual in nature, and most individual characters (N = 82) were major players on a show (n = 68, 82.9%). The total amount of time couples were portrayed interacting or appearing together on screen, regardless of whether they were engaging in conflict or not, averaged only 4 minutes (M = 236 seconds, *SD* = 225.8) per show. However, individual couples' interactions ranged from less than 1 second to more than 14 minutes (875 seconds) per show.

Characteristics of Conflict Episodes

As stated previously, a total of 123 conflict episodes were coded in sitcoms over a period of 1 week. During these conflict episodes, females (n = 73, 59.3%) initiated conflict more frequently than did males (n = 50, 40.7%). The target of the conflict was most frequently partner's behavior (n = 74, 60.2%), followed by the situation (n = 17, 13.8%), other people (n = 15, 12.2%), the partner's personality (n = 14, 11.4%), or another cause (n = 3, 2.4%).

Conflict episodes ranged widely in duration, from 2 to 245 seconds, with an average length just over half a minute (M = 34.2 seconds, SD = 38.8). Over an entire sitcom episode, the frequency of conflict episodes also varied, from 0 to 9 conflicts per couple, with an average of 3 conflicts (M = 3.00, SD = 2.70) for the 41 romantic couples portrayed. The total amount of time spent in conflict ranged from 0 seconds to more than 8 minutes (508 seconds) per romantic couple (M = 102.5 seconds, SD = 122.7). A comparison of conflict versus nonconflict interaction revealed that an average of almost 40% (M = .38, SD = .29) of couples' time together was spent in conflict.

Portrayals of Media Myths

Because 8 of the 41 romantic couples portrayed in the sitcoms viewed for this study did not engage in direct conflict during the week data were collected, conflict behaviors were analyzed for a total of 33 couples. Relationship types of the 33 couples were similar to the original 41 couples reported above: married (n = 20, 60.6%), engaged (n = 2, 6.1%), dating (n = 9, 27.3%), and ex-daters (n = 2, 6.1%). Also as before, most characters (n = 66) played a major part on a show (n = 57, 86.4%).

Media stereotypes were prominent in the romantic conflicts portrayed in television sitcoms, with most conflicts perpetuating Myth #8, bickering and fighting a lot are the key to a loving relationship (n = 85, 69.1%). Although general bickering predominated, other myths also factored into causes of some conflicts, as some characters tried to transform their partner's "beastly" behaviors (Myth #7, n = 13, 10.6%) or became upset because they expected their partner to be able to ascertain their wants and needs without being told (Myth #3, *n* = 9, 7.3%). Portrayals of Galician's (2004) prescriptions made up fewer than 15% of the strategies used by characters to address conflict situations (courtesy, n = 8, 6.5%; courage to ask, n = 5, 4.1%; cease controlling, n = 3, 2.4%).

More frequently than not, the individual conflict episode resulted in a negatively valenced outcome (n = 93, 75.6%). Using chi-square analysis, this finding was probed further, revealing a significant difference between the valance of conflicts when a myth versus a prescription was portrayed, $X^2(1, N = 123) = 39.7$, p< 001. When myths were portrayed, 85% of the time they were negatively valenced (n = 91), whereas prescriptions were negatively valenced only 12.5% of the time (n = 2). The reverse of this pattern was seen when positively valenced conflict episodes were evaluated. Only 15% of conflict episodes depicting myths (n= 16) were viewed as having positively valenced outcomes, whereas 87.5% (n = 14) of conflicts depicting prescriptions were evaluated as having positive outcomes.

Furthermore, conflicts that had a positively valenced outcome (m = 55.6 seconds, SD = 55.32) took twice as long on average as conflicts that where negatively valenced (m = 27.3 seconds, SD = 28.9). Similarly, conflict episodes in which Galician's (2004) prescriptions were demonstrated (m = 46.4 seconds, SD = 44.0) generally took longer than conflict episodes that illustrated media myths (m = 32.4 seconds, SD = 37.9).

Discussion

The proportion of time partners were shown in conflict with each other during a show might suggest to viewers that conflict is frequent, natural, and expected as a significant part of one's romantic relationships. For example, on the aptly titled *Still Standing* (Filisha, Hamil, & Weyman, 2003), married couple Bill and Judy spent more than 75% of .their time together in conflict, bickering about each other's behavior ("How come you didn't answer the phone?"; "Aren't you over-reacting a little?"; "How come you're still watching the game? You're supposed to be taking this box to Goodwill"), and expectations of mind reading:

> **Judy:** I can t believe you told [our daughter] about Gina Morelli.
> **Bill:** If you're going to lie, you have to tell me.

If, as Gottman (1994) suggested, couples should experience five positive interactions for every one negative interaction, many couples in today's sitcoms are falling far short of this goal. Although engaging in conflict is better than ignoring or being indifferent to one's partner (Gottman & DeClaire, 2001), it is still a risky endeavor when excessive. However, the prevalence of conflict between romantic partners in television sitcoms may be interpreted by viewers as endorsement of this classic media myth (Galician, 2004).

Furthermore, television sitcoms send mixed messages about the impact of conflict on relationships. On one hand, individual conflict episodes usually imply a negative (short-term) outcome, yet by the end of a show episode, the long-term impact on the relationship appears to be a positive one, as the couple expresses love or other positive regard for each other. For example, Dylan and Gavin (*Good Morning, Miami*; Goldstein & Bonerz, 2003) have negative conflicts related to all three myths coded in the current study: mind reading ("If you don't get why this is so important to me, [then you should go to St. Barts alone]"); transforming ("Can't you pretend to be gracious?"); and bickering ("Why do you have to be like that?"). In the end, however, the couple has renewed its commitment to the relationship, proving that love conquers all. The happy ending prevalent in sitcom romantic relationships seems to reinforce the myth that conflict is good for relationships, regardless of its valence.

However, when prescriptions are presented in sitcoms, they are not presented in a way that is rewarding to the audience. They are frequently associated with serious moments, not humorous ones, or when funny they are sometimes associated with a negative impact on the character. In an episode in which Malcolm (*Malcolm in the Middle;* Murphy, Thompson, & Melman, 2003) is uncharacteristically courteous in conflict situations with his girlfriend (and others), he is hospitalized with a peptic ulcer later in the show. His courtesy is shown to have a positive impact on his relationships, but the price for being courteous is his health. In a different example, Christine *(Yes, Dear;* Bowman, Pennie, & Meyer, 2003) ceases trying to control the beastly behavior of her husband, Jimmy, only to find that Jimmy's hurtful comments are overheard by their son, who runs from the room upset. The underlying message in this instance seems to be that Christine's (normally) controlling behavior is necessary for the happiness of the family.

However, in some instances, sitcoms do seem to depict the complexity of real conflict episodes. Some conflicts are shown to change as they progress, illustrating how a negative interaction can be altered by the introduction of positive communication behaviors like those prescribed by Galician (2004). For example, the final conflict between Cheryl and Jim *(According to Jim;* Driscoll & MacKenzie, 2003), which lasted over 4 minutes, began as Cheryl gave Jim the silent treatment, because of a previous transgression in the show. As it evolved, the conflict behavior shifted from an expectation of mind reading (the origin of the conflict), to having the courage to ask in an attempt to understand each other. A courteous discussion followed, resulting in Jim's finally understanding Cheryl's position and Cheryl's proclaiming, "You get it!" The lengthiness of Cheryl and Jim's final interaction aligns with previous conflict research (e.g., Wilmot & Hocker, 2001) that suggested that it takes time and effort to collaboratively work through conflict to achieve a positive outcome. The role of time in conflict is reinforced by the current study's findings, that positively valenced outcomes and those conflicts that included prescriptions took longer than negative-outcome and myth conflicts.

Conclusion

Although the primary purpose of sitcoms is to entertain, the messages sitcoms send can tech harmful lessons about how romantic couples should handle conflict. By prominently portraying bickering, mind reading, and transforming as regular and humorous behavior enacted by couple in romantic relationships, the belief that such behavior are good for relationship is reinforced, In turn, the prescriptions to be courteous, to have the courage to ask, and to cease controlling are frequently presented as either the serious, less exiting side of relationship or as negatively consequential. Humor often from conflict in sitcoms, but the repercussions of hurtful and harmful couple interactions are rarely shown. Audiences may know that they should not take sitcoms seriously, but regular associations between the fun of humor in harmful interactions and the outcome of happy relationships may be difficult to overcome.

Study Questions/Recommended Exercises

1. In this study, Buslig and Ocaña found that conflicts that involved one or more of Galician's prescriptions took longer to resolve than conflicts involving only myths. Why do you think this is?

2. Buslig and Ocaña also found that female characters are more likely to initiate conflict with their partners than male characters, which is consistent with research in actual interpersonal relationships. Do you think the differences in conflict initiation are due to gender, or are there other factors that might explain the difference in conflict initiation.

3. Do you think situation comedies would be as interesting if they primarily represented Galician's prescriptions for healthy relationships rather than the myths about love? What is the role of conflict as a driving force behind many of the story lines in sitcoms? In other words, why does conflict seem to be more interesting to watch than healthy interactions between couples?

4. How do you think sitcoms compare to dramas in terms of their portrayals of the conflict myths discussed in this selection? Observe how conflict is handled between romantic partners in a television drama. Are the consequences of handling conflict poorly different in dramatic series than in humorous ones?

5. Choose an episode of your favorite sitcom, and watch for portrayals of the myths studied in this selection. For each instance of bickering (Myth #8), transforming (Myth #7), or mind reading (Myth #3) that you observe, how would you use Galician's prescriptions to rewrite the script to result in healthy and effective interaction?

References

Auter, P. J. (1990). Analysis of the ratings for television comedy programs 19501959: The end of "Berlesque." *Mass Communication Review, 17*, 23–32.

Bowman, B. (Writer), Pennie, M. (Writer), & Meyer, J. (Director) (2003). Trophy husband [Television series episode]. In A. Kirschenbaum, & G. T. Garcia (Producers) *Yes, dear*. New York: Columbia Broadcasting System.

Buslig, A. L. S., & Oca–a, A. M. (2003). *"I love you, Dr. Slutbunny": Hurtful gender messages in TV sitcoms*. Paper presented at the annual meeting of the Central States Communication Association, Omaha, NE.

Cantor, M. G. (1980). *Prime-time television: Content and control.* Beverly Hills, CA: Sage.

Cantor, J., & Venus, P (1980). The effect of humor on recall of a radio advertisement. *Journal Broadcasting, 24,* 13–22.

Cohen, J. (1960). A coefficient of agreement for nominal scales. *Educational and Psychological Measurement, 20,* 37–46.

Driscoll, M. (Writer), & MacKenzie, P. C. (Director). (2003). Moral dilemma [Televisionseries episode]. In J. Belushi, T. Newman, J. Stark, S. Bukinik, & M. Gurvitz (Producers) *According to Jim.* Burbank, CA: American Broadcasting Company.

Filisha, C. (Writer), Hamil, J. (Writer), & Weyman, A. D. (Director). (2003). Still bullying [Television series episode]. In D. Burroughs, T. Doyle, & J. Gutierrez (Producers), *Still standing.* New York: Columbia Broadcasting System.

Freud, S. *(1963). Jokes and their relation to the unconscious* (J. Strachey, Trans.). New York: *W.W.* Norton.

Galician, M.-L. (2004). *Sex, love, and romance in the mass media: Analysis and criticism of unrealistic portrayals and their influence.* Mahwah, Nj: Lawrence Erlbaum Associates.

Goldstein, J. (Writer), & Bonerz, E (Director). (2003). The big leap [Television series episode]. In D. Kohan & M. Mutchnick (Producers). *Good morning, Miami.* New York: National Broadcasting Company.

Gottman, J. M. (1994). *Why marriages succeed or fail* New York: Simon & Schuster.

Gottman, J. M., & DeClaire, J. (2001). *The relationship cure: A 5 step guide for building better connections with family, friends, and lovers.* New York: Crown.

Grotjahn, M. (1966). *Beyond laughter: Humor and the subconscious.* New York: McGraw-Hill. (Original work published 1957)

Guilford, J. E (1954). *Psychometric methods.* New York: McGraw-Hill

Hough, A. (1981). Trials and tribulations: Thirty years of sitcoms. In R. P Adler (Ed.) *Understanding television: Essays on television as a social and cultural force* (pp. 201–224). New York: Praeger.

McGhee, P E. (1979). *Humor: Its origin and development.* San Francisco: W. H. Freeman.

McGhee, P E. (1980). Toward the integration of entertainment and educational functions of television: The role of humor. In P. H. Tannenbaum (Ed.), *The entertainment functions of television* (pp. 18–208). Hillsdale, NJ: Lawrence Erlbaum Associates.

Murphy, G. (Writer), Thompson, N. (Writer), & Melman, J. (Director). (2003). Malcolm holds his tongue [Television series episode]. In L. Boomer (Producer), *Malcolm in the middle.* Beverly Hills, CA: Fox Broadcasting Company.

Oppliger, P. A. (2003). Humor and learning. In J. Bryant, D. Roskos-Ewoldsen, &. J. Cantor (Eds.), *Communication and emotion: Essays in honor of Dolf Zillmann* (pp. 255273). Mahwah, NJ: Lawrence Erlbaum Associates.

Perkinson, H. J. (1991). *Getting better: Television and moral progress*. New Brunswick, NJ: transaction.

Schmidt, S. S. (1994). Effects of humor on sentence memory. *Journal of Experimental Psychology* 20,953–967.

Wilmot, W. W., & Hocker, J. L. (2001). *Interpersonal conflict* (6th ed.). New York: McGraw-Hill.

Aileen L. S. Buslig (B.ARCH., *University of Miami, 1989; M.A. and Ph.D., University of Arizona, 1991, 1996*) has been *studying and teaching interpersonal communication for 15 years, although she has been an observer of relationships for as long as she can remember. A "Southerner" living in Fargo, ND, Dr. Buslig loves being an associate professor and codirector of the honors program for the Communication Studies and Theatre Art Department at Concordia College in Moorhead, MN, where she teaches a variety of courses, including interpersonal communication, communication theory, and research methods, as well as a special topics course on communication and gender. As an undergraduate, Dr. Buslig studied architecture, but after discovering some communication courses by accident, she decided to change directions after graduation. Following her desire to combine the study of architecture with her interest in communication behavior and interaction, Dr. Buslig earned her masters and doctorate at the University of Arizona. Reflecting her diverse interests, she has presented and published research on interpersonal privacy and deception, gender images in the media, the effects of architecture on emotional reactions and human interactions, and ethnocentrism in the United States before and after September 11. Dr. Buslig practices her communication skills with her husband, Anthony Ocaña, with whom she almost always has constructive conflict.*

Anthony M Ocaña (B.A., *University of California, Santa Barbara, 1996) is a Presidential Fellow completing his Ph.D. in the Department of Communication at North Dakota State University in Fargo, ND. While studying communication as an undergraduate, Anthony developed his interest in mediation and conflict resolution. He applies his training in both traditional and transformative styles of alternative dispute resolution to his research on roommate conflict, conflict process and outcome satisfaction among divorcing couples, and the role of listening in mediation. In addition to conflict research, Anthony participates in and presents research on communication assertiveness, persuasive message effectiveness, organizational change and communication, media gender messages, and jury decision-making processes, and he recently received a "top three" paper award in the communication theory division of the Western States Communication Association for his research on Door-inThe-Face theory. While completing his degree, Anthony teaches undergraduate courses in communication and conflict, public speaking, business and professional communication, and research methods. In his spare time, Anthony enjoys traveling to different international locations with his wife, Dr. Aileen Buslig, and collecting stamps from the various countries they visit.*

Worldview Perspective

If the people and issues represented within a program reflect how the producer sees the world, how would we describe what he or she sees? How does this vision limit or enable what occurs in the program? What ideologies predominate?

The term "worldview" denotes a comprehensive set of opinions, seen as an organic unity, about the world as the medium and exercise of human existence. It serves as a framework for generating various dimensions of human perception and experience like knowledge, politics, economics, religion, culture, science, and ethics. For example, worldview of causality as unidirectional, cyclic, or spiral generates a framework of the world that reflects these systems of causality. A unidirectional view of causality is present in some monotheistic (i.e., believing there is only one God) views of the world with a beginning and an end and a single great force with a single end (e.g., Christianity and Islam). A cyclic worldview of causality is present in religious traditions that are seasonal and events recur in cyclical patterns (e.g., Zoroastrianism, Mithraism, and Hinduism). These worldviews not only underlie religion but also other belief systems such as history, political and economic theory, and political systems like democracy, authoritarianism, anarchism, capitalism, socialism, and communism.

It's important to recognize who exists in this world that the producer creates for us for 30 to 60 minutes per week. Who (people) and what (ideas) are included within the province of the program? More importantly, who and what are ignored or not included?

If the producer's perspective, production elements, characters, ideologies, cultural perspectives, and characters represented in a program reflect how the producer sees the world, how could we describe it? How does it zero in on some aspects of our non-TV reality when contrasted to the reality of our environment? Is it a world composed of white middle-class liberals? Suburban white conservatives? Rural staunch individualists? A world that meets the American ideal of a "melting pot" of cultures, ethnicities, races, and religions? A Judeo-Christian world?

How does the worldview intersect with the belief systems or ideologies that dominate on American television, including:

- A world preoccupied by the self rather than the collective good (narcissism, staunch individualism)
- A world of immediate gratification
- A world that expects simple solutions to complex problems
- A world where consumerism is the cardinal ideology
- A world where style is more importance than substance.

Elements from each of these critical perspectives are included within the following media-literacy assessment of *The Simpsons* (episode, "Radio Bart") authored by NYU Media Professor Douglas Rushkoff. Look for the contribution made possible through exploring the program from a producer perspective, production perspective, ideological perspective, cultural perspective, character perspective, and worldview perspective.

A Media Literate Perspective:
Douglas Rushkoff on The Simpsons

Mediasprawl: Springfield U.S.A.

The Simpsons are the closest thing in America to a national media literacy program. By pretending to be a kids' cartoon, the show gets away with murder: that is, the virtual murder of our most coercive media iconography and techniques. For what began as entertaining interstitial material for an alternative network variety show has revealed itself, in the twenty-first century, as nothing short of a media revolution. Maybe that's the very reason The Simpsons works so well. The Simpsons were born to provide The Tracey Ullman Show with a way of cutting to commercial breaks. Their very function as a form of media was to bridge the discontinuity inherent to broadcast television. They existed to pave over the breaks. But rather than dampening the effects of these gaps in the broadcast stream, they heightened them. They acknowledged the jagged edges and recombinant forms behind the glossy patina of American television and, by doing so, initiated its deconstruction. They exist in the outlying suburbs of the American media landscape: the hinterlands of the Fox network. And living as they do—simultaneously a part of yet separate from the mainstream, primetime fare—they are able to bear witness to our cultural formulations and then comment upon them.

Consider, for a moment, the way we thought of media before this cartoon family quite literally satirized us into consciousness. Media used to be a top-down affair. A few rich guys in suits sat in offices at the tops of tall buildings and decided which stories would be in the headlines or on the evening news and how they would be told. As a result, we came to think of information as something that got fed to us from above. We counted on the editors of the New York Times to deliver "all the news that's fit to print" and Walter Cronkite to tell us "that's the way it was." We had no reason not to trust the editorial decisions of the media managers upon whom we depended to present, accurately, what was going on in the world around us. In fact, most of us didn't even realize such decisions were being made at all. The TV became America's unquestioned window to the world, as The Simpsons' opening sequence—which shows each family member rushing home to gather at the TV set—plainly acknowledges.

But we call the stuff on television programming for a reason. No, television programmers are not programming television sets or evening schedules; they're programming the viewers. Whether they are convincing us to buy a product, vote for a candidate, adopt an ideology, or simply confirm a moral platitude, the underlying reason for making television is to hold onto our attention and then sell us a bill of goods. Since the time of the Bible and Aristotle through today's over-determined three-act action movies, the best tool at the programmer's disposal has been the story. But thanks to interactive technologies like the remote control, and cynical attitudes like Bart Simpson's, the story just doesn't hold together anymore.

For the most part, television stories program their audiences by bringing them into a state of tension. The author creates a character we like and gets us to identify with the hero's plight. Then the character is put into jeopardy of one sort or another. As the character moves up the incline plane towards crisis, we follow him vicariously, while taking on his anxiety as our own. Helplessly we follow him into danger, disease, or divorce, and just when we can't take any more tension without bursting, our hero finds a way out. He finds a moral, a product, an agenda, or a strategy—the one preferred by the screenwriter or his sponsor, of course—that rescues him from danger and his audience from the awful vicarious anxiety. Then everyone lives happily ever after. This is what it means to "enter-tain"—literally "to hold within"—and it only works on a captive audience.

In the old days of television, when a character would get into danger, the viewer had little choice but to submit To change the channel would have required getting up out of the La-Z-Boy chair, walking up to the television set, and turning the dial. 50 calories of human effort. That's too much effort for a man of Homer's generation, anyway.

The remote control changed all that. With an expenditure of, perhaps, .0001 calories, the anxious viewer is liberated from tortuous imprisonment and free to watch another program. Although most well-behaved adult viewers will soldier on through a story, kids raised with remotes in their hands have much less reverence for well-crafted story arcs and zap away without a moment's hesitation. Instead of watching one program, they skim through ten at a time. They don't watch TV, they watch the television, guiding their own paths through the entirety of media rather than following the prescribed course of any one programmer. No matter how much we complain about our kids' short attention spans or even their Attention Deficit Disorders, their ability to disconnect from programming has released them from the hypnotic spell of even the best TV mesmerizers.

The Nintendo joystick further empowers them while compounding the programmer's dilemma. In the old days, the TV image was unchangeable. Gospel truth piped into the home from the top of some glass building. Today, kids have the experience of manipulating the image on the screen. This has fundamentally altered their perception of and reverence for the television image. Just as the remote control allows viewers to deconstruct the television image, the joystick has demystified the pixel itself. The newsreader is just another middle-aged man manipulating his joystick. Hierarchy and authority are diminished, and the programmers' weapons neutralized. Sure, they might sit back and watch a program now and again, but they do so voluntarily and with full knowledge of their complicity. It is not an involuntary surrender.

A person who is doing rather than receiving is much less easily provoked into a state of tension. The people I call "screenagers," those raised with interactive devices in their media arsenals, are natives in a mediaspace where even the best television producers are immigrants. Like Bart, they speak the language better and see through those clumsy attempts to program them into submission. They never forget for a moment that they are watching media and resent those who try to draw them in and sell them something. They will not be part of a "target market." At least not without a fight.

So, then, what kind of television does appeal to such an audience? Programs that celebrate the screenager's irreverence for the image, while providing a new sort of narrative arc for the sponsor-wary audience. It's the ethos and behavior embodied by screenager role-model and anti-hero Bart Simpson. His name intended as an anagram for "brat," Bart embodies youth culture's ironic distance from media and its willingness to dissemble and re-splice even the most sacred meme constructs. With the plastic safety of his incarnation as an animated character, Bart can do much more than just watch and comment on media iconography. Once a media figure has entered his animated world, Bart can interact with it, satirize it, or even become it. Although The Simpsons began on adult television, these animated tidbits became more popular than the live-action portion of The Tracey Ullman Show and Fox decided to give the Simpson family their own series. It is not coincidental that what began as a bridging device between a show and its commercials—a media paste—developed into a self-similar media pastiche.

The Simpsons' creator, comic-strip artist Matt Groening (rhymes with "raining"), has long understood the way to mask his countercultural agenda. "I find you can get away with all sorts of unusual ideas if you present them with a smile on your face," he said in an early 1990s interview. In fact, the show's mischievous ten-year-old protagonist is really just the screen presence of Groening's true inner nature. For his self-portrait in a Spin magazine article, Groening simply drew a picture of Bart and then scribbled the likeness of his own glasses and beard over it. Bart functions as Matt Groening's "smile," and the child permits him—and the show's young, Harvard-educated writing staff—to get away with a hell of a lot.

The Simpsons takes place in a town called Springfield, named after the fictional location of Father Knows Best, making it clear that the Simpson family is meant as a '90s answer to the media reality presented to us in the '50s and '60s. Suburban sitcoms of those decades, like Father Knows Best, The Dick Van Dyke Show, Leave it to Beaver, and even The Brady Bunch, all tended to promote life in the suburbs as somehow more wholesome than the city for a postwar American family. In the 'burbs, there was time and room to work out the family's problems, all in the safety of an ample living room and at the arm of daddy's big chair.

The ability of these families to solve their problems in half-an-hour at the most was really an advertisement for the suburbs. These shows made it okay for daddy to go all the way to the city to work and only show up at home by nightfall. Evenings and weekends were all the fathering these children required. Besides, equipped with 1950s space age technologies in the home, such as washing machines and canister vacuums, mommies were empowered to wrestle with more important matters once left for dad: meetings with teachers, driving the kids to baseball practice, and, of course, keeping up on local gossip. It shouldn't be surprising that along with Levittown and its built-in televisions rose the sitcom, pandering to its new constituency while advertising the appliances of GE and Westinghouse as well as the lifestyle and happiness they promised. In fact, the utopian fantasy of these programs did depend on the selling of more washing machines and television sets. Our postwar economy was busy absorbing hundreds of thousands of veterans while relegating women back to the kitchen. A consumer culture needed to be developed by any means necessary.

But if Father Knows Best was a hopeful projection into the future, The Simpsons is what actually came to pass. The Simpsons is the American media family turned on its head, told from the point of view of not the smartest member of the family, but the most ironic. Audiences delight in watching Bart effortlessly outwit his parents, teachers, and local institutions. This show is so irreverent that it provoked an attack from George Bush, who pleaded for the American family to be more like the Waltons than the Simpsons. The show's writers quickly responded, letting Bart say during one episode, "Hey, man, we're just like the Waltons. Both families are praying for an end to the depression."

The show shares many of the viral features of other '90s programs. Murphy Brown's office dartboard, for example, was used as a meme slot; in each episode it has a different satirical note pinned to it. The Simpsons' writers also create little slots for the most attentive viewers to glean extra memes. The opening credits always begin with Bart writing a different message on his classroom bulletin board and contain a different saxophone solo from his sister, Lisa. Every episode has at least one film reenactment, usually from Hitchcock or Kubrick, to satirize an aspect of the modern cultural experience. In a spoof of modern American child care, writers re-created a scene from The Birds, except here Homer Simpson rescues his baby daughter from a daycare center by passing through a playground of menacingly perched babies.

These media references form the basis for the show's role as a media literacy primer. The joy of traditional television storytelling is simply getting to the ending. The reward is making it through to the character's escape from danger. While most episodes of The Simpsons incorporate a dramatic nod to such storytelling conventions, the screenagers watching the program couldn't care less about whether Principal Skinner gets married or Homer finds his donut. These story arcs are there for the adult viewers only. No, the pleasure of watching The Simpsons for its media-literate (read: younger) viewers is the joy of pattern recognition. The show provides a succession of "a-ha" moments—those moments when we recognize which other forms of media are being parodied. We are rewarded with self-congratulatory laughter whenever we make a connection between the scene we are watching and the movie, commercial, or television program on which it is based.

The Simpsons serves as an alternative strategy for dealing with both virtual suburbs of the television dial and the very real suburbs of Springfield, U.S.A. The pervasive choice in confronting the monotony of planned residential communities is to invent theme environments and then superimpose them over the otherwise bland. A steak house becomes an Outback Australian theme environment and a strip mall becomes the Wild West. Like the narrative and happy ending superimposed on the otherwise random and utterly meaningless day of a suburban family in a 1950s sitcom, these manufactured realities combat the underlying dearth of cultural evolution or any foundation whatsoever. In this sense, The Simpsons deconstructs and informs the media soup of which it is a part. Rather than drawing us into the hypnotic spell of the traditional storyteller, the program invites us to make active and conscious comparisons of its own scenes with those of other, less transparent media forms. By doing so, the show's writers help us in our efforts to develop immunity to their coercive effects. By deconstructing the narrative veneer of the media with which it cohabitates, The Simpsons re-urbanizes the media suburbs. It adds a first layer of reflection: a bracket of self-consciousness through which a genuine relationship between us and its characters can begin. And what we have in common is that we all live in the artificially quaintified themepark of the American suburbs.

The show's supervisors through The Simpsons' golden years of the mid-1990s, Mike Reiss and Al Jean, were both Harvard Lampoon veterans. When I met with them on the Fox lot, they told me how they delighted in animation's ability to serve as a platform for sophisticated social and media satire. "About two thirds of the writers have been Harvard graduates," explained Jean, "so it's one of the most literate shows on TV." "We take subjects on the show," added Reiss, who was Jean's classmate, "that we can parody. Homer goes to college or onto a game show. We'll take Super Bowl Sunday and then parody the Bud Bowl and how merchants capitalize on the event." Having been raised on media themselves, the Diet Coke-drinking, baseball-jacketed pair gravitate toward parodying the media aspects of the subjects they pick. They did not comment on social issues as much as they did the media imagery around a particular social issue. "These days television in general seems to be feeding on itself, parodying itself," Jean told me. "Some of the most creative stuff we write comes from just having the Simpsons watch TV." Which they often did.

Many episodes are still about what happens on the Simpsons' own TV set, allowing the characters to feed off television, which itself is feeding off other television. In this self-reflexive circus, it is only Bart who refuses to be fooled by anything. His father, Homer, represents an earlier generation and can easily be manipulated by TV commercials and publicity stunts like clear beer. "Homer certainly falls for every trick," admitted Reiss, "even believing the Publishers Clearing House mailing that he is a winner." When Homer acquired an illegal cable TV hookup, he became so addicted to the tube that he almost died. Lisa, the brilliant member of the family, maintains a faith in the social institutions of her world, works hard to get good grades in school, and even entered and won a Reader's Digest essay contest about patriotism. "But Lisa feels completely alienated by the media around her," Jean warned me.

The writers empathize with her more than any other character. She has a more intellectual reaction to how disquieting her life has become. When Homer believes he may die from a heart attack, he tells the children, "I have some terrible news." Lisa answers, "Oh, we can take anything. We're the MTV generation. We feel neither highs nor lows." Homer asks what it's like, and she just goes, "Eh." It was right out there.

Bart's reaction to his cultural alienation, on the other hand, is much more of a lesson in GenX strategy. Bart is a ten-year-old media strategist—or at least an unconscious media manipulator—and his exploits reveal the complexity of the current pop media from the inside out. In one episode, the show that earned Reiss and Jean their first Emmy nomination, Homer sees a commercial for a product he feels will make a great birthday gift for Bart: a microphone that can be used to broadcast to a special radio from many feet away (a parody of a toy called Mr. Microphone). At first Bart is bored with the gift and plays with a labeler he also received instead. Bart has fun renaming things and leaving messages like "property of Bart Simpson" on every object in his home; one such label on a beer in the fridge convinces Homer that the can is off limits. Bart's joy, clearly, is media and subversive disinformation.

Homer plays with the radio instead, trying to get Bart's interest, but the boy knows the toy does not really send messages into the mediaspace; it only broadcasts to one little radio. Bart finally takes interest in the toy when he realizes its subversive value. After playing several smaller-scale pranks, he accidentally drops the radio down a well and gets the idea for his master plan. Co-opting a media event out of real history, when a little girl struggled for life at the bottom of a well as rescuers worked to save her and the world listened via radio, Bart uses his toy radio to fool the world and launch his own media virus. He creates a little boy named Timmy O'Toole, who cries for help from the bottom of the well. When police and rescuers prove too fat to get into the well to rescue the boy, a tremendous media event develops. News teams set up camp around the well, much in the fashion they gather around any real-world media event, like the O. J. trial or the Waco stand-off. They conduct interviews with the unseen Timmy—an opportunity Bart exploits to make political progress against his mean school principal. In Timmy's voice, he tells reporters the story of how he came to fall into the well: he is an orphan, new to the neighborhood, and was rejected for admission to the local school by the principal because his clothes were too shabby. The next day, front-page stories calling for the principal's dismissal appear. Eventually the virus grows to the point where real-world pop musician Sting and Krusty the Clown, a TV personality from within the world of The Simpsons, record an aid song and video to raise money for the Timmy O'Toole cause called "We're Sending Our Love Down the Well." The song hits number one on the charts.

So Bart, by unconsciously exploiting a do-it-yourself media toy to launch viruses, feeds back to mainstream culture. He does this both as a character in Springfield, U.S.A., and as a media icon in our datasphere, satirizing the real Sting's charity recordings. The character Bart gets revenge against his principal and enjoys a terrific prank. The icon Bart conducts a lesson in advanced media activism. But, most importantly, it is through Bart that the writers of The Simpsons are enabled to voice their own, more self-conscious comments on the media.

Finally, in the story, Bart remembers that he has put a label on his radio toy, earmarking it "property of Bart Simpson." He decides he better get it out of the well before the radio, and his own identity, is discovered. In his attempt to get the damning evidence out from the bottom of the well, however, Bart really does fall in. He calls for help, admitting what he has done. But once there is a real child in the well—and one who had attempted to play a prank on the media—everyone loses interest in the tragedy. The virus is blown. The Sting song plummets on the charts, and the TV news crews pack up and leave. It is left to Bart's mom and dad to dig him out by hand. In our current self-fed media, according to the writers of The Simpsons, a real event can have much less impact than a constructed virus, especially when its intention is revealed.

No matter how activist the show appears, its creators insist that they have no particular agenda. Reiss insisted he promoted no point of view on any issue. In fact, he claimed to have picked the show's subjects and targets almost randomly:

The show eats up so much material that we're constantly just stoking it like a furnace when we parody a lot of movies and TV. And now so many of our writers are themselves the children of TV writers. There's already a second generation rolling in of people who not only watched TV but watched tons of it. And this is our mass culture. Where everyone used to know the catechism, now they all know episodes of The Twilight Zone, our common frame of reference.

Reiss was being deceptively casual. Even if he and the other writers claim to have no particular agenda (which is debatable), they readily admit to serving the media machine as a whole. As writers, they see themselves as "feeding" the show and using other media references as the fodder. It is as if the show is a living thing, consuming media culture, recombining it, and spitting it out as second-generation media. With a spin.

Even Bart is in on the gag. In one episode, when Homer is in the hospital, the family stands around his sick bed recalling incidents from the past, leading to a satire of the flashback format used by shows to create a new episode out of "greatest hit" scenes from old ones. As the family reminisces together about past events, Bart raises a seeming non sequitur. His mother, Marge, asks him, "Why did you bring that up?" "It was an amusing episode," replies Bart, half looking at the camera, before he quickly adds "… of our … lives." Bart knows he's on a TV show and knows the kinds of tricks his own writers use to fill up airtime.

Such self-consciousness is what allows The Simpsons to serve as a lesson in modern media discontinuity. Bart skateboards through each episode, demonstrating the necessary ironic detachment needed to move through increasingly disorienting edits. "It's animation," explained Jean, who has since returned to writing for the program. "It's very segmented, so we just lift things in and out. If you watch an old episode of I Love Lucy, you'll find it laborious because they take so long to set something up. The thesis of The Simpsons is nihilism. There's nothing to believe in anymore once you assume that organized structures and institutions are out to get you." "Right," chimed in Reiss, finally admitting to an agenda. "The overarching point is that the media's stupid and manipulative, TV is a narcotic, and all big institutions are corrupt and evil." These writers make their points both in the plots of the particular episodes and in the cut-and-paste style of the show. By deconstructing and reframing the images in our media, they allow us to see them more objectively, or at least with more ironic distance. They encourage us to question the ways institutional forces are presented to us through the media and urge us to see the fickle nature of our own responses. Figures from the television world are represented as cartoon characters not just to accentuate certain features, but to allow for total recontextualization of their identities. These are not simple caricatures, but pop cultural samples, juxtaposed in order to illuminate the way they affect us.

As writers and producers, Reiss and Jean served almost as "channels" for the media, as received through their own attitudinal filters. While they experience their function as simply to "stoke the furnace," the media images they choose to dissemble are the ones they feel need to be exposed and criticized. Reiss admitted to me,

I feel that in this way The Simpsons is the ultimate of what you call a media virus. It sounds a little insidious because I have kids of my own, and the reason we're a hit is because so many kids watch us and make us a huge enterprise. But we're feeding them a lot of ideas and notions that they didn't sign on for. That's not what they're watching for. We all come from this background of comedy that has never been big and popular—it's this Letterman school or Saturday Night Live, Harvard Lampoon, National Lampoon. We used to be there, too.

The Simpsons provided its writers with a durable viral shell for their most irreverent memes: "It's as though we finally found a vehicle for this sensibility, where we can do the kind of humor and the attitudes, yet in a package that more people are willing to embrace. I think if it were a live-action show, it wouldn't be a hit," Reiss concluded quite accurately. In the mainstream media, only kids' TV appears sufficiently innocuous to permit such high levels of irreverence. Like a Trojan horse, The Simpsons sneaks into our homes looking like one thing, before releasing something else, far different, into our lives. The audience interested in the program's subversive doctrine may not be large enough to keep the show in prime time, but the millions of kids who tune in every week to watch Bart's antics are.

Just as the show raises our awareness of media's false promise of a happy ending and our culture's many false commercial idols, it also brings suburban American consciousness to the next level. Land zoning regulations, almost intentionally planned to flatten the perspective and reduce the potential for ironic, urban cynicism to emerge, have now become the canvas for social satire. Abu's Quik-E-Mart, Krusty Burger, the nuclear power plant, and Springfield Elementary all irrevocably change our relationship to the equivalent locales on our own suburban landscapes. They have been recontextualized experientially. They are points of reference for social satire. They are no longer functional façades, but have been transformed into breaks in the veneer: portals through which to deconstruct the rest of suburban experience. The tube that was once used to sell us the suburban utopia is now the lens through which we can demystify its symbols and smash its myths.

If The Simpsons fades in popularity in the coming decade it will merely be a testament to the show having accomplished its purpose. Once we fully recognize the way that our media attempts to make us care about things we ought best not care about, from the labels on our sneakers to the ones on our fertilizer, Bart's lesson in media literacy and cultural activism will be complete.

An Analysis of Futurama

Do you ever sit back during your favorite television series and think about why what is happening is happening? It is very common for a show especially within sitcoms for the creator to shape the show the way they do. *Futurama* is a great example of a sitcom that is shaped with a certain purpose and intention behind its actions. Futurama which originally aired on Fox before being canceled and eventually being revived years later by Comedy Central is proof that there is more going on than pure entertainment value. Fox did not agree with the manner in which Futurama went about business which led to its original cancellation and its resurrection by Comedy Central. These programs can be analyzed to get down to what the core values and what is trying to be conveyed to the audience through the use of different analytical perspectives. These perspectives are the producer, production, ideological, cultural, character, and worldview perspectives. Through each of these perspectives we delve deeper into the inner workings of a television program in order to pull out the message hidden behind all the laughs and gags. *Futurama* does a fantastic job of conveying important themes under the guise of an animated sitcom through the use of its production and characters.

The guiding hand so to speak behind *Futurama* is creator Matt Groening along with his long time cohort David X. Cohen with whom he has teamed with on The Simpsons since 1993. Ken Keeler joined Groening and Cohen as executive producers in 2002 during season four of the series after serving as a co-executive producer since 1999. Groening identifies himself as agnostic while it is well known that he is a liberal and both of these views can be seen within the work he has done on *Futurama*. A prime example of his agnostic views is seen in season threes twentieth episode *Godfellas*. In this episode Bender becomes God to a civilization of small aliens called Shrimpkins after being jettisoned from a torpedo tube into the deep depths of space. Hailing bender as a God the Shrimpkins pray for miracles from him such as for sunlight to help their crops grow. Each time Bender attempts to answer their prayers he causes them more harm than help such as when he answers their prayer for sunlight only to set their plantations on fire. Bender tries to fix this mistake by blowing the fire out only to blow some of his worshippers off of his stomach and into the depths of space. This causes some of Bender's followers to migrate to his rear end and become atheists as their prayers were not answered by God and felt forsaken. The atheist Shrimpkins threaten Bender's followers with war and as they pray for his assistance he refuses because of all the misfortune he has caused them. This leads to a war between the two factions eventually ending in a nuclear war which kills off the last of the Shrimpkins leaving Bender devastated. Bender floats on into the depths of space until he encounters what he believes to be the real God who explains to him how it does not directly intervene in the affairs of its worshippers as it had much the same experience Bender did with the Shrimpkins. Instead God tells Bender that light-touches are best used when dealing with its worshippers which he relates to things such as pick pocketing to help Bender relate and understand how minor God's actions are in the lives of its worshippers. That episode really displays the agnostic belief of Groening as it is never confirmed that Bender is talking to God but what he believes to be God not much different than the Shrimpkins viewing Bender as their God. Groening also takes to task issues such as global warming and pollution in different episodes which shows that he has an interest in them or the way the world reacts and deals with said issues. Social issues also manifest themselves in the works of Futurama such as the completely obvious episode *Proposition Infinity* which was the fourth episode of the shows sixth season. This episode was clearly a play on California's Proposition 8 which restricted same-sex marriages in the state. The episode involves Amy and everyone's favorite robot Bender entering a robosexual relationship which is frowned upon not much unlike how homosexuality is frowned upon in our world today. While most of their co-workers are supportive of their relationship Professor Farnsworth who is adamantly against robosexualism immediately breaks the couple up by calling Amy's parents to take her home to Mars and Reverend Preacherbot to send Bender to a rehabilitation camp. Fry becomes Amy's fake boyfriend to get her away from her parents where they immediately rescue Bender from his rehabilitation camp. Once they return to Planet Express Bender proposes but the Professor reminds them that robosexual marriage is illegal in New New York. This causes Amy and Bender to launch Proposition Infinity which would make robosexual marriage legal. With the odds against them entering the final debate Bender tells Amy that the amendment will pass when they win the debate against none other than Professor Farnsworth of the robosexualism opposition party. Bender delivers giving a rousing speech which causes Farnsworth to tell them that his one time love Eunice was caught sleeping with a robot and that is why he hated robosexualism. Unfazed by the Professor's sob story he accidently admits that his Eunice was actually named Unit, a robot, and that he hated robosexualism after having his heart broken by that robot. Soon after Farnsworth joins the support of Proposition Infinity and it is passed the next day only for Bender to dump Amy because he doesn't want to be tied down to one woman. As previously stated the parallels between the real social issue and the episode are extremely clear as they are both clear pushes to allow same-sex and or robot-human relationships by fighting through the legal system for their right to marry whom they want to and who they love. This episode clearly shows and interest of Groening, the producers, and the writers in this big social issue that is being more prominent across the country now and not just in California. This is just one of the most obvious social issue parallels made by Groening as there are more examples across the shows many seasons. When it comes to his agenda for *Futurama* Groening is very open in an interview with the magazine *Mother Jones*. Groening flat out says that Futurama will both satirize and honor modern conventions of science fiction in the form of a cartoon. Groening said with *Futurama* his goal is to find a happy medium between the common apocalyptic and gloomy futures such as in movies such as *The Fifth Element* while also not making it all happy go lucky like in *The Jetsons* creating a feel of how things are in our present just in the future with new toys. He does admit though that his direction is a reaction to the fact the previously mentioned shows and movies have already been done and he wants to provide and alternative to what has already been done.

Groening reaffirms that his vision for the show is to create a future based on the present with more robots, "toys", and mutants running about. One of the main parts of Groening's agenda with this show is to "point out the way TV is unconsciously structured in a way to keep us all distracted" as he says to *Mother Jones* in his interview. While admitting he may be biting off more than he can chew he states through entertainment he wants to show wake people up and make them aware of some of the ways they are being exploited and manipulated. He also insists that he is trying to in his own way hit on unspoken rules of our culture today and get away with it by casting it off as a futuristic fantasy. Though these are some personal aspects of Groening that may be manifest in *Futurama* it is to be noted that it is a collaborative work between him, David X. Cohen, the writers, and animators that puts the show together so some of the beliefs held by him may be shared among the team to run some of these episodes that play off of things such as social issues and religion.

Futurama at the time of it's of creation was revolutionary in the way it was produced for an animated television series. The show was one of the first to use entirely computer colored cells and computer animated into 2D. The process of producing an episode of a show of *Futurama's* nature is typically a three step process consisting of writing, voice acting, and animating in that order. All three phases are usually being executed at the same time for different episodes to keep production moving along and to push out episodes faster on schedule. The characters of the show stick with what Groening was going for which was a present in the future with costumes that were consistent throughout the series and not unlike what you would see if you were out and about today. There was no laugh track used in the making of *Futurama* and generally speaking the sounds were very common. Sound effects would accompany corresponding actions and music would be used when the scene is transitioned to signify the shift. Lighting and camera were also fairly typical in terms of how they were used. Most of the time the whole frame would be illuminated to show us what is going on where the characters are but different amounts of fill and key lighting would be used to create moods which are typical lighting techniques to set the mood or tone for a scene if it helps serve the purpose of the director. Camera angles usually were pointed head on and straight at characters. When emphasis was being placed on a character or a character was giving a big important powerful speech sometimes a low angle shot would be used to show the importance of what is going on with what is being said by the character. Also used would be high angles in such cases that a superior is talking down to people of lower rank then him like the Supreme Court of the show when the characters end up on trials multiple times. Scenes often open up with establishing shots to show the viewer where the scene is taking place sometimes it is a planet like Omicron Persei 8 or a specific place on a planet such as Planet Express. Framing is pretty general as most of the time a character with relevance to the scene is present and centered or surrounded by other relevant characters. If a character is speaking they are usually within the frame unless they are not present where the scene is taking place in which case the device they are speaking through tends to be a focal point of the scene along with the person on the other side of the communication. These elements together keep a consistent image for the series while also keep the important parts of the episode in the middle of the action and so that the viewers can tell where they are and so they can focus in on them through the lighting and camera techniques. This conveys the way the production techniques are used to highlight the key points of the episodes and series of *Futurama*.

The series has different ideological systems displayed through the different characters and groupings of characters that help progress issues and causes they are concerned with. Within the Planet Express organization the crew is pretty close knit and act towards the same goal a lot of the time which is their current mission. Professor Farnsworth acts the part of the boss and just blindly sends them on any mission requested of them. Leela being a strong independent woman and believing in that system and acting as the captain welcomes any job that the Professor gives them because she wants to prove herself capable of handling it. Leela believes in trying her hardest and best and proving that woman are every bit as good as men at doing things such as being a space captain when many people would laugh at that thought in the show. Fry and Bender the two goons for the main crew both like to take a laid back approach and resist exerting too much effort when out and about on missions. This causes Leela to have to push those two sometimes to get the job requested of them done. Fry is set in a belief system that you can get through life being lazy and on minimum wage and still enjoy life. Bender on the other hand while similar to Fry in his desire to be lazy also believes that drinking, smoking, and generally speaking doing whatever you want such as committing crimes is socially acceptable. A lot of laughs within Planet Express are results of shots at our current culture or world while also laughs are taken at the expense of Doctor Zoidberg because he is poor and because of that his opinion holds little value which represents the ideology that if you are poor you are unimportant. Another person who has to deal with jokes at their expense is Fry because he is not used to the year 3000 and everything it has to offer when he first arrives all his ideas and past conventions are laughed at as they don't make sense to the people in the future. Mom represents the ideology that money translates to power and that with money you can do what you want without consequence because you can get out of trouble. Zapp Brannigan embodies the thought that as a military or person in some authoritative position you have the ability to do what you want and take matters into your own hands. These are some of the main ideological values and the characters that represent them throughout the series.

Futurama has an interesting way of dealing with pecking order since there are different levels of pecking orders within the show. Most notably it would appear income is a high influence of power as can be demonstrated through the character Mom. Mom is the head of Momcorp which is a mega corporation which has divisions such as Mom's Friendly Robot Company and Mom's Friendly Delivery Service. Mom in the public eye comes across as a gentle and sweet old woman and uses that image to push her product on people and make a lot of money. This money allows Mom to push whoever she wants around and do whatever she wants. This is demonstrated in the episode *A Fishful of Dollars* the sixth episode of the shows first season. In the episode Fry being broke now 1000 years in the future goes to an ATM machine having realized he still had his card and remember his pin number which was conveniently the price of a cheese pizza and large soda at his former place of employment all those years ago Panucci's Pizza. The interest over all those years left Fry with $4.3 billion dollars causing him to go on a spending spree at an auction to buy things that reminded him of the time he came from. When a can of anchovies came up for auction Fry went all out bidding against Mom to get them to eat. Mom thinks Fry is trying to put her out of business by using the anchovy oil to rival her robot oil business. This causes Mom to send her sons to trick Fry into giving them his PIN number with the help of the head of Pamela Anderson by pretending the year was 2000 and he was working at Panucci's again. The brothers quickly empty Fry's account and Mom offers to buy the anchovies after Fry loses everything to repossession. Fry refuses and states his desire to eat the little fish on pizza which causes Mom to back off realizing her grasp on the industry is not in danger. Fry ends up sharing the anchovy pizza with his friends who are completely disgusted by it and don't bother eating more. This episode best demonstrates how those with power rule in the world of *Futurama*. Though this power structure is also seen within the Planet Express business as well as generally speaking the workers are all pretty obedient to do the missions that Professor Farnsworth sends them on because he is the one who is supposed to be writing their paychecks. The bottom of the totem pole within the business though is Doctor Zoidberg who has no money and lives in a dumpster. Everyone bashes Zoidberg's ideas and treats him like dirt most of the time which really reaffirms that his lack of any money at all makes him the equivalent of dirt. While money is one power structure position also is very relevant as the President of Earth and members of the military such as Captain Zapp Brannigan can get away with most anything they choose because of their position and occupation within Earth. Race is usually not an issue of power in *Futurama* as some of the most successful characters in the show are of multiple races such as the robot actor Calculon and the alien super chef Elzar. Gender is sometimes referenced as sometimes people refuse to listen to the women of shows ideas because they are assumed not to know anything about certain topics being women. Professor Farnsworth is usually one of the people who disregard women's opinions in certain episodes though he also believes that Leela, a woman, is best suited to be the captain of his delivery ship meaning that gender usually isn't a determination of power but sometimes just used as an issue of equality. Once again Mom really best represents that gender does not matter in terms of power as she is one of the most powerful characters in the show and she is obviously a woman. When you boil it down *Futurama* has an income and rank based power structure allowing the rich and political or military characters to more or less do what they please.

Futurama is a melting pot in the sense that a lot of different characters manage to get along and portray different views of a world that is meant to be a future based at least socially on modern times. Being a workplace sitcom it focuses on many different personalities in the workplace. The original main character and our hero to start out is Philip J. Fry a pizza delivery boy from 1999 who is frozen on New Year's Eve for 1000 years waking up in 2999. Fry represents your typical stupid character that really has no real idea of what's going on and acts based out of desire. A quick example of Fry doing stuff for gratification would be in the episode *Fry and the Slurm Factory* where in *Willy Wonka* fashion Fry cannot wait to taste what the factory is famous for and dangles over the edge of the boat on the Slurm river to taste his favorite drink only to fall in and get separated from the group because he could not wait until the end of the tour. As the show moves along Fry is abandoned as the sole focus of the show as it broadens to the other characters such as the shows heroine Turanga Leela. Leela is a beautiful one-eyed mutant from the sewers of New New York that serves as the captain of the Planet Express ship. Leela is a powerful character in the sense that she takes her job seriously and tries to get the job done the right away without causing any shenanigans. Leela is also very strong in her belief to stand up for what she thinks is right and at times serves as an activist for various causes such as getting together with a group of women called the Feministas to stop the destruction of the dazzling Violet Dwarf Star by Leo Wong in the movie *Into the Wild Green Yonder*. The next main character is Bender the ever lovable robot. Bender is the exact opposite of a role model as he smokes, drinks constantly, has a foul mouth, and commits many crimes of various degrees. While Bender is by no means someone you want to emulate Groening explains in an interview with the *L.A. Times* that Bender can get away with all this and not be ripped apart by critics because he is a robot, science fiction, he is not someone you would ever look at and take seriously and that is how he gets away with his actions. Professor Farnsworth is Fry's distant nephew and the last known relative of Fry. Farnsworth is an old scientist who creates many weird gadgets and owns Planet Express. He is a mix of your typical boss telling you to get the job done with the obvious signs of being very old with naps out of nowhere and forgetting what was going on at times. Hermes Conrad is the Jamaican accountant and bureaucrat. Hermes fulfills the typical role of an accountant he can be found mentioning missions as well as the monetary situation of the company. Hermes is a character that gets more involved as the series goes on. Another character who starts out more minor is Amy Wong who has a rich daddy who lives on Mars. Amy is usually portrayed as the flirty type as she is seen to flirt with many different men while also being known to have a thing for bad boys. Rounding out the Planet Express crew is Doctor John Zoidberg who is usually the punch line that everyone laughs off and treats like dirt. Zoidberg has no money and lives in a dumpster and is treated as such in the workplace power structure. Zoidberg represents that person that is working and still not managing to get by while the other characters are living the typical low wage job lives in apartments. Nibbler while technically within the workplace very rarely gets involves in matters unless it is for the greater good. The problem is nibbler most of the time feigns being a stupid adorable little alien wearing a cape and diaper. Nibbler only reveals his intelligence when it is necessary like to Fry when he must destroy the Infosphere in the episode *The Why of Fry* episode eight of the shows fifth season. Due to Nibbler's fake demeanor most of the time he is not taken seriously at first until the situation is made clear to

Fry by the rest of Nibbler's race. Mom in charge of Momcorp in a sense is like the people behind what in media known as The Big Five in the sense that she spreads her views and is out for control of the flow of products to the characters within the show like The Big Five are to the media and information made available through media to the people of our world. Mom has lots of money and it translates to her power and ability to do what she wants as she has a kind and gentle public image but behind the scenes is a tyrannical monster out to control the world with her products such as the EyePhone in the episode *Attack of the Killer App*. Zapp Brannigan represents the military force and due to his rank as Captain of Earth's army he is allowed to do almost anything he wants. Zapp is very unintelligent and is usually short sighted in his approach to situations. Zapp is also the clueless womanizer with cheesy inappropriate pickup lines that never work and always has his mind on sex. Zapp has someone behind him though his second in command Kif Kroker who always tries to help Zapp take the right approach and make the right decision. The problem is Kif is a subordinate and is treated as such as his opinion is disregarded or Zapp takes credit for it if the plan is followed through and succeeds. The relationship between these two characters closely represents the big ego that comes with rank and how in a workplace the superior will take advantage of the rank of the lesser by stealing ideas or just flat out ignoring them because the their lower status. While not a main character there is one smaller character that represents a pretty big ideology and that is Hypnotoad. Hypnotoad hypnotizes people who look into his eyes and can influence their opinions and actions. This is important because Hypnotoad gets across one of Groening's biggest themes and that is to make people aware of the fact that we are being manipulated and exploited by TV and the media. All of these characters no matter how big a role they play in the show represent very different entities in the everyday workplace now and in the future of *Futurama* along with some strong ideological values.

When you view *Futurama* from a Worldview you can very easily see quite a few of them spread across the series. One of these views if of a world of immediate gratification. This is present in the show by the previously mentioned episode *Fry and the Slurm Factory*. As mentioned Fry can clearly wait until his tour of the Slurm factory is complete to get drink all the Slurm he desires but Fry is unable to wait and needs his gratifications immediately which results in him falling over a railing into a river of Slurm and being separated from all of his friends. Another prominent worldview that is ever present in *Futurama* is a world of simple solutions to complex problems. The episodes *Crimes of the Hot* (Season 5 Episode 1) and *A Big Piece of Garbage* (Season 1 Episode 8) both display complex problems that are solved by simple solutions as the people want the problem taken care of quickly without much thought into the solution. In Crimes of the Hot the issues of global warming is taken to task during a giant heat wave. The solution used for many years to solve this problem is none other than dropping a giant ice cube into the ocean, The Planet Express crew is charged with dropping the cube which they fail to do leading them to Hailey's comet to gather the ice required to make a new cube. The only problem is the comet is out of ice which causes them to come up with another simple solution to the problem. The emissions of robots are causing most of the green house gases causing global warming so the plan is to kill them all with a giant electromagnet on the Galapagos Islands. At the end of the day the robots use their combined emissions to blast Earth farther from the sun causing the magnet to not kill the robots and the intense heat wave to cease. This demonstrates how our societies desire to have problems solved rapidly with simple solutions to complex problems don't always work out. In *A Big Piece of Garbage* a similar situation arises where a giant garbage ball is discovered while the Professor is using his smell-o-scope. Farnsworth warns the mayor but his science advisor and Farnsworth's nemesis Wernstrom says that it is all nonsense so it is up to Planet Express to save the day. Farnsworth gives the crew of Fry, Leela, and Bender a bomb to plant on the garbage ball to blow it up but unfortunately once planted they realize that the Professor had set the timer wrong and instead of having 25 minutes they had 52 seconds to get clear of the garbage ball which required them to dispose of the bomb. With the garbage ball now evident to the rest of the city they decide the right course of action is to blast another garbage ball to deflect the first one. Fry teaches the people of New New York how to litter and be filthy messes so that they can collect enough trash to make the second ball. They succeed and destroy the old garbage ball with a new one. This is just another example of a simple solution to a complex problem. Something is about to destroy our planet what do we do? Blow it up! We can't blow it up! Then let's give that garbage ball a taste of it's own medicine! There are so many things to consider in such a situation but the simple solution is to destroy it or deflect it. While both are valid ways of doing things the way they go about it in the episode are simplistic and crude. Deflecting a garbage ball with a garbage ball is not the best course of action but it's the easy route so it is the first one taken. A world with consumerism as a cardinal idea is also referenced in certain episodes where everyone and their mother are lined up to get the new greatest product such as the EyePhone from *Attack of the Killer App*. These are the most prominent worldviews taken on by *Futurama* and displayed in various ways throughout the series.

The many levels of analysis that help paint the full picture of a creator's vision and message are astounding. By using the producer, production, ideological, cultural, character, and worldview perspectives together we can look deeper into our own world and the things going on around us that we may not have seen before. It all starts with the creator or producer's vision and their way of conveying that through a program that uses production techniques and interesting characters to convey different messages and ideologies. *Futurama* does a phenomenal job of fitting a set core number of values and messages into the program while also bringing up different issues that are going around us. These different methods are used across many a program to put messages out there that with enough effort can be unearthed by any viewer of the program. Next time you sit down and watch your favorite show and think to yourself how funny and that is was made strictly for your entertainment remember that there is more there than meets the eye if you just look under the surface.

—Brandon Neborsky

Works Cited

Cohen, David X. "The Why of Fry." *Futurama*. Dir. Wes Archer. Fox. Los Angeles, California, 6 Apr. 2003. Television.

Doherty, Brian. "Matt Groening." *Mother Jones*. Mother Jones, Mar.-Apr. 1999. Web. 17 Dec. 2013.

Ehasz, Aaron. "Crimes of the Hot." *Futurama*. Dir. Peter Avanzino. Fox. Los Angeles, California, 10 Nov. 2002. Television.

"Futurama Full Cast & Crew." *IMDb*. IMDb.com, n.d. Web. 17 Dec. 2013.

Futurama Into the Wild Green Yonder. Dir. Peter Avanzino, Ken Keeler, and David X. Cohen. Prod. Claudia Katz and Lee Supercinski. 2009. DVD.

Gage, Simon. "Matt Groening: I Could Easily Fill up My Entire Life Just Working On Futurama." *Metro Matt Groening I Could Easily Fill up My Entire Life Just Working On Futurama Comments*. METRO UK, 8 Mar. 2012. Web. 17 Dec. 2013.

Keeler, Ken. "Godfellas." *Futurama*. Dir. Susan Dietter. Fox. Los Angeles, California, 17 Mar. 2002. Television.

"Ken Keeler." *IMDb*. IMDb.com, n.d. Web. 17 Dec. 2013.

Lloyd, Robert. "'Futurama' Ends: The Matt Groening Interview, Part 2." *Los Angeles Times*. Los Angeles Times, 24 July 2013. Web. 17 Dec. 2013.

Lloyd, Robert. "Matt Groening's 'Futurama' Is Ready for Its Intergalactic Send-off." *Los Angeles Times*. Los Angeles Times, 05 July 2013. Web. 17 Dec. 2013.

Morton, Lewis. "A Big Piece of Garbage." *Futurama*. Dir. Susan Dietter. Fox. Los Angeles, California, 11 May 1999. Television.

Morton, Lewis. "Fry and the Slurm Factory." *Futurama*. Dir. Ron Hughart. Fox. Los Angeles, California, 14 Nov. 1999. Television.

"ON SUNDAY, DECEMBER 27, 1998: QUESTIONS FOR:; Matt Groening." *The New York Times*. The New York Times, 27 Dec. 1998. Web. 17 Dec. 2013.

Rowe, Michael. "Proposition Infinity." *Futurama*. Dir. Crystal Chesney-Thompson. Comedy Central. New York City, New York, 8 July 2010. Television.

Verrone, Patric M. "Attack of the Killer App." *Futurama*. Dir. Stephen Sandoval. Comedy Central. New York City, New York, 1 July 2010. Television.

Verrone, Patric M. "A Fishful of Dollars." *Futurama*. Dir. Ron Hughart and Gregg Vanzo. Fox. Los Angeles, California, 27 Apr. 1999. Television.

The Assignment:
Media Literacy Analysis Specifications

Critiquing a Situation Comedy

After identifying the program and the station or network that it was (originally, currently) aired on, please answer the following questions. They require you to view, consider, and analyze the program carefully. You are also required to conduct extensive research on the program (websites, library books, magazine articles, scholarly journals, etc.). You may also choose to use a DVD so you can review it and/or find Youtube or other web-streamed clips. You must completely satisfy the following perspectives in preparing your presentation:

Producer Perspective

The producer of a television program is its guiding force, its creator, dictator, and head writer. The producer has an agenda...a story he or she is really trying to tell...that's encapsulated within the rule-set of an entertainment genre. The producer needs to placate advertisers and networks, has his eye on maximizing revenues, but typically has a social issue, cultural perspective, ideological frame of reference, or worldview that he/she would like to share. This is done using the program that you're about to analyze.

Who is the executive producer or creator of this program?
Conduct research on this person. Many keep low-profiles and require lots of digging beyond google searches. Try industry periodicals (variety.com, broadcast&cable.com) and search wikipedia.com (and follow sources/citations to non-peer created information sources—wikipedia.com may NOT be used as a primary reference). Check Youtube.com for interviews. At the same time, others producers maintain high profiles. When you're done with your research on the executive producer/creator, be sure that you can answer the following based on direct quotations or other coverage:

    a.   What is the producer's area(s) of interest socially, politically, economically, and/or spiritually? Are any of these manifest in the program?

    b.   What causes or social issues is the producer interest in? Is this manifest in the program?

    c.   Is there an agenda, either inferred (suggested) or clear about why this program is being produced? What is the producer trying to accomplish?

Production Perspective

Among the producer's critical tools are production techniques that have a mild to strong impact on how we perceive the action and dialog taking place in the program. Framing, camera angles, lighting, costumes, and sound, among others, play a critical role in how we feel as we watch a program.

Based on your understanding of production techniques, and their influence on audiences, what did you see that reinforces the Producer's perspective from the Production perspective?

Show us a clip (or two) that demonstrates your conclusion(s).

Ideological Perspective

What is the system of beliefs, or ideology, that drive the thinking and behavior of the characters? This perspective is typically noted at the sub-text level which is reinforced, or signaled through, body language, tone of voice, audience reaction, and other production techniques.

    a.   What ideologies are embodied in the lead character? Supportive characters? Antagonistic characters?

    b.   What system of beliefs or values seemed to underscore the story, how characters related with one another, how the story turned out?

    c.   What evidence supports your perspective? How was it reinforced through body language, tone of voice, and/or production techniques (HINT: What triggers laugh lines? Who gets to laugh at whom? Why?)

Cultural Perspective

This is a sociological viewpoint that presumes there is always an inequitable distribution of power within a culture, setting, or context (in this case within the television program). How is power allocated and demonstrated? Who is dominant and who is submissive? Is the "pecking order" based on gender, class, race, education, sexual preference, or some other obvious demarcation between groups of people (which can be stereotyped and reflected in a single character).

    a.   What is the pecking order (of power) based upon in this program? Gender? Class? Race? Income? Or something else?

    b.   Is there a confrontation between these powers? Describe it and tell us how it turned out.

Character Perspective

Each character in a program typically represents an ideology (set of beliefs, perhaps demonstrated in lifestyle) or embody ideological positions based on the interests they represent. Protagonists typically epitomize characteristics considered admirable by the producer (or society) while antagonists are not. If you plot the characters in the program along with the ideologies they represent, you can learn some interesting things about what is endorsed and not endorsed by the producer (or society).

    a.   What did the character perspective teach you that's new/different from the other perspectives? If it's something significant, share it with us.

    b.   What aspects (or whole parts) of main characters are endorsed and not endorsed by the producer (or society)?

Worldview Perspective

If the people and issues represented within a program reflect how the producer sees the world (note link to #1 above), how can this worldview be described? How does it limit or enable what occurs in this world? What ideologies (note link to #3 above) predominate? Television worldviews/ideologies typically encountered include:

a. world preoccupied by self rather than the collective good (narcissism)
b. world of immediate gratification
c. world that expects simple solutions to complex problems
d. world where consumerism is the cardinal ideology
e. world where style is more important than substance.

Which of these worldviews applied to your program? How do these fit into the rest of your analysis?

Make sure that you also include the following in your analysis. They may hold keys to, and potentially change, your perspective on what's happening from a critical perspective with your sitcom:

What comedic elements were utilized? Which comedic elements were used to build the tension in this episode of your program?

What does your program sell?. This means providing a listing of the advertisements that ran during the program. Sitcoms are 22:00 in length and 8:00 of commercials (ads) run throughout during the 30:00 of airtime. Who were the advertisers? Also consider, what products were placed within the program? This is another key source of revenue, particularly to offset production costs. How did these advertisers influence the program content?

Who owns the channel? The network that originally airs a program (ABC, NBS, CBS, FOX) may, and generally does, have an agenda or a reason why they are running it. Do you have any thoughts on why this network chose to take the risk of running your program for the first time?

What did you learn by thinking critically about this program? This is generally good material which provides an opportunity for you to share any additional insights you've gained by doing this analysis.

Presentations should summarize these findings in a concise 15-minute presentation. Clips from the episode you've selected to analyze, or representative "best clips" from multiple episodes, may be presented to reinforce your perspectives.

Optionally, students may elect to submit written reports (rather than the class presentation. Reports should be 15–20 pages in length to adequately cover the goals outlined above.

FUTURE THINKING

Digitization and the Internet Can Take Us Anywhere

From the perspective of a Digital Native, identity is not broken up into online and offline identities, or personal and social identities. Because these forms of identity exist simultaneously and are so closely linked to one another, Digital Natives almost never distinguish between the online and off-line versions of themselves. They establish and communicate their identities simultaneously in the physical and digital worlds.

—John Palfrey and Urs Gasser, *Born Digital*

"People whose governing habit is the relinquishment of power, competence, and responsibility, and whose characteristic suffering is the anxiety of futility, make excellent spenders," wrote Wendell Berry in The Unsettling of America. *"They are the ideal consumers. By inducing in them little panics of boredom, powerlessness, sexual failure, mortality, paranoia, they can be made to buy (or vote for) virtually anything that is 'attractively packaged.'" And there are no shortages of experiences and products that, for a price, promise to stimulate us, make us powerful, sexy, invincible, admired, beautiful, and unique.*

—Chris Hedges, *Empire of Illusion: The End of Literacy and the Triumph of Spectacle*

The one sure thing that we can say about the future of the mass media is that no one really knows what's going to happen in the next ten, twenty, or thirty years. We don't know what the content will look like or what devices people will use. The two technologies that make it so difficult to predict what will happen, above and beyond the miniaturization and declining pricing of processing power, are: 1) digitization and 2) distribution. Digitization is the process of recreating images, sound, and text into computer-readable formats. For instance, an MP3 sound file or a .jpg image file is simply a coded (think 0s and 1s) representation of the actual sound or image that has been recorded. The amazing thing about digital files is that they do not suffer from reproduction noise. Every copy sounds and looks just as good as any other copy. In the analog (pre-digital) world, copies of sounds or images introduced increased noise levels. For example, if I typed a paper, each time I made a copy of it and then a copy of the copy, and then another copy of that copy, the text would look a little worse each time. When I was in high school, I would make cassette tapes of albums and sometimes friends would ask me to make a copy of the tape. Unfortunately, the copy of the tape wouldn't sound nearly as good.

Digitization and electronic distribution have changed and will continue to significantly change the entertainment industry. According to Kevin Zhu's analysis ("Internet-based Distribution of Digital Videos: The Economic Impacts of Digitization on the Motion Picture Industry," 2001, *Electronic Markets*, Routledge), video distribution over the Internet will continue to result in "disintermediation," or the eradication of intermediaries (or middlemen in the distribution chain), currently involved in the delivery of video and other entertainment. As more of us stream movies from Netflix or purchase episodes of *LOST* on Amazon.com, the production and distribution of DVDs, traffic into video rental stores, use of Redbox vending machines, and syndication through broadcast television stations are affected. Video streaming, similar to MP3 downloading, can be defined as a "disruptive technology" in that it drastically changes the way businesses are traditionally run. In the past, powerful movie studios produced high-budget feature films that were, in turn, duplicated and distributed to theaters by way of a handful of companies called "distributors" who would market the film (including advertising) and

Figure 5.1 City of the Future: Seoul, South Korea. Seoul is the only city in the world featuring DMB, a digital mobile TV technology and WiBro, a wireless high-speed mobile internet service, as well as the world's fastest, and most penetrated, 100Mbps fiber-optic broadband network, which is being upgraded to 1Gbps by the end of this year (2013).

also account for revenues generated by the theaters and alternative distribution methods such as DVD sales. Distributors would also account for revenues generated from video rental stores. Video streaming also threatens other traditional channels such as broadcast television and cable systems, which rely on an "appointment-based" rather than on-demand-based business models. The appointment-based model—which carried the film, radio, and television industries for decades—means, that viewers need to wait until the film or program "airs." On-demand models allow us to watch the show any time we feel like it. Zhu believes distributors, brick-and-mortar retail sales and rentals, and appointment-based broadcasters, which once were critical to the traditional value chain linking production to customers, are threatened by streaming video on-demand dissemination of entertainment content.

Film Distribution Standard Operating Procedures

In the US, a Hollywood movie is traditionally first released through movie theaters, which the industry calls the "theatrical window." After about four months, the film is released on DVD, or the "video window." After several months, the film is licensed to Pay TV and VOD services like Netflix. About two years after the theatrical window opens, it is syndicated on free-to-air broadcast TV.

More recently, the studios, concerned with declining DVD sales (which had peaked in 2004 and were down 25% by 2010), have considered shortening the theatrical window to three months, shortening the opening of the video window by 4 weeks. The studios are also mulling a 30-day theatrical window followed by a premium pay-per-view window where consumers could watch the film via cable systems for $20-$30. This would be followed by a shortened video window prior to release to VOD and free-to-air broadcast TV.

But Zhu is focused primarily on the technological impacts on the traditional media system. Historically, other factors have influenced the adoption and use of media on the one hand, and the production and dissemination of media on the other. These include social factors (i.e., how have the technologies affected the social scene and vice versa as in the case of Facebook), economic factors, political factors, and the pervasive content of the media. Each of these factors will play into our exploration, or structured "brainstorming" of possible outcomes, into the evolution of the U.S. media system. They also form the basis of a future-thinking methodology called "scenario planning" that we will use to predict how our media will change over the course of the next ten years.

SCENARIO PLANNING: ENVISIONING THE FUTURE

When business environments are unstable and difficult to predict, as in the case of the media, forecasters and planners in corporate, government, and other settings often rely on a research and visioning methodology called "scenario planning." Scenario planning is a structured method for developing a picture of the future by identifying and understanding the driving forces or trends affecting our world today that are likely shape the future as well. By looking at trends driving our social, political, economic, technological, and media environments, we can seek to understand broader trends that underlie them. Likewise, trends may converge from two or more of environments that scenario planners believe will contribute to otherwise unforeseen outcomes.

Scenario planning is used as a strategic business management tool and is frequently found employed by government agencies, educational institutions, and other places where operating environments are considered unstable or uncertain. As a communication consultant working on advertising strategies for the computer industry in the 1980s and 1990s, I would frequently conduct scenario-planning sessions with group we called HTAP (for high technology advisory council) composed of strategic planners, venture capitalists, product developers, and others. The methodology was our preferred approach to anticipating the condition of consumer and business markets five to ten years into the future.

The development of scenario planning is generally attributed to Herman Kahn and Anthony J. Wiener of the Hudson Institute during the 1960s. The Hudson Institute remains as a nonpartisan policy research center that explores global security and prosperity. Founded in 1961 by Herman Kahn, the institute challenges conventional thinking and helps government agencies and other organizations manage strategic transitions to the future by using the scenario-planning methodology.

The methodology was subsequently adopted fairly widely, including within the military and State Departments and the electronics and oil industries in the private sector. Shell Oil's scenario-planning process is well documented and helped the global oil company anticipate various oil shocks and economic trends from the early 1970s onward.

Figure 5.2a Scenario planning typically takes place in conference centers like this one set up in a rectangular configuration so participants can clearly see one another while engaging in the brainstorming phase of the methodology.

HOW SCENARIO PLANNING WORKS

Scenario planning is like a structured brainstorming session. Prior to the session, which typically runs over a two-day period, participants are briefed on the goal of the exercise (e.g., what will the computer industry look like in 2023?) and are encouraged to investigate the social, political, economic, technological, and industry trends that may affect the industry's future. Many times, briefing books containing relevant information are sent several weeks in advance to the scenario-planning team.

In a comfortable setting, typically in a focus-group suite equipped with a video camera, lots of white boards, and a one-way mirror where observers can watch without distracting the participants, 6 to 8 scenario planners are asked to brainstorm these key trends. A group leader, or moderator, writes their thoughts down on the white boards under one of five headings:

- Social trends
- Political trends
- Economic trends
- Technological trends
- Industry trends

Typically 15 to 20 trends are recorded per category over the period of a half day.

Another white board contains a different kind of heading. It reads Key uncertainties.

Under this heading, participants also suggest, and the moderator writes down, key anticipated unknowns. For example, for the future of the entertainment industry, key uncertainties may include: Will the Democrats launch a propaganda news channel to counter Fox News? Will one or more of the movie studios be further consolidated? Will one or more of the broadcast networks forgo broadcast television to better focus on Internet streaming to portable devices?

After all of the trends and uncertainties are recorded, the moderator leads a discussion designed to identify the most important trends, or combination of trends, that the participants believe will have the greatest impact on the future of that industry. In many cases, participants are asked to score each of the trends and factors recorded. Scoring takes into account the likelihood that the trend will continue and the resultant impact it will have on the industry. A typical scoring protocol appears in figure 5.2b.

Notice that participants are offered the opportunity to provide a range of scores for each of the quadrants they believe the trend falls within. In this way, they can provide even more (or less) weight to each of the trends as necessary. Recording these scores individually is a good way to ensure that each respondent has equal weight in identifying the most important, or key, trends. During a break, the moderator and her assistant

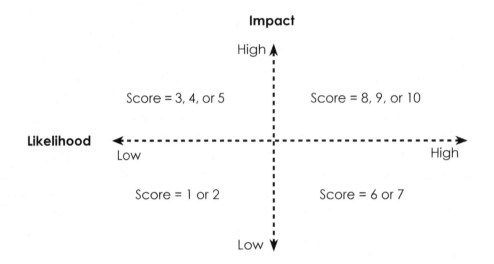

Figure 5.2b Scenario Planning Scoring Protocol

calculate the average (mean) score for each trend. These are then listed in order of highest to lowest score.

After the break, respondents are shown the trends and scores. A discussion begins as the moderator asks how the ordering of the trends has confirmed or changed any of the respondents' thinking about the power or weight of each trend. Respondents are also afforded the opportunity to appeal for a higher score for a trend that may have been under-scored by the group. Many times, this leads to the inclusion of an additional trend in the top 5 or top 10 trends overall.

Next, the group considers the trends in light of the "key uncertainties" factors. Would movement in any direction relative to the unknown factors change the relative importance of the trends? If so, how? These questions generally lead to some fascinating discussion and provide the research team with qualifying information that they can incorporate into the findings report.

Next, the moderator leads a discussion on how the key trends will play themselves out over a 10-year timeframe. Some group participants may over-estimate the advance of a technology while others temper their enthusiasm. After further discussion, the group tends to settle on the velocity of each trend over time.

At the end of the first day, the moderator asks respondents to begin formulating, again in a brainstorm-like fashion, a vision of the future. In the case of our example here, she may ask, "What will we use a computer for in 2023?" Here, a few short questions can yield some very interesting insights from the 6 to 8 respondents who have been grounded in trends for the past 8 or so hours. The goal here is not to generate findings, but to establish a mind-set. At the end of the long day, the scenario planners are asked to enjoy their dinner but return to their laptops to write a descriptive piece on their vision of the future. I've found that asking respondents, and now students, to simply write a narrative piece, a day-in-the-life essay, in this case describing their experience with computers over a one-day period in 2023 from the time they wake up until going to bed yields the most insights and granularity. Armed with the trending data and a day's worth of discussion, the respondents put in another 3 to 4 hours writing their stories, which are emailed to the moderator and shared with the others the next morning.

On the second day, the moderator circulates copies of the essays that the respondents spend an hour or so reading. Informal comments are shared between the participants. After the essays are read, the moderator works with the participants to build a single group scenario. She begins the exercise by asking, "So, which of the passages that you've just read do you find to be most compelling?" She may follow up by asking, "And which do you feel are most realistic?" The group works to take sections from each respondent's essay, edit them, and compile a single rough draft that incorporates the best thinking from each individual and the group as a whole.

SUMMIT ON THE FUTURE: HOW SCENARIO PLANNING IS APPLIED TO UNDERSTANDING THE FUTURE OF THE ENTERTAINMENT INDUSTRY

One of my favorite experiences while teaching Introduction to Mass Communication each semester is convening students in a scenario-planning exercise with the goal of understanding what the mass media will look like ten years from now. We call the exercise Summit on the Future. Here's how the exercise works:

First, students need to review a set of common resources. For several semesters, I had circulated copies of industry reports including the annual Electronic Industry Association (EIA), Motion Picture Association of America (MPAA), Magazine Publishers Association (MPA), Entertainment Software Association (ESA) that chronicles and projects videogame sales, National Cable Television Association (NCTA), Recording Industry Association of America (RIAA), and National Broadcasters Association (radio and broadcast television) reports. Subsequently, I made these reports available along with compelling futuristic videos and other data on a wiki—a website that allows users to both create and edit content, which offers students the opportunity to submit materials that they would like their counterparts to experience before participating in the Summit.

After reviewing these resources and conducting independent research, my Introduction to Mass Communication classes convene a brainstorming session. The sessions follow the guidelines from the Scenario Planning methodology as follows. Initially, students will brainstorm key trends affecting the future mass media from several different perspectives. These include:

1. <u>Technological trends</u>: What current trends in technology, or those that we can envision, will impact the entertainment industry's future?
2. <u>Social trends</u>: What social or societal trends do we see affecting the industry in the future?
3. <u>Economic trends</u>: What current or anticipated trends regarding economic conditions will affect the entertainment industry in the future?
4. <u>Political trends</u>: What national and international political trends do we believe will impact the industry?
5. <u>Entertainment industry trends</u>: Within the industry itself, what trends do we see continuing that can affect its future?
6. <u>Key uncertainties</u>: What don't we know about that we should so we can be certain about the effects of the trends that we've documented?

Trends and uncertainties are described and not judged. During brainstorming, all ideas are recorded. Brief descriptions of each are written down on the white boards or screens in the classroom. Students also take notes to help prepare for their own analysis.

Students are asked to rank order the trends in terms of their likelihood of being an important trend ten years from now and on their likelihood of having an impact on the future of the entertainment industry using the same scoring mechanism shown in figure 5.2b.

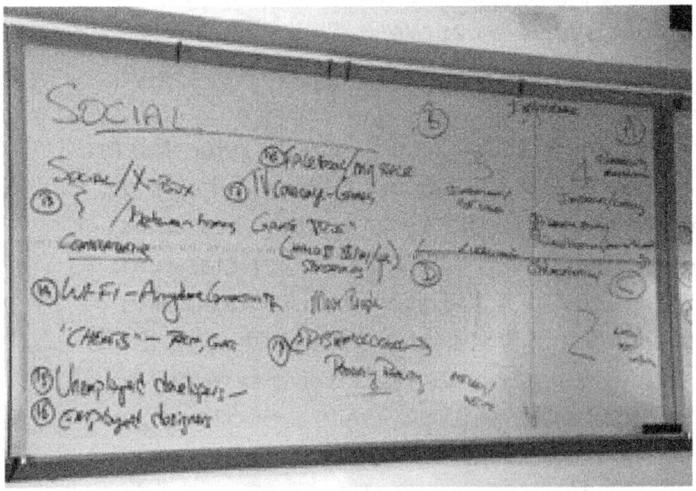

Figure 5.3 White board with notes on social issues that student participants believe will effect the future of the media industry in 2022.

During the second day of the Summit on the Future, students review their scorings of the trends and a discussion begins on how the key trends will affect the future of the industry. These key trends are extrapolated to the most radical extreme. For example, if the class mentions miniaturization as a technological trend, how far could this go? Contact lenses as display devices? Retinal implants? DNA coding? Then, the class discusses and agrees upon "reasonable" progress for that trend within the 10-year window.

Upon completion of the second class discussion, students have 1 week to write personal narratives on their vision of the future. In the future that's envisioned, what happens when you wake up? What do you do? How and what media do you consume from that moment until you go back to sleep that night? How and what do you watch, do, and experience? What is the technology like? Society? Economic conditions? Politics? Entertainment? Typical papers run 5–10 pages in length.

Findings from Summer 2012 Brainstorming Session

A small class of summer Introduction to Mass Communication students (2012) brainstormed top social, economic, political, technological, and entertainment industry trends that they see affecting the media landscape in ten years (2022). These were later analyzed to identify key trends affecting multiple categories. Key trends included continued piracy of content to the extent that streaming movies, television, music, and text were not made available. Further discussion revealed a willingness to adopt advertising supported streaming content, just so long as the content could be made available on an on-demand basis. In other words, a roadblock to access to some of the content is reliance on appointment-based (i.e., scheduled broadcast) distribution. The students believe that network, especially prime-time, television, for example, may not entirely go away in ten years, but ratings will be sharply curtailed by those streaming video on an on-demand basis. The "pull" for much of this content is toward another key trend which the students called "evolving multimedia devices" that includes cell phones and other portable wi-fi based devices that stream content portably. Movies and television will be streamed into devices used whenever there's some downtime or need for diversion.

Streaming video and further digitization of books may spawn social movements that threaten the status quo as news on the misdistribution of wealth in the United State, further fall-out from the economic malfeasance of large corporate entities, enhanced coverage of white collar crimes, decline in real incomes, job dislocation, and the widening gap between the privileged and the rest of us are disseminated to wider audiences. Homegrown video content, through

Figure 5.4 Author leads Summit on the Future scenario planning exercise with a Raritan Valley Community College Introduction to Mass Communication class.

channels like YouTube, and self-publishing, through outlets like Amazon, will bring such content to large audiences absent the corporatized controls that stymie their production under the existing "Big Five" cartel. Additionally, the co-opting of social media by the Republicans and Democrats during the 2012 campaign are beginning to show signs of weakening as alternative perspectives are presented using their time tested methodologies. Students called this trend the "Socialization of political media" where more populist political perspectives gain traction in areas like supporting the causes of labor unions, more stringent environmental policies, migration away from laissez-faire regulation of corporate misbehavior (e.g., bank scandals), support for universal health care—issues that enhance the well-being of the people rather than the bottom lines of large corporate entities, many of whom including GE (part owner of NBC), with profits exceeding $14 billion, paid no taxes to the Federal Government in 2010. Interesting, NBC failed to cover the story. Students see these populist campaigns resulting in the resurgence of protest movements similar to those seen in the United States in the 1960s.

In 2022, students believe the current premium on speed, offered by capabilities like Twitter, will outpace the need for the increased content and contextualizing provided in news stories today. News will be delivered as headlines—sufficient enough to get through the day. Knowledge of the story, or better yet, being the first to know about it, will trump understanding the details or shades of meaning associated with it. And, news stories will coalesce with social media and people at work "allowing for no real disconnect between media and standard reality, unlike what you see today with people learning about a news story after they leave work," as one student offered.

Students also anticipate highly personalized information, mostly in the form of advertising, delivered to them based on their physical location (GPS), web sites visited (cookies), buying history (Axiom Corporation), knowledge (recent tweets, sites, and scrolls on facebook), finger prints, or retinal eye scans. While many worry about the implications intelligence services could gain from these technologies, most worry about their effect on purchasing, personal debt, and overall well-being.

In 2010, most students believed the economy would drive media content and delivery by suggesting near post-apocalyptic themes regarding life in 2020. More recently, students fear political implications—particularly as the nation moves more to the left. This fear isn't based on the policies of the left, but from the fear of the right-wing's backlash to the normal, pendulum-like, swing between such policies as learned in political science classes.

In 2022, students believe hot career choices will include:

1. Advertising, particularly web-based
2. Game development and sales, particularly through portals like Kickstarter.com
3. Digital video production

WHAT WE LEARNED IN OUR FIRST SUMMIT (2006)

Meta-Universe: The World in 2016

So, where are technology, entertainment, and the rest of the world headed and how will it affect our lives? This report summarizes findings from The Summit on the Future, a scenario-planning conference held by Prof. Bick Treut's Introduction to Mass Communication class at Raritan Valley Community College in North Branch, NJ, on November 15 and 17, 2006. Students identified 25 trends affecting the future of technology, entertainment, global economics, society, and politics. These were then rated on an importance/likelihood scale to discern five key trends. Students brainstormed likely scenarios as a result of these key trends to paint a picture of the world in 2016.

Key trends that will change the way we live, work, and play in the next ten years include:

1. Increased socialization through virtual worlds
2. Cradle-to-grave mediation of communication and gaming
3. Increased portability as devices used to tap this meta-universe get smaller
4. Ubiquitous accessibility via Wi-Fi and other technologies
5. Migration of advertising dollars now earmarked for traditional media (TV, radio, newspapers) into web-enabled game/socialization networks.

A Description of the Scenario: Welcome to the Meta-Universe

Students already see the Net as their "3rd Place," a virtual rather than physical gathering of friends. It is a place where you can look any way and be anything you want. Social networks like MySpace or gaming environments like World of War craft will continue to grow and merge into "meta-universes" like Second Life (secondlife.com), but with vastly improved gaming engines. The meta-universe will expand to accommodate other brick-and-mortar environments: school, church, concert hall, community center, corner bar, movie theater, streetscape, casino, etc., while also displacing traditional media distribution methods (broadcasting, CATV, print). Films, music, television, radio, newspapers, magazines, and books will be consumed within the meta-universe. Let's go on a virtual date and go to the movies together. I'm going to run down to the virtual corner newsstand to buy the *New York Times*. Let's see what's on the television while we relax on this virtual couch.

Imagine a room where the walls and ceiling are flat panel display screens. You could be looking in five different directions and interact with your environment. Why fly to

France, a resort, or anywhere else for that matter? Just download the software. It would be the meta-universe's equivalent to surround sound and a great way to learn a new language or culture.

Instead of shopping at a mall, an avatar (maybe an iguana or a poodle) will ask you questions about your height, weight, and measurements. A .jpg file will be created of your face. In a matter of moments, an avatar is sent off to every clothing store imaginable to locate, based on your tastes, two or three dresses to try on. The avatar does all the work and returns to show you what you look like with them on. Have the dress you like best sent to you. The same technology will make it possible to "troll for dates" by sending an avatar into the meta-universe to find a match.

Increased portability via miniaturization will allow for access via glasses in the near term and contact lenses or surgical implants in the more distant future. New communication forms like "virtual meeting mail" provide non-real-time conversations between your avatar and someone else's (kind of like sitting in a waiting room and then meeting the person you'd like to speak with). Thought control (think "walk" and you start to walk) and thought-to-text technologies will result in "the ultimate in text messaging" and feel more like telepathic communication than the real thing. The combined ubiquity and availability of others will eliminate the fear of being alone. But the fear may be replaced by State monitoring (NSA style) in the form of Orwellian Thought Police. You'll never be able to lie again. Many students thought that this would put an end to politicians and the legal profession. "Who needs a trial?" asked one student. "Just replay everything and listen to what they're thinking."

Software developers will make it attractive to hook up kids as quickly as possible. Programs that virtually parent children (including virtual cuddling and discipline) will be written by child psychologists and do a much better job than real moms and dads. "Real imaginary friends" are included in the experience that leads, when appropriate, to virtual pre-school and K–12 without ever having to leave home. Pencils, pens, and keyboards will become obsolete as hard drives record all of these experiences and the lessons will be readily searchable when needed. "Who needs paper and pens anymore?" asked one student.

Education will shift from its current reliance on presentation to simulation. Instead of attending a lecture about Aristotle, students put on their glasses and arrive in ancient Greece to hear the philosopher in person. Math will be taught through real-life experience that will "make physics a great deal of fun," according to one of the students. The idea of sitting in a classroom sounds foreign in light of the technology and software, right?

Living between the real and virtual world will feel uncomfortable at first as people, institutions, and infrastructures prepare for the mass migration to virtual realities. Attending college or school, for instance, will seem foreign while multi-tasking between two very real dimensions. You may be sitting in class but want to meet with friends when you put on your glasses (or think about them) at a cafe in Paris. The virtual world (more colorful, interesting, and ordered) will attract more and more attention as the uncertainty and less-glamorous aspects of the "real world" fade from the eyes of humankind.

The students mulled the loss of reality as we know it. "It's just weird," said one student. Another suggested that we might not be able to handle events that happen in one world but not in the other. "What if you're shot and killed on one dimension? You wouldn't necessarily be dead in the other, would you?" Another philosophically, "Could it get to the point where we're really not sure which dimension is real?"

Here are some other key observations:

Socialization
- TV will cover the virtual world as if it's real
- Parents will lose the need to live vicariously through their children
- New psychological problems will emerge; others will disappear
- Virtual survival kits and roadmaps
- Virtual worlds will incorporate tactile sensations (haptics)
- New laws, forms of government will emerge within the meta-universe

Cradle-to-Grave Meta-Universe
- Age won't matter. Ten-year-olds will earn six figures
- Clinically tested "time outs" for bad behavior
- Kids will no longer need to read or write
- 3-D and food "printers" will result in a "Jetson's"-like lifestyle
- More games are targeted to younger markets
- Virtual capabilities will be marketed for huge improvements in lifestyle; followed by wave of fascism
- Mass protests, similar to 1960s, will result; Watch out for Berkeley in 2016

Portability
- "Surgical screens" will be implanted with visual cortex
- Telepathic waves will be used to move virtual "controls"
- Watch out for Big Brother
- English evolves into dominant "universal" language

Rank ordering of the 25 trends identified by the students
- Socialization via games
- Cradle-to-grave games (marketed to infants through senior citizens)
- Portability of game devices
- Increase in game sales

- Ubiquitous access to the Internet and games
- In-game advertising
- Growth market for game designers
- Halo-fication of game content (into traditional forms of media)
- Music releases via games
- Epistemological effects of simulated reality
- Piracy
- Game pros become celebrities
- Health benefits of gaming (DDR)
- Episodic games
- Growth in social networks
- Lego-ization of games (they can fit together for a customized game)
- Government "push back" on sex/violence in games
- Real-time spin-free news from diverse sources
- Increase in info-scandals (e.g., Foley case)
- Booming market for in-game "cheats"
- Unemployed game programmers
- Gold farmers (resell levels in games)
- Ninja-fication (traditional media offerings morphed into games)
- TV coverage of games
- Increase in "info glut"

Here's how the student newspaper, *The Record*, covered the first Summit at Raritan Valley Community College:

Summit Predicts: Not Your Father's Games

Students in Professor Bick Treut's "Introduction to Mass Communication" class may not have a crystal ball, but they did try to get a glimpse of the future.

On Nov. 15 and 17, the 20 women and nine men in the class gathered in a large classroom on the third floor in Somerset Hall for the first "Summit on the Future." Desks were moved in a large "U" shape as students took their seats with name placards in front of them.

The Summit on the Future is basically a structured brainstorming session on a specific topic—in this case, video games and the digital gaming industry. Treut moderated the summit, but the students did most of the talking.

In a search for ways to excite and involve his students in the learning process, Treut came up with the summit from his vast experience conducting scenario-planning sessions for Fortune 1000 companies. "I just threw all the pieces together—the briefing book and the outline for discussion," said Treut.

Scenario-planning is a strategic-planning method used by organizations to make flexible long-term plans. Treut chose the Pentagon Scenario Method, one of many quantitative-analysis methods. It's the easiest to present in the classroom setting because it contains fewer steps and takes less time to complete, he said.

He had three objectives in mind when choosing this method: to cover the content in an efficient manner; to get the students to think creatively and not just mirror the things that read; and to come up with something the students had ownership in. The key questions to answer were, "What will the future game industry look like? How will it affect traditional media and our way of life (work, social and school)?"

The scope of the analysis would cover a five- to 10-year look into a probable future. The categories in this summit included industry, economic, social, technological, political and consumer.

The summit required students to analyze current trends across these categories, considering what trends are out there today and what impact these trends will have in the future. They then mapped the driving trends for each category, determining what the outcome will be and identifying extreme and possible outcomes for each.

Twenty-six different trends were identified, including personal gaming devices (portability), in-game advertising, growth of digital gaming as a sanctioned "sport," and employment in game development/design. Each participant ranked and scored the 26 trends, with 4 being important and likely and 1 being not important and not likely.

The participants turned in their personal trend rankings to be compiled by Treut. In turn, the compilation will be brainstormed for possible outcomes to see if a scenario of the future of the gaming industry can be constructed.

Treut was very positive about the summit and told the participants that the scenario they come up with will be accessed by the people in the industry. These people "are always really hungry and thirsty for trend-line information, particularly from people in your age group because you have a whole different perspective as to where things are going," said Treut.

He also said this type of quantitative analysis is a nice thing for students' portfolios when they go looking for jobs.

Justin Shapp, a Web development major who participated in the event, said, "This was a great place to be able to have an open discussion of what the future is going to be. We usually get an adult perspective; it's nice to get my generation's perspective."

Alex Clauss, a liberal arts major who participated in the event, said "it was nice to discuss gaming in a classroom setting and that gaming is essentially going mainstream."

Treut said that by hosting this summit, he is "letting the students help change the curriculum (in the Mass Communication class) —basically how I'm going to cover it and what I'm going to cover. I'll probably do the same exercise again (next semester) because it will be really interesting to see how the scenarios change.

CONSERVATIVE CHRISTIANITY IN THE USA

Interpretive and Normative Perspectives

Introduction

It is not difficult to see the many ways religion is present in contemporary public life, from politics to public religious symbols and to contributions to civil society. In the USA, religion has been especially important over the past three decades in political culture. This chapter begins by examining empirical research on religious affiliation and voting behaviour, giving special attention to conservative Protestantism. It then explores two interpretive frameworks to explain these patterns, offered by two prominent American sociologists. It places these frameworks in a model of practical theology that involves four distinct, but interrelated tasks: the descriptive-empirical, interpretive, normative, and pragmatic (Osmer, 2008). While giving special attention to competing understandings of evangelicalism in American public life, it raises normative questions that flow from these different interpretations.

The Religious Factor in American Politics

In recent decades, a great deal of attention has been given to the religious factor in American politics, one of the most prominent modes of religious participation in public life in the USA. Following the 2004 presidential race between George W. Bush and John Kerry, the media highlighted the importance of the 'God gap' and 'values voters' in Bush's re-election. In an election that Bush won by only one percent of the two-party vote, the overwhelming support of white evangelical Protestants for Bush was the subject of highly charged rhetoric (Green, 2007, pp. 1–3). Liberal New York Times columnist, Maureen Dowd, wrote:

> The president got re-elected by dividing the country along fault lines of fear, intolerance, ignorance and religious rule ... W. ran a jihad in America so he can fight one in Iraq—drawing a devoted flock ... to the polls by opposing abortion, suffocating stem cell research and supporting a constitutional amendment against gay marriage.

Conservative New York Times columnist, Nicholas Kristof, saw things differently:

> America is driven today by a 'God gulf' of distrust, dividing churchgoing Republicans from relatively secular Democrats. A new Great Awakening is sweeping the country ... All this is good news for Bush Republicans, who are in tune with heartland religious values, and bad news for Dean Democrats who don't know John from Job.

While differing sharply in their evaluations, Dowd and Kristof both draw attention to the religious factor in Bush's re-election. The descriptive-empirical task of practical theology asks the question: What is going on in a particular context? Then it uses the methods of empirical research to answer this question. Here, I simply draw on two tables (see Tables 1 and 2) that summarize research by John Green, a senior fellow in Religion and American Politics at the Pew Forum on Religion & Public Life (Green, 2007, pp. 7–9).[1]

At first glance, these tables appear to underscore Maureen Dowd's point: the evangelicals did it! White Evangelical Protestants voted overwhelmingly for Bush, reaching as high as 82% among those attending church weekly. But a closer look complicates the picture. Bush pieced together a coalition in which he received a majority of the votes by Latino Protestants, Mainline Protestants, Roman Catholics who are not Latino, and Other Christians (Jehovah's Witnesses, Mormons, Christian Scientists, etc.). As the second table indicates, moreover, in every one of these constituencies, Bush's support was higher among those who attend church weekly.

Operationalizing Strategies

This sort of highly charged debate over the role of religion in American politics is not new, and consequently social scientists have carried out quite a bit of research on conservative Christianity since the election of Jimmy Carter, a self-avowed, born-again evangelical. Important methodological issues are

---

1   In addition to the research cited in these notes, some of the more important research includes Kohut (2000), Lakoff (2006), Greeley, A (2006), and Lindsay (2007).

TABLE 1. RELIGIOUS BELONGING AND THE 2004 TWO-PARTY VOTE.

	BUSH %	KERRY %	ELECTORATE%
White Evangelical Protestants	78.8	21.2	21.8
White mainline Protestants	53.3	46.7	19.7
Black Protestants	13.5	86.5	7.6
Latino Protestants	56.6	43.4	2.5
Non-Latino Catholics	55.3	44.7	22.7
Latino Catholics	31.9	63.1	3.8
Other Christians	74.0	26.0	3.8
Other faiths	17.6	82.4	2.5
Jews	23.4	76.6	2.4
Unaffiliated	27.1	72.9	12.7
All	51.0	49.0	100

Source: 2004 National Election Pool (NEP).

at stake in how this research is carried out. Social scientists have operationalized and thus measured the population of evangelicals in very different ways, resulting in remarkably diverse findings and interpretations. Much of this research has relied on social surveys. As Conrad Hackett and Michael Lindsay (2008) note, almost all of this survey research has used one of three methods: sorting by denomination or tradition, self-identification, or belief affirmations.[2]

Perhaps the most common method until recently has been to classify people as evangelical (or fundamentalist or conservative Protestant, depending on the umbrella category used by the researcher) on the basis of denominational affiliation. Tom Smith (1990, pp. 225–245) devised a classification method, FUND, that aggregates all 150 denominational groups in the General Social Survey into three groups: fundamentalist, moderate, and liberal. Smith's classification was criticized by Guth, Kellstedt, Smidt, and Green in the mid-1990s and, more recently, by Steensland as imprecise.[3] They argue for a model of religious traditions based on traditionalist, centrist, and modernist categories and distinguish subgroups on the basis of religious history and race. Their classification method, RELTRAD, locates conservative Protestant denominations under the label of evangelical Protestants and separates African-American denominations into a separate black Protestant category. Acknowledging this sort

---

2   See also Kellstedt and Smidt (1996).
3   For an overview of these issues, see Steensland (2000) and Green's discussion (2007, chs 2–3 and *The American religious landscape and political attitudes: A baseline for 2004*— accessed via the Internet).

TABLE 2. RELIGIOUS AFFILIATION AND ATTENDANCE, AND THE 2004 TWO-PARTY

	BUSH %	KERRY %	ELECTORATE%
Weekly attending Evangelical Protestants	82.5	17.5	14.3
Less observant Evangelical Protestants	71.9	28.1	7.5
Latino Protestants	56.6	43.4	2.5
Weekly attending mainline Protestants	57.3	42.7	4.5
Less observant mainline Protestants	52.1	47.9	15.2
Weekly attending black Protestants	16.9	83.1	4.4
Less observant black Protestants	8.5	91.5	3.2
Weekly attending Catholics	59.9	40.1	10.3
Less observant Catholics	51.4	48.6	12.4
Latino Catholics	36.9	63.1	4.3
Other Christians	74.0	26.0	3.8
Other faiths	17.6	82.4	2.5
Jews	23.4	76.6	2.4
Unaffiliated	27.1	72.9	12.7
All	51.0	49.0	100

Source: 2004 National Election Pool (NEP).

of variation is important, for it allows us to see the differences between white evangelical Protestants (who voted overwhelmingly for Bush) and African-American Protestants (who voted overwhelmingly for Kerry), even though both traditions share many features of conservative Protestantism.

Sorting by denomination or tradition has one major disadvantage. It fails to capture variation across and within denominations. Thus, a second method has come to be used by social scientists: self-identification. This has the advantage of allowing the members of different denominations to classify themselves as evangelical, born-again, or conservative, depending on the sorting category used. Starting in 1986, for example, the Gallup Organization began using the question 'Would you describe yourself as a born-again, or evangelical Christian?' to identify evangelicals. Aggregating Gallup polling data between 1992 and 1998, Hackett and Lindsay (2008, p. 501) find that 54% of all Protestants self-identify as evangelical, 21% of Catholics, and 31% of the members of Orthodox churches. This method, thus, has the advantage of identifying conservative Christians across denominations. It also has the advantage of capturing variation *within* denominations. The Presbyterian Panel, which is the research unit of my own denomination, the Presbyterian Church (USA), regularly carries out survey research on a broad range of issues. Using the method of self-identification in a 2002 survey, 12% of PCUSA members identified themselves as evangelical, over 33% as theologically conservative, and 30% as born again.[4]

One of the problems with self-identification is that people commonly do not understand religious categories in the same way as social scientists. For example, Gallup equates born-again and evangelical. Yet other research indicates that only 38% of respondents who describe themselves as 'born-again' also describe themselves as evangelical (Hackett & Lind-say, 2008, p. 510).[5] This has led to the use of a third method to identify evangelicals: belief affirmations. George Barna, for example, of the Barna Research Group, conceptualizes evangelicals as a subset of born-again Christians (Hackett & Lindsay, 2008, p. 503). Respondents are classified as born-again if they have (1) made a personal commitment to Jesus Christ that is still important in their life today, and (2) believe that after they die they will go to Heaven because they have confessed their sins and accepted Jesus Christ as their saviour. To be classified as evangelical, born-agains must agree with seven belief affirmations, historically important to evangelical Protestantism. These include such beliefs as the importance of sharing the faith with non-Christians, the existence of Satan, the accuracy of the Bible in all that it teaches (inerrancy), and so forth. Using a particular set of belief affirmations, Barna found that nearly 40% of the adult population can be classified as born-again but only 7% as evangelical. One of the problems with this method is the adequacy of the belief affirmations used to identify evangelicals. Using the criterion of biblical literalism, or inerrancy, to sort out evangelicals, for example, excludes better educated evangelicals, who often believe that the Bible is God's true Word but is not to be read literally.[6] It is no surprise, thus, that when evangelicals are identified in this way, they end up being characterized as having less education, as holding poorer-paying jobs, and, in general, as situated in social locations furthest removed from modernity.

To summarize, three different methods have been widely used by American social scientists in recent decades to identify and describe evangelicals. Given the strengths and limitations of each method, some social scientists have begun to combine these methods.[7] Some also have begun to combine survey research with in-depth, face-to-face interviews in order to explore the meaning of beliefs for individuals in ways that survey research cannot.[8] Others have noted that more qualitative research is needed to understand better the variation among conservative Christians—the differences, for example, between

---

4   Markum, J. *How Many Evangelicals? PC (USA) 2004*, [Online] Available at: www.pcusa.org/tody/department/go-figure/past/2004/gf-0404.htm, [Accessed July 2004].

5   Hackett and Lindsay were provided this information by David Kinnaman, senior vice president of the organization.

6   Nancy Ammerman (1982, 1987) argues that the debate over biblical inerrancy among Southern Baptists has left many unwilling to use this category.

7   Green, for example, (2007).

8   This is the method used by Christian Smith and his colleagues (1998, 2000).

white conservative Catholics and conservative Pentecostal Latinos or between evangelical Southern Baptists and evangelical mainline Protestants.[9]

Robert Wuthnow's Restructuring of American Religion Thesis

Practical theologians who are committed to empirical research are sensitive to the sorts of methodological issues raised above, but they also are aware that research is not self-interpreting. As we have seen, theoretical decisions (like the historic belief affirmations of evangelicals) inform research, and theory, in turn, is shaped by findings. In this section and the next, I move to the interpretive task of practical theology, in which practical theologians enter an interdisciplinary dialogue with social scientists to develop theoretical understandings and explanations of why certain patterns or actions are taking place in a socio-historical context. In this section I describe the widely influential theory of Robert Wuth-now (1988) (Princeton University) on the realignment of American religion since World War 2, found in *The restructuring of American religion*.[10] Wuthnow's theory sets the stage for the examination of two quite different theoretical interpretations of evangelical Protestantism during this period, offered by James Hunter and Christian Smith in the section that follows. Hunter and Smith portray and evaluate the contribution of conservative Protestants to American public life quite differently.

Wuthnow situates his interpretation of recent religion in the USA in the longer story of denominationalism across American history (1988, ch. 2). In 1800, there were about three dozen major denominations in the USA; by 1900, this had risen to more than 200, as a result of immigration, schism, regionalism, and revivalism. Between 1870 and 1910, 20 million immigrants arrived in the USA, swelling the ranks of Roman Catholics to 14.2 million by 1906 and increasing the number of Lutherans as well. Between 1881 and 1920, 2 million Jews immigrated to the USA, mostly from Eastern Europe, swelling their membership to 3.4 million. Denominations, moreover, continued to grow internally throughout this period and into the twentieth century. Between 1870 and the end of World War 1, the number of congregations grew from around 70,000 to over 225,000. Only the Great Depression brought a halt to this growth.

Wuthnow tells this story to underscore the importance of denomina-tionalism in the structuring of American religion. H. Richard Niebuhr (1929) gave classic expression to this pattern in *The social sources of denominationalism*, which described (and criticized) the ways American denominations were rooted in the social divisions of class, race, region, and ethnicity. All this was to change after

---

9   One of the best in-depth, qualitative studies of an American congregation remains Warner (1988). Nancy Tatom Ammerman (1997) uses mixed methods of research, combining quantitative and qualitative approaches.
10   See Wuthnow (1989) for a discussion of the struggles between evangelicals and liberals during this period.

World War 2. Although denominations grew rapidly during the 1950s, social changes already were beginning to unfold that would undercut denominationalism from the 1960s forward.

Wuthnow's description of these changes is rich, and I can only offer a summary here. First, he describes the shift to a post-industrial economy, eroding the manufacturing base of the American economy and heightening the importance of higher education for professionals, managers, researchers, and other participants in the newly emerging knowledge industry. Second, he notes the Cold War, prompting large investments by the USA government and corporations in scientific research and technology. Third, he draws attention to the USA government's enormous investment in higher education immediately after World War 2, through the G.I. Bill, land grants, and university-based research funding. Fourth, he notes expansion of the functions of the national government, particularly in areas of welfare, education, equal rights legislation and judicial decisions, all of which affected the day to day activities of citizens.

These and other social changes were to have a lasting impact on the structuring of American religion. Here again, Wuthnow's story is complex, and I will only trace the impact of the expansion of higher education and the functions of the state. Between 1950 and 1980, enrolment in higher education rose from 2.6 million to 12.1 million (the latter represented 40% of young people age 18 to 24) (Wuthnow, 1988, pp. 155, 167). One of the most important consequences was a sharp reduction of the 'education gap' separating denominations. In the 1950s, fewer than one Baptist, Lutheran, or Catholic in seven had ever been to college and only one Methodist in five and one Presbyterian in three. By the early 1970s, at least one person in four had been to college in most denominations, and this percentage would have been even higher if so many college graduates had not stopped participating in the church. By 1980, a very substantial minority of most denominations were college educated.

Even as the 'education gap' *between* denominations was diminishing, it was growing *within* denominations. A consistent finding of studies during the 1960s and 1970s was the liberalizing impact of higher education on young people on a wide range of issues, including divorce, premarital sex, religious tolerance, abortion, interracial dating, and so forth. College graduates who remained involved in organized religion brought these attitudes with them, creating an 'education gap' between less educated laity holding more conservative views and college educated, more liberal laity.

Higher education impacted denominationalism in other ways. Many college goers stopped participating in organized religion during these years and, often, never returned or only did so after marriage and the arrival of children. Moreover, college graduates no longer felt compelled to return to the denomination in which they were raised and felt freer across adulthood to shift from one denomination to another, commonly known as religious switching.

In short, the expansion of higher education following World War 2 impacted the structuring of American religion in a number of ways: reducing the 'education gap' between denominations, increasing the 'education gap' within denominations, and lessening the importance of affiliation with a particular denomination during young adulthood and beyond. This led to another social change noted by Wuthnow, the expansion of the functions of the national government. Arguably, this began during the administration of Franklin Delano Roosevelt to combat the effects of the Great Depression and to mobilize the country for World War 2. Generally, the expanded role of the state by Roosevelt was approved by most Americans, and even many political conservatives viewed it as a necessary emergency measure.

More controversial and socially divisive, however, were legislative and judicial actions during the 1960s, which expanded entitlement programmes, made abortion legal and prayer in school illegal, and guaranteed civil rights through court-ordered desegregation of public schools, voter registration, and affirmation action. Many Americans viewed these actions as the state's intrusion into their local cultures and everyday lives. Cultural cleavages began to appear that had a major impact on the structuring of American religion and politics.

One response to these emerging cultural divisions was the growth of what Wuthnow calls special purpose groups. He uses this concept quite broadly to refer to a wide range of organizations, not only in religious communities but also in civil society. They range from Bird-watching groups and Alcoholics Anonymous meetings to politically activist organizations like the National Organization of Women and The National Right to Life Committee. These are voluntary associations oriented toward a specific, limited objective that mobilizes members and resources to meet this objective. Wuthnow describes their impact on religion:

> In a complex, highly diverse, highly specialized society such as the USA, therefore, special purpose groups constitute a valuable way of sustaining religious commitment. People can participate in these organizations for limited periods of time. When their interests change, or when a more pressing issue emerges, they can switch to a different organization ... The same kind of adaptation has occurred in almost all sectors of social life. In the marketplace occupations and products have become more specialized ... and political interest groups have learned the value of organizing around single issues.
>
> Wuthnow, 1988, pp. 124–125)

As denominations have become more alike (in terms of education, income level, social status, etc.) and their identities less important in affiliation, they 'have become to a greater extent diverse federations of special purpose groups rather than monolithic, homogeneous structures' (Wuthnow, 1988, p. 125). The result has been a major restructuring of American religion in which denominationalism has not disappeared but is far less important along a number of dimensions (i.e. individual affiliation, congregational identity, the role of denominational bureaucracies, etc.).

Wuthnow's restructuring thesis has implications for some of the empirical issues raised above. At a minimum, it rules out identifying conservative or evangelical Christians exclusively by sorting them into denominations or traditions. Moreover, the rise of special purpose groups that bring people together across denominational lines appears to call for new ways of identifying what conservative Catholics, evangelical Mainliners, Pentecostals, and Evangelicals have in common, as well as what distinguishes them. The sort of belief affirmation criteria used to this point are either too narrow (Barna) or too broad (Gallup) for this purpose. My primary reason for sharing Wuthnow's restructuring thesis, however, is to set the stage for an examination of two different interpretations of American evangelicalism during this period, which are found in the writings of James Hunter (University of Virginia) and Christian Smith (University of Notre Dame). Hunter and Smith portray evangelical Protestantism's contribution to public life along very different lines.

After Restructuring: Two Interpretations of Evangelical Protestantism

One way of reading Wuthnow's theory is to view it as an account of the impact of late modernity on American religion. The social changes he notes (post-industrialism, the spread of scientific research and technology, the expansion of higher education, and a broader role of the state) have undercut denomi-nationalism and given rise to new patterns of religious identity and affiliation in which special purpose groups are more prominent. It also has led to different forms of participation in public life. Yet how this participation is interpreted and evaluated is remarkably different, as we see in the writings of James Hunter and Christian Smith on conservative Protestantism.

James Hunter and the Culture Wars Thesis

James Hunter (1980, 1983) was one of the first sociologists to examine American evangelicalism during the period of restructuring described by Wuthnow. In *American evangelicalism*, Hunter (1983) draws on a 1979 Gallup study conducted for *Christianity Today*. He limits evangelicals to Protestants and identifies them through belief affirmations along three lines: the inerrancy of the Bible, the divinity of Jesus, and a confessional or conversional Christocentric soteriology.[11] Using these criteria, Hunter es-timated evangelicals as 22% of the American adult population and as disproportionately female, older, rural, with low education and income, and located in the Southern and Midwestern parts of the USA. Drawing on the theory of Peter Berger, among others, he argues that the functional rationality, cultural pluralism, and structural differentiation of modernity erode the plausibility of religion. Evangelicals are able to maintain their doctrinal orthodoxy only because they are located 'furthest away from moder-nity' (Hunter, 1983, p. 59). Even here, however, Hunter detects some accommodation to modernity as

---

11   The confessional category includes belief that 'the only hope for heaven is through personal faith in Jesus Christ' and the conversional category includes affirmation of four items about religious experience: (1) having a 'particularly powerful religious insight or awakening', (2) involving Jesus Christ, (3) that is 'still important' to them in everyday life, and (4) entailing 'an identifi-able turning point that included asking Jesus Christ to be [one's] personal savior'.

evangelicals de-emphasize offensive aspects of their belief system (e.g. sin, hell, damnation), focus on subjectivity, and adopt modern marketing and selling techniques.

Hunter (1987) explores this sort of accommodation more fully in *Evangelicalism: The coming generation*. In this book, he studies evangelicals who are not on the edges of modernity but are students in the best evangelical liberal arts colleges and seminaries and, as such, are in the very midst of encountering modernity. These are the future leaders of evangelical Protestantism and, as such, serve as a leading indicator of the emerging contours of evangelicalism as a cultural system. Hunter finds that the 'coming generation' of evangelicals are actively engaged in 'cognitive bargaining' with modernity, even though they remain far more orthodox theologically than the secular university students of a comparison group. Their theological orthodoxy is more open and diverse, as is their moral stance on politics, the family, and education.

In 1991, Hunter (1991) published *Culture wars: The struggle to define America*. Hunter's thesis in this book was widely discussed and, commonly, misrepresented in the media. Hunter views this book as an 'extension' of Wuthnow's description of the restructuring of American religion, focusing primarily on the cultural realignment taking place in religion (and more generally) during this period.[12] With the decline of denominational identity and the rise of special purpose groups, American religion and culture generally has polarized around two markedly different worldviews: Orthodox and Progressive. This has resulted in what Hunter calls the new ecumenism of American religion: alliance-building among the orthodox and progressive members of different traditions, bringing together people from traditions that historically have been antagonistic toward one another (e.g. Protestant fundamentalism and Roman Catholicism). Orthodox and Progressives across different religious traditions often find they have more in common with one another than with other members of their own denomination or congregation.

Hunter argues that at the heart of the worldviews of Orthodox and Progressives are very different understandings of moral authority (1991, ch. 4). The Orthodox in their various forms share a commitment to an external, definable, and transcendent source of authority, revealed in texts or tradition. From this authority, they derive a measure of value, goodness, and identity that is consistent, definable (often in propositional terms), and absolute. All other forms of truth (be they personal experience or modern science) are secondary in relation to external, transcendent authority. Progressives in their various forms view authority as residing in the process of resymbolizing traditional ideas and norms in ways that are relevant to the contemporary world. Moral and religious truths are neither static nor propositional; rather they are dynamic and emergent, and, as such, conditional and relative. Progressives ascribe authority to science and contemporary experience and seek to reinterpret traditional doctrines and norms in ways that take these authorities into account, along with traditional sources of religious authority.

---

12   See his comments in Ibid, endnote 19, p. 329.

Hunter contends that these understandings of moral authority commonly are vague among ordinary people. It is elites—which include academics, political activists, media pundits and newscasters, and the leaders of politically-oriented, religious special purpose groups—who tap into these impulses and polarize them in public rhetoric, often, for partisan political gain.[13] Accordingly, he distinguishes the 'politics of culture', in which elites and interest groups polarize public discourse for political purposes, and the 'culture of politics', which are the symbolic frameworks shaping how people interpret and engage political institutions and contests, as well as other spheres of life like the family, education, and work (Hunter, 2006, pp. 90ff.).

Throughout *Culture wars*, Hunter portrays Protestant evangelicalism as the paradigm case of the Orthodox worldview. He does not discuss his earlier research on evangelicals, however, and we are left to speculate whether he maintains or revises his earlier portrait. It may be that he continues to view evangelicalism as a defensive reaction to modernity, which is maintained in enclaves distant from modernity or must engage in cognitive bargaining as its members enter modern spheres like higher education and the professions, which will have a secularizing impact in the long-run. But it may be that Hunter has changed his mind. In *Culture wars*, he appears to portray evangelicalism and progressivism as two distinct ways of engaging late modernity, which draw on very different cultural systems embedded in different institutions. Evangelicalism resists certain features of modernity, even as it accommodates others, revising its traditions in the process.

Religious Fundamentalism and the Culture Wars

While Hunter focuses entirely on the American scene and explores the tensions between Orthodox and Progressives, his description of symbolic warfare by elites, which polarize the cultural frameworks of their loyal followers, may have broader implications. It is not difficult to detect analogues to the American culture wars across national and religious borders. Especially worrisome is the sort of conflict emerging when religious fundamentalists (which are not to be confused with American evangelicals[14]) set their sights, not only on the progressive elements in their societies, but also on one another. The intensity of symbolic warfare between the Christian fundamentalism of the American Religious Right and various forms of Islamic fundamentalism preceded and accompanies the actual warfare of terrorism and the American invasion of Afghanistan and Iraq. It makes the title of Hunter's 1994 book, *Before the shooting begins*, appear prescient.

The Fundamentalism Project, a research project conducted under the auspices of the American Academy of Arts and Sciences, helps us to understand better the rise of religious fundamentalism

---

13   See Hunter (1994) where he has further clarified his argument.
14   Wuthnow, Hunter, and Smith all distinguish American evangelicals from American fundamentalists, a split taking place in the 1940s when a new generation of conservative Protestant leaders broke with the older leaders of the fundamentalist/modernist conflict of the 1920s.

around the world during the twentieth century, studying fundamentalist movements in a variety of religions and regions. In the final book of this five-volume series, Almond, Sivan, and Appleby (1995, ch. 16) attempt to identify the formal properties of modern fundamentalism as a distinct type of religion. They identify nine such characteristics.

The first five characteristics are ideological:

- reactivity: a defensive reaction toward secularization and modernization, especially the erosion of religion and its proper role in society;
- selectivity: the selection and reshaping of particular aspects of a tradition, particularly those distinguishing the fundamentalists from the mainstream;
- dualism: projecting a symbolic framework that divides the world into good and evil;
- absolutism and inerrancy: basing their moral and religious claims on an 'inerrant' text which can only be correctly interpreted using certain strategies;
- millennialism and messianism: history has a culmination in which good triumphs over evil, ushered in by a messiah or elect group.

The remaining four characteristics are organizational:

- an elect, or divinely called membership;
- sharp boundaries, separating the elect from the sinful, which are established symbolically and in practice;
- authoritarian organization, commonly organized around a charismatic leader;
- behavioural requirements, which distinguish members from others (especially the compromising mainstream) and create a powerful sense of in-group identity.

Even a cursory glance at these ideological and organizational properties of religious fundamentalism reveals the potential for mutual demonization that may occur when religious fundamentalists begin to wage symbolic or actual warfare on one another. It raises the ominous spectre of global culture wars outside the moderating effects of democratic institutions and cultures. If this is the context in which we find ourselves, it raises important questions for practical theology. How do practical theologians best conceptualize the tasks of political theology in a context of extreme cultural polarization? Do the older approaches to political theology, which drew heavily on Marxism, provide an adequate account of cultural and religious difference? Does the American example of polarization of Orthodox and Progressive perspectives during a time of social change hold true in other parts of the world and, if so, what sort of religious postures ought practical theologians commend in such contexts? These normative questions are raised by Hunter's culture wars thesis, although they cannot be answered on the basis of his sociological theory alone. They are profoundly important, however, for practical theology's evaluation of the positive and negative contributions of religion to public life.

Christian Smith: Subcultural Identity Theory and Evangelical Protestantism

Chris Smith (1997, p. 175) strongly disagrees with Hunter's culture wars thesis. As he puts it: 'Culture wars is a myth. The conventional wisdom that Americans are divided into two warring camps slugging it out over abortion, prayer in schools, and homosexuality is greatly exaggerated. Growing empirical evidence suggests it just is not true.' The empirical research to which Smith refers here is a major study of American evangelicals carried out by a team of twelve sociologists, which he led over a three-year period, called the Evangelical Identity and Influence Project.[15] His criticism of Hunter's thesis receives further support from research by the sociologist Alan Wolfe (1998) and political scientist Morris Fiorina (2005).[16] Smith's national study of evangelicals used a variety of research methods at different points, but relied primarily on self-identification to sort out evangelicals (after screening a theologically diverse sample of Protestants to include only people who attend church at least 2–3 times per month or who regard religion as 'extremely important' in their lives). While 29% of the American population self-identify as conservative Protestant, only 11.2% self-identify as evangelical.

In *Christian America?* Smith draws on the Evangelical Identity and Influence Project to charge advocates of the culture wars thesis like Hunter with committing four fallacies:

- *the representative elite fallacy*: presuming that evangelical leaders represent the views of ordinary evangelicals and that evangelicals have a single elite;
- *the factual survey fallacy*: assuming that public opinion surveys alone accurately and adequately capture the views of ordinary people;
- *the ideological consistency fallacy*: assuming that people hold ideologically consistent worldviews when, in fact, cultural identities are internally contradictory and loosely integrated;
- *the monolithic bloc fallacy*: treating conservative Protestants as a monolithic social group and, thus, failing to acknowledge the diversity and historic tensions between Pentecostals, fundamentalists, evangelicals, and charismatics.

Smith draws on his research to paint a picture of evangelicals as theologically diverse and as holding a range of moral stances on sexuality, the family, education, and politics. Most evangelicals, he notes,

15   For a detailed description, see Smith (1998, 2000).
16   See also their contributions to Hunter (2006).

are unfamiliar with the so-called culture wars. The issues they care about most are jobs, quality education for their children, economic pressures on the family, and the rise of violent crime. Particularly noteworthy is Smith's contention that evangelicals, like the members of all cultural groups, hold beliefs that often are in tension with one another. Many evangelicals, for example, bemoan the diminished importance of America's Christian heritage in the public square and commonly vote for candidates who hold traditionalist positions on moral issues. Yet this is counterbalanced by beliefs that are central to evangelical subculture: for example, the root of the human problem is in the human heart and can only be overcome by conversion and spiritual transformation which cannot be coerced; belief in the power of personal example and relationships, not political systems, leading to ambivalence about what really can be accomplished through electoral politics. In short, it is misleading to interpret the voter preferences of evangelicals as indicative of a culture war, for evangelicalism is characterized by 'an enormous amount of diversity, complexity, ambivalence, and disagreement' (Smith, 2000, pp. 127–128).

In *American evangelicalism: Embattled and thriving*, Smith (1998) draws on the same body of research to portray American evangelicalism as the paradigm case of how religion can adapt successfully to late modernity, calling into question the secularization thesis that Hunter used in his early writings on evangelicalism. In comparison with mainline, liberal, and fundamentalist forms of Protestantism, Smith's research reveals that evangelicalism is stronger along six dimensions: adherence to beliefs, salience of faith, robustness of faith, group participation, commitment to mission, and retention and recruitment of members (Smith, 1998, pp. 21–22). He explains its strength with a subcultural identity theory of religious persistence.

Smith summarizes his argument as follows: 'Religion survives and can thrive in pluralistic, modern society by embedding itself in subcultures that offer satisfying morally orienting collective identities which provide adherents meaning and belonging' (Smith, 1998, p. 118). He unpacks this thesis in the form of eight propositions (Smith, 1998, ch. 4). I will offer them here and then comment briefly.

- Proposition 1: The human drives for meaning and belonging are satisfied primarily by locating human selves within social groups that sustain distinctive, morally orienting collective identities.
- Proposition 2: Social groups construct and maintain collective identities by drawing symbolic boundaries that create distinction between themselves and relevant out-groups.
- Proposition 3: Religious traditions have always strategically renegotiated their collective identities by continually reformulating the ways their constructed orthodoxies engage the changing sociocultural environments they confront.
- Proposition 4: Because the socially normative bases of identity-legitimation are historically variable, modern religious believers can establish strong religious identities and commitments on the basis of individual choice rather than through ascription.

- Proposition 5: Individuals and groups define their values and norms and evaluate their identities and actions in relation to specific, chosen reference groups; dissimilar and antagonistic out-groups may serve as negative reference groups.
- Proposition 6: Modern pluralism promotes the formation of strong subcultures and potentially 'deviant' identities, including religious subcultures and identities.
- Proposition 7: Intergroup conflict in a pluralistic context typically strengthens in-group identity, solidarity, resources mobilization and membership retention.
- Proposition 8: Modernity can actually increase religion's appeal, by creating social conditions that intensify the kinds of felt needs and desires that religion is especially well-positioned to satisfy.

The force of Smith's theory is best seen by contrasting it with Hunter and Berger. The latter portray modern rationalization, institutional differentiation, and cultural pluralism as destroying the sacred canopy of traditional societies and as creating cognitive quandaries at the individual level, which necessitate the heretical imperative, in Berger's famous phrase (each individual must choose and piece together their own faith). In contrast, Smith locates the problems of human meaning and belonging within the larger problem of collective identity, especially at the level of subcultural groups. Such groups may not provide a 'sacred canopy' for American society as a whole, but they do provide a 'sacred umbrella' for their members (Smith, 1998, p. 106). American evangelicalism has thrived precisely because its congregations, parachurch groups, and special purpose organizations serve as reference groups in which their members can establish strong religious identities. What may appear as polarized culture war rhetoric among evangelicals, moreover, actually is not directed toward out-groups but is primarily in-group talk designed to strengthen subcultural identity boundaries.

In short, many features of late modernity which are commonly interpreted as having a secularizing impact, actually create social conditions that may increase religion's appeal, intensifying 'the felt needs and desires that religion is especially well-positioned to satisfy' (Proposition 8). The key is whether religious communities, be they evangelical or not, can foster subcultural identities that satisfy the human need for meaning and belonging by serving as reference groups with which people identify affectively and by forming religious identities among their members strong enough to shape their engagement of modern institutions. This theory and Smith's research on American evangelicals raises two set of issues, both of which are important for our understanding of their role in public life.

First, if American evangelicals are not best viewed as willing participants in a culture war but as theologically and socially diverse, are there more possibilities than is commonly recognized for meaningful discussion of contemporary social issues across theological lines? If this is the case, then should not more attention be given to the forms this sort of conversation might take both within and across denominations? While denominational debate over issues like abortion and the ordination of gay and lesbians has looked very much like a culture war, is this necessarily the case? What if other issues are in view, like global warming, the growing disparity between rich and poor, and commitment to more egalitarian forms of marriage and family? Moreover, should not more attention be given to the complexity of centrist perspectives, which too often are ignored or shouted down in the midst of polarized debate?[17] Perhaps there is more room for meaningful debate and discussion of public issues across theological lines than is commonly perceived, if Smith is correct. It is political elites who high-jack issues and polarize them for partisan political gain.

Second, if Smith's subcultural identity theory is correct, what implications does this hold for mainline Protestant congregations, which commonly are so loosely-bound that they play a minimal role in shaping the cultural identities of their members? Would it be helpful if practical theologians began to reflect theologically on subcultural identity theory with the concept of the church as a contrast society? What are the implications of the very different understandings of this concept found in the writings of Stanley Hauerwas, Jürgen Moltmann, and Gerhard Lohfink, to name but a few? While Moltmann portrays the church as a contrast society, for example, he does so in ways that leave it open to learning from other religious and non-religious groups, which contribute to the common good.

Concluding Reflections

We now have before us two interpretations of evangelicalism in the context of the restructuring of American religion. Practical theologians will take careful note of the empirical research strategies on which they rest, especially the way they operationalize evangelicalism. They also will attend to the social science traditions in which these interpretations are located, which make assumptions about modernity, secularization, culture, and religion. Such traditions are open to the findings of empirical research, but they are never completely derived from or falsified by such research. The processes of justifying, comparing, revising, and falsifying traditions of interpretation take place at a different level, which frequently includes discussion of the nature of social science.

Hunter's and Smith's interpretation of evangelicalism raise different normative issues, which I have noted in passing. Addressing such issues more fully is the normative task of practical theology in which constructive theological and ethical proposals are developed about what *ought* to take place in response to cultural polarization, for example, or in light of the importance of religious subcultures in late modernity. Such proposals open out to pragmatic guidance about how to embody such norms in a particular social context. What I have done in this chapter, thus, is only part of what I consider to be the full research programme of practical theology. But it is a starting point that opens out to future discussion.

---

17   Two interesting attempts to define centrist positions are Weston (2003) and Gushee (2008).

References

Almond, G.A., Sivan, E., & Appleby, R.S. (1995). Explaining fundamentalisms. In M. Marty, & R.S. Appleby (Eds.), *Fundamentalisms comprehended*: *The fundamentalism Project, Volume 5* (pp. 405–408). Chicago: University of Chicago Press.

Ammerman, N. (1982). Operationalizing evangelicalism: An amendment. *Sociological Analysis*, 43(2), 170–171.

Ammerman, N. (1987). *Bible believers: Fundamentalists in the modern world*.New Brunswick, NJ: Rutgers University Press.

Ammerman. N. (1997). *Congregation & community*. New Brunswick, NJ: Rutgers Univ. Press.

Fiorina, M. (2005). *Culture war? The myth of a polarized America*. New York: Pearson Longman.

Greeley, A. (2006). *The truth about conservative Christians: What they think and what they believe*. Chicago, IL: University of Chicago Press.

Green, J. (2007). *The faith factor: How religion influences American elections*. Westport, CN.: Praeger Publishers.

Gushee. D. (2008). *The future of faith in American politics: The public witness of the evangelical center*. Waco, TX: Baylor University Press.

Hackett, C., & Lindsay, S.M. (2008) Measuring evangelicalism: Consequences of different operationalization strategies. *Journal for the Scientific Study of Religion, 47*(3), 499–514.

Hunter, J. (1980). The new class and the young evangelicals. *Review of Religious Research, 22*(2), 155–169.

Hunter, J. (1983). *American evangelicalism: Conservative religion and the quandary of modernity*. New Brunswick, NJ: Rutgers University Press.

Hunter. J. (1987). *Evangelicalism: The coming generation*. Chicago, IL: University of Chicago Press.

Hunter, J. (1991). *Culture wars: The struggle to define America*. New York: BasicBooks

Hunter, J. (1994). *Before the shooting begins: Searching for democracy in America's culture war*. Toronto; New York: Free Press; Maxwell Macmillan Canada; Maxwell Macmillan International.

Hunter, J. (1996). Response to Davis and Robinson: Remembering Durkheim. *Journal for the Scientific Study of Religion, 35*(3), 246.

Hunter, J. (2006). *Is there a culture war? A dialogue on values and American public life*. Washington, DC: Pew Research Center; Brookings Institution Press.

Kellstedt, L., & Smidt, C. (1996). Measuring fundamentalism: An analysis of different operational strategies. In J. Green (Ed.), *Religion and the culture wars: Dispatches from the front* (pp. 193–218). Lanham, MD: Rowman & Littlefield.

Kohut, A. (2000). *The diminishing divide: Religion's changing role in American politics*. Washington, DC: Brookings Institution Press.

Lakoff, G. (2006). *Moral politics: How liberals and conservatives think* 2nd ed. Chicago, ILL: University of Chicago Press.

Lindsay, D. (2007). *Faith in the halls of power: How evangelicals joined the American elite.* New York: Oxford University Press.

Niebuhr, H. (1929). *The social sources of denominationalism.* New York: H. Holt and Co.

Osmer, R. (2008). *Practical theology: An introduction,* Grand Rapids, MI.: William B. Eerdmans Pub. Co.

Smith, C. (1998). *American evangelicalism: Embattled and thriving.* Chicago, IL.: University of Chicago Press.

Smith, C. (2000). *Christian America? What evangelicals really want.* Berkeley, CA: University of California Press.

Smith, T.W. (1990). Classifying Protestant Denominations. *Review of Religious Research, 31*(3), 225.

Steensland, B. et al. (2000). The Measure of American religion: Toward improving the state of the art. *Social Forces, 79*(1), 291–324.

Warner, R. (1988). *New wine in old wineskins: Evangelicals and liberals in a small-town church.* Berkeley, CA: University of California Press.

Weston, W. (2003). *Leading from the center: Strengthening the pillars of the church.* Louisville, KY: Geneva Press.

Wolfe, A. (1998). *One nation, after all: what middle-class Americans really think about: God, country, family, racism, welfare, immigration, homosexuality, work, the right, the left, and each other.* New York: Viking.

Wuthnow, R. (1988). *The restructuring of American religion: Society and faith since World War II.* Princeton, N.J.: Princeton University Press.

Wuthnow, R. (1989). *The struggle for America's soul: evangelicals, liberals, and secularism,* Grand Rapids, MI: W.B. Eerdmans.

STUDENT PERSPECTIVES

An Analysis of Seinfeld

The sitcom I chose to use as my subject for my media literacy analysis is Seinfeld. Fans and creators considered Seinfeld as "a show about nothing." The show followed the four main characters, Jerry, George, Elaine, and Kramer as they live in New York City and encounter problems, which they discuss in a comedic fashion through their nuances and idiosyncrasies. Those problems were something everyone can relate to, which is why Seinfeld had such a wide audience. Seinfeld was one of the highest rated shows on TV throughout the 90s and was led by head writers and producers, Jerry Seinfeld and Larry David

Before a sitcom star, Jerry Seinfeld was a stand-up comedian. He style of stand-up was that of "observational humor," where he focused on uncomfortable social situations and relationships. Jerry Seinfeld was of Jewish ancestry, and his conventional qualities from this showed through his humor, as he seemed to be a normal person, from the outside looking in at the absurdity of everyday situations. This manifested itself it the program, as traditional cultural, social, and ethnic groups were poked fun at without crossing the line and becoming controversial. Poking fun at stereotypes was done as well, but this was used in a way to relate to the audience.

Larry David was much like George Costanza, the character that was based upon him, as someone that seemed to be a failure. He came from humble beginnings and did not fit in with the "Johnny Carson" type comics, but he did not compromise in his comedic career. He also used "observational humor," like his partner, Jerry Seinfeld had an interesting outlook on life and he had insights to life that people didn't seem to notice. When Jerry, was given the offer by NBC to make a sit-com pilot, he thought Larry could help him. And he definitely did.

The episode I chose to analyze is called "The Bizaro Jerry." The premise of the episode, is the Elaine breaks up with her boyfriend Kevin and much like Elaine and Jerry, they decide to be "just friends." She starts hanging out with Kevin and his friends and she finds that his friends are the exact opposite of Jerry and the other main characters. Jerry suggests to Elaine that they are from "Bizarro World," which is a reference to the Superman comics. Meanwhile, Kramer gets a job at company called Brandt/Leland. He actually gets the job by accident when he is wandering the halls and finds himself in a meeting. He works this job for no pay and says he's doing it "just for me." Jerry starts dating a woman named Jillian who is very beautiful, but also has "man hands," meaning her hands are large and strong like a man's. George uses a picture of Jillian to get into the "forbidden city," a club full of models, and says the picture of Jillian is his late wife in order to gain sympathy from them, but then he accidently burns the picture with a hair dryer. By the end of the episode, Elaine gets shunned from her new, "bizarro" friends, Kramer gets fired from his job, George is banned from the "forbidden city," and Jerry tells Jillian he just wants to be friends which she does not take too well.

From the production perspective, we see a lot of different perspectives and aspects of the episode. In the scene where Jerry, George and Elaine are at the diner and Elaine is telling Jerry about her situation with Kevin and Jerry is told about Jillian and George get the picture of Jillian from Elaine, I see that the characters in the frame are all above midline, which shows the dominance of the characters, because in the beginning of the episode they all seem to be on a positive path. Jerry is also above midline when he meets Jillian and the camera is tilted upwards, and the camera is titled downwards towards Jillian. And when they shake hands, her hands are in the center of the frame. When Kramer tells Jerry he is working at Brant/Leland, he is now wearing a different costume. He is wearing a suit, because that coincides with the story of the episode. In this scene as well, the laugh track is used to laugh at Kramer. When Elaine and Jerry are talking about Kevin and how he is the total opposite of Jerry the laugh track is used to laugh at the situation of Kevin being the "Bizarro Jerry." In the same scene Kramer comes home from work the laugh track is used laugh at Kramer. When George finds his way into the "forbidden city," he is marginalized in the frame, which shows the beginning of his character on the path to his negative out come with-in the episode. Jerry is also marginalized on his first date with Jillian as this starts out his negative outcome with Jillian in the episode. When Jerry and Kramer are discussing how they "never do anything anymore," due to Kramer's hectic work schedule the camera is pointed down towards Kramer. The camera also follows Jerry during this scene during the episode. The camera also follows Jerry when he breaks up with Jillian. In the scene where the Bizarro friends meet the main characters the Bizarro friends are in the background behind Elaine and come in the foreground as Elaine chooses to go with them over the main characters for the night. In the scene where Kramer gets fired from his job he is marginalized. When Elaine gets shunned from the Bizarro friends she is also marginalized.

By looking at the ideological perspective of the episode we can see that there are different aspects of the episode portrayed, through the characters ideologies and cultural social norms. At the subtext level, the show is anti-establishment. It rejects social norms, by having the characters value things that are for their own personal gain, rather then the whole collective good of everyone involved.

The system of beliefs that drive Jerry, is that he is from the outside looking in, giving advice to the characters about their situations. When it comes to the situation of him and Jillian though, he is driven by the fact he cannot get over the idiosyncrasies and characteristics of certain women he dates have. When it comes to the situation between him and Kramer, he is driven by the fact Kramer is not paying him enough attention to him due to Kramer's hectic work schedule.

George is selfish and inconsiderate towards Jerry when he doesn't allow Jerry to come with him to the Forbidden City. He is trying to achieve success in his quest to gain acceptance from the attractive women by doing minimal work, such as presenting a picture of Jillian and calling her his late wife in order to gain sympathy from the attractive women.

Elaine is driven by and values wanting to be "normal," with the good and attractive Bizarro friends, and not caught up in the world of the craziness that surrounds her with the main characters.

Kramer is driven by and values the fact he wants to be useful, and accepted by the real world, something that deviates from his normal character (which I will get into later with the character perspective).

This episode is about a dominant ideology, as we see with what drives the characters and their system of beliefs. The subcultures with-in the episode interacts with the dominant ideology. With Elaine's Bizarro friends who are seemingly normal and good, they reject Elaine's behaviors and in turn, reject the dominant ideology. The subculture of the attractive women of the Forbidden City rejects George's ideology. The subculture of the people at Kramer's job rejects his dominant ideology because he is inept at his job.

In this particular episode, the power is allocated differently amongst the main characters. Jerry seems to be submissive in this episode. He is submissive when George comes to him only when he needs something, or when Elaine chooses to leave her friends for the Bizarro friends or when Kramer begins to focus on his work and not Jerry and their friendship and because of these Jerry loses control of his social circle, something he is usually dominant in. Elaine is dominant, as she chooses to leave her current crazy social circle of friends for something more normal. Kramer is dominant when he begins to focus on his job but then becomes submissive when he fails and gets "fired." George is submissive because he tries to gain access to the Forbidden City and ultimately fails and makes a fool of him self. This says about the programs as a whole, that women can be in dominant roles, because of Elaine, which she usually is, and men can be submissive.

Members of the dominant class in society represent their own interests as being in the interests and welfare of society as a whole. The program does not do this. The characters and stories of the episodes are a parody of this concept. The characters are usually selfish and have their own interests in mind. They are projected in this episode when Jerry finds the quality of a woman he is dating (Jillian) unattractive and chooses to not see her anymore because of this. George uses a picture of Jillian who he says is his deceased wife, which is appalling, to gain acceptance from attractive women. Elaine seemingly does not care about her friends anymore and chooses a new group of friends over the main characters because they are more "normal." Kramer is a person in the series who is selfish and leeches off of Jerry, and usually has no consideration for others.

In this episode, there is a pecking order amongst the main characters that is of power or influence. Elaine is at the top of the pecking order, because she is in a dominant role in this episode. I would say Kramer is at the second spot of the pecking order, because he is taking action and deviating from his normal routine, plus he is abandoning Jerry, even though this is done in a comedic fashion. Jerry is next in the pecking order; because he is still showing power when he chooses not to see the woman he is dating anymore. George is last in the pecking order, because he is the perennial failure of the series and in this episode. I believe the pecking order is based off of gender, because each of the characters fills certain types of male and female stereotypes.

The characters in Seinfeld all represent different ideologies and perspectives on life. Each is either dominant or submissive. Either a character that takes life by the horns or a person that is caught in the whirlwind of life, trying to find a way to achieve success, but ultimately failing. There is also the voice of reason, and the quirkiness of a character that is content with living a life amounting to nothing.

Jerry Seinfeld is a successful comedian, both in real life and on the show. He uses his observational humor to point out the obscurity of other characters lives as well as his own. He provokes his friends and audience to think about their lives by bringing up points that the characters would not be aware of. This leads to hilarity. He can be admired for this, as I think with George (who I'll get into later) are the most sympathetic characters, but for different reasons of course. I believe Jerry deviates from the dominant culture, by observing and bringing up points about life that deviate from the norm. The subculture that Jerry represents effect the dominant ideology promoting the idea that culture should be viewed upon from an objective perspective. These ironies and insights he provides help guide us and the other characters through their social lives, by questioning the absurd rules, or the norms, that they and us, originally thought were supposed to guide social lives.

On the other hand there is the character of George Constanza, who is the model for a continuous failure. He's cynical, bald, short, and throughout the series has lived with his parents for periods of time. You might even call him a "loser." George has no self-respect. He tries to go through life trying to achieve success by doing minimal work. He makes devious plans, when the right way to go about doing things is being honest. An example would be in one of my favorite episodes called "The Invitations," where George is getting married to the character of Susan and is trying to find a way to get out of his impending wedding. Jerry makes the suggestion of starting smoking, thinking Susan would reject him for this since she hates smoking. Of course, he fails at this. In a passive-aggressive way, he decides to buy the cheapest invitations for the wedding. It turns out that the glue on the invitations is toxic and Susan gets poisoned and later on in the episode actually dies. George could have been honest, but instead he schemed, which led to disastrous results. I believe George deviates from the norm, as he is not a successful person and his attempts to achieve success are deviant. He accepts the ends but not means to those ends. So George's subculture he represents affect the dominant ideology in a negative way by presenting statements like "Jerry... It's not a lie, if you believe it." (http://youtu.be/lqfgOlm-w2U).

Elaine Benes is the model for a single, successful, career driven woman. She is a "guys girl," as she fits in like one of the boys. She often is in the power role of her sexual and romantic relationships. I believe she conforms to the dominant ideological perspective, as she is a seemingly sane woman, she provides stability to the craziness that surrounds her. As a somewhat feminist, her representative subculture affects the dominant ideology, by showing what a strong woman can do in society.

Kramer is the model of zany, eccentric man who moves from situation to situation, drifting without deviating from his root character. No one knows where his money comes from and he is seemingly doesn't even have a job. In the episode I chose to analyze, "The Bizzaro Jerry," Kramer falls in to a job for a company where he doesn't even receive pay, he's just "T.C.B." a.k.a "Takin' Care of Buisness." And what's in his briefcase? Crackers. (http://youtu.be/PKs6y9_d2ps). Kramer deviates from the dominant cultural perspective because of this. Where a rigid schedule and conformity dominate social and professional life, Kramer has none of these objectives. I believe the subculture Kramer represents doesn't even come close to affecting our dominant ideology, because he lives in a world of fantasy.

The worldview definition of this program is that the self rather than the collective good preoccupies the world. An example that the self rather than the collective good preoccupies the world in this episode is George. George is preoccupied with himself, because he is selfishly using a picture of the woman Jerry is dating to gain access to the "Forbidden City." He is saying the picture is of his deceased wife, which is just wrong. He also doesn't allow Jerry to come with him to the club. The initial woman he attracts with the picture, he dumps in order to see other woman. He accidently burns the picture with a blow dryer, and calls Jerry up to get another one. Jerry fails at this and then George cuts a picture out of the magazine to say it's his wife. He ultimately fails at attracting the women he wants. And he did all of this to satisfy himself. The characters in the show that compromise this world do similar things. Jerry is seen often dating a new girl every week and usually dumps them because they have a certain and single odd quality about themselves that Jerry finds unattractive. Elaine is a person in the power role of her relationships and focuses on what she can do to improve her standing and not the others in the relationship. George is a selfish person; often seeking ways to plot and scheme is ways into things by doing minimal work. Kramer is a person who leeches off the people around him, using others for personal gain. The types of people who comprise this world are characters that lack empathy and compassion. The types of people who are stereotyped are those of particular races, even though this is not seen in the particular episode I am analyzing. There is an example from another episode called "The Diplomats Club." In this episode, George makes a comment to his workplace superior, whom is African American, that he looks like "Sugar" Ray Leonard. His boss says, "I guess we all look alike to you." George then goes on a quest to make his boss realize he is not a racist, which leads to a disastrous outcome. Races are often stereotyped, not for racist reasons, but to find humor in the stereotype everyone can relate to. I believe the characters are not in control of their own destinies in this world. They seem to be in control of their antagonists, as they all seem to be in the losing end of their efforts. I think what defines success in this world is for people to be good people and have healthy relationships. The reason why I say this is because this program is a parody of that, and it often shows how the characters are not successful in these endeavors. What is rewarded is not often seen, but what is punished is. Selfish behaviors, and when the characters are preoccupied with themselves are often punished.

http://thesubaltern.com/2012/01/31/seinfeld-reinforcing-rejecting-and-establishing-cultural-norms/

Pretty, Pretty, Pretty Good: Larry David and the Making of Seinfeld and Curb Your Enthusiasm

—**Stephen J. Kwiecien**
Intro to Mass Communications
Professor Treut
December 12, 2013

References

See episode #137 – "The Bizarro Jerry." Directed by Andy Ackerman and written by David Mandel. Original airdate, October 3, 1996.

See episode #108 – "The Diplomat's Club" Directed Andy Ackerman and written by Tom Gammill and Max Pross. Original airdate, May, 4 1995.

http://miniblooms.com/soci326/Goffman&Humor.pdf

http://homepage.ntlworld.com/alan.dawson87/rd286/rock/seinfeld.html

BIBLIOGRAPHY

Anderson, C. (2006). *The Long Tail: Why the Future of Business is Selling Less of More*. New York, NY: Hyperion.

Bagdikian, B. (2004). *The New Media Monopoly*. Boston, MA: Beacon Press.

Baran, S. J. (2008; 2011). *Introduction to Mass Communication: Media Literacy and Culture*. New York, NY: McGraw-Hill.

Berger, P. L., & Luckmann, T. (1966). *The Social Construction of Reality: A Treatise in the Sociology of Knowledge*. New York, NY: Anchor Books.

Blondheim, M. (2004). *News Over the Wires: The Telegraph and the Flow of Public Information in America (1844-1897)*. Boston, MA: Harvard College.

Bowser, E. (1990). *The Transformation of the Cinema 1907-1915*. New York, NY: Scribner.

Brock, D., & Rabin-Havt, A. (2012). *The Fox Effect: How Roger Ailes Turned a Network Into a Propaganda Machine*. New York, NY: Anchor Books.

Byrne, E., & McQuillan, M. (1999). *Deconstructing Disney*. London, UK: Pluto Press.

Campbell, R., Martin, C. R., & Fabos, B. (2011). *Media & Culture: An Introduction to Mass Communication*. New York, NY: Bedford St. Martin's.

Carr, N. (2011). *The Shallows: What the Internet is Doing to Our Brains*. New York, NY: W. W. Norton.

Cassirer, E. (1956). *An Essay on Man*. New Haven, CT: Yale University Press.

Colman, A. M. (2006). *Oxford Dictionary of Psychology*. New York, NY: Oxford University Press.

Cowley, E., & and Janus, E. (2004) "Not Necessarily Better, but Certainly Different: A Limit to the Advertising Misinformation Effect" *Journal of Consumer Research*, 30 (3), 443-454.

Czitrom, D. J. (1982). *Media and the American Mind: From Morse to McLuhan*. Chapel Hill, NC: University of North Carolina Press.

Entertainment Software Association. (2010). *Industry Facts*. Retrieved from http://www.theesa.com/facts

Dill, K. (2009). *How Fantasy Becomes Reality: Seeing Through Media Influence*. New York, NY: Oxford University Press.

Dill, K. (2013). *The Oxford Handbook of Media Psychology*. New York, NY: Oxford University Press.

Evans, T. W. (2007). *The Education of Ronald Reagan: The General Electric Years and the Untold Story of His Conversion to Conservatism*. New York, NY: Columbia University Press.

Fiske, J. (1997). *Television Culture*. New York, NY: Routledge.

Four Arrows, & Fetzer, J. (2004). *American Assassination: The Strange Death of Senator Paul Wellstone*. Brooklyn, NY: Vox Pop.

Gerbner, George. (1972). "Communication and Social Environment." *Scientific American*, 227(3), 152-160. Reprinted in *Communication: A Scientific American Book*. San Francisco: W.H. Freeman, pp. 111-118.

Giles, D. (2009). *Media Psychology*. New York, NY: Routledge.

Giles, D. (2010). *Psychology of the Media*. New York, NY: Palgrave Macmillan.

Giroux, H. A., & Pollack, G. (2010). *The Mouse that Roared: Disney and the End of Innocence*. New York, NY: Rowman and Littlefield.

Goffman, E. (1959). *The Presentation of Self in Everyday Life*. New York, NY: Penguin Books.

Gopal, B.S., Ramakrishnan, R. and R. Shums, R. (2008). "The US Newspaper Industry at Crossroads?" The Case Centre (ecch).

Gross, Larry. (1977). "Television as a Trojan Horse." *School Media Quarterly*, 5(3), 175-180.

Hall, S., et al. (1980). *Culture, Media, Language: Working Papers in Cultural Studies, 1972-1979*. London, UK: Taylor and Francis.

Hallin, D. C., & Mancini, P. (2004). *Comparing Media Systems: Three Models of Media and Politics*. New York, NY: Cambridge University Press.

Hanson, R. E. (2008). *Mass Communication: Living in a Media World*. Washington, DC: CQ Press.

Hedges, C. (2009). *Empire of Illusion: The End of Literacy and the Triumph of Spectacle*. New York, NY: Nation Books.

IBIS World. (2013). "Newspaper Publishing in the U.S.: Market Research Report." Retrieved from http://www.ibisworld.com/industry/default.aspx?indid=1231

Kassin, S., Fein, S., & Markus, H. S. (2008). *Social Psychology*. Belmont, CA: Wadsworth.

Kilbourne, J. (2012). *Can't Buy My Love: How Advertising Changes the Way We Think and Feel*. New York, NY: Free Press.

Klapper, J. (1960). *The Effects of Mass Communication: An Analysis of Research on the Effectiveness and Limitations of Mass Media in Influencing the Opinions, Values, and Behavior of their Audiences*. New York, NY: Free Press of Glencoe.

Klinenberg, E. (2010). *Fighting for Air: The Battle for Control of America's Media*. New York, NY: Macmillon.

Lewis, J. (1991). *The Ideological Octopus: An Exploration of Television & Its Audience*. New York, NY: Routledge.

"Liberals Want GE CEO Jeff Immelt out of Obama Administration." March 29, 2011. Retrieved from www.cbsnews.com

Lindstrom, M. (2008). *Buyology: Truth and Lies About What We Buy*. New York, NY: Crown Business.

Lodziak, C. (1986). *The Power of Television: A Critical Appraisal*. New York, NY: Palgrave Macmillan.

Livingstone, S. (1998). *Making Sense of Television: The Psychology of Audience Interpretation*. London, UK: Routledge.

Mander, J. (2002). *Four Arguments for the Elimination of Television*. New York, NY: Harper Collins.

McChesney, R. W. (2004). *The Problem of the Media: U.S. Communication Politics in the 21st Century*. New York, NY: Monthly Review Press.

McChesney, R. W. (1999). *Rich Media Poor Democracy: Communication Politics in Dubious Times*. Chicago, IL: University of Illinois Press.

McQuail, D. (2000). *McQuail's Mass Communication Theory* (4th ed.). Thousand Oaks, CA: Sage.

McLuhan, M. (1964). *Understanding Media: The Extensions of Man*. Boston, MA: MIT Press.

McQuown, D. (2013). "The Chicago School of Media Theory: Radio." Retrieved from http://lucian.uchicago.edu/blogs/mediatheory/keywords/radio/

Miller, M. C. (2006). "The Death of News." *The Nation*. New York, NY.

Morgan, Michael. (1989). "Cultivation Analysis." In Eric Barnouw (ed.), *The International Encyclopedia of Communications, Vol I*. New York: Oxford University Press, pp. 430-433.

Morgan, M. & Shanahan, J. (2010). "The state of cultivation." *Journal of Broadcasting & Electronic Media*, 54(2), 337-355.

Morgan, M. (2012). *George Gerbner: A critical introduction to media and communication theory*. New York: Peter Lang.

Munk, N. (2004). *Fools Rush In: Steve Case, Jerry Levin, and the Unmaking of AOL Time Warner*. New York, NY: Harper Business.

Motion Picture Association of America (2012). "Theatrical Market Statistics." Retrieved from: http://www.mpaa.org/policy/industry

Newspaper Association of America. (2013). "Trends and Numbers." Retrieved from http://www.naa.org/Trends-and-Numbers.aspx

Palfrey, J., & Gasser, U. (2008). *Born Digital: Understanding the First Generation of Digital Natives*. New York, NY: Basic Books.

Postman, N. (1985). *Amusing Ourselves to Death: Public Discourse in the Age of Show Business*. New York, NY: Penguin Books.

Postman, N., & Powers, S. (1992). *How to Watch TV News*. New York, NY: Penguin Books.

Project for Excellence in Journalism (2004). "Magazine Audience." Pew Research Center. Retrieved from: http://stateofthemedia.org/2004/magazines-intro/

Schudson, M. (1978). *Discovering the News: A Social History of American Newspapers*. New York, NY: Basic Books.

Sigman, A. (2005). *Remotely Controlled: How Television is Damaging Our Lives*. London, UK: Vermilion.

Silverblatt, A., & Elicieri, E. (1997). *Dictionary of Media Literacy*. Westport, CT: Greenwood Press.

Silverblatt, A. (2008). *Media Literacy: The Keys to Interpreting Media Messages* (3rd ed.). San Francisco, CA: Praeger.

Starr, P. (2004). *The Creation of the Media: Political Origins of Modern Communication*. New York, NY: Basic Books.

Sterling, C. H., & Kittross, J.M. (1978). *Stay Tuned: A Concise History of American Broadcasting*. Belmont, CA: Wadsworth Publishing Company.

Television Bureau of Advertising (2012). *TV Basics: A Report on the Growth and Scope of Television*. New York: TVBA.

Thoreau, H. D. (1882). *Walden*. Amazon Digital Publishing (Public Domain).

Tupper, D., & Cicerone, K, (1990). *The Neuropsychology of Everyday Life: Assessment and Basic Competencies*. Norwell, MA: Kluwer Academic Publishing.

Viacom/CBS Merger: Media Competition and Consolidation in the New Millennium. (1999). Committee on the Judiciary United States Senate. Washington, DC: US Government Printing Office.

West, R., & Turner, L. H. (2010). *Introducing Communication Theory: Analysis and Application* (4th ed.). New York, NY: McGraw-Hill Higher Education.

Williamson, J. (2010). *Decoding Advertisements: Ideology and Meaning in Advertising*. New York, NY: Marion Boyars Publishing.

Zhu, K. (2001). "Internet based distribution of digital videos: The economic impacts of digitization on the motion picture industry." *Electronic Markets*, 11 (4), 273-280.

IMAGE CREDITS

Introduction

Fig I.1   Copyright © 2004 by Glogger at the English language Wikipedia, (CC BY-SA 3.0) at: http://commons.wikimedia.org/wiki/File:Mediated-reality-easel.jpg.
Fig I.2   Copyright in the Public Domain.
Fig I.3   Copyright © 2007 by Victor Bezrukov, (CC BY 2.0) at: http://commons.wikimedia.org/wiki/File:Scared_Girl.jpg.
Fig I.5   Copyright © 2011 by Krish Dulal, (CC BY-SA 3.0) at: http://commons.wikimedia.org/wiki/File:Television_studio_HTV.jpg.

Media History

Fig 1.1   Copyright © 2011 by Visitor7, (CC BY-SA 3.0) at: http://commons.wikimedia.org/wiki/File:Pike_Place_Newstand_2_(Seattle,_Washington).jpg.
Fig 1.2   Copyright in the Public Domain.
Fig 1.3   Copyright © 1967 by John Reeves. Reprinted with permission.
Fig 1.4   Copyright in the Public Domain.
Fig 1.5   Copyright in the Public Domain.
Fig 1.6   Copyright in the Public Domain.
Fig 1.7   Copyright in the Public Domain.

Fig 1.8   Source: National Portrait Gallery, London. Copyright in the Public Domain.
Fig 1.9   Source: Yale Center for British Art, New Haven. Copyright in the Public Domain.
Fig 1.10   Copyright in the Public Domain.
Fig 1.11   Copyright © 2008 by David Flanders, (CC BY-SA 2.0) at: http://commons.wikimedia.org/wiki/File:2008_reading_book_3124785808.jpg.
Fig 1.12   Copyright in the Public Domain.
Fig 1.13   Copyright in the Public Domain.
Fig 1.14   Copyright in the Public Domain.
Fig 1.15   Copyright in the Public Domain.
Fig 1.16   Copyright © 2004 by Alterego, (CC BY-SA 3.0) at: http://commons.wikimedia.org/wiki/File:The_associated_press_building_in_new_york_city.jpg.
Fig 1.17   Copyright in the Public Domain.
Fig 1.18   Copyright in the Public Domain.
Fig 1.19   Copyright in the Public Domain.
Fig 1.20   Copyright © 2004 by Tomás Fano, (CC BY-SA 2.0) at: http://commons.wikimedia.org/wiki/File:Times_Square_Newsstand.jpg.
Fig 1.21   Chris Anderson, "[image]: The New Market Place (The Long Tail)," http://www.thelongtail.com/about.html, ~1. Copyright © 2004 by . Reprinted with permission.
Fig 1.22   Copyright in the Public Domain.
Fig 1.23a   Copyright in the Public Domain.
Fig 1.23b   Copyright © 2011 by Lionel Allorge, (CC BY-SA 3.0) at: http://commons.wikimedia.org/wiki/

Media Ownership and the Corporatization of Thought

The Effects of Media Exposure

Media Literacy

Future Thinking

CPSIA information can be obtained at www.ICGtesting.com
Printed in the USA
LVOW03s0710300115

425014LV00002B/6/P